Commentaries On St. Paul's Epistles To The Galatians And Ephesians

JOHN CALVIN

Commentaries On St. Paul's Epistles To The Galatians And Ephesians, J. Calvin
Jazzybee Verlag Jürgen Beck
86450 Altenmünster, Loschberg 9
Deutschland

ISBN: 9783849688875

Translated by John King (1789 – 1858)

www.jazzybee-verlag.de
www.facebook.com/jazzybeeverlag
admin@jazzybee-verlag.de

Printed by Createspace, North Charleston, SC, USA

CONTENTS:

TRANSLATOR'S PREFACE

The extraordinary ability and skill displayed by Calvin, in his Commentaries on the Inspired Writings, have been set forth by almost all the Translators of this Series. I have always thought, and am happy to have the support of his latest Editor, Dr. Tholuck, that he is more successful in expounding the Epistles Of Paul than in any other portion of Scripture. This might arise in part from having studied them with uncommon ardor and perseverance. The times in which he lived held out strong inducements to examine the great peculiarities of the Christian Faith. And where were these so likely to be found as in the writings of an Apostle whom the Spirit of God employed, more than all the others, in unfolding to the Church "the unsearchable riches of Christ?" (Eph 3:8.)

How far that success might be promoted by the resemblance of character which an able and eloquent writer [1] asserts to have existed between the great Apostle and the Reformer, I leave undetermined. But the chief cause unquestionably lay in his singularly clear perception of that scheme of doctrine which Paul was honored to declare. This enabled him to penetrate the design of the Apostle, and to follow closely the course of his argument. In discussions of the greatest intricacy he seldom loses his way.

Various authors, who cannot be named without awakening gratitude, and to whom it would be impossible to do justice in this brief sketch, have supplied the materials of valuable Notes to this volume. From their pages it would have been easy to select many a warm tribute to the Genevan Reformer, to whom they were deeply indebted, and whose writings were consulted by them with acknowledged deference. The greatest lights of our age have not superseded the labors of Calvin, and ablest divines vie with each other in doing homage to his great sagacity as an interpreter of the Holy Scriptures.

To my younger brethren in the ministry may I take the liberty of recommending these Commentaries as an excellent model for expounding the inspired Epistles? The frequent mention of Popery does not lessen the value of this recommendation. How far it may be necessary, at all times, to fortify our hearers against the attacks of the "man of sin," (2Th 2:3,) I do not now stay to inquire. But as a skillful, natural, and impressive application of divine truth to the controversies of the day, the warnings against Popery deserve careful study. They are appropriately introduced, and serve to illustrate more fully the mind of the Spirit.

In describing them as models, it may be proper to mention that they are strictly what their title bears, Commentaries, unaccompanied by those illustrations which, in public instruction, are indispensably necessary. To devout minds they will have many attractions. They are imbued with the ardent piety and that copious use of the language of Scripture by which all the writings of Calvin are so eminently distinguished.

Achtebarder,
6th September 1854.

Footnotes

1

"The Paul of the Reformation. More than two hundred and fifty years have elapsed since he went to join the Apostle whom he so much resembled in the kingdom of God." — Dr. Mason on Catholic Communion.

DEDICATION

TO THE MOST ILLUSTRIOUS PRINCE
CHRISTOPER,
DUKE OF WIRTEMBERG, EARL OF MONTEBELIARD, ETC.

Though personally unknown to you, most illustrious Prince, I venture unhesitatingly [2] to dedicate to you one of my productions. It may be thought that so bold a step will be censured by some persons as rash, and therefore demands an apology. Nothing is more easy. A few words shall suffice. My motives to address you are chiefly two.

You have hitherto, indeed, pursued the right course with great spirit and energy. Yet I thought that it might not be altogether unnecessary to excite you, by a direct appeal, to the perusal of a work not a little fitted to strengthen your resolutions. Onc advantagc you po33c33, in thc kind providcncc of God, abovc mo3t princc3 of the present day. Having enjoyed an early and liberal education in the Latin language, you are enabled to employ your leisure in reading profitable and religious books. If ever there was a time when the consolations derived from religious instruction were necessary, what other resource is left to the most heroic minds by the present distress of the Church, and by greater and heavier distresses which appear to be approaching? Whoever, therefore, wishes to remain unmoved to the last, let him rely entirely on this support; whoever desires to have a sure protection, let him learn to betake himself to this refuge. Besides, in these four Epistles, [3] of which I now present to you my Expositions, you will find, noble Prince, many subjects of consolation exceedingly adapted to the present times; but to which I do not now more particularly refer, because they will occur to yourself with much better effect in their own places.

I come now to my second reason for dedicating to you this work. During the present confusion of affairs, while some are shaken, and others are entirely thrown down, you have preserved an astonishing composure and moderation, accompanied by a remarkable steadfastness, amidst all the storms which have arisen. I consider, therefore, that it is highly advantageous to the whole Church, to hold out in you, as in a bright mirror, an example which all may imitate. For, while the Son of God enjoins on all his followers, without exception, that they shall choose rather to fight under the banner of his cross than to triumph with the world, yet very few are found who are ready to engage in that kind of warfare. It is the more necessary that all should be stimulated and taught, by such uncommon examples as yours, to correct their effeminacy.

Of my Commentaries I shall only say, that they perhaps contain more than it would become me to acknowledge. On this point, however, I wish you to read and judge for yourself. Farewell, most illustrious Prince. May the Lord Jesus long preserve you for himself and his Church, and guide you by His Spirit!

Geneva,
1st February 1548.

Footnotes

2

"Sans En Faire Difficulte." "Without Any Scruple"

3

The Volume To Which This Dedication Was Prefixed, Contained The Commentaries On The Epistles To The Galatians, Ephesians, Philippians, And Colossians. — *Ed.*

THE ARGUMENT OF THE EPISTLE OF PAUL TO THE GALATIANS.

What part of Asia was inhabited by the Galatians, and what were the boundaries of their country, is well known; but whence they originally came [4] is not agreed among historians. It is universally admitted that they were Gauls, and, on that account, were denominated Gallo-Grecians. But from what part of Gaul they came it is more difficult to determine.

Strabo thought that the Tectosages came from Gallia Narbonensis, and that the remainder were Celtae; [5] and this opinion has been generally adopted. But, as Pliny enumerates the Ambiani [6] among the Tectosagi, and as it is universally agreed that they were allied to the Tolistobogi, who dwelt on the banks of the Rhine, I think it more probable that, they were Belgians, whose territory extended from a very distant part of the course of the Rhine to the English Channel. The Tolistobogi inhabited that part which receives from its present inhabitants the names of Cleves and Brabant.

The mistake originated, I think, in this way. A band of Tectosagi, who had made all irruption into Gallia Narbonensis, retained their own name, and gave it to the country which they had conquered. This is intimated by Ausonius, [7] who says, "As far as the Teutosagi, whose original name was Belgians; [8] for he calls them Belgians, and says that they were first called Teutosagi, and afterwards Tectosagi. Caesar, [9] indeed, places the Tectosagi in the Hercynian [10] forest; but I consider this to have been in consequence of their emigration, which indeed appears from that very passage.

But more than enough has now been said as to the origin of the nation, so far as relates to the present passage. Pliny informs us that the Galatians, who inhabited that part of Asia to which they gave their name, were divided into three chief nations, Tectosagi, Tolistobogi, and Trocmi, and accordingly occupied three chief cities. So great was the power which they at one time swayed over their unwarlike neighbors, that they received tribute from a great part of Lesser Asia. Losing at length their ancient valor, and giving themselves up to pleasure and luxury, they were vanquished in war and subdued, with little difficulty, by Cneius Manlius, a Roman consul.

At the time of the Apostle Paul they were under the dominion of the Romans. He had purely and faithfully instructed them in the Gospel; but false apostles had entered, during his absence, and had corrupted the true seed by false and erroneous doctrines. They taught that the observation of ceremonies was still necessary. This might appear to be a trivial matter; but Paul very properly contends as for a fundamental article of the Christian faith. It is no small evil to quench the light of the Gospel, to lay a snare for consciences, and to remove the distinction between the Old and New Testaments. He perceived that these errors were also connected with a wicked and dangerous opinion as to the manner in which justification is obtained. This is the reason why he fights with so much earnestness and vehemence; and, having learned from him the important and serious nature of the controversy, it is our duty to read with greater attention.

One who forms his views of the subject from the Commentaries of Origen and Jerome, will be astonished that Paul should take so deep an interest in external rites; but whoever goes to the fountain will acknowledge that there was abundant reason for all this sharpness of reproof. The Galatians had allowed themselves to be drawn aside from the right course by excessive credulity, or rather by lightness and folly. He therefore censures them more severely; for I do not agree with those who attribute the harshness of his language to their slowness of apprehension. The Ephesians and Colossians had been subjected to the same temptations. If they had lent as ready an ear to the tale of the impostors, do we imagine that Paul would have treated them with greater gentleness? This boldness of rebuke was not suggested by the disposition of the people, but extorted by the baseness of their conduct.

Having ascertained what was the design of writing the Epistle, let us attend to the order in which it is treated. In the *first* and *second* Chapters (Galatians 1 and Galatians 2) he maintains the authority of his Apostleship, except that, towards the close of the second chapter, he touches incidentally on his main point, the question of Man's Justification, which, however, is avowedly and directly argued in the *third* Chapter, Galatians 3. Although he appears in those two Chapters to have many objects in view, yet his sole object is to prove that He is equal to the highest apostles, and that there is no reason why he should not be considered to hold an equally honorable rank with any of them.

But it is of importance to know why he labors so hard in establishing his own claim to respect. Provided that Christ reigns, and that the purity of doctrine remains uncontaminated, what matters it whether he is higher or lower than Peter, or whether they are all on a footing of equality? If all must "decrease," that Christ alone may "increase," (Joh 3:30,) it is idle to dispute about human ranks. Besides, it may be asked, why does he draw a comparison between himself and other apostles? What dispute had he with Peter, and James, and John? What good purpose did it serve to bring into collision those who were united in sentiment, and in the closest friendship?

I reply, the false apostles, who had deceived the Galatians, endeavored to obtain favor by pretending that they had received a commission from the Apostles. Their chief influence arose from insinuating the belief that they represented the Apostles, and delivered their message. To Paul, on the other hand, they refused the name and authority of an Apostle. They objected that he had not been chosen by our Lord as one of the Twelve; that he had never been acknowledged as such by the college of the Apostles; that he did not receive his doctrine from Christ, or even from the Apostles themselves. All this tended not only to lower Paul's authority, but to rank him with the ordinary members of the Church, and therefore to place him far below those persons who made these insinuations.

If this had been merely a personal matter, it would have given no uneasiness to Paul to be reckoned an ordinary disciple. But when he saw that his doctrine was beginning to lose its weight and authority, he was not entitled to be silent. It became his duty to make a bold resistance. When Satan does not venture openly to attack doctrine, his next stratagem is to diminish its influence by indirect attacks. Let us remember, then, that in the person of Paul the truth of the Gospel was assailed; for, if he had allowed himself to be stripped of the honor of apostleship, it followed that he had hitherto claimed what he had no title to enjoy; and this false boasting would have made him liable to suspicion in other matters. The estimation in which his doctrine was held depended on the question, whether it came, as some had begun to think, from an ordinary disciple, or from an apostle of Christ.

He was overwhelmed, on the other hand, by the lustre of great names. Those who referred, in a boastful manner, to Peter, and James, and John, pretended to apostolical authority. If Paul had not manfully resisted this boasting, he would have given way to falsehood, and would have allowed the truth of God [11] to suffer again in his own person. He therefore contends earnestly for both points: that he was appointed by the Lord to be an apostle, and that he was in no respect inferior to the rest, but enjoyed the same title, and was equal to them in authority and rank. He might, indeed, have denied that those men were either sent, or hold any commission from Peter and his associates. But he takes far higher ground, that he does not yield to the Apostles themselves; and if he had declined doing so, he would have been supposed to have distrusted his cause.

Jerusalem was, at that time, the Mother of all the Churches; for the Gospel had spread from it over the whole world, and it might be said to be the principal seat of the kingdom of Christ. Any one who came from it into other churches was received with due respect. But many were foolishly elated with the thought that they had enjoyed the friendship of the Apostles, or at least had been taught in their school; and therefore nothing pleased them but what they had seen at Jerusalem. Every custom that had not been practiced there was not only disliked, but unsparingly condemned by them. This peevish manner becomes highly pernicious, when the custom of a single church is attempted to be enforced as a universal law. We are sometimes so devoted to an instructor or a place, that, without exercising any judgment of our own, we make the opinion of one man the standard for all men, and the customs of one place the standard for every other place. Such attachment is ridiculous, if there be not always in it a mixture of ambition; or rather we should say, excessive peevishness is always ambitious.

To return to those false apostles, if they had only attempted, through wicked contention, to establish everywhere the use of those ceremonies, which they had seen observed at Jerusalem, that would have been no slight offense; for, when a custom is forthwith converted into a law, injustice is perpetrated. But a more serious evil was involved in the wicked and dangerous doctrine, which held consciences to be bound to them by religious considerations, which made justification to depend on the observation of them. Such were the reasons why Paul defended his Apostleship with so much earnestness, and why he contrasted himself with the rest of the Apostles.

He pursues this subject to the end of the *second* Chapter, Galatians 2, when he proceeds to argue the doctrine, that we are justified in the sight of God by Free Grace, and not by the Works of the Law. His argument is this: If Ceremonies have not the power of bestowing Justification, the observation of them is therefore unnecessary. We must remark, however, that he does not confine himself entirely to Ceremonies, but argues generally about Works, otherwise the whole discussion would be trifling.

If any person thinks that we are thus straining the matter too far, let him attend to the two following reasons. First, the question could not be settled without assuming the general principle, that we are justified by the free grace of God; and this principle sets aside not only ceremonies, but every other kind of works. Secondly, Paul did not attach so much importance to Ceremonies as to the wicked doctrine of obtaining Salvation by Works. Let it be observed, therefore, that Paul had good reasons for recurring to first principles. It was necessary to go to the fountain, and to warn his readers that the controversy related, not to some insignificant trifle, but to the most important of all matters — the method of obtaining salvation.

It is a mistake, therefore, to suppose that the Apostle confined himself wholly to the special question about Ceremonies, a subject which did not admit of being settled by itself. A similar instance occurs in history. (Ac 15:2.) Strife and contention had arisen out of the question, whether or not Ceremonies were necessary to be observed. In the course of the discussion, the Apostles dwell largely on the intolerable yoke of the Law, and on the Forgiveness of Sins through Free Grace. What was the object of this? It appears to be a foolish departure from the point in hand; but the contrary is the fact, for a particular error cannot be satisfactorily refuted without assuming a universal principle. As, for instance, if I am called to dispute about, forbidding the use of flesh, I shall not speak merely about the different kinds of food, but shall arm myself with the general doctrine: What authority have the Traditions of men for binding the conscience? I shall quote the declaration, that

"There is one Lawgiver, who has power to save and to destroy." (Jas 4:12.)

In short, Paul here argues negatively from general to particular propositions, which is the ordinary and most natural method of reasoning. By what evidences and arguments he proves this principle, that we are justified by the grace of God alone, we shall see when we come to the passage. He pursues this topic till the end of the *third* Chapter, Galatians 3.

In the commencement of the *fourth* Chapter, Galatians 4, he inquires into the proper use of Ceremonies, and the reason why they were appointed; shewing, at the same time, that they are now abolished. It became necessary to meet this silly objection, which might occur to some minds. What, then, was the purpose of Ceremonies? Were they useless? Were the Fathers idly employed in observing them? He illustrates briefly two statements, that in their own time they were not superfluous, and that they have now been abolished by the coming of Christ, because He is the truth and end of them; and therefore he shews that we must abide by Him. Glancing briefly at the difference between our condition and that of the Fathers, he infers that the doctrine of the false apostles is wicked and dangerous, because it darkens the clearness of the gospel by ancient shadows. The Apostle's doctrine is now intermingled with some affecting exhortations. Towards the close of the Chapter his argument is enlivened by a beautiful allegory.

In the *fifth* Chapter, Galatians 5, he exhorts them to hold fast the Liberty which has been obtained by the blood of Christ, that they may not surrender their consciences to be ensnared by the opinions of men. But he reminds them, at the same time, in what manner Liberty may be lawfully used. [12] He then takes occasion to point out the proper employments of Christians, that they may not uselessly spend their time in Ceremonies, and neglect matters of real importance.

Footnotes

4

"Mais quant a leur origine, et le lieu dont ils sont premieremerit partis, les anciens autheurs ne se trouvent d'accord." "But as to their lineage, and the place from which they originally came, ancient authors are not agreed."

5

"Strabo geographe pense que ceux d'entre eux qui avoyent le nom de Tectosagois estoyent venus du pays de Provence, et les antres de la Gaule Celtique." "Strabo, the geographer, thinks that those of them who bore the name of Tectosages had come from Provence, and the remainder from Celtic Gaul."

6

"Ceux d'Amiens." "Those of Amiens."

7

"Ausone poete Bordelois, qui a escrit en Latin." "Ausonius, the poet, a native of Bourdeaux, who wrote in Latin."

8

"Usque in Teutosagos primaevo nomine Belgas."

9

Bell. Gall. 50 6 100 24.

10

A forest in Germany, which Caesar describes to be nine days' journey in breadth, and, at least, sixty days' journey in length. How much more he was unable to say, as he had never found any person who had traveled farther, or could tell where the forest terminated. He regrets the necessity of employing these vague terms, having placed little reliance on the skill or accuracy of his informers. It is mentioned, he adds, by Eratosthenes and other Greek writers, under the name of *Orcynia. — Ed.*

11

"La verite de Dieu."

12

"En quoy consiste ceste liberte, et quel en est le vray et droit usage" "In what that liberty consists, and what is the true and lawful use of it."

CHAPTER 1

Galatians 1:1-5

1. Paul, an apostle, (not of men, neither by man, but by Jesus Christ, and God the Father, who raised him from the dead,)
1. Paulus apostolus, non ab hominibus, neque per hominem, sed per Iesum Christum, et Deum Patrem, qui suscitavit illum ex mortuis,
2. And all the brethren which are with me, unto the churches of Galatia:
2. Et qui mecum sunt fratres omnes, ecclesiis Galatiae:
3. Grace *be* to you, and peace, from God the Father, and *from* our Lord Jesus Christ,
3. Gratia vobis et pax a Deo Patre, et Domino nostro Iesu Christo,
4. Who gave himself for our sins, that he might deliver us from this present evil world, according to the will of God and our Father:
4. Qui dedit se ipsum pro peccatis nostris, ut nos eriperet a praesenti saeculo maligno, secundum voluntatem Dei et Patris nostri,
5. To whom *be* glory for ever and ever. Amen.
5. Cui gloria in saecula saeculorum. Amen.

1. *Paul, an apostle.* In the salutations with which he commenced his Epistles, Paul was accustomed to claim the title of "an Apostle." His object in doing so, as we have remarked on former occasions, was to employ the authority of his station, for the purpose of enforcing his doctrine. This authority depends not on the judgment or opinion of men, but exclusively on the calling of God; and therefore he demands a hearing on the ground of his being "an Apostle." Let us always bear this in mind, that in the church we ought to listen to God alone, and to Jesus Christ, whom he has appointed to be our teacher. Whoever assumes a right to instruct us, must speak in the name of God or of Christ.

But as the calling of Paul was more vehemently disputed among the Galatians, he asserts it more strongly in his address to that church, than in his other Epistles; for he does not simply affirm that he was called by God, but states expressly that it was *not either from men or by men.* This statement, be it observed, applies not to the office which he held in common with other pastors, but to the apostleship. The authors of the calumnies which he has in his eye did not venture to deprive him altogether of the honor of the Christian ministry. They merely refused to allow him the name and rank of an apostle.

We are now speaking of the apostleship in the strictest sense; for the word is employed in two different ways. Sometimes, it denotes preachers of the Gospel, to whatever class they might belong; but here it bears a distinct reference to the highest rank in the church; so that Paul is equal to Peter and to the other twelve.

The first clause, that he was called *not from men*, he had in common with all the true ministers of Christ. As no man ought to "take this honor unto himself," (Heb 5:4,) so it is not in the power of men to bestow it on whomsoever they choose. It belongs to God alone to govern his church; and therefore the calling cannot be lawful, unless it proceed from Him. So far as the church is concerned, a man who has been led to the ministry, not by a good conscience, but by ungodly motives, may happen to be regularly called. But Paul is here speaking of a call ascertained in so perfect, a manner, that nothing farther can be desired.

It will, perhaps, be objected — Do not the false apostles frequently indulge in the same kind of boasting? I admit they do, and in a more haughty and disdainful style than the servants of the Lord venture to employ; but they want that actual call from Heaven to which Paul was entitled to lay claim.

The second clause, that he was called *not by man*, belonged in a peculiar manner to the apostles; for in an ordinary pastor, this would have implied nothing wrong. Paul himself, when travelling through various cities in company with Barnabas, "ordained elders in every church," by the votes of the people, (Ac 14:23;) and he enjoins Titus and Timothy to proceed in the same work. (1Ti 5:17 Titus 1:5.) Such is the ordinary method of electing pastors; for we are not entitled to wait until God shall reveal from heaven the names of the persons whom he has chosen.

But if human agency was not improper, if it was even commendable, why does Paul disclaim it in reference to himself? I have already mentioned that something more was necessary to be proved than that Paul was a pastor, or that he belonged to the number of the ministers of the Gospel; for the point in dispute was the apostleship. It was necessary that the apostles should be elected, not in the same manner as other pastors, but by the direct agency of the Lord himself. Thus, Christ himself (Mt 10:1) called the Twelve; and when a successor was to be appointed in the room of Judas, the church does not venture to choose one by votes, but has recourse to *lot.* (Ac 1:26.) We are certain that the lot was not employed in electing pastors. Why was it resorted to in the election of Matthias? To mark the express agency of God for it was proper that the apostles should be distinguished from other ministers. And thus Paul, in order to shew that he does not belong to the ordinary rank of ministers, contends that his calling proceeded immediately from God. [13]

But how does Paul affirm that he was *not* called *by men*, while Luke records that Paul and Barnabas were called by the church at Antioch? Some have replied, that he had previously discharged the duties of an apostle, and that, consequently, his apostleship was not founded on his appointment by that church. But here, again, it may be objected, that this was his first designation to be the apostle of the Gentiles, to which class the Galatians belonged. The more correct, and obvious reply is, that he did not intend here to set aside entirely the calling of that church, but merely to shew that his apostleship rests on a higher title. This is true; for even those who laid their hands on Paul at Antioch did so, not of their own accord, but in obedience to express revelation.

"As they ministered to the Lord, and fasted, the Holy Ghost said, Separate me Barnabas and Saul for the work whereunto I have called them. And when they had fasted and prayed, and laid their hands on them, they sent them away." (Acts 13:2, 3.)

Since, therefore, he was called by Divine revelation, and was also appointed and declared by the Holy Spirit to be the apostle of the Gentiles, it follows, that he was not brought forward *by men*, although the customary rite of ordination was afterwards added. [14]

It will, perhaps, be thought that an indirect contrast between Paul and the false apostles is here intended. I have no objection to that view; for they were in the habit of glorying in the name of men. His meaning will therefore stand thus: "Whoever may be the persons by whom others boast that they have been sent, I shall be superior to them; for I hold my commission from God and Christ."

By Jesus Christ and God the Father He asserts that God the Father and Christ had bestowed on him his apostleship. Christ is first named, because it is his prerogative to send, and because we are his ambassadors. But to make the statement more complete, the Father is also mentioned; as if he had said, "If there be any one whom the name of Christ is not sufficient to inspire with reverence, let him know that I have also received my office from God the Father."

Who raised him from the dead. The resurrection of Christ is the commencement of his reign, and is therefore closely connected with the present subject. It was a reproach brought by them against Paul that he had held no communication with Christ, while he was on the earth. He argues, on the other hand, that, as Christ was glorified by his resurrection, so he has actually exercised his authority in the government of his church. The calling of Paul is therefore more illustrious than it would have been, if Christ, while still a mortal, had ordained him to the office. And this circumstance deserves attention; for Paul intimates that the attempt to set aside his authority, involved a malignant opposition to the astonishing power of God, which was displayed in the resurrection of Christ; because the same heavenly Father, who raised Christ from the dead, commanded Paul to make known that exertion of his power.

2. *And all the brethren who are with me.* — He appears to have usually written in the name of many persons, judging that, if those to whom he wrote should attach less weight to a solitary individual, they might listen to a greater number, and would not despise a whole congregation. His general practice is, to insert the salutations from brethren at the conclusion, instead of introducing them at the commencement as joint authors of the epistle: at least, he never mentions more than two names, and those very well known. But here he includes all the brethren; and thus adopts, though not without good reason, an opposite method. The concurrence of so many godly persons must have had some degree of influence in softening the minds of the Galatians, and preparing them to receive instruction.

To the churches of Galatia. It was an extensive country, and therefore contained many churches scattered through it. But is it not wonderful that the term "Church", which always implies unity of faith, should have been applied to the Galatians, who had almost entirely revolted from Christ? I reply, so long as they professed Christianity, worshipped one God, observed the sacraments, and enjoyed some kind of Gospel ministry, they retained the external marks of a church. We do not always find in churches such a measure of purity as might be desired. The purest have their blemishes; and some are marked, not by a few spots, but by general deformity. Though the doctrines and practices of any society may not, in all respects, meet our wishes, we must not instantly pronounce its defects to be a sufficient reason for withholding from it the appellation of a Church. Paul manifests here a gentleness of disposition utterly at variance with such a course. Yet our acknowledgment of societies to be churches of Christ must be accompanied by an explicit condemnation of everything in them that is improper or defective; for we must not imagine, that, wherever there is some kind of church, everything in it that ought to be desired in a church is perfect.

I make this observation, because the Papists, seizing on the single word *Church*, think that whatever they choose to force upon us is sanctioned; though the condition and aspect of the Church of Rome are widely different from what existed in Galatia. If Paul were alive at the present day, he would perceive the miserable and dreadfully shattered remains of a church; but he would perceive no building. In short, the word Church is often applied by a figure of speech in which a part is taken for the whole, to any portion of the church, even though it may not fully answer to the name.

3. *Grace be to you and peace.* This form of salutation, which occurred in the other epistles, has received an explanation, to which I still adhere. Paul wishes for the Galatians a state of friendship with God, and, along with it, all good things; for the favor of God is the source from which we derive every kind of prosperity. He presents both petitions to Christ, as well as to the Father; because without Christ neither grace, nor any real prosperity, can be obtained.

4. *Who gave himself for our sins.* He begins with commending the grace of Christ, in order to recall and fix on Him the attention of the Galatians; for, if they had justly appreciated this benefit of redemption, they would never have fallen into opposite views of religion. He who knows Christ in a proper manner beholds him earnestly, embraces him with the warmest affection, is absorbed in the contemplation of him, and desires no other object. The best remedy for purifying our minds from any kind of errors or superstitions, is to keep in remembrance our relation to Christ, and the benefits which he has conferred upon us.

These words, *who gave himself for our sins*, were intended to convey to the Galatians a doctrine of vast importance; that no other satisfactions can lawfully be brought into comparison with that sacrifice of himself which Christ offered to the Father; that in Christ, therefore, and in him alone, atonement for sin, and perfect righteousness, must be sought; and that the manner in which we are redeemed by him ought to excite our highest admiration. What Paul here ascribes to Christ is, with equal propriety, ascribed in other parts of Scripture to God the Father; for, on the one hand, the Father, by an eternal purpose, decreed this atonement, and gave this proof of his love to us, that he "spared not his only-begotten Son, (Ro 8:32,) but delivered him up for us all;" and Christ, on the other hand, offered himself a sacrifice in order to reconcile us to God. Hence it follows, that his death is the satisfaction for sins. [15]

That he might deliver us. He likewise declares the design of our redemption to be, that Christ, by his death, might purchase us to be his own property. This takes place when we are separated from the world; for so long as we are of the world, we do not belong to Christ. The word αἰών, (*age*,) is here put for the corruption which is in the world; in the same manner as in the first Epistle of John, (1Jo 5:19) where it is said that "the whole world lieth in the wicked one," and in his Gospel, (Joh 17:15,) where the Savior says,

"I pray not that thou shouldst take them out of the world, but that thou shouldst keep them from the evil;"

for there it signifies the present life.

What then is meant by the word "World" in this passage? Men separated from the kingdom of God and the grace of Christ. So long as a man lives to himself, he is altogether condemned. The World is, therefore, contrasted with regeneration, as nature with grace, or the flesh with the spirit. Those who are born of the world have nothing but sin and wickedness, not by creation, but by corruption. [16] Christ, therefore, died for our sins, in order to redeem or separate us from the world.

From the present wicked age. By adding the epithet "wicked", he intended to shew that he is speaking of the corruption or depravity which proceeds from sin, and not of God's creatures, or of the bodily life. And yet by this single word, as by a thunderbolt, he lays low all human pride; for he declares, that, apart from that renewal of the nature which is bestowed by the grace of Christ, there is nothing in us but unmixed wickedness. We are of the world; and, till Christ take us out of it, the world reigns in us, and we live to the world. Whatever delight men may take in their fancied excellence, they are worthless and depraved; not indeed in their own opinion, but in the judgment of our Lord, which is here pronounced by the mouth of Paul, and which ought to satisfy our minds.

According to the will. He points out the original fountain of grace, namely, the purpose of God;

"for God so loved the world, that he gave his only-begotten Son." (Joh 3:16.)

But it deserves notice, that Paul is accustomed to represent the decree of God as setting aside all compensation or merit on the part of men, and so *Will* denotes here what is commonly called "good pleasure." [17] The meaning is, that Christ suffered for us, not because we were worthy, or because anything done by us moved him to the act, but because such was the purpose of God. *Of God and our Father* is of the same import as if he had said, "Of God who is our Father." [18]

5. *To whom be glory.* By this sudden exclamation of thanksgiving, he intends to awaken powerfully in his readers the contemplation of that invaluable gift which they had received from God, and in this manner to prepare their minds more fully for receiving instruction. It must at the same time be viewed as a general exhortation. Every instance in which the mercy of God occurs to our remembrance, ought to be embraced by us as an occasion of ascribing glory to God.

Galatians 1:6-9

6. I marvel that ye are so soon removed from him that called you into the grace of Christ unto another gospel:

6. Miror quod ita cito transferimini a Christo, qui vos vocavit in gratia, ad aliud evangehum;

7. Which is not another; but there be some that trouble you, and would pervert the gospel of Christ.

7. Quod non est aliud, nisi quod sunt quidant, qui vos turbant, ae volunt evertere evangelium Christi.

8. But though we, or an angel from heaven, preach any other gospel unto you than that which we have preached unto you, let him be accursed.

8. Verum etiamsi nos, aut Angelus e coelo evangelizet vobis praeter id quod evangelizavimus vobis, anathema sit.

9. As we said before, so say I now again, If any *man* preach any other gospel unto you than that ye have received, let him be accursed.

9. Quemadmodum praediximus, nunc quoque iterum dico; si quis vobis evangelizaverit praeterquam quod accepistis, anathema sit.

6. *I wonder.* He commences by administering a rebuke, though a somewhat milder one than they deserved; but his greatest severity of language is directed, as we shall see, against the false apostles. He charges them with turning aside, not only from his gospel, but from Christ; for it was impossible for them to retain their attachment to Christ, without acknowledging that he has graciously delivered us from the bondage of the law. But such a belief cannot be reconciled with those notions respecting the obligation of ceremonial observance which the false apostles inculcated. They were *removed from* Christ; not that they entirely rejected Christianity, but that the corruption of their doctrines was such as to leave them nothing more than an imaginary Christ.

Thus, in our own times, the Papists, choosing to have a divided and mangled Christ, have none, and are therefore "removed from Christ." They are full of superstitions, which are directly at variance with the nature of Christ. Let it be carefully observed, that we are *removed from Christ,* when we fall into those views which are inconsistent with his mediatorial office; for light can have no fellowship with darkness.

On the same principle, he calls it *another gospel,* that is, a gospel different from the true one. And yet the false apostles professed that they preached the gospel of Christ; but, mingling with it their own inventions, [19] by which its principal efficacy was destroyed, they held a false, corrupt, and spurious gospel. By using the present tense, ("ye are removed") he appears to say that they were only in the *act* of failing. As if he had said, "I do not yet say that ye have been removed; for then it would be more difficult to return to the right path. But now, at the critical moment, do not advance a single step, but instantly retreat."

From Christ, who called you by grace. Others read it, "from him who called you by the grace of Christ," understanding it to refer to the Father; but the reading which we have followed is more simple. When he says that they were called by Christ through grace, this tends to heighten the criminality of their ingratitude. To revolt from the Son of God under any circumstances, is unworthy and disgraceful; but to revolt from him, after being invited to partake salvation by grace, is more eminently base. His goodness to us renders our ingratitude to him more dreadfully heinous.

So soon. When it is considered how *soon* they had discovered a want of steadfastness, their guilt is still further heightened. A proper season, indeed, for departing from Christ cannot be imagined. But the fact, that no sooner had Paul left them than the Galatians were led away from the truth, inferred still deeper blame. As the consideration of the grace by which they had been called was adduced to aggravate their ingratitude, so the circumstance of the time when they were removed is now adduced to aggravate their levity.

7. *Which is not another thing* [20] Some explain it thus, "though there is not another gospel;" as if it were a sort of correction of the Apostle's language, to guard against the supposition that there were more gospels than one. So far as the explanation of the words is concerned, I take a more simple view of them; for he speaks contemptuously of the doctrine of the false apostles, as being nothing else than a mass of confusion and destruction. As if he had said, "What do those persons allege? On what grounds do they attack the doctrine which I have delivered? They merely trouble you, and subvert the gospel. They do nothing more." But it amounts to the same meaning; for this, too, I acknowledge, is a correction of the language he had used about *another gospel.* He declares that it is not a gospel, but a mere disturbance. All I intended to say was, that, in my opinion, the word *another* means *another thing.* It resembles strongly the expression in common use, "this amounts to *nothing, but that* you wish to deceive."

And wish to pervert. He charges them with the additional crime of doing an injury to Christ, by endeavoring to subvert his gospel. Subversion is an enormous crime. It is worse than corruption. And with good reason does he fasten on them this charge. When the glow of justification is ascribed to another, and a snare is laid for the consciences of men, the Savior no longer occupies his place, and the doctrine of the gospel is utterly ruined.

The gospel of Christ. To know what are the leading points of the gospel, is a matter of unceasing importance. When these are attacked, the gospel is destroyed. When he adds the words, *of Christ,* this may be explained in two ways; either that it has come from Christ as its author, or that it purely exhibits Christ. The apostle's reason for employing that expression unquestionably was to describe the true and genuine gospel, which alone is worthy of the name.

8. *But though we.* As he proceeds in defending the authority of his doctrine, his confidence swells. First of all, he declares that the doctrine which he had preached is the only gospel, and that the attempt to set it aside is highly criminal. But then he was aware, the false apostles might object: "We will not yield to you in our desire to maintain the gospel, or in those feelings of respect for it which we are accustomed to cherish." Just as, at the present day, the Papists describe in the strongest terms the sacredness with which they regard the gospel, and kiss the very name with the deepest reverence, and yet, when brought to the trial, are found to persecute fiercely the pure and simple doctrine of the gospel. Accordingly, Paul does not rest satisfied with this general declaration, but proceeds to define what the gospel is, and what it contains, and declares boldly that his doctrine is the true gospel; so as to resist all further inquiry.

Of what avail was it to profess respect for the gospel, and not to know what it meant? With Papists, who hold themselves bound to render *implicit faith*, that might be perfectly sufficient; but with Christians, where there is no knowledge, there is no faith. That the Galatians, who were otherwise disposed to obey the gospel, might not wander hither and thither, and "find no rest for the sole of their foot," (Ge 8:9,) Paul enjoins them to stand steadfastly by his doctrine. He demands such unhesitating belief of his preaching, that he pronounces a curse on all who dared to contradict it.

And here it is not a little remarkable, that he begins with himself; for thus he anticipates a slander with which his enemies would have loaded him. "You wish to have everything which comes from you received without hesitation, because it is your own." To show that there is no foundation for such a statement, he instantly surrenders the right of advancing anything against his own doctrine. He claims no superiority, in this respect, over other men, but justly demands from all, equally with himself, subjection to the word of God.

Or an angel from heaven. In order to destroy more completely the pretensions of the false apostles, he rises so high as to speak of angels; and, on the supposition that they taught a different doctrine, he does not satisfy himself with saying that they were not entitled to be heard, but declares that they ought to be held accursed. Some may think, that it was absurd to engage in a controversy with angels about his doctrine; but a just view of the whole matter will enable any one to perceive, that this part of the apostle's proceedings was proper and necessary. It is impossible, no doubt, for angels from heaven to teach anything else than the certain truth of God. But when the credit due to doctrines which God had revealed concerning the salvation of men was the subject of controversy, he did not reckon it enough to disclaim the judgment of men, without declining, at the same time, the authority of angels.

And thus, when he pronounces a curse on angels who should teach any other doctrine [21] though his argument is derived from an impossibility, it is not superfluous. This exaggerated language must, have contributed greatly to strengthen the confidence in Paul's preaching. His opponents, by employing the lofty titles of men, attempted to press hard on him and on his doctrine. He meets them by the bold assertion, that even angels are unable to shake his authority. This is no disparagement to angels. To promote the glory of God by every possible means was the design of their creation. He who endeavors, in a pious manner, to accomplish this object, by an apparently desrespectful mention of their name, detracts nothing from their high rank. This language not only exhibits, in an impressive manner, the majesty of the word of God, but yields, also, a powerful confirmation to our faith while, in reliance on that word, we feel ourselves at liberty to treat even angels with defiance and scorn. When he says, "let him be accursed," the meaning must be, "let him be held by you as accursed." In expounding 1Co 12:3, we had occasion to speak of the word ἀνάθεμα. [22] . Here it denotes cursing, and answers to the Hebrew word, חרם (hherem.)

9. *As we said before.* Leaving out, in this instance, the mention of himself and of angels, he repeats the former assertion, that it is unlawful for any man to teach anything contrary to what they had learned. [23] Observe the expression —*ye have received*; for he uniformly insists, that they must not regard the gospel as something unknown, existing in the air, or in their own imaginations. He exhorts them to entertain a firm and serious conviction, that the doctrine which they had received and embraced is the true gospel of Christ. Nothing can be more inconsistent with the nature of faith than a feeble, wavering assent. What, then, must be the consequence, if ignorance of the nature and character of the gospel shall lead to hesitation? Accordingly he enjoins them to regard as devils those who shall dare to bring forward a gospel different from his, — meaning by *another gospel,* one to which the inventions of other men are added; [24] for the doctrine of the false apostles was not entirely contrary, or even different, from that of Paul, but corrupted by false additions.

To what poor subterfuges do the Papists resort, in order to escape from the Apostle's declaration! First, they tell us, that we have not in our possession the whole of Paul's preaching, and cannot know what it contained, unless the Galatians who heard it shall be raised from the dead, in order to appear as witnesses. Next, they assert, that it is not every kind of addition which is forbidden, but that *other gospels* only are condemned. What Paul's doctrine was, so far as it concerns us to know, may be learned with sufficient clearness from his writings. Of this gospel, it is plain, the whole of Popery is a dreadful perversion. And from the nature of the case, we remark in conclusion, it is manifest that any spurious doctrine whatever is at variance with Paul's preaching; so that these cavils will avail them nothing.

Galatians 1:10-14

10. For do I now persuade men, or God? or do I seek to please men? for if I yet pleased men, I should not be the servant of Christ.

10. Nunc enim suadeone secundum homines, an secundum Deum? vel quaero hominibus placere? si enim adhuc hominibus placerem, Christi servus non essem.

11. But I certify you, brethren, that the gospel which was preached of me is not after man.

11. Notum autem vobis faeio, fratres, Deuteronomy Evangelio, quod evangelizatum est a me, quod non est secundum hominem;

12. For I neither received it of man, neither was I taught *it*, but by the revelation of Jesus Christ.

12. Neque enim ego ab hormine accepi illud, neque didici; sed per revelationem Iesu Christi.

13. For ye have heard of my conversation in time past in the Jews' religion, how that beyond measure I persecuted the church of God, and wasted it;

13. Audistis enim conversationem meam, quae aliquando fuit in Iudaismo; quod supra modum persequebar ecclesiam Dei, et vastabam illam,

14. And profited in the Jews' religion above many my equals in mine own nation, being more exceedingly zealous of the traditions of my fathers.

14. Et proficiebam in Iudaismo supra multos aequales meos in gernere meo, quum vehementius studiosus essem paternarum traditionum.

Having extolled so confidently his own preaching, he now shows that this was no idle or empty boast. He supports his assertion by two arguments. The first is, that he was not prompted by ambition, or flattery, or any similar passion, to accommodate himself to the views of men. The second and far stronger argument is, that he was not the author of the gospel, but delivered faithfully what he had received from God.

10. *For do I now persuade according to men or according to God?* The ambiguity of the Greek construction in this passage, has given rise to a variety of expositions. Some render it, *Do I now persuade men or God?* [25] Others interpret the words "God" and "men," as meaning divine and human concerns. This sense would agree very well with the context, if it were not too wide a departure from the words. The view which I have preferred is more natural; for nothing is more common with the Greeks than to leave the preposition κατὰ, *according to*, to be understood.

Paul is speaking, not about the subject of his preaching, but about the purpose of his own mind, which could not refer so properly to men as to God. The disposition of the speaker, it must be owned, may have some influence on his doctrine. As corruption of doctrine springs from ambition, avarice, or any other sinful passion, so the truth is maintained in its purity by an upright conscience. And so he contends that his doctrine is sound, because it is not modified so as to gratify men.

Or, do I seek to please men? This second clause differs not much, and yet it differs somewhat from the former; for the desire of obtaining favor is one motive for speaking "according to men." When there reigns in our hearts such ambition, that we desire to regulate our discourse so as to obtain the favor of men, our instructions cannot be sincere. Paul therefore declares, that he is in no degree chargeable with this vice; and, the more boldly to repel the calumnious insinuation, he employs the interrogative form of speech; for interrogations carry the greater weight, when our opponents are allowed an opportunity of replying, if they have anything to say. This expresses the great boldness which Paul derived from the testimony of a good conscience; for he knew that he had discharged his duty in such a manner as not to be liable to any reproach of that kind. (Ac 23:1; 2Co 1:12.)

If I yet pleased men This is a remarkable sentiment; that ambitious persons, that is, those who hunt after the applause of men, cannot serve Christ. He declares for himself, that he had freely renounced the estimation of men, in order to devote himself entirely to the service of Christ; and, in this respect, he contrasts his present position with that which he occupied at a former period of life. He had been regarded with the highest esteem, had received from every quarter loud applause; and, therefore, if he had chosen to please men, he would not have found it necessary to change his condition. But we may draw from it the general doctrine which I have stated, that those who resolve to serve Christ faithfully, must have boldness to despise the favor of men.

The word *men* is here employed in a limited sense; for the ministers of Christ ought not to labor for the express purpose of displeasing men. But there are various classes of men. Those to whom Christ "is precious," (1Pe 2:7,) are men whom we should endeavor to please in Christ; while they who choose that the true doctrine shall give place to their own passions, are men to whom we must give no countenance. And godly, upright pastors, will always find it necessary to contend with the offenses of those who choose that, on all points, their own wishes shall be gratified; for the Church will always contain hypocrites and wicked men, by whom their own lusts will be preferred to the word of God. And even good men, either through ignorance, or through weak prejudice, are sometimes tempted by the devil to be displeased with the faithful warnings of their pastor. Our duty, therefore, is not to take alarm at any kind of offenses, provided, at the same time, that we do not excite in weak minds a prejudice against Christ himself.

Many interpret this passage in a different manner, as implying an admission to the following effect: "If I pleased men, *then I should not be the servant of Christ.* I own it, but who shall bring such a charge against me? Who does not see that I do not court the favor of men?" But I prefer the former view, that Paul is relating how large an amount of the estimation of men he had relinquished, in order to devote himself to the service of Christ.

11. *Now I make known to you.* This is the most powerful argument, the main hinge on which the question turns, that he has not received the gospel from men, but that it has been revealed to him by God. As this might be denied, he offers a proof, drawn from a narrative of facts. To give his declaration the greater weight, he sets out with stating that the matter is not doubtful, [26] but one which he is prepared to prove; and thus introduces himself in a manner well adapted to a serious subject. He affirms that it is *not according to man*; that it savours of nothing human, or, that it was not of human contrivance; and in proof of this he afterwards adds, that he had not been instructed by any earthly teacher. [27]

12. *For I neither received it from man.* What then? shall the authority of the word be diminished, because one who has been instructed by the instrumentality of men shall afterwards become a teacher? We must take into account, all along, the weapons with which the false apostles attacked him, alleging that his gospel was defective and spurious; that he had obtained it from an inferior and incompetent teacher; and that his imperfect education led him to make unguarded statements. They boasted, on the other hand, that they had been instructed by the highest apostles, with whose views they were most intimately acquainted. It was therefore necessary that Paul should state his doctrine in opposition to the whole world, and should rest it on this ground, that he had acquired it not in the school of any man, but by revelation from God. In no other way could he have set aside the reproaches of the false apostles.

The objection, that Ananias (Ac 9:10) was his teacher, may be easily answered. His divine instruction, communicated to him by immediate inspiration, did not render it improper that a man should be employed in teaching him, were it only to give weight to his public ministry. In like manner, we have already shown, that he had a direct call from God by revelation, and that he was ordained by the votes and the solemn approbation of men. These statements are not inconsistent with each other.

13. *For ye have heard of my conversation.* The whole of this narrative was added as a part of his argument. He relates that, during his whole life, he had such an abhorrence of the gospel, that he was a mortal enemy of it, and a destroyer of the name of Christianity. Hence we infer that his conversion was divine. And indeed he calls them as witnesses of a matter not at all doubtful, so as to place beyond controversy what he is about to say.

His *equals* were those of his own age; for a comparison with older persons would have been unsuitable. When he speaks of *the traditions of the fathers*, he means, not those additions by which the law of God had been corrupted, but the law of God itself, in which he had been educated from his childhood, and which he had received through the hands of his parents and ancestors. Having been strongly attached to the customs of his fathers, it would have been no easy matter to tear him from them, had not the Lord drawn him by a miracle.

Galatians 1:15-24

15. But when it pleased God, who separated me from my mother's womb, and called *me* by his grace,

15. At postquam placuit Deo, qui me segregaverat ab utero matris meae, et vocavit per gratiam suam,

16. To reveal his Son in me, that I might preach him among the heathen; immediately I conferred not with flesh and blood:

16. Revelare Filium suum mihi, ut praedicarem ipsnm inter Gentes, continuo non contuli cum carne et sanguine;

17. Neither went I up to Jerusalem to them which were apostles before me; but I went into Arabia, and returned again unto Damascus.

17. Neque redii Hierosolymam, ad eos qui ante me fuerunt Apestoli; sed abii in Arabiam, ac denuo reversus sum Damascum.

18. Then, after three years, I went up to Jerusalem to see Peter, and abode with him fifteen days.

18. Deinde post annos tres redii Hierosolymam, ut viderein Petrum; et mansi apud illum dies quindecim.

19. But other of the apostles saw I none, save James the Lord's brother.

19. Alium antem ex Apostolis non vidi quenquam, nisi Iacobum fratrem Domini.

20. Now the things which I write unto you, behold, before God, I lie not.

20. Porro quae scribo vobis, ecce coram Deo, non mentier.

21. Afterwards I came into the regions of Syria and Cilicia;

21. Deinde vent in regiones Syriae ac Ciliciae.

22. And was unknown by face unto the churches of Judea which were in Christ:

22. Eram autem facie ignotus Ecclesiis Iudaeae, qute erant in Christo.

23. But they had heard only, that he which persecuted us in times past, now preacheth the faith which once he destroyed.

23. Sed tantum hic rumor apud illos erat; Qui persequebatur nos aliquando, nunc praedicat fidem quam quondam expugnabat.

24. And they glorified God in me.

24. Et glorificabant in me Deum.

15. *But after that it pleased God.* This is the second part of the narrative, and relates to his miraculous conversion. He tells us, first, that he had been called by the grace of God to preach Christ among the Gentiles; and, next, that as soon as he had been called, without consulting the apostles, he unhesitatingly proceeded to the performance of the work, which, he felt assured, had been enjoined upon him by the appointment of God. In the construction of the words, Erasmus differs from the Vulgate. He connects them in the following manner: "When it pleased God that I should preach Christ among the Gentiles, who called me for this purpose that he might reveal him *by me*." But I prefer the old translation; for Christ had been revealed to Paul before he received a command to preach. Admitting that Erasmus were right in translating ἐν ἐμοὶ, *by me*, still the clause, *that I might preach*, is added for the purpose of describing the kind of revelation.

Paul's reasoning does not, at first sight, appear so strong; for although, when he had been converted to Christianity, he instantly, and without consulting the apostles, entered into the office of preaching the gospel, it does not thence follow that he had been appointed to that office by the revelation of Christ. But the arguments which he employs are various, and, when they are all collected, will be found sufficiently strong to establish his conclusion. He argues, first, that he had been called by the grace of God; next, that his apostleship had been acknowledged by the other apostles; and the other arguments follow. Let the reader, therefore, remember to read the whole narrative together, and to draw the inference, not from single parts, but from the whole.

Who had separated me. This separation was the purpose of God, by which Paul was appointed to the apostolic office, before he knew that he was born. The calling followed afterwards at the proper time, when the Lord made known his will concerning him, and commanded him to proceed to the work. God had, no doubt, decreed, before the foundation of the world, what he would do with regard to every one of us, and had assigned to every one, by his secret counsel, his respective place. But the sacred writers frequently introduce those three steps: the eternal predestination of God, the destination from the womb, and the calling, which is the effect and accomplishment of both.

The word of the Lord which came to Jeremiah, though expressed a little differently from this passage, has entirely the same meaning.

"Before I formed thee in the belly, I knew thee; and before thou camest forth from the womb I sanctified thee; a prophet to the nations have I made thee." (Jer 1:5.)

Before they even existed, Jeremiah had been set apart to the office of a prophet, and Paul to that of an apostle; but he is said to separate us from the womb, because the design of our being sent into the world is, that he may accomplish, in us, what he has decreed. The calling is delayed till its proper time, when God has prepared us for the office which he commands us to undertake.

Paul's words may therefore be read thus: "When it pleased God to reveal his Son, by me, who called me, as he had formerly separated me." He intended to assert, that his calling depends on the secret election of God; and that he was ordained an apostle, not because by his own industry he had fitted himself for undertaking so high an office, or because God had accounted him worthy of having it bestowed upon him, but because, before he was born, he had been set apart by the secret purpose of God.

Thus, in his usual manner, he traces his calling to the good pleasure of God. This deserves our careful attention; for it shows us that we owe it to the goodness of God, not only that we have been elected and adopted to everlasting life, but that he deigns to make use of our services, who would otherwise have been altogether useless, and that he assigns to us a lawful calling, in which we may be employed. What had Paul, before he was born, to entitle him to so high an honor? In like manner we ought to believe, that it is entirely the gift of God, and not obtained by our own industry, that we have been called to govern the Church.

The subtle distinctions into which some commentators have entered in explaining the word *separated*, are altogether foreign to the subject. God is said to *separate* us, not because he bestows any peculiar disposition of mind which distinguishes us from others, but because he appoints us by his own purpose [28]. Although the apostle had most explicitly attributed his calling to the free grace of God, when he pronounced that voluntary separation from the womb to be the origin of it, yet he repeats the direct statement, both that, by his commendation of Divine grace, he may take away all grounds of boasting, and that he may testify his own gratitude to God. On this subject he is wont freely to expatiate, even when he has no controversy with the false apostles.

16. *To reveal his Son to me.* If we read it, "to reveal *by me*," it will express the design of the apostleship, which is to make Christ known. And how was this to be accomplished? By preaching him among the Gentiles, which the false apostles treated as a crime. But I consider the Greek phrase ἐν ἐμοὶ [29] to be a Hebrew idiom for *to me*; for the Hebrew particle ב (beth) is frequently redundant, as all who know that language are well aware. The meaning will therefore be, that Christ was revealed *to* Paul, not that he might alone enjoy, and silently retain in his own bosom the knowledge of Christ, but that he might preach among the Gentiles the Savior whom he had known.

Immediately I conferred not. To *confer with flesh and blood*, is to consult with flesh and blood. So far as the meaning of these words is concerned, his intention was absolutely to have nothing to do with any human counsels. The general expression, as will presently appear from the context, includes all men, and all the prudence or wisdom which they may possess. [30] He even makes a direct reference to the apostles, for the express purpose of exhibiting, in a stronger light, the immediate calling of God. Relying on the authority of God alone, and asking nothing more, he proceeded to discharge the duty of preaching the gospel.

17. *Neither did I return to Jerusalem.* What he had just written is now explained, and more fully stated. As if he had said, "I did not ask the authority of any man," not even of the apostles themselves. It is a mistake to suppose, that, because the apostles are now separately mentioned, they are not included in the words, *flesh and blood.* Nothing new or different is here added, but merely a clearer explanation of what had been already said. And no disrespect to the apostles is implied in that expression. For the purpose of shewing that he did not owe his commission to man, the false boasting of unprincipled men laid him under the necessity of contrasting. the authority of the apostles themselves with the authority of God. When a creature is brought into comparison with God, however contemptuous or humiliating may be the language employed, he has no reason to complain.

But I went into Arabia. In the Acts of the Apostles, Luke has omitted these three years. In like manner, there are other passages of the history which he does not touch; and hence the slander of those who seek to build on this a charge of inconsistency in the narratives is ridiculous. Let godly readers consider the severe temptation with which Paul was called to struggle at the very commencement of his course. He who but yesterday, for the sake of doing him honor, had been sent to Damascus with a magnificent retinue, is now compelled to wander as an exile in a foreign land: but he does not lose his courage.

18. *Then after three years.* It was not till three years after he had begun to discharge the apostolic office, that he *went up to Jerusalem.* Thus, he did not, at the outset, receive the calling of men. But lest it should be supposed that he had separate interests from theirs, and was desirous to avoid their society, he tells us that he went up for the express purpose *to see* [31] *Peter.* [32] Although he had not waited for their sanction before undertaking the office, yet it was not against their will, but with their full consent and approbation, that he held the rank of an apostle. He is desirous to shew that at no period was he at variance with the apostles, and that even now he is in full harmony with all their views. By mentioning the short time that he remained there, he shews that he had come, not with a view to learn, but solely for mutual intercourse.

19. *But I saw no other of the apostles.* This is added to make it evident that he had but one object in his journey, and attended to nothing else.

Except James. Who this James was, deserves inquiry. Almost all the ancients are agreed that he was one of the disciples, whose surname was "Oblias" and "The Just," and that he presided over the church at Jerusalem. [33] Yet others think that he was the son of Joseph by another wife, and others (which is more probable) that he was the cousin of Christ by the mother's side: [34] but as he is here mentioned among the apostles, I do not hold that opinion. Nor is there any force in the defense offered by Jerome, that the word Apostle is sometimes applied to others besides the twelve; for the subject under consideration is the highest rank of apostleship, and we shall presently see that he was considered one of the chief *pillars.* (Ga 2:9.) It appears to me, therefore, far more probable, that the person of whom he is speaking is the son of Alpheus. [35]

The rest of the apostles, there is reason to believe, were scattered through various countries; for they did not idly remain in one place. Luke relates that Paul was brought by Barnabas to the apostles. (Ac 9:27.) This must be understood to relate, not to the twelve, but to these two apostles, who alone were at that time residing in Jerusalem.

20. *Now the things which I write to you.* This affirmation extends to the whole narrative. The vast earnestness of Paul on this subject is evinced by his resorting to an oath, which cannot lawfully be employed but on great and weighty occasions. Nor is it wonderful that he insists with so much earnestness on this point; for we have already seen to what expedients the impostors had recourse in order to take from him the name and credit of an apostle. Now the modes of swearing used by good men deserve our attention; for we learn from them that an oath must be viewed simply as an appeal to the judgment-seat of God for the integrity and truth of our words and actions; and such a transaction ought to be guided by religion and the fear of God.

22. *And was unknown by face.* This appears to be added for the sake of shewing more strongly the wickedness and malignity of his slanderers. If the churches of Judea who *had only heard* respecting him, were led to give glory to God for the astonishing change which he had wrought in Paul, how disgraceful was it that those who had beheld the fruits of his amazing labors should not have acted a similar part! If the mere report was enough for the former, why did not the facts before their eyes satisfy the latter?

23. *Which once he destroyed.* This does not mean that *faith* [36] may actually be destroyed, but that he lessened its influence on the minds of weak men. Besides, it is the will, rather than the deed, that is here expressed.

24. *And they glorified God in me* [37] This was an evident proof that his ministry was approved by all the churches of Judea, and approved in such a manner, that they broke out into admiration and praise of the wonderful power of God. Thus he indirectly reproves their malice, by showing that their venom and slanders could have no other effect than to hide the glory of God, which, as the apostles admitted and openly acknowledged, shone brightly in the apostleship of Paul.

This reminds us of the light in which the saints of the Lord ought to be regarded by us. When we behold men adorned with the gifts of God, such is our depravity, or ingratitude, or proneness to superstition, that we worship them as gods, unmindful of Him by whom those gifts were bestowed. These words remind us, on the contrary, to lift up our eyes to the Great Author, and to ascribe to Him what is his own, while they at the same time inform us that an occasion of offering praise to God was furnished by the change produced on Paul, from being an enemy to becoming a minister of Christ.

Footnotes

13

"C'est a dire, sans aucun moyen des hommes." "That is, without any agency of men."

14

"Quoy que depuis on ait observe la ceremonie accoustumee en l'ordination des ministeres." "Although the ceremony usually performed at the ordination of ministers was afterwards added."

15

"Pour nos pechez." "For our sins."

16

"Non pas que cela viene de la creation, mais de leur corruption." "Not that this comes from creation, but from their corruption."

17

Οὐκ εἶπε κατ ' ἐπιταγὴν τοῦ Πατρὸς ἀλλὰ κατὰ τὸ θέλημα, τουτέστι τὴν εὐδοκίαν "He did not say, according to the command, but according to the will, that is, according to the good pleasure, of the Father." — Theophylact.

18

"An English reader would readily suppose that 'God and our Father' are two different persons. The original text suggests no such idea. The meaning is, 'our God and Father'. — The particle καὶ (and) is here hermeneutic. As Crellius says, it is equivalent to 'that is' or 'who is;' or rather, it does not connect different persons, but different descriptions of the same person: 1Co 2:2; Eph 1:3; Eph 4:6; 1Th 1:3; 1Th 3:11; 1Pe 1:2 Ἡμῶν belongs equally to both nouns, Θεοῦ and Πατρός — *Brown.*

19

"Leurs songes et inventions." "Their dreams and inventions."

20

"ὃ οὐκ ἔστιν ἄλλο. Some have questioned the genuineness of ἄλλο,— conjecturing that some one first introduced ἀλλὰ into the margin as an interpretation of εἰ μή, and then some other person changed it into ἄλλο, *per incuriam*, and introduced it into the text. This is ingenious, but, like all conjectural criticism on the New Testament, is of no value." — *Brown*

21

"Quand il denonce les anges pour excommuniez et pour abominables, s'ils enseignent autre chose." "When he denounces the angels as excommunicated and detestable persons, if they teach anything else."

22

" 'Ανάθεμα. This word, which we render *accursed*, doth not signify 'accursed or condemned of God to the punishments of another world.' This the Apostle would not wish to the worst of men. The meaning is, 'Let him be as a person excommunicated, or wholly cut off from the synagogue, or church, with whom it is unlawful to have any commerce or correspondence whatever.' And so it is not properly a wish of the apostle, but a direction to the Galatians how to behave, *Let him be* ἀνάθεμα. 'Hold him, and treat him as an excommunicated and accursed person.'" — Chandler.

23

"D'enseigner autre doctrine que cello qu'il avoit enseignee aux Galatiens." "To teach any other doctrine than that which he had taught to the Galatians."

24

"Quand on y mesle des inventions humaines, et des choses qui ne sont point de mesme." "When it is mixed up with human inventions, and with things that are contrary to it."

25

"Πείθω. This word, which we render *persuade*, frequently signifies 'to obtain by treaty,' or, 'to endeavor the friendship and good will of any person.' Thus in Mt 28:14, the chief-priests tell the soldiers, whom they corrupted, to give a false report: 'If this come to the governor's ears, we will *persuade* him, and secure you, that is, prevail with him to be favorable to you, and save you from punishment.' Thus, Ac 12:20, πείσαντες Βλάστον, we render, 'having made Blastus their friend.' Vid. Pind. Ol. 3:28. And in the Apocryphal book of Maccabees, (2Ma 4:45,) when Menelaus found himself convicted of his crimes, he promised Ptolemy a large sum of money, πεῖσαι τὸν βασιλέα, 'to pacify the king,' to prevent his displeasure, and secure his favor. And thus, in the place before us, 'to persuade God,' is to endeavor to secure his approbation; which, the Apostle assures the Galatians, was his great and only view, as well as his great support, under the censure and displeasure of men, for preaching the pure and uncorrupted doctrines of the gospel." — Chandler.

26

"Qu'il ne parle point d'une chose incertaine ou incognue." "That he does not speak about a thing uncertain or unknown."

27

"The idiom by which there is a transposition of ὅτι is frequent, and may here, Schott thinks, have been made use of, in order to place a highly important topic in the most prominent point of view" — Bloomfield.

28

"Quand par son conseil il nous destine a quelque chose." "When he appoints us to any thing by his purpose."

29

" 'Εν ἐμοὶ, that is, 'to me;' but yet it appears to denote something more." — Beza. "The ancient commentators, and, of the moderns, Winer, Schott, and Scott, seem right in regarding this as a strong expression for 'in my mind and heart.'" — Bloomfield.

30

"The expression, 'flesh and blood,' is used to denote men. Thus when Peter confessed to our Lord, 'Thou art Christ, the Son of the living God,' Jesus answered, 'Flesh and blood hath not revealed it unto thee.' (Mt 16:17.) That is, no man hath made this discovery; and thus it hath the same meaning in the place before us. But as the apostle speaks of his countrymen and equals in age, in the verses before, I apprehend he particularly means them, and that he intends to assure the Galatians, that, notwithstanding his former zeal for the law and the traditions of the Jews, yet that, after his extraordinary conversion, he had no longer any dependence on them, nor sought the least direction from the wisest among them." — Chandler.

31

" ἱστορεῖν signifies either 'to ascertain any *thing* by inquiry, or any *person* by personal examination;' but sometimes, as here, to visit for the purpose of becoming acquainted with any one by personal communication.' So Josephus, Bell. 6:1-8, ὃν (scil. Julianum), ἱστόρησα, 'whom when I came to know and be with.' See Acts 9:26, 27." — Bloomfield.

32

"The distinguished guest of a distinguished host." — Grotius.

33

"Qui estoit pasteur en l'eglise de Jerusalem." "Who was pastor in the church at Jerusalem."

34

"Qu'il estoit cousin-germain de Jesus Christ, fils de la soeur de sa mere." "That he was cousin-german of Jesus Christ, his mother's sister's son."

35

This is fully consistent with the opinion commonly held, that Alpheus or Cleopas was the husband of the sister of Mary, the mother of our Lord, and consequently that James, the son of Alpheus, was our Lord's cousin-german. — *Ed.*

36

"The word πίστις denotes not only the act of believing, but that which is believed." — Beza.

37

"He does not say, They praised or glorified me, but, They glorified God. He says, They glorified God in me; for all that belongs to me was from the grace of God." — OEcumenius.

CHAPTER 2

Galatians 2:1-5

1. Then, fourteen years after, I went up again to Jerusalem with Barnabas, and took Titus with *me* also.

1. Deinde post annos quatuordecim ascendi rursus Hierosolymam una cum Barnaba, assumpto simul et Tito.

2. And I went up by revelation, and communicated unto them that gospel which I preach among the Gentiles, but privately to them which were of reputation, lest by any means I should run, or had run, in vain.

2. Ascendi autem secundum revelationera, et contuli cum illis evangelium, quod praedico inter Gentes; privatim vero cum iis qui in pretio erant, ne quo mode in vahum currerem, aut cucurrssem,

3. But neither Titus, who was with me, being a Greek, was compelled to be circumcised:

3. Sed neque Titus, qui mecum erat, quum esset Graecus, compulsus fuit circumcidi;

4. And that because of false brethren unawares brought in, who came in privily to spy out our liberty which we have in Christ Jesus, that they might bring us into bondage:

4. Propter subingresses falsos fratres, qui subintroierant ad explorandum libertatem nostram, quam habemus in Christo Iesu; quo nos in servitutem adigerent;

5. To whom we gave place by subjection, no, not for an hour, that the truth of the gospel might continue with you.

5. Quibus ne ad heram quidem cessimus per subjectionem, ut veri tas evangelii maneret apud vos.

1. *Fourteen years after*. This cannot with certainty be affirmed to be the same journey mentioned by Luke. (Ac 15:2.) The connection of the history leads us rather to an opposite conclusion. We find that Paul performed four journeys to Jerusalem. Of the first we have already spoken. The second took place when, in company with Barnabas, he brought the charitable contributions of the Greek and Asiatic Churches. (Ac 15:25.) My belief that this second journey is referred to in the present passage rests on various grounds. On any other supposition, the statements of Paul and Luke cannot be reconciled. Besides, there is ground for conjecturing that the rebuke was administered to Peter at Antioch while Paul was residing there. Now, this happened before he was sent to Jerusalem by the Churches to settle the dispute which had arisen about ceremonial observances. (Ac 15:2.) It is not reasonable to suppose that Peter would have used such dissimulation, if that controversy had been settled and the decree of the Apostles published. But Paul writes that he came to Jerusalem, and afterwards adds that he had rebuked Peter for an act of dissimulation, an act which Peter certainly would not have committed except in matters that were doubtful. [38]

Besides, he would scarcely have alluded, at any time, to that journey [39] undertaken with the consent of all the believers, without mentioning the occasion of it, and the memorable decision which was passed. It is not even certain at what time the Epistle was written, only that the Greeks conjecture that it was sent from Rome, and the Latins from Ephesus. For my own part, I think that it was written, not only before Paul had seen Rome, but before that consultation had been held, and the decision of the Apostles given about ceremonial observances. While his opponents were falsely pleading the name of the apostles, and earnestly striving to ruin the reputation of Paul, what carelessness would it have angered in him to pass by the decree universally circulated among them, which struck at those very persons! [40] Undoubtedly, this one word would have shut their mouth: "You bring against me the authority of the apostles, but who does not know their decision? and therefore I hold you convicted of unblushing falsehood. In their name, you oblige the Gentiles to keep the law, but I appeal to their own writing, which sets the consciences of men at liberty."

We may likewise observe, that, in the commencement of the Epistle, he reproved the Galatians for having so soon revolted from the gospel which had been delivered to them. But we may readily conclude, that, after they had been brought to believe the gospel, some time must have elapsed before that dispute about the ceremonial law arose. I consider, therefore, that the fourteen years are to be reckoned, not from one journey to another, but from Paul's conversion. The space of time between the two journeys was eleven years.

2. *And I went up according to revelation.* [41] He now proceeds to prove his apostleship and his doctrine, not only by works, but also by a Divine revelation. Since God directed that journey, which had for its object the confirmation of his doctrine, the doctrine was confirmed, not by the concurrence of men only, but likewise by the authority of God. This ought to have been more than enough to overcome the obstinacy of those who blamed Paul by holding up the names of the apostles. For although, up to this time, there had been some room for debate, the communication of the mind of God put an end to all discussion.

I communicated to them. The word *communicated* claims our first attention; for the apostles do not describe to him what he ought to teach, but, after listening to his own account of his doctrine, express their concurrence and approbation. But, as his opponents might allege that, by cunning dissimulation on many points, he had gained the favor of the apostles, he expressly states that he "communicated to them that doctrine which he preacheth among the Gentiles;" which removes all suspicion of hypocrisy or imposture. We shall see what followed; for the apostles did not take it amiss that he had not waited to obtain their sanction. On the contrary, without dispute or expostulation, they approved of his labors; and did so by the direction of the same Spirit, under whose guidance Paul had performed his journey to Jerusalem. Thus, he was not made an apostle by them, but acknowledged to be an apostle. But this point will be treated more fully afterwards.

Lest by any means. What then? Shall the word of God fall, when it is unsupported by the testimony of men? Though the whole world were unbelieving, yet the word of God remains firm and unshaken: and they who preach the gospel by the command of God are not uselessly employed, even when no fruit is produced by their labors. This is not Paul's meaning; but, as the consciences of men, so long as they doubt and hesitate, derive no benefit from the ministry of the word, so a preacher is said, so far as men is concerned, to *run in vain*, when his labors are ineffectual, and unaccompanied by proper edification.

It was, therefore, a formidable weapon for shaking weak consciences, when the doctrine which Paul preached was falsely declared by impostors to be at variance with the doctrine of the apostles. Multitudes in this manner fell away. The certainty of faith, indeed, does not depend on the agreement of human opinions; but, on the contrary, it is our duty to rest in the naked truth of God, so that neither men nor all the angels together, could shake our faith. Yet ignorant persons, who have imperfectly understood, and never have cordially embraced, sound doctrine, feel the temptation to be almost irresistible, while teachers of acknowledged eminence are found to entertain opposite views. Nay, strong believers are sometimes powerfully affected by this stratagem of Satan, when he holds out to their view the "strife and divisions" (1Co 3:3) of those who ought to have been

"perfectly joined together in the same mind and in the same judgment." (1Co 1:10.)

It is hard to tell how many were driven from the gospel, how many had their faith shaken, by the mournful controversy about the bodily presence of Christ in the Lord's Supper, because, on a question of the highest moment, very distinguished men were observed to take opposite sides.

On the other hand, the agreement of all who teach in the Church is a powerful aid for the confirmation of faith. Since, therefore, Satan was laboring so insidiously to hinder the progress of the gospel, Paul resolved to meet him. When he had succeeded in demonstrating that he held the same views with all the apostles, every hinderance was removed. Weak disciples were no longer perplexed by the inquiry, whom they ought to follow. His meaning may be thus summed up: "That my former labors might not be thrown away and rendered useless, I have set at rest the question which disturbed many minds, whether I or Peter deserved your confidence; for in all that I had ever taught we were perfectly at one." If many teachers in our own day were as heartily desirous as Paul was to edify the Church, they would take more pains to be agreed among themselves.

3. *But neither Titus.* This is an additional argument to prove that the Apostles held the same views with himself; for he had brought to them an uncircumcised man, whom they did not hesitate to acknowledge as a brother. The reason is assigned why he was not circumcised; for circumcision, being a matter of indifference, might be neglected or practiced as edification required. Our invariable rule of action is, that, if "all things are lawful for us," (1Co 10:23) we ought to inquire what is expedient. He circumcises Timothy, (Ac 16:3,) in order to take away a ground of offense from weak minds; for he was at that time dealing with weak minds, which it was his duty to treat with tenderness. And he would gladly have done the same thing with Titus, for he was unwearied in his endeavors to "support (Ac 20:35) the weak;" but the case was different. For some false brethren were watching for an opportunity of slandering his doctrine, and would immediately have spread the report: "See how the valiant champion of liberty, when he comes into the presence of the apostles, lays aside the bold and fierce aspect which he is wont to assume among the ignorant!" Now, as it is our duty to "bear the infirmities of the weak," (Ro 15:1,) so concealed foes, who purposely watch for our liberty, must, be vigorously resisted. The duties of love to our neighbor ought never to be injurious to faith; and therefore, in matters of indifference, the love of our neighbour will be our best guide, provided that faith shall always receive our first regard.

4. *And that because of false brethren.* This may mean either that false brethren made it the subject of wicked accusation, and endeavored to compel him; or that Paul purposely did not circumcise him, because he saw that they would immediately make it an occasion of slander. They had insinuated themselves into Paul's company with the hope of gaining one of two objects. Either he would treat with open scorn the ceremonial law, and then they would rouse the indignation of the Jews against him; or he would refrain entirely from the exercise of his liberty, and in that case they would exult over him among the Gentiles as one who, overwhelmed with shame, had retracted his doctrine.

I prefer the second interpretation, that Paul, having discovered the snares laid for him, determined not to circumcise Titus. When he says that he was not "compelled," the reader is led to understand that circumcision is not condemned as a bad thing in itself, but that the obligation to observe it was the subject of dispute. As if he had said, "I would have been prepared to circumcise Titus if higher matters had not been involved." Their intention was to lay down a law; and to such compulsion he would not yield.

5. *To whom we gave place by subjection, no, not for an hour.* This steadiness was the seal of Paul's doctrine. For when false brethren, who wished nothing more than a ground of accusation against him, exerted themselves to the utmost, and he stood firm, there could no longer be any room for doubt. It cannot now be insinuated that he deceived the apostles. He asserts that he did not for a moment *give place* to them *by subjection*, that is, by such a mode of yielding as would have implied that his liberty had been crushed. In every other respect, he was prepared, to the very close of his life, to exercise mildness and forbearance toward all men.

That the truth of the gospel. There was no danger that Paul would be deprived of his liberty even by yielding to them; but the example would have done harm to others, and therefore he prudently inquired what was expedient. This shows us how far offenses must be avoided, and points us to edification as the object which ought to be kept in view in all matters of indifference. The amount, is this: "We are the servants of the brethren, but still keeping in view that we all serve the Lord, and that the liberty of our conscience shall remain unimpaired." When false brethren wished to bring the saints in to bondage, it was their duty not to yield to them.

The truth of the gospel denotes its genuine purity, or, which means the same thing, its pure and entire doctrine. For the false apostles did not altogether set aside the gospel, but mixed up with it their own notions, so as to give it a false and disguised aspect, which it always has when we make the smallest departure "from the simplicity that is in Christ." (2Co 11:3.)

With what effrontery then will the Papists boast that they possess the gospel, which is not only corrupted by many inventions, but more than adulterated by many wicked doctrines? Let us remember that it is not enough to retain the name of the gospel, and some kind of summary of its doctrines, if its solid purity do not remain untouched. Where are the men who, by pretended moderation, endeavor to bring about a reconciliation between us and the Papists? as if the doctrine of religion, like a matter affecting money or property, could be compromised. With what abhorrence would such a transaction have been regarded by Paul, who affirms that it is not the true gospel, if it is not pure!

Galatians 2:6-10

6. But of those who seemed to be somewhat, (whatsoever they were, it maketh no matter to me: God accepteth no man's person:) for they who seemed *to be somewhat* in conference added nothing to me:

6. Ab iis autem qui videbantur aliquid esse, quales aliquando fuerint, nihil mea refert (personam hominis Deus non accipit, Deut. 10:17, 2 Chr. 19:7Job 34:19; Wis. 6:8, Sir. 35:15; Ac 10:34; Ro 2:11; Eph 6:9; Col 3:25; 1Pe 1:17) nam mihi, qui videbantur esse in pretio nihil contulerunt

7. But contrariwise, when they saw that the gospel of the uncircumcision was committed unto me, as *the gospel* of the circumcision *was* unto Peter;

7. Imo contra, quum vidissent mihi concreditum fuisse evangelium praeprputii, quemadmodum Petro Circumcisionis;

8. (For he that wrought effectually in Peter to the apostleship of the circumcision, the same was mighty in me toward the Gentiles:)

8. (Nam qui efficax fuit in Petro ad apostolatum Circumcisionis efficax fuit et in me erga Gentes);

9. And when James, Cephas, and John, who seemed to be pillars, perceived the grace that was given unto me, they gave to me and Barnabas right hands of fellowship; that we *should go* unto the heathen, and they unto the circumcision.

9. Quumque cognovissent gratiam mihi datam Iaeobus et Cephas et Ioannes, qui videbantur columnae esse, dextras dederunt mihi ac Barnabae societatis, ut nos inter Gentes, ipsi vore in Circumcisionem, apestolatu fungerenur.

10. Only *they would* that we should remember the poor; the same which I also was forward to do.

10. Tanturn ut pauperurn memores essenms, in quo et diligens fui, ut hoc ipsum facerem.

6. *Of those who seemed to be somewhat.* [42] Paul is not yet satisfied, without making the Galatians understand that he had learned nothing from Peter and the apostles. Hence Porphyry and Julian [43] accuse the holy man of pride, because he claims so much for himself that he cannot endure to learn anything from others; because he boasts of having become a teacher without any instruction or assistance; and because he labors so hard not to appear in an inferior character. But any one who will consider how necessary that boasting was, will acknowledge that it was holy boasting, and worthy of the highest praise; for, if he had yielded this point to his opponents, that he had profited under the apostles, he would have furnished them with two charges against him. They would immediately have said, "And so you made some progress; you corrected your past errors, and did not repeat your former rashness." Thus, in the first place, the whole doctrine which he had hitherto taught would have fallen under suspicion; and, secondly, he would ever afterwards have possessed less authority, because he would have been reckoned but an ordinary disciple. We find, therefore, that it was not on his own account, but by the necessity under which he lay to establish the doctrine, that he was led to this holy boasting. The controversy has no reference to individuals, and therefore cannot be a struggle of ambition; but Paul's determination was that no man, however eminent, should throw into the shade his apostleship, on which the authority of his doctrine depended. If this be not enough to silence those dogs, their barking is sufficiently answered.

Whatsoever they were. These words must be read as a separate clause; for the parenthesis was intended to assure his opponents that he did not concern himself with the opinions of men. This passage has been variously interpreted. Ambrose thinks that it is a passing reference to the folly of attempting to lower Paul by holding up the apostles; and represents him as saying; "As if I were not equally at liberty to object that they were poor, illiterate men, while I, from my early years, enjoyed a liberal education under the care of Gamaliel. But I pass over all this, because I know that there is no respect of persons with God." Chrysostom and Jerome take a harsher view of the words, as an indirect threatening of the most distinguished apostles. "Whatsoever they may be, if they swerve from duty, they shall not escape the judgment of God; neither the dignity of their office, nor the estimation of men, shall protect them." But another interpretation appears to me more simple, and more agreeable to Paul's design. He admits that they were first in the order of time, but contends that this did not prevent him from being their equal in rank. He does not say that it is of no consequence to him what they are at present; but he is speaking of a period now past, when they were already apostles, and when he was opposed to the faith of Christ. In short, he does not choose that what is past shall decide the matter; and refuses to admit the proverb, that he who comes first has the best right.

No man's person. Besides the interpretations which I have mentioned, a third is not unworthy of notice, — that in the government of the world distinctions of rank are admitted, but in the spiritual kingdom of Christ they can have no place. There is plausibility in the statement, but it is in reference to worldly government, that it is said,

"Ye shall not respect persons in judgment,."

(De 1:17.)

But I do not enter into that argument, for it does not affect this passage. Paul simply means, that the honorable rank which the apostles had attained did not prevent him from being called by God, and raised, all at once, from the lowest condition to be their equal. The difference between them, though great, is of no value in the sight of God, who does not accept persons, and whose calling is not influenced by any prejudices. But this view may likewise appear liable to objection; for, granting it to be true, and a truth which must be carefully maintained, that in our intercourse with God there is no respect of persons, how does this apply to Peter and his fellow-apostles, who were venerable, not merely for their rank, but for true holiness and spiritual gifts?

The word *person* is contrasted with the fear of God and a good conscience; and this is its ordinary acceptation in Scripture. (Acts 10:34, 35 1Pe 1:17.) But piety, zeal, holiness, and other similar graces, were the principal grounds of the esteem and respect in which the apostles were held; while Paul speaks contemptuously of them, as if they had possessed nothing but the outward forms.

I reply: Paul is not discussing the real worth of the apostles, but the idle boasting of his adversaries. In order to support their own unfounded pretensions, they talked in lofty terms of Peter, and James, and John, and took advantage of the veneration with which they were regarded by the Church, for accomplishing their earnest desire of degrading Paul. His object is not to inquire what the apostles are, or what opinion must be formed respecting them when controversy is laid aside, but to tear off the disguises which the false apostles wore. As in a subsequent part of the Epistle he treats of circumcision, not in its real character, but in the false and impious notion attached to it by those impostors, so he now declares that the apostles were in the sight of God disguises, by which those persons attempted to shine in the world; and this is evident from the words. Why did they prefer them to Paul? because they were his predecessors in office. This was a mere disguise. In any other point of view, they would have been highly esteemed, and the gifts of God manifested in them would have been warmly admired by one so singularly modest as the apostle Paul, who elsewhere acknowledges that he was "the least of the apostles," and unworthy to occupy so exalted a station.

"I am the least of the apostles, and not worthy to be called an apostle, because I persecuted the Church of God."

(1Co 15:9.)

They communicated nothing to me. It might also be rendered, "they communicated nothing with me;" for it is the same word which he formerly used twice. [44] But the meaning is the same. When the apostles had heard Paul's gospel, they did not on the other side bring forward their own, (as is commonly done when something better and more perfect is desired,) but were satisfied with his explanation, and simply and unhesitatingly embraced his doctrine, so that not even on the most doubtful point did a single word of debate pass between them. Nor are we to suppose that Paul, presuming on his superiority, took the lead in the discussion, and dictated to his brethren. On the contrary, his faith, about which unfavourable rumors had been spread, was fully explained by him, and sanctioned by their appropation.

7. *But, on the contrary.* They immediately *gave him the right hand of fellowship.* (Ga 2:9.) Consequently they gave their testimony to his doctrine, and without any exception; for they produced nothing on the other side, as is commonly done on debated points, but acknowledged that he held the same gospel in common with them, and was therefore entitled to the honors and rank of an associate. Now, one condition of this *fellowship* was, that they distributed the provinces among themselves. They were therefore equal, and there was no subjection on the part of Paul. To "give the right hands of fellowship" means here, to have a partnership settled by mutual agreement.

When they saw that the gospel of the uncircumcision was committed to me. He asserts that he was not indebted to the apostles for the favor of being made an apostle by their consent and approbation, but that, in conceding to him the apostleship, they only refused to take away what God had given. He constantly urges that he was made an apostle by the gift and appointment of God, but adds here that he was acknowledged as such by the apostles themselves. Hence it followed, that those unprincipled men were attempting, what the apostles durst not have attempted, to oppose the election of God.

And here he begins to claim what belonged to himself in preference to others, the apostleship of the uncircumcision. For Paul and Barnabas differed from the rest in this respect, that they had been appointed to be apostles of the Gentiles. (Ac 13:2.) That had been done by a Divine revelation, which the apostles not only did not oppose, but determined to ratify, because not to obey it, would have been impious. This shows us in what manner they arranged their respective duties, in compliance with a Divine revelation, namely, that Paul and Barnabas should be the apostles of the Gentiles, and that the others should be the apostles of the Jews.

But this appears to be at variance with the command of Christ, which enjoins that the twelve shall

"go unto all the world, and preach the gospel to every creature." (Mr 16:15.)

I reply, that command was not intended to apply specifically to each individual, but describes in general terms the design of the apostolic office, which was, that salvation must be proclaimed to all nations by the doctrine of the gospel. For the apostles evidently did not travel over the whole world; nay, it is probable that not one of the twelve ever passed into Europe. What they allege about Peter may, for aught I know, be fabulous, and is, at all events, quite uncertain.

All of them, it will be objected, had still a commission both to Gentiles and to Jews. I own they had, as occasion offered. Each apostle, I grant, was entrusted with the publication of the gospel both among Gentiles and Jews; for the distribution was not of such a nature as to assign them fixed boundaries, like those of kingdoms, principalities, and provinces, which could not lawfully be passed. We see that Paul, wherever he went, uniformly offered his labors and services, in the first instance, to the Jews. As he had a right, while living among the Gentiles, to offer himself as an apostle and teacher to the Jews; so the others were at liberty, wherever they had it in their power, to bring Gentiles to Christ; and we find Peter exercising this privilege with regard to Cornelius and others. (Ac 10:1.) But as there were other apostles in that district, which was almost wholly inhabited by Jews, Paul traveled through Asia, Greece, and other distant parts, and on this occasion was specially ordained to be an apostle to the Gentiles. Nay, when the Lord first commanded him to be set apart, he directed him to leave Antioch and Syria, and perform voyages to distant countries for the sake of the Gentiles. On ordinary occasions, therefore, he was the apostle of the Gentiles, and on extraordinary occasions, he was the apostle of the Jews. The other apostles, again, took the Jews for their own department, but with the understanding that, when an opportunity occurred, they would be at liberty to direct their ministrations to the Gentiles; this last, however, being in their case an extraordinary service.

But if Peter's apostleship had a peculiar reference to the Jews, let the Romanists see on what ground they derive from him their succession to the primacy. If the Pope of Rome claims the primacy because he is Peter's successor, he ought to exercise it over the Jews. Paul is here declared to be the chief apostle of the Gentiles, yet they affirm that he was not bishop of Rome; and, therefore, if the Pope would establish any claim to his primacy, let him gather churches from among the Jews. He who by a decree of the Holy Spirit, and by the consent of the whole apostolic college, has been solemnly declared to be one of the apostles, cannot but be acknowledged by us in that character. Those who would transfer that right to Peter set aside all ordination, both human and divine. It is unnecessary to explain here the well-known metaphor in the words *circumcision* and *uncircumcision*, as applied to Jews and Gentiles.

8. *He that wrought effectually.* That the province which had been assigned to him was truly his own, is proved by the exertion of divine power during his ministry. Now, this manifestation of divine energy, as we have frequently seen, is the seal by which his doctrine was attested, and his office as a teacher sanctioned. Whether Paul refers God's *effectual working* to the success of his preaching, or to the graces of the Holy Spirit which were then bestowed on believers, is doubtful. I do not understand it as denoting the mere success, but the spiritual power and efficacy, [45] which he has elsewhere mentioned. (1Co 2:4.) The amount of the whole is, that it was no idle bargain which the apostles had made among themselves, but a decision which God had sealed.

9. *And when they perceived the grace.* They who treated with contempt the grace of God, by which the most eminent apostles had been led to admire and reverence Paul, are charged with hateful and proud disdain. If they should allege that they were ignorant of that which the apostles knew from the beginning, the hypocritical pretense was not to be endured. This admonishes us to yield to the grace of God, wherever it is perceived, unless we choose to contend with the Holy Spirit, whose will it is that his gifts shall not remain unemployed. The grace which the apostles perceived to have been given to Paul and Barnabas, induced them to sanction their ministry by receiving them as their associates.

James and Cephas. I have already stated, that James was the son of Alpheus. He could not be "the brother of John" who had been lately put to death by Herod, (Ac 12:2,) and to suppose that one of the disciples had been placed above the apostles would be absurd. That he held the highest rank among the apostles, is made evident by Luke, who ascribes to him the summing up and decision of the cause in the council, (Ac 15:13,) and afterwards mentions his having assembled "all the elders" of the church of Jerusalem. (Ac 21:18.) When he says, that they *seemed to be pillars*, he does not speak contemptuously, but quotes the general opinion, arguing from it, that what was done by such men ought not to be lightly set aside. In a question relating to diversity of rank, it is surprising that James should be mentioned before Peter; but the reason perhaps is, that he presided over the church at Jerusalem. As to the word *pillar*, we know that, from the nature of things, those who excel in ability, prudence, or other gifts, possess greater authority. And even in the Church of God, he who enjoys a larger measure of grace ought, on that account, to receive the higher honor. It argues ingratitude, nay impiety, not to worship the Spirit of God wherever he appears in his gifts; and as a people cannot want a pastor, so the assemblies of pastors require a moderator. But in all cases let the rule be followed,

"He that is greatest among you shall be your servant" (Mt 23:11.)

10. *That we should remember the poor.* It is evident that the brethren who were in Judea labored under extreme poverty: otherwise they would not have burdened other churches. That might arise both from the various calamities which befell the whole nation, and from the cruel rage of their own countrymen, by which they were every day stript of their possessions. It was proper that they should receive assistance from the Gentiles, who owed to them the inestimable benefit of the gospel. Paul says, that he was *forward to do*, that he faithfully performed, what the apostles had requested from him, and thus he takes away from his adversaries a pretext which they were desirous to seize.

Galatians 2:11-16

11. But when Peter was come to Antioch, I withstood him to the face, because he was to be blamed.

11. Quum autem venisset Petrus Antiochiam, palam ei restiti, eo quod reprehensione dignus esset.

12. For, before that certain came from James, he did eat with the Gentiles: but when they were come, he withdrew, and separated himself, fearing them which were of the circumcision.

12. Nam antequam venissent quidam ab Iacobo, una cum Gentibus sumebat cibum; quum autem venissent, subduxit ac separavit se ab illis, metuens eos qui erant ex Circumcisione.

13. And the other Jews dissembled likewise with him; insomuch that Barnabas also was carried away with their dissimulation.

13. Acts simulabant una cum illo caeteri quoque Iudeai, adeo ut Barnabas simul abduceretur in illorum simulationem.

14. But when I saw that they walked not uprightly, according to the truth of the gospel, I said unto Peter before *them* all, If thou, being a Jew, livest after the manner of Gentiles, and not as do the Jews, why compellest thou the Gentiles to live as do the Jews?

14. Verum ubi vidissem, quod non recto pede incederent ad veritatem evangelii, dixi Petro coram omnibus: Si tu, quum sis Iudaeus, Gentiliter vivis, et non Iudaice; cur cogis Gentes Iudaizare?

15. We *who are* Jews by nature, and not sinners of the Gentiles,

15. Nos natura Iudaei, et non ex Gentibus peccatores,

16. Knowing that a man is not justified by the works of the law, but by the faith of Jesus Christ, even we have believed in Jesus Christ, that we might be justified by the faith of Christ, and not by the works of the law: for by the works of the law shall no flesh be justified.

16. Cognito, non justificari hominem ex operibus legis, nisi per fidem Iesu Christi, et nos in Iesum Christum credidimus, ut justificaremur ex fide Christi, et non ex operibus legis; propterea quod non justificabitur ex operibus legis onmis care.

11. *When Peter was come.* Whoever will carefully examine all the circumstances, will, I trust, agree with me in thinking, that this happened before the apostles had decided that the Gentiles should receive no annoyance about ceremonial observances. (Ac 15:28.) For Peter would have entertained no dread of offending James, or those sent by him, after that decision had been passed: but such was the dissimulation of Peter, that, in opposing it, Paul was driven to assert "the truth of the gospel." At first he said, that the certainty of his gospel does not in any degree depend on Peter and the apostles, so as to stand or fall by their judgment. Secondly, he said, that it had been approved by all without any exception or contradiction, and particularly by those who were universally admitted to hold the highest place. Now, as I have said, he goes further, and asserts that he had blamed Peter for leaning to the other side; and he proceeds to explain the cause of the dispute. It was no ordinary proof of the strength of his doctrine, that he not only obtained their cordial approbation, but firmly maintained it in a debate with Peter, and came off victorious. What reason could there now be for hesitating to receive it as certain and undoubted truth?

At the same time, this is a reply to another calumny, that Paul was but an ordinary disciple, far below the rank of an apostle: for the reproof which he administered was an evidence that the parties were on an equal footing. The highest, I acknowledge, are sometimes properly reproved by the lowest, for this liberty on the part of inferiors towards their superiors is permitted by God; and so it does not follow, that he who reproves another must be his equal. But the nature of the reproof deserves notice. Paul did not simply reprove Peter, as a Christian might reprove a Christian, but he did it officially, as the phrase is; that is, in the exercise of the apostolic character which he sustained.

This is another thunderbolt which strikes the Papacy of Rome. It exposes the impudent pretensions of the Roman Antichrist, who boasts that he is not bound to assign a reason, and sets at defiance the judgment of the whole Church. Without rashness, without undue boldness, but in the exercise of the power granted him by God, this single individual chastises Peter, in the presence of the whole Church; and Peter submissively bows to the chastisement. Nay, the whole debate on those two points was nothing less than a manifest overthrow of that tyrannical primacy, which the Romanists foolishly enough allege to be founded on divine right. If they wish to have God appearing on their side, a new Bible must be manufactured; if they do not wish to have him for an open enemy, those two chapters of the Holy Scriptures must be expunged.

Because he was worthy of blame. The Greek participle, κατεγνωσμένος, signifies Blamed, so that the words run, "because he was blamed;" but I have no doubt whatever, that the word was intended to express, "one who deserves just blame." Chrysostom makes the meaning to be, that others had previously indulged in complaint and accusation; but this is really trifling. It was customary with the Greeks to give to their participles the signification of nouns, which, every person must see, is applicable to this passage. This will enable us to perceive the absurdity of the interpretation given by Jerome and Chrysostom, who represent the whole transaction as a feigned debate, which the apostles had previously arranged to take place in presence of the people. They are not even supported by the phrase, "I withstood him *to the face*, κατὰ πρόσωπον, which means that "to the face," or "being present," Peter was chastised and struck dumb. The observation of Chrysostom, that, for the sake of avoiding scandal, they would have talked in private if they had any difference, is frivolous. The less important must be disregarded in comparison of the most dangerous of all scandals, that the Church would be rent, that Christian liberty was in danger, that the doctrine of the grace of Christ was overthrown; and therefore this public offense must be publicly corrected.

The chief argument on which Jerome rests is excessively trifling. "Why should Paul," says he, "condemn in another what he takes praise for in himself? for he boasts that 'to the Jews he became as a Jew.'" (1Co 9:20.) I reply, that what Peter did is totally different. Paul accommodated himself to the Jews no farther than was consistent with the doctrine of liberty; and therefore he refused to circumcise Titus, that the truth of the gospel might remain unimpaired. But Peter Judaized in such a manner as to "compel the Gentiles" to suffer bondage, and at the same time to create a prejudice against Paul's doctrine. He did not, therefore, observe the proper limit; for he was more desirous to please than to edify, and more solicitous to inquire what would gratify the Jews than what would be expedient for the whole body. Augustine is therefore right in asserting, that this was no previously arranged plan, but that Paul, out of Christian zeal, opposed the sinful and unseasonable dissimulation of Peter, because he saw that it would be injurious to the Church.

12. *For before that certain persons came.* The state of the case is here laid down. For the sake of the Jews, Peter had withdrawn himself from the Gentiles, in order to drive them from the communion of the Church, unless they would relinquish the liberty of the Gospel, and submit to the yoke of the Law. If Paul had been silent here, his whole doctrine fell; all the edification obtained by his ministry was ruined. It was therefore necessary that he should rise manfully, and fight with courage. This shews us how cautiously we ought to guard against giving way to the opinions of men, lest an immoderate desire to please, or an undue dread of giving offense, should turn us aside from the right path. If this might happen to Peter, how much more easily may it happen to us, if we are not duly careful!

14. *But when I saw that they walked not uprightly.* Some apply these words to the Gentiles, who, perplexed by Peter's example, were beginning to give way; but it is more natural to understand them as referring to Peter and Barnabas, and their followers. The proper road to the truth of the gospel was, to unite the Gentiles with the Jews in such a manner that the true doctrine should not be injured. But to bind the consciences of godly men by an obligation to keep the law, and to bury in silence the doctrine of liberty, was to purchase unity at an exorbitant price.

The truth of the gospel is here used, by Paul, in the same sense as before, and is contrasted with those disguises by which Peter and others concealed its beauty. In such a case, the struggle which Paul had to maintain must unquestionably have been serious. They were perfectly agreed about doctrine; [46] but since, laying doctrine out of view, Peter yielded too submissively to the Jews, he is accused of halting. There are some who apologize for Peter on another ground, because, being the apostle of the circumcision, he was bound to take a particular concern in the salvation of the Jews; while they at the same time admit that Paul did right in pleading the cause of the Gentiles. But it is foolish to defend what the Holy Spirit by the mouth of Paul has condemned. This was no affair of men, but involved the purity of the gospel, which was in danger of being contaminated by Jewish leaven.

Before them all. This example instructs us, that those who have sinned publicly must be publicly chastised, so far as concerns the Church. The intention is, that their sin may not, by remaining unpunished, form a dangerous example; and Paul elsewhere (1Ti 5:20) lays down this rule expressly, to be observed in the case of elders,

"Them that sin rebuke before all, that others also may fear;"

because the station which they hold renders their example more pernicious. It was particularly advantageous, that the good cause, in which all had an interest, should be openly defended in presence of the people, that Paul might have a better opportunity of shewing that he did not shrink from the broad light of day.

If thou, being a Jew. Paul's address to Peter consists of two parts. In the first, he expostulates with him for his injustice toward the Gentiles, in compelling them to keep the law, from the obligations of which he wished himself to be exempted. For, not to mention that every man is bound to keep the law which he lays down for others, his conduct was greatly aggravated by compelling the Gentiles to observe Jewish ceremonies, while he, being a Jew, left himself at liberty. The law was given to Jews, not to Gentiles; so that he argues from the less to the greater.

Next, it is argued, that, in a harsh and violent manner, he *compelled the Gentiles*, by withdrawing from their communion, unless they chose to submit to the yoke of the law; and thus imposed on them an unjust condition. And, indeed, the whole force of the reproof lies in this word, which neither Chrysostom nor Jerome has remarked. The use of ceremonies was free for the purposes of edification, provided that believers were not deprived of their liberty, or laid under any restraint from which the gospel sets them free.

15. *We who are Jews by nature.* Some, I am aware, think that this is stated in the form of an objection, (ἀνθυποφορὰ,) anticipating what might be urged on the other side, that the Jews possessed higher privileges; not that they would boast of exemption from the law, (for it would have been highly absurd, that they to whom the Law was given should make this their boast,) but that there was a propriety in retaining some points of distinction between them and the Gentiles. I do not entirely reject, and yet, as will afterwards appear, I do not altogether adopt this view. Some, again, consider that it is Paul himself who uses this argument, "If you were to lay upon the Jews the burden of the law, it would be more reasonable, because it is theirs by inheritance." But neither do I approve of this view.

He is now proceeding to the second part of his speech, which commences with an anticipation. The Gentiles differed from them in this respect, that they were "unholy and profane," (1Ti 1:9;) while the Jews, being holy, so far as God had chosen them for his people, might contend for this superiority. Skilfully anticipating the objection, Paul turns it to the opposite conclusion. Since the Jews themselves, with all their advantages, were forced to betake themselves to the faith of Christ, how much more necessary was it that the Gentiles should look for salvation through faith? Paul's meaning therefore is: "We, who appear to excel others, — we, who, by means of the covenant, have always enjoyed the privilege of being nigh to God, (De 4:7,) have found no method of obtaining salvation, but by believing in Christ: why, then, should we prescribe another method to the Gentiles? For, if the law were necessary or advantageous for salvation to those who observed its enactments, it must have been most of all advantageous to us to whom it was given; but if we relinquished it, and betook ourselves to Christ, much less ought compliance with it to be urged upon the Gentiles."

The word *sinner*, signifies here, as in many other places, a "profane person," (Heb 12:16,) or one who is lost and alienated from God. Such were the Gentiles, who had no intercourse with God; while the Jews were, by adoption, the children of God, and therefore set apart to holiness. *By nature*, does not mean that they were naturally free from the corruption of the human race; for David, who was a descendant of Abraham, acknowledges,

"Behold, I was shapen in iniquity, and in sin did my mother conceive me," (Ps 51:5,)

but the corruption of nature, to which they were liable, had been met by the remedy of sanctifying grace. Now, as the promise made the blessing hereditary, so this benefit is called natural; just as, in the Epistle to the Romans, he says, that they were sprung from a "holy root." (Ro 11:16.)

When he says, *we are Jews by nature,* his meaning is, "We are born holy: not certainly by our own merit, but because God hath chosen us to be his people." Well, then, we who were by nature Jews, what have we done? "We have believed in Jesus Christ." What was the design of our believing? "That we might be justified by the faith of Christ." For what reason? Because we "know that a man is not justified by the works of the law." From the nature and effect of faith, he reasons that the Jews are in no degree justified by the law. For, as they who

"go about to establish their own righteousness have not submitted themselves to the righteousness of God," (Ro 10:3,)

so, on the contrary, they who believe in Christ, confess that they are sinners, and renounce justification by works. This involves the main question, or rather, in this single proposition nearly the whole controversy is embodied. It is the more necessary to bestow some care on the examination of this passage.

The first thing to be noticed is, that we must seek justification by the faith of Christ, because we cannot be justified by works. Now, the question is, what is meant by *the works of the law*? The Papists, misled by Origen and Jerome, are of opinion, and lay it down as certain, that the dispute relates to shadows; and accordingly assert, that by "the works of the law" are meant ceremonies. As if Paul were not reasoning about the free justification which is bestowed on us by Christ. For they see no absurdity in maintaining that "no man is justified by the works of the law," and yet that, by the merit of works, we are accounted righteous in the sight of God. In short, they hold that no mention is here made of the works of the moral law. But the context clearly proves that the moral law is also comprehended in these words; for almost everything which Paul afterwards advances belongs more properly to the moral than to the ceremonial law; and he is continually employed in contrasting the righteousness of the law with the free acceptance which God is pleased to bestow.

It is objected by our opponents, that the term "works" must have been employed without any addition, if Paul had not intended to limit it to a particular class. But I reply, there is the best of all reasons for this mode of expression; for, though a man were to excel all the angels in holiness, no reward is due to works, but on the footing of a Divine promise. Perfect obedience to the law is righteousness, and has a promise of eternal life annexed to it; but it derives this character from God, who declares that "they who have fulfilled them shall live." (Le 18:5.) On this point we shall afterwards treat more fully in its own place. [47] Besides, the controversy with the Jews was about the law. Paul, therefore, chose rather to bring the matter to an issue, by meeting them at once on their own ground, than to adopt a more circuitous route, which might wear the aspect of evading the subject, or distrusting his cause. Accordingly he resolves to have a close debate about the law.

Their second objection is, that the whole question raised was about ceremonies, which we readily allow. Why then, say they, would the apostle pass suddenly from a particular department to the whole subject? This was the sole cause of the mistake into which Origen and Jerome were betrayed; for they did not think it natural that, while the false apostles were contending about ceremonies alone, Paul should take in a larger field. But they did not consider that the very reason for disputing so keenly was, that the doctrine led to more serious consequences than at first view appeared. It would not have given so much uneasiness to Paul that ceremonies should be observed, as that the confident hope and the glory of salvation should be made to rest on works; just as, in the dispute about forbidding flesh on certain days, we do not look so much to the importance of the prohibition itself, as to the snare which is laid for the consciences of men. Paul, therefore, does not wander from the subject, when he enters into a controversy about the whole law, although the arguments of the false apostles were confined wholly to ceremonies. Their object in pressing ceremonies was, that men might seek salvation by obedience to the law, which, they falsely maintained, was meritorious; and accordingly, Paul meets them, not with the moral law, but with the grace of Christ alone. And yet this extended discussion does not occupy the whole of the Epistle; he comes at length to the specific question of ceremonies: but as the most serious difficulty was, whether justification is to be obtained by works or by faith, it was proper that this should be first settled. As the Papists of the present day are uneasy when we extort from them the acknowledgment that men are justified by faith alone, they reluctantly admit that "the works of the law" include those of a moral nature. Many of them, however, by quoting Jerome's gloss, imagine that they have made a good defense; but the context will show that the words relate also to the moral law. [48]

16. *But by the faith of Jesus Christ.* He does not merely state that ceremonies, or works of any kind, are insufficient without the assistance of faith, but meets their denial by a statement admitting of no exception, as if he had said, "Not by works, but by the Gift of Christ alone." In any other point of view, the sentiment would have been trivial and foreign to the purpose; for the false apostles did not reject Christ nor faith, but demanded that ceremonies should be joined with them. If Paul had admitted this claim, they would have been perfectly at one, and he would have been under no necessity to agitate the church by this unpleasant debate. Let it therefore remain settled, that the proposition is so framed as to admit of no exception, "that we are justified in no other way than by faith," or, "that we are not justified but by faith," or, which amounts to the same thing, "that we are justified by faith alone."

Hence it appears with what silly trifling the Papists of our day dispute with us about the word, as if it had been a word of our contrivance. But Paul was unacquainted with the theology of the Papists, who declare that a man is justified by faith, and yet make a part of justification to consist in works. Of such half-justification Paul knew nothing. For, when he instructs us that we are justified by faith, because we cannot be justified by works, he takes for granted what is true, that we cannot be justified through the righteousness of Christ, unless we are poor and destitute of a righteousness of our own. [49] Consequently, either nothing or all must be ascribed to faith or to works. As to the word justification, and the manner in which faith is the cause of it, we shall afterwards see.

By the works of the law shall no flesh be justified. He had already appealed to the consciences of Peter and others, and now confirms it more fully by affirming that such is the actual truth, that by the works of the law no mortal will obtain justification. This is the foundation of a freely bestowed righteousness, when we are stripped of a righteousness of our own. Besides, when he asserts that no mortal is justified by the righteousness of the law, the assertion amounts to this, that from such a mode of justification all mortals are excluded, and that none can possibly reach it.

Galatians 2:17-21

17. But if, while we seek to be justified by Christ, we ourselves also are found sinners, *is* therefore Christ the minister of sin? God forbid.

17. Porro si quaerentes justificari in Christo, inventi sumus ipsi quoque peccatores, ergo Christus peceati minister est? absit.

18. For if I build again the things which I destroyed, I make myself a transgressor.

18. Nam si quae destruxi haec rursum aedifieo, praevaricatorem me ipsum constituo.

19. For I through the law am dead to the law, that I might live unto God.

19. Ego enim per Legem Legi mortuus sum. Ut Deo viverem,

20. I am crucified with Christ: nevertheless I live; yet not I, but Christ liveth in me: and the life which I now live in the flesh I live by the faith of the Son of God, who loved me, and gave himself for me.

20. Cum Christo sum crucifixus; vivo autem non amplius ego, sed vivit in me Christus; quod autem nunc vivo in carne, in fide vivo Filii Dei, qui dilexit me, et tradidit se ipsum pro me.

21. I do not frustrate the grace of God: for if righteousness *come* by the law, then Christ is dead in vain.

21. Non abjicio gratiam Dei; si enim per Legem justitia, ergo Christus gratis mortuus est.

17. *If, while we seek to be justified.* He now returns to the Galatians. We must take care not to connect this verse with the preceding one, as if it were a part of the speech addressed to Peter: for what had Peter to do with this argument? It certainly has very little, if anything, to do with the speech; but let every one form his own opinion.

Chrysostom, and some other commentators, make the whole passage to be an affirmation, and interpret it thus: "If, while we seek to be justified by Christ, we are not yet perfectly righteous, but still unholy, and if, consequently, Christ is not sufficient for our righteousness, it follows that Christ is the minister of the doctrine which leaves men in sin:" supposing that, by this absurd proposition, Paul insinuates a charge of blasphemy against those who attribute a part of justification to the law. But as the expression of indignant abhorrence immediately follows, which Paul is never accustomed to employ but in answer to questions, I am rather inclined to think that the statement is made for the purpose of setting aside an absurd conclusion which his doctrine appeared to warrant. He puts a question, in his usual manner, into the mouth of his antagonists. "If, in consequence of the righteousness of faith, we, who are Jews and were 'sanctified from the womb,' (Jer 1:5 Ga 1:15,) are reckoned guilty and polluted, shall we say that Christ makes sin to be powerful in his own people, and that he is therefore the author of sin?"

This suspicion arose from his having said that Jews, by believing in Christ, renounce the righteousness of the law; for, while they are still at a distance from Christ, Jews, separated from the ordinary pollution of the Gentiles, appear to be in some respects exempted from the appellation of sinners. The grace of Christ places them on a level with the Gentiles; and the remedy, which is common to both, shews that both had labored under the same disease. This is the force of the particle also, — *we ourselves also*, — meaning not any description of men, but the Jews, who stood highest.

Far from it. He properly rejects that inference. Christ, who discovers the sin which lay concealed, is not therefore the minister of sin; as if, by depriving us of righteousness, he opened the gate to sin, or strengthened its dominion. [50] The Jews were mistaken in claiming any holiness for themselves apart from Christ, while they had none. Hence arose the complaint: "Did Christ come to take from us the righteousness of the law, to change saints into polluted men, to subject us to sin and guilt?" Paul denies it, and repels the blasphemy with abhorrence. Christ did not bring sin, but unveiled it; he did not take away righteousness, but stripped the Jews of a false disguise.

18. *For if I build again.* The reply consists of two parts. This is the first part, and informs us that the supposition now made is at variance with his whole doctrine, since he had preached the faith of Christ in such a manner as to connect with it the ruin and destruction of sin. For, as we are taught by John, that Christ came not to build up the kingdom of sin, but "that he might destroy the works of the devil," (1Jo 3:8,) so Paul declares, that, in preaching the gospel, he had restoreth true righteousness, in order that sin might be destroyed. It was, therefore, in the highest degree improbable, that the same person who destroyed sin should renew its power; and, by stating the absurdity, he repels the calumny.

19. *For I through the law.* Now follows the direct reply, that we must not ascribe to Christ that work which properly belongs to the law. It was not necessary that Christ should destroy the righteousness of the law, for the law itself slays its disciples. As if he had said, "You deceive wretched men by the false notion, that they must live by the law; and, under that pretext, you keep them in the law. And yet you bring it as a charge against the Gospel, that it annihilates the righteousness which we have by the law. But it is the law which forces us to die to itself; for it threatens our destruction, leaves us nothing but despair, and thus drives us away from trusting to the law."

This passage will be better understood by comparing it with Ro 7. There Paul describes beautifully, that no man lives to the law, but he to whom the law is dead, that is, has lost all power and efficacy; for, as soon as the law begins to live in us, it inflicts a fatal wound by which we die, and at the same time breathes life into the man who is already dead to sin. Those who live to the law, therefore, have never felt the power of the law, or properly understood what the law means; for the law, when truly perceived, makes us die to itself, and it is from this source, and not from Christ, that sin proceeds.

To die to the law, may either mean that we renounce it, and are delivered from its dominion, so that we have no confidence in it, and, on the other hand, that it does not hold us captives under the yoke of slavery; or it may mean, that, as it allures us all to destruction, we find in it no life. The latter view appears to be preferable. It is not to Christ, he tells us, that it is owing that the law is more hurtful than beneficial; but the law carries within itself the curse which slays us. Hence it follows, that the death which is brought on by the law is truly deadly. With this is contrasted another kind of death, in the life-giving fellowship of the cross of Christ. He says, that he is crucified together with Christ, that he might live unto God. The ordinary punctuation of this passage obscures the true meaning. It is this: "I through the law am dead to the law, that I might live to God." But the context will read more smoothly thus: "I through the law am dead to the law;" then, in a separate sentence, "That I might live to God, I am crucified with Christ."

That I might live to God. He shews that the kind of death, on which the false apostles seized as a ground of quarrel, is a proper object of desire; for he declares that we are dead to the law, not by any means that we may live to sin, but that we may live to God. *To live to God,* sometimes means to regulate our life according to his will, so as to study nothing else in our whole life but to gain his approbation; but here it means to live, if we may be allowed the expression, the life of God. In this way the various points of the contrast are preserved; for in whatever sense we are said to die to sin, in the same sense do we live to God. In short, Paul informs us that this death is not mortal, but is the cause of a better life; because God snatches us from the shipwreck of the law, and by his grace raises us up to another life. I say nothing of other interpretations; but this appears to be the apostle's real meaning.

20. *I am crucified with Christ.* This explains the manner in which we, who are dead to the law, live to God. Ingrafted into the death of Christ, we derive from it a secret energy, as the twig does from the root. Again, the handwriting of the law,

"which was contrary to us, Christ has nailed to his cross." (Col 2:14.)

Being then crucified with him, we are freed from all the curse and guilt of the law. He who endeavors to set aside that deliverance makes void the cross of Christ. But let us remember, that we are delivered from the yoke of the law, only by becoming one with Christ, as the twig draws its sap from the root, only by growing into one nature.

Nevertheless I live. To the feelings of man, the word Death is always unpleasant. Having said that we are "crucified with Christ," he therefore adds, "that this makes us alive."

Yet not I, but Christ liveth in me. This explains what he meant by "living to God." He does not live by his own life, but is animated by the secret power of Christ; so that Christ may be said to live and grow in him; for, as the soul enlivens the body, so Christ imparts life to his members. It is a remarkable sentiment, that believers live out of themselves, that is, they live in Christ; which can only be accomplished by holding real and actual communication with him. Christ lives in us in two ways. The one life consists in governing us by his Spirit, and directing all our actions; the other, in making us partakers of his righteousness; so that, while we can do nothing of ourselves, we are accepted in the sight of God. The first relates to regeneration, the second to justification by free grace. This passage may be understood in the latter sense; but if it is thought better to apply it to both, I will cheerfully adopt that view.

And the life which I now live in the flesh. There is hardly a sentence here which has not been torn by a variety of interpretations. Some understand by the word *flesh*, the depravity of sinful nature; but Paul means by it simply the bodily life, and it is to this that the objection applies. "You live a bodily life; but while this corruptible body performs its functions, — while it is supported by eating and drinking, this is not the heavenly life of Christ. It is therefore an unreasonable paradox to assert, that, while you are openly living after the ordinary manner of men, your life is not your own."

Paul replies, that it consists in faith; which intimates that it is a secret hidden from the senses of man. The life, therefore, which we attain by faith is not visible to the bodily eye, but is inwardly perceived in the conscience by the power of the Spirit; so that the bodily life does not prevent us from enjoying, by faith, a heavenly life.

"He hath made us sit together in heavenly places in Christ Jesus." (Eph 2:6.)

Again,

"You are fellow-citizens with the saints and of the household of God." (Eph 2:19.)

And again,

"Our conversation is in heaven." (Php 3:20.)

Paul's writings are full of similar assertions, that, while we live in the world, we at the same time live in heaven; not only because our Head is there, but because, in virtue of union, we enjoy a life in common with him. (Joh 14:23.)

Who loved me. This is added to express the power of faith; for it would immediately occur to any one, — whence does faith derive such power as to convey into our souls the life of Christ? He accordingly informs us, that the love of Christ, and his death, are the objects on which faith rests; for it is in this manner that the effect of faith must be judged. How comes it that we live by the faith of Christ? Because "he loved us, and gave himself for us." The love of Christ led him to unite himself to us, and he completed the union by his death. By giving himself for us, he suffered in our own person; as, on the other hand, faith makes us partakers of every thing which it finds in Christ. The mention of love is in accordance with the saying of the apostle John,

"Not that we loved God, but he anticipated us by his love."

(1Jo 4:10)

For if any merit of ours had moved him to redeem us, this reason would have been stated; but now Paul ascribes the whole to love: it is therefore of free grace. Let us observe the order: "He loved us, and gave himself for us." As if he had said, "He had no other reason for dying, but because he loved us," and that "when we were enemies," (Ro 5:10,) as he argues in another Epistle.

He gave himself. No words can properly express what this means; for who can find language to declare the excellency of the Son of God? Yet he it is who gave himself as a price for our redemption. Atonement, cleansing, satisfaction, and all the benefits which we derive from the death of Christ, are here represented. [51] The words *for me*, are very emphatic. It will not be enough for any man to contemplate

Christ as having died for the salvation of the world, unless he has experienced the consequences of this death, and is enabled to claim it as his own. [52]

21. *I do not reject.* There is great emphasis in this expression; for how dreadful is the ingratitude manifested in despising the grace of God, so invaluable in itself, and obtained at such a price! Yet this heinous offense is charged against the false apostles, who were not satisfied with having Christ alone, but introduced some other aids towards obtaining salvation. For, if we do not renounce all other hopes, and embrace Christ alone, we reject the grace of God. And what resource is left to the man, who "puts from him" the grace of God, "and judges himself unworthy of everlasting life?" (Ac 13:46.)

Christ is dead in vain [53] There would then have been no value in the death of Christ; or, Christ would have died without any reward; for the reward of his death is, that he has reconciled us to the Father by making an atonement for our sins. Hence it follows, that we are justified by his grace, and, therefore, not by works. The Papists explain this in reference to the ceremonial law; but who does not see that it applies to the whole law? If we could produce a righteousness of our own, then Christ has suffered in vain; for the intention of his sufferings was to procure it for us, and what need was there that a work which we could accomplish for ourselves should be obtained from another? If the death of Christ be our redemption, then we were captives; if it be satisfaction, we were debtors; if it be atonement, we were guilty; if it be cleansing, we were unclean. On the contrary, he who ascribes to works his sanctification, pardon, atonement, righteousness, or deliverance, makes void the death of Christ.

This argument, we shall perhaps be told, is of no weight against those who propose to unite the grace of Christ with works; which, it is universally admitted, was done by the false apostles. The two doctrines, it is alleged, stand together, that righteousness is by the law, and that we are redeemed by the death of Christ. True; supposing it were granted that a part of our righteousness is obtained by works, and a part comes from grace. But such theology, it may easily be proved, was unknown to Paul. His argument with his opponents is either conclusive or inconclusive. If any blasphemer shall dare to accuse him of bad reasoning, a powerful defense is at hand; for that justification in the sight of God of which he treats, is not what men may imagine to be sufficient, but what is absolutely perfect.

But we are not now called to plead in behalf of Paul against blasphemers, who venture to speak in reproachful language of the Holy Spirit himself. Our present business is with the Papists. They ridicule us, when we argue with Paul that, if righteousness come by works, Christ is dead in vain. They imagine it to be a beautiful reply, with which their sophists furnish them, that Christ merited for us the first grace, that is, the opportunity of meriting; and that the merit of his death concurs with the satisfactions of works for the daily pardon of sins. Let them ridicule Paul, whose language we quote. They must refute him before they can refute us. We know that he had to deal with men, who did not entirely reject the grace of Christ, but ascribed the half of salvation to works. In opposition to them he argues, that "if righteousness is by the law, then Christ is dead in vain;" and by so doing, he certainly does not allow to works one drop of righteousness. Between those men and the Papists there is no difference; and therefore, in refuting them, we are at liberty to employ Paul's argument.

Footnotes

38

"Sinon les choses estant douteuses et non resolues encore." "Except in matters that were doubtful and not yet settled."

39

"Ce voyage-la qui est escrit au quinzieme chapitre" "That journey which is recorded in the fifteenth chapter" (of the Acts of the Apostles.)

40

"De la quelle il eust au assez pour les vaincre du tout." "Which would have been sufficient for gaining a complete victory over them."

41

"Et y montai par revelation." "And I went up thither by revelation."

42

"Τῶν δοκούντων εἶναί τι, the men 'who appeared to be somewhat,' that is, persons of highest character and estimation. For though this word signifies to 'appear,' or 'seem,' yet it is not always used in a diminutive or disparaging sense, but to denote what they really are, and what others think them to be. Thus, τῶν 'Ελλήνων δοκοῦντες διαφέρειν (AElian) are persons esteemed as the principal men of Greece; and Aristotle is said σόφος ἄνηρ καὶ ὢν καὶ εἶναι δοκῶν, both to be, and to be esteemed as a wise man.' "Chandler.

43

Porphyry, (Πορφύριος.) a Greek philosopher, (whose original name was Malchus,) and Julian, the Roman emperor, (commonly called "the apostate,") were able and virulent opponents of Christianity. Their writings drew forth powerful defences, by which all their arguments were triumphantly confuted. — *Ed.*

44

"ἀνεθέμην αὐτοῖς", Ga 2:2

45

"La vertu et efficace spiriluelle."

46

"From this portion of sacred history, we are not at liberty to conclude that either of those two apostles had fallen into error in faith; or that they differed from each other about doctrine. Unquestionably, so far as relates to doctrine, Peter was of the same opinion with Paul on this subject, that it was lawful for a Jew to live on terms of friendship with believing Gentiles. — The whole of this controversy related, not to the doctrine of Christian liberty, but to the exercise of it at different times and places; and on this point the rules of prudence were better understood by Paul than by Peter." — Witsius.

47

See p. 90.

48

"The Papists will readily acknowledge that we are justified by faith; but they add that it is in part. Now this gloss spoils all; for they are convinced that we cannot be righteous before God, unless it be accomplished by our Lord Jesus Christ, and unless we rely on that salvation which he has procured for us. The Papists see this very well; and therefore, with a careless air, they will say, We are justified by faith.

But by faith alone? No. On this point they give battle, and this is the chief article on which we differ from them." — Calvin's Sermons.

49

Sinon en nous recognoissant despourveus et du tout desnuez de justice propre a nons." "Unless by acknowledging that we are poor and utterly destitute of any righteousness of our own."

50

Εἰ παράβασις τιῦτο νεν□ ομισται ὅτι τὸν νόμον καταλιπόντες ἐν Χριστῷ ζητοῦμεν δικαιωθῶναι, ἡ αἰτία εἰς αὐτὸν Χριστὸν χωρήσει. "If this be reckoned an offence, that we have forsaken the law, and seek to be justified through Christ, the blame will fall on Christ himself." — Theodoret.

51

Χριστός ἐστι πάντα ἐν ὑμῖν καὶ κρατῶν καὶ δεσπόζων· Καὶ τὸ μὲν ἡμέτερον θέλημα νεκρόν ἐστι. Τὸ δὲ ἐκείνου ζῶ καὶ κυθερνᾷ τὴν ζωὴν ἡμῶν. "It is Christ who does and rules and governs all in you; and our will is dead, but his will lives and directs our life." — Theophylact.

52

"Car cene seroit point assez de considerer que Christ est mort pour le salut du monde, si avec cela un chaeun n'applique particulierement a sa personne l'efficace et jouissance de ceste grace." "For it would not be enough to consider that Christ died for the salvation of the world, unless each individual specially apply to his own person the efficacy and enjoyment of that grace."

53

"Δωρεὰν ἀπέθανε does not mean 'in vain,' 'uselessly,' 'ineffectually,' but 'without just cause;' for if righteousness be by the law, there was no reason why he should die." — Tittmann.

Εἰ γὰρ ἀπέθανεν ὁ Χριστός εὔδηλον ὅτι διὰ τὸ μὴ ἰσχύειν τὸν νόμον ἡμᾶς δικαιοῦν· εἰ δ ' ὁ νόμος δικαιοῖ περιττὸς ὁ τοῦ Χριστοῦ θάνατος. "For if Christ died, it is very evident that it was because the law was unable to justify us; and if the law justifies us, the death of Christ was superfluous." — Chrysostom.

CHAPTER 3

Galatians 3:1-5

1. O foolish Galatians, who hath bewitched you, that ye should not obey the truth, before whose eyes Jesus Christ hath been evidently set forth, crucified among you?

1. O stulti Galatae, quis vos fascinavit, ut non obediatis veritati? quibus ante oculos Iesus Christus depictus est inter vos crucifixus.

2. This only would I learn of you, Received ye the Spirit by the works of the law, or by the hearing of faith?

2. Hoc solum volo discere a vobis: Ex operibus Legis Spiritum accepistis, an ex praedicatione fidei?

3. Are ye so foolish? having begun in the Spirit, are ye now made perfect by the flesh?

3. Ita stulti estis, ut, exorsi a Spiritu, nunc carne eonsummemini?

4. Have ye suffered so many things in vain? if *it be* yet in vain.

4. Tanta passi estis frustra? si tamen etiam frustra.

5. He therefore that ministereth to you the Spirit, and worketh miracles among you, *doeth he it* by the works of the law, or by the hearing of faith?

5. Qui ergo subministrat vobis Spiritum, et operatur in vobis virtutes; ex operibus legis, an ex praedieatione fidei id (facit)?

1. *O foolish Galatians.* An expostulation is here interwoven — I should rather say, inserted — amidst his doctrinal statements. Some will wonder that he did not delay it to the close of the Epistle, but the very serious nature of the errors which he has brought forward unquestionably roused him to a burst of passion. When we hear that the Son of God, with all his benefits, is rejected, that his death is esteemed as nothing, what pious mind would not break out into indignation? He therefore declares that those who allowed themselves to be involved in so heinous a crime must have been ἀνόητοι, that is, "disordered in mind." He accuses them not only of having suffered themselves to be deceived, but of having been carried away by some sort of magical enchantment, [54] which is a still more serious charge. He insinuates that their fall partook more of madness than of folly.

Some think that Paul refers to the temper of the nation, that, being sprung from barbarians, it was more difficult to train them; but I rather think that he refers to the subject itself. It looks like something supernatural, that, after enjoying the gospel in such clearness, they should be affected by the delusions of Satan. He does not merely say that they were "bewitched" and "disordered in mind," because they did not obey the truth; but because, after having received instruction so clear, so full, so tender, and so powerful, they immediately fell away. Erasmus has chosen to interpret the words, "that ye should not *believe* the truth." I am not quite prepared to set aside that rendering, but would prefer the word *obey*, because Paul does not charge them with having, from the outset, rejected the gospel, but with not having persevered in obedience.

Before whose eyes. This is intended, as I have already hinted, to express an aggravation; for, the better opportunities they had of knowing Christ, the more heinous was the criminality of forsaking him. Such, he tells them, was the clearness of his doctrine, that it was not naked doctrine, but the express, living image of Christ. [55] They had known Christ in such a manner, that they might be almost said to have seen him.

Jesus Christ hath been evidently set forth. Augustine's interpretation of the word προεγράφη, ("hath been set forth,") is harsh, and inconsistent with Paul's design. He makes it to signify that Christ was to be thrust out from possession. Others propose a different phrase, (*proscriptus,*) which, if used in the sense of "openly proclaimed," would not be inapplicable. The Greeks, accordingly, borrow from this verb the word προγράμματα, to denote boards on which property intended to be sold was published, so as to be exposed to the view of all. But the participle, *painted,* is less ambiguous, and, in my own opinion, is exceedingly appropriate. To shew how energetic his preaching was, Paul first compares it to a picture, which exhibited to them, in a lively manner, the image of Christ.

But, not satisfied with this comparison, he adds, *Christ hath been crucified among you,* intimating that the actual sight of Christ's death could not have affected them more powerfully than his own preaching. The view given by some, that the Galatians had "crucified to themselves (Heb 6:6) the Son of God afresh, and put him to an open shame;" that they had withdrawn from the purity of the gospel; or, at least, had lent their ear, and given their confidence, to impostors who crucified him, — appears to me overstrained. The meaning therefore is, that Paul's doctrine had instructed them concerning Christ in such a manner as if he had been exhibited to them in a picture, nay, "crucified among them." Such a representation could not have been made by any eloquence, or by "enticing words of man's wisdom," (1Co 2:4,) had it not been accompanied by that power of the Spirit, of which Paul has treated largely in both the Epistles to the Corinthians.

Let those who would discharge aright the ministry of the gospel learn, not merely to speak and declaim, but to penetrate into the consciences of men, to make them see Christ crucified, and feel the shedding of his blood. [56] When the Church has painters such as these, she no longer needs the dead images of wood and stone, she no longer requires pictures; both of which, unquestionably, were first admitted to Christian temples when the pastors had become dumb and been converted into mere idols, or when they uttered a few words from the pulpit in such a cold and careless manner, that the power and efficacy of the ministry were utterly extinguished.

2. *This one I wish to learn from you.* He now proceeds to support his cause by additional arguments. The first is drawn from their experience, for he reminds them in what manner the gospel was introduced among themselves. When they heard the gospel, they received the Spirit. It was not to the law, therefore, but to faith, that they owed the reception of this benefit. This same argument is employed by Peter in the defense which he makes to his brethren for having baptized uncircumcised persons. (Ac 10:47.) Paul and Barnabas followed the same course in the debate which they maintained at Jerusalem on this subject. (Acts 15:2, 12.) There was therefore manifest ingratitude in not submitting to the doctrine, by means of which they had received the Holy Spirit. The opportunity which he gives them to reply is expressive not of doubt, but of greater confidence: for their convictions, founded on their own experience, forced them to acknowledge that it was true.

Faith is here put, by a figure of speech, for the gospel, which is elsewhere called "the law of faith," (Ro 3:27,) because it exhibits to us the free grace of God in Christ, without any merit of works. *The Spirit* means here, I think, the grace of regeneration, which is common to all believers; though I have no objection to understand it as referring to the peculiar gifts by which the Lord, at that period, honored the preaching of the gospel. [57]

It may be objected, that the Spirit was not, in this respect, given to all. But, it was enough for Paul's purpose, that the Galatians knew that the power of the Holy Spirit in his Church had accompanied Paul's doctrine, and that believers were variously endowed with the gifts of the Spirit for general edification. It may likewise be objected, that those gifts were not infallible signs of adoption, and so do not apply to the present question. I reply, that it was enough that the Lord had confirmed the doctrine of Paul by the visible gifts of his Spirit. A still simpler view of the case is, that they had been distinguished by the ordinary privilege of adoption, before those impostors had brought forward their additions. "In whom," says he to the Ephesians,

"ye also trusted, after that ye heard the word of truth, the gospel of your salvation; in whom also, after that ye believed, ye were sealed with that Holy Spirit of promise." (Eph 1:13.)

3. *Are ye so foolish?* Commentators are not agreed as to what he means by *the Spirit* and by *the flesh*. He alludes, in my opinion, to what he had said about the Spirit. As if he had said, "As the doctrine of the gospel brought to you the Holy Spirit, the commencement of your course was spiritual; but now ye have fallen into a worse condition, and may be said to have fallen from the Spirit into the flesh." The flesh denotes either outward and fading flyings, such as ceremonies are, particularly when they are separated from Christ; or it denotes dead and fading doctrine. There was a strange inconsistency between their splendid commencement and their future progress.

4. *Have ye suffered so many things?* This is another argument. Having suffered so many things in behalf of the gospel, would they now, in an instant, lose it all? Nay, he puts it in the way of reproach, if they were willing to lose the advantage of so many illustrious struggles which they had made for the faith. If the true faith had not been delivered to them by Paul, it was rash to suffer anything in defense of a bad cause; but they had experienced the presence of God amidst their persecutions. Accordingly, he charges the false apostles with ill-will in depriving the Galatians of such valuable ornaments. But to mitigate the severity of this complaint, he adds, *if it be yet in vain*; thus inspiring their minds with the expectation of something better, and rousing them to the exercise of repentance. For the intention of all chastisement is, not to drive men to despair, but to lead them to a better course.

5. *He therefore that ministereth.* He is not now speaking of the grace of regeneration, but of the other gifts of the Spirit; for a subject different from the preceding one is manifestly introduced. He warns them that all the gifts of the Holy Spirit, in which they excelled, are the fruits of the gospel, of that gospel which had been preached among them by his own lips. Their new teachers deprived them of those gifts when they left the gospel, and fled to another kind of doctrine. In proportion to the value which they attached to those gifts, to which the apostle here adds *miracles*, they ought the more carefully and resolutely to adhere to the gospel.

Galatians 3:6-9

6. Even as Abraham believed God, and it was accounted to him for righteousness.
6. Quemadmodum Abraham credidit Deo, et imputatum est illi in justitiam. (Ge 15:6 Ro 4:3 Jas 2:23.)
7. Know ye therefore, that they which are of faith, the same are the children of Abraham.
7. Cognoscite ergo, quod qui ex fide sunt, ii sunt filii Abrahae.
8. And the scripture, foreseeing that God would justify the heathen through faith, preached before the gospel unto Abraham, *saying*, In thee shall all nations be blessed.
8. Scriptura autem, quia praevidebat, quod ex fide justificet Deus Gentes, ante evangelizavit Abrahae: In to benedicentur omnes Gentes. (Ge 22:18.)
9. So then they which be of faith are blessed with faithful Abraham.
9. Itaque qui ex fide sunt, benedicuntur cure fideli Abraham.

Having appealed to facts and experience, he now gives quotations from Scripture. And first, he brings forward the example of Abraham. Arguments drawn from examples are not always so conclusive, but this is one of the most powerful, because neither in the subject nor in the person is there any ground of exception. There is no variety of roads to righteousness, and so Abraham is called "the father of all them that believe," (Ro 4:11,) because he is a pattern adapted to all; nay, in his person has been laid down to us the universal rule for obtaining righteousness.

6. *Even as Abraham.* We must here supply some such phrase as *but rather*, for, having put a question, he resolved instantly to cut off every ground of hesitation. At least the phrase "*even as*," (καθὼς,) refers only to the verse immediately preceding, to the "ministration of the Spirit and of miracles by the hearing of faith;" as if he had said, that, in the grace bestowed on them, a similarity might be found to the case of Abraham.

Believed God. By this quotation he proves both here, and in the 4th chapter of the Epistle to the Romans, that men are justified by faith, because the faith of Abraham *was accounted to him, for righteousness.* (Ro 4:3.) We must here inquire briefly, first, what Paul intends by *faith*; secondly, what is *righteousness*; and thirdly, why faith is represented to be a cause of justification. Faith does not mean any kind of conviction which men may have of the truth of God; for though Cain had a hundred times exercised faith in God when denouncing punishment against him, this had nothing to do with obtaining righteousness. Abraham was justified by believing, because, when he received from God a promise of fatherly kindness, he embraced it as certain. Faith therefore has a relation and respect to such a divine promise as may enable men to place their trust and confidence in God.

As to the word *righteousness*, we must attend to the phraseology of Moses. When he says, that

"he believed in the Lord,

and he counted it to him for righteousness," (Ge 15:6,)

he intimates that that person is righteous who is reckoned as such in the sight of God. Now, since men have not righteousness dwelling within themselves, they obtain this by imputation; because God holds their faith as accounted for righteousness. We are therefore said to be "justified by faith," (Rom. 3:28, Rom. 5:1,) not because faith infuses into us a habit or quality, but because we are accepted by God.

But why does faith receive such honor as to be entitled a cause of our justification? First, we must observe, that it is merely an instrumental cause; for, strictly speaking, our righteousness is nothing else than God's free acceptance of us, on which our salvation is founded. But as the Lord testifies his love and grace in the gospel, by offering to us that righteousness of which I have spoken, so we receive it by faith. And thus, when we ascribe to faith a man's justification, we are not treating of the principal cause, but merely pointing out the way in which men arrive at true righteousness. For this righteousness is not a quality which exists in men, but is the mere gift of God, and is enjoyed by faith only; and not even as a reward justly due to faith, but because we receive by faith what God freely gives. All such expressions as the following are of similar import: We are "justified freely by his grace." (Ro 3:24.) Christ is our righteousness. The mercy of God is the cause of our righteousness. By the death and resurrection of Christ, righteousness has been procured for us. Righteousness is bestowed on us through the gospel. We obtain righteousness by faith.

Hence appears the ridiculousness of the blunder of attempting to reconcile the two propositions, that we are justified by faith, and that we are justified at the same time by works; for he who is "just by faith" (Hab 2:4 Heb 10:38) is poor and destitute of personal righteousness, and relies on the grace of God alone. And this is the reason why Paul, in the Epistle to the Romans, concludes that Abraham, having obtained righteousness by faith, had no right to glory before God. (Ro 4:2.) For it is not said that faith was imputed to him for a part of righteousness, but simply for righteousness; so that his faith was truly his righteousness. Besides, faith looks at nothing but the mercy of God, and a dead and risen Christ. All merit of works is thus excluded from being the cause of justification, when the whole is ascribed to faith. For faith, — so far as it embraces the undeserved goodness of God, Christ with all his benefits, the testimony of our adoption which is contained in the gospel, — is universally contrasted with the law, with the merit of works, and with human excellence. The notion of the sophists, that it is contrasted with ceremonies alone, will presently be disproved, with little difficulty, from the context. Let us therefore remember, that those who are righteous by faith, are righteous out of themselves, that is, in Christ.

Hence, too, we obtain a refutation of the idle cavilling of certain persons who evade Paul's reasoning. Moses they tell us, gives the name of righteousness to goodness; and so means nothing more than that Abraham was reckoned a good man, because he believed God. Giddy minds of this description, raised up in our time by Satan, endeavor, by indirect slanders, to undermine the certainty of

Scripture. Paul knew that Moses was not there giving lessons to boys in grammar, but was speaking of a decision which God had pronounced, and very properly viewed the word righteousness in a theological sense. For it is not in that sense in which goodness is mentioned with approbation among men, that we are accounted righteous in the sight of God, but only where we render perfect obedience to the law. Righteousness is contrasted with the transgression of the law, even in its smallest point; and because we have it not from ourselves, it is freely given to us by God.

But here the Jews object that Paul has completely tortured the words of Moses to suit his own purpose; for Moses does not here treat of Christ, or of eternal life, but only mentions an earthly inheritance. The Papists are not very different from the Jews; for, though they do not venture to inveigh against Paul, they entirely evade his meaning. Paul, we reply, takes for granted, what Christians hold to be a first principle, that whatever promises the Lord made to Abraham were appendages of that first promise,

"I am thy shield, and thy exceeding great reward."

(Ge 15:1.)

When Abraham received the promise,

"In multiplying I will multiply thy seed as the stars of the heavens, and as the sand which is upon the sea-shore" (Ge 22:17,)

he did not limit his view to that word, but included it in the grace of adoption as a part of the whole, and, in the same manner, every other promise was viewed by him as a testimony of God's fatherly kindness, which tended to strengthen his hope of salvation. Unbelievers differ from the children of God in this respect, that, while they enjoy in common with them the bounties of Providence, they devour them like cattle, and look no higher. The children of God, on the other hand, knowing that all their blessings have been sanctified by the promises, acknowledge God in them as their Father. They are often directed, in this way, to the hope of eternal life; for they begin with the faith of their adoption, which is the foundation of the whole. Abraham was not justified merely because he believed that God would "multiply his seed," (Ge 22:17,) but because he embraced the grace of God, trusting to the promised Mediator, in whom, as Paul elsewhere declares, "all the promises of God are yea and amen." (2Co 1:20.)

7. *Know ye therefore*, or, *ye know*; for both readings are equally agreeable to the Greek termination γινώσκετε. But it matters little which is preferred, for the meaning is the same, only that the old translation, (*know ye*,) which I have followed, is more energetic. [58] He says that those "are of faith," who have relinquished all confidence in works, and rely on the promise of God alone. It is on the authority of Paul himself that we give this interpretation; for in the Epistle to the Romans he thus writes:

"To him that worketh is the reward not reckoned of grace, but of debt. But to him that worketh not, but believeth on him that justifieth the ungodly, his faith is accounted for righteousness." (Rom. 4:4, 5.)

To be *of faith*, therefore, is to rest their righteousness and hope of salvation on the mercy of God. That such are the children of God he concludes from the preceding statement; for if Abraham was justified by faith those who wish to be his children must likewise abide firmly by faith. He has omitted one remark, which will be readily supplied, that there is no place in the church for any man who is not a son of Abraham.

8. *The scripture foreseeing.* What he had said in a general manner is now applied expressly to the Gentiles; for the calling of the Gentiles was a new and extraordinary occurrence. Doubts existed as to the manner in which they should be called. Some thought that they were required "to be circumcised and to keep the law," (Ac 15:24,) and that otherwise they were shut out from having a share in the covenant. But Paul shews, on the other hand, that by faith they arrive at the blessing, and by faith they must be "in grafted" (Rom. 11:17, 24,) into the family of Abraham. How does he prove this? Because it is said, *In thee shall all nations be blessed.* These words unquestionably recall that all must be blessed in the same manner as Abraham; for he is the model, nay, the rule, to be universally observed. Now, he obtained the blessing by faith, and in the same manner must it be obtained by all.

9. *Faithful Abraham.* This expression is very emphatic. They *are blessed*, not with Abraham as circumcised, nor as entitled to boast of the works of the law, nor as a Hebrew, nor as relying on his own excellence, but with Abraham, who by faith alone obtained the blessing; for no personal quality is here taken into the account, but faith alone. The word Blessing is variously employed in Scripture: but here it signifies Adoption into the inheritance of eternal life.

Galatians 3:10-14

10. For as many as are of the works of the law are under the curse: for it is written, Cursed *is* every one that continueth not in all things which are written in the book of the law to do them.

10. Quictrnque enim ex operibus Legis sunt, sub maledictione sunt. Scripture est enim (De 27:26): Maledictus omnis, qui non permanet in omnibus, quae scripta sunt in libro Legis, ut facial ca.

11. But that no man is justified by the law in the sight of God, *it is* evident: for, The just shall live by faith.

11. Quod autem in Lege nerno justificetur apud Deum, patet, quia justus ex fide rivet. (Hab 2:4 Ro 1:17 Heb 10:38.)

12. And the law is not of faith: but, The man that doeth them shall live in them.

12. Lex autern non estex fide, sed, Qui fecerit haec homo, rivet in ipsis. (Le 18:5.)

13. Christ hath redeemed us from the curse of the law, being made a curse for us: for it is written, Cursed *is* every one that hangeth on a tree:

13. Christus nos redemit a maledictione Legis, factus pro nobis maledictio: (scriptum est enim, maledictus omnis qui pependerit in ligno, (De 21:23,)

14. That the blessing of Abraham might come on the Gentiles through Jesus Christ; that we might receive the promise of the Spirit through faith.

14. Ut in Gentes benedictio Abrabae perveniat per Christum Iesnrn; quo promissionern Spiritus aecipiaruns per fidem.

10. *For as many as are of the works of the law.* The argument is drawn from the contradictory nature of the two schemes; for the same fountain does not yield both hot and cold. The law holds all living men under its curse; and from the law, therefore, it is in vain to expect a blessing. They are declared to be *of the works of the law* who place their trust for salvation in those works; for such modes of expression must always be interpreted by the state of the question. Now, we know that the controversy here relates to righteousness. All who wish to be justified by the works of the law are declared to be liable to the curse. But how does he prove this? The sentence of the law is, that all who have transgressed any part of the law are cursed. Let us now see if there be any living man who fulfils the law. But no such person, it is evident, has been, or ever can be found. All to a man are here condemned. The minor and the conclusion are wanting, for the entire syllogism would run thus: "Whoever has come short in any part of the law is cursed; all are held chargeable with this guilt; therefore all are cursed." This argument of Paul would not stand, if we had sufficient strength to fulfill the law; for there would then be a fatal objection to the minor proposition. Either Paul reasons badly, or it is impossible for men to fulfill the law.

An antagonist might now object: "I admit that all transgressors are accursed; what then? Men will be found who keep the law; for they are free to choose good or evil." But Paul places here beyond controversy, what the Papists at this day hold to be a detestable doctrine, that men are destitute of strength to keep the law. And so he concludes boldly that all are cursed, because all have been commanded to keep the law perfectly; which implies that in the present corruption of our nature the power of keeping it perfectly is wanting. Hence we conclude that the curse which the law pronounces, though, in the phrase of logicians, it is *accidental,* is here perpetual and inseparable from its nature. The blessing which it offers to us is excluded by our depravity, so that the curse alone remains.

11. *But that no man, is justified by the law.* He again argues from a comparison of contradictory schemes. "If we are justified by faith, it is not by the law: but we are justified by faith therefore it is not by the law." The minor is proved by a passage from Habakkuk, which is also quoted in the Epistle to the Romans. (Hab 2:4; Ro 1:17.) The major is proved by the difference in the methods of justification. The law justifies him who fulfils all its precepts, while faith justifies those who are destitute of the merit of works, and who rely on Christ alone. To be justified by our own merit, and to be justified by the grace of another, are two schemes which cannot be reconciled: one of them must be overturned by the other. Such is the amount of the argument: let us now attend to the separate clauses.

The just shall live by faith. As we had occasion to expound this passage where it occurs in the Epistle to the Romans, it will be unnecessary to repeat the exposition of it here. The prophet evidently describes a proud confidence in the flesh as contrasted with true faith. He declares, that "the just shall live;" by which he means, not that they are supported for a short period, and liable to be overwhelmed by an approaching storm; but that they shall continue to live, and that, even amidst the most imminent danger, their life shall be preserved. There is therefore no weight in the scornful reproaches of our adversaries, who allege that the prophet there employs the word Faith in a wider acceptation than Paul does in this passage. By Faith he evidently means the exercise of a calm, steady conscience, relying on God alone; so that Paul's quotation is properly applied.

12. *And the law is not of faith.* The law evidently is not contrary to faith; otherwise God would be unlike himself; but we must return to a principle already noticed, that Paul's language is modified by the present aspect of the case. The contradiction between the law and faith lies in the matter of justification. You will more easily unite fire and water, than reconcile these two statements, that men are justified by faith, and that they are justified by the law. "The law is not of faith;" that is, it has a method of justifying a man which is wholly at variance with faith.

But the man who shall do these things. The difference lies in this, that man, when he fulfils the law, is reckoned righteous by a legal righteousness, which he proves by a quotation from Moses. (Le 18:5.) Now, what is the righteousness of faith? He defines it in the Epistle to the Romans,

"If thou shalt confess with thy mouth the Lord Jesus, and shalt believe in thine heart that God hath raised him from the dead,

thou shalt be saved." (Ro 10:9.)

And yet it does not follow from this, that faith is inactive, or that it sets believers free from good works. For the present question is not, whether believers ought to keep the law as far as they can, (which is beyond all doubt,) but whether they can obtain righteousness by works, which is impossible. But since God promises life to the doers of the law, why does Paul affirm that they are not righteous? The reply to this objection is easy. There are none righteous by the works of the law, because there are none who do those works. We admit that the doers of the law, if there were any such, are righteous; but since that is a conditional agreement, all are excluded from life, because no man performs that righteousness which he ought. We must bear in memory what I have already stated, that to do the law is not to obey it in part, but to fulfill everything which belongs to righteousness; and all are at the greatest distance from such perfection.

13. *Christ hath redeemed us.* The apostle had made all who are under the law subject to the curse; from which arose this great difficulty, that the Jews could not free themselves from the curse of the law. Having stated this difficulty, he meets it, by shewing that Christ hath made us free, which still farther aids his purpose. If we are saved, because we have been freed from the curse of the law, then righteousness is not by the law. He next points out the manner in which we are made free.

It is written, Cursed is every one that hangeth on a tree. Now, Christ hung upon the cross, therefore he fell under that curse. But it is certain that he did not suffer that punishment on his own account. It follows, therefore, either that he was crucified in vain, or that our curse was laid upon him, in order that we might be delivered from it. Now, he does not say that Christ was cursed, but, which is still more, that he was *a curse*, — intimating, that the curse "of all men [59] was laid upon him" (Isa 53:6.) If any man think this language harsh, let him be ashamed of the cross of Christ, in the confession of which we glory. It was not unknown to God what death his own Son would die, when he pronounced the law, "He that is hanged is accursed of God." (De 21:23.)

But how does it happen, it will be asked, that a beloved Son is cursed by his Father? We reply, there are two things which must be considered, not only in the person of Christ, but even in his human nature. The one is, that he was the unspotted Lamb of God, full of blessing and of grace; the other is, that he placed himself in our room, and thus became a sinner, and subject to the curse, not in himself indeed, but in us, yet in such a manner, that it became necessary for him to occupy our place. He could not cease to be the object of his Father's love, and yet he endured his wrath. For how could he reconcile the Father to us, if he had incurred his hatred and displeasure? We conclude, that he "did always those things that pleased" (Joh 8:29) his Father. Again, how would he have freed us from the wrath of God, if he had not transferred it from us to himself? Thus, "he was wounded for our transgressions," (Isa 53:5,) and had to deal with God as an angry judge. This is the foolishness of the cross, (1Co 1:18,) and the admiration of angels, (1Pe 1:12,) which not only exceeds, but swallows up, all the wisdom of the world.

14. *That the blessing of Abraham.* Having said that "Christ hath redeemed us from the curse of the law" he now applies that statement more closely to his purpose. The promised blessing of Abraham is founded on this, and flows from it to the Gentiles. If the Jews must be delivered from the law, in order to become the heirs of Abraham, what shall hinder the Gentiles from obtaining the same benefit? And if that blessing is found in Christ alone, it is faith in Christ which alone brings it into our possession.

The promise of the Spirit appears to me to mean, agreeably to a Hebrew idiom, a spiritual promise. Although that promise relates to the New Testament, "I will pour out my Spirit upon all flesh," (Joe 2:28,) yet, in this passage, Paul refers to another subject. The spirit is here contrasted with all outward things, not with ceremonies merely, but with lineal descent, so as to leave no room for diversity of rank. From the nature of the promise, he proves that Jews differ nothing from Gentiles; because, if it is spiritual, it is received by faith alone.

Galatians 3:15-18

15. Brethren, I speak after the manner of men; Though *it be* but a man's covenant, yet *if it be* confirmed, no man disannulleth, or addeth thereto.

15. Fratres, (secundum hominem dico) Hominis licet pactum, tamen si sit comprobatum, nemo rejicit aut addit aliquid.

16. Now to Abraham and his seed were the promises made. He saith not, And to seeds, as of many; but as of one, And to thy seed, which is Christ.

16. Porro Abrahae dictae sunt promissiones, et semini ejus. Non dicit, Et seminibus, tanquam Deuteronomy multis, sed tanquam Deuteronomy uno, Et semini tuo, qui est Christus.

17. And this I say, *that* the covenant, that was confirmed before of God in Christ, the law, which was four hundred and thirty years after, cannot disannul, that it should make the promise of none effect.

17. Hoc autem dico: pactum ante comprobatum a Deo erga Christum, Lex, quae post annos quadringentos et triginta coepit, non facit irritum, ut abroget Promissionem.

18. For if the inheritance *be* of the law, *it is* no more of promise: but God gave *it* to Abraham by promise.

18. Nam si ex Lege haereditas, non jam ex Promissione; atqui Abrahae per Promissionem donavit Deus.

15. *I speak after the manner of men.* By this expression he intended to put them to the blush. It is highly disgraceful and base that the testimony of God should have less weight with us than that of a mortal man. In demanding that the sacred covenant of God shall receive not less deference than is commonly yielded to ordinary human transactions, he does not place God on a level with men. The immense distance between God and men is still left for their consideration.

Though it be but a man's covenant. This is an argument from the less to the greater. Human contracts are admitted on all hands to be binding: how much more what God has established? The Greek word διαθήκη, here used, signifies more frequently, what the Latin versions here render it, (*testamentum,*) a *testament*; but sometimes too, a *covenant*, though in this latter sense the plural number is more generally employed. It is of little importance to the present passage, whether you explain it *covenant* or *testament.* The case is different with the Epistle to the Hebrews, where the apostle unquestionably alludes to testaments, (Heb. 9:16, 17;) but here I prefer to take it simply for the covenant which God made. The analogy from which the apostle argues, would not apply so strictly to a testament as to a covenant. The apostle appears to reason from human bargains to that solemn covenant into which God entered with Abraham. If human bargains be so firm that they can receive no addition, how much more must this covenant remain inviolable?

16. *Now to Abraham, and his seed.* Before pursuing his argument, he introduces an observation about the substance of the covenant, that it rests on Christ alone. But if Christ be the foundation of the bargain, it follows that it is of free grace; and this too is the meaning of the word *promise.* As the law has respect to men and to their works, so the promise has respect to the grace of God and to faith.

He saith not, And to seeds. To prove that in this place God speaks of Christ, he calls attention to the singular number as denoting some particular seed. I have often been astonished that Christians, when they saw this passage so perversely tortured by the Jews, did not make a more determined resistance; for all pass it slightly as if it were an indisputed territory. And yet there is much plausibility in their objection. Since the word *seed* is a collective noun, Paul appears to reason inconclusively, when he contends that a single individual is denoted by this word, under which all the descendants of Abraham are comprehended in a passage already quoted, "In multiplying I will multiply thy seed, ערז (*zerang,*) or ךערז (*zargnacha,*) as the stars of the heaven, and as the sand which is upon the sea-shore." (Ge 22:17.) Having, as they imagine, detected the fallacy of the argument, they treat us with haughty triumph.

I am the more surprised that our own writers should have been silent on this head, as we have abundant means of repelling their slander. Among Abraham's own sons a division began, for one of the sons was cut off from the family. "In Isaac shall thy seed be called." (Ge 21:12.) Consequently Ishmael is not included in the reckoning. Let us come a step lower. Do the Jews allow that the posterity of Esau are the blessed seed? nay, it will be maintained that their father, though the first-born, was struck off. And how many nations have sprung from the stock of Abraham who have no share in this "calling?" The twelve patriarchs, at length, formed twelve heads, not because they were descended from the line of Abraham, but because they had been appointed by a particular election of God. Since the ten tribes were carried away, (Ho 9:17,) how many thousands have so degenerated that they no longer hold a name among the seed of Abraham? Lastly, a trial was made of the tribe of Judah, that the real succession to the blessing might be transmitted among a small people. And this had been predicted by Isaiah,

"Though thy people Israel be as the sand of the sea,
yet a remnant of them shall return." (Isa 10:22.)

Hitherto I have said nothing which the Jews themselves do not acknowledge. Let them answer me then; how comes it that the thirteen tribes sprung from the twelve patriarchs were the seed of Abraham, in preference to Ishmaelites and Edomites? Why do they exclusively glory in that name, and set aside the others as a spurious seed? They will, no doubt, boast that they have obtained it by their own merit; but Scripture, on the contrary, asserts that all depends on the calling of God; for we must constantly return to the privilege conveyed in these words, "In Isaac shall thy seed be called." (Ge 21:12.) The uninterrupted succession to this privilege must have been in force until Christ; for, in the person of David, the Lord afterwards brought back by recovery, as we might say, the promise which had been made to Abraham. In proving, therefore, that this prediction applies to a single individual, Paul does not make his argument rest on the use of the singular number. He merely shews that the word *seed* must denote one who was not only descended from Abraham according to the flesh, but had been likewise appointed for this purpose by the calling of God. If the Jews deny this, they will only make themselves ridiculous by their obstinacy.

But as Paul likewise argues from these words, that a covenant had been made in Christ, or to Christ, let us inquire into the force of that expression,

"In thy seed shall all the nations of the earth be blessed."
(Ge 22:18.)

The Jews taunt the apostle with making a comparison, as if the seed of Abraham were to be quoted as an example in all disastrous omens and prayers; while, on the contrary, to curse in Sodom or Israel is to employ the name of Sodom or Israel in forms of cursing. This, I own, is sometimes the case, but not always; for to bless one's self in God has quite a different meaning, as the Jews themselves admit. Since, therefore, the phrase is ambiguous, denoting sometimes a cause and sometimes a comparison, wherever, it occurs, it must be explained by the context. We have ascertained, then, that we are all cursed by nature, and that the blessing of Abraham has been promised to all nations. Do all indiscriminately reach it? Certainly not, but those only who are "gathered" (Isa 66:8) to the Messiah; for when, under His government and direction, they are collected into one body, they then become one people. Whoever then, laying disputing aside, shall inquire into the truth, will readily acknowledge that the words here signify not a mere comparison but a cause; and hence it follows that Paul had good ground for saying, that the covenant was made in Christ, or in reference to Christ.

17. *The law which was four hundred and thirty years after.* If we listen to Origen and Jerome and all the Papists, there will be little difficulty in refuting this argument. Paul reasons thus: "A promise was given to Abraham four hundred and thirty years before the publication of the law; therefore the law which came after could not disannul the promise; and hence he concludes that ceremonies are not necessary." But it may be objected, the sacraments were given in order to preserve the faith, and why should Paul separate them from the promise? He does so separate them, and proceeds to argue on the matter. The ceremonies themselves are not so much considered by him as something higher, — the effect of justification which was attributed to them by false apostles, and the obligation on the conscience. From ceremonies, accordingly, he takes occasion to discuss the whole subject of faith and works. If the point in dispute had no connection with obtaining righteousness, with the merit of works, or with ensnaring the conscience, ceremonies would be quite consistent with the promise.

What, then, is meant by this *disannulling* of the promise, against which the apostle contends? The impostors denied that salvation is freely promised to men, and received by faith, and, as we shall presently see, urged the necessity of works in order to merit salvation. I return to Paul's own language. "The law," he says, "is later than the promise, and therefore does not revoke it; for a covenant once sanctioned must remain perpetually binding." I again repeat, if you do not understand that the promise is free, there will be no force in the statement; for the law and the promise are not at variance but on this single point, that the law justifies a man by the merit of works, and the promise bestows righteousness freely. This is made abundantly clear when he calls it a *covenant* founded on Christ.

But here we shall have the Papists to oppose us, for they will find a ready method of evading this argument. "We do not require," they will say, "that the old ceremonies shall be any longer binding; let them be laid out of the question; nevertheless a man is justified by the moral law. For this law, which is as old as the creation of man, went before God's covenant with Abraham; so that Paul's reasoning is either frivolous, or it holds against ceremonies alone." I answer, Paul took into account what was certainly true, that, except by a covenant with God, no reward is due to works. Admitting, then, that the law justifies, yet before the law men could not merit salvation by works, because there was no covenant. All that I am now affirming is granted by the scholastic theologians: for they maintain that works are meritorious of salvation, not by their intrinsic worth, but by the acceptance of God, (to use their own phrase,) and on the ground of a covenant. Consequently, where no divine covenant, no declaration of acceptance is found, — no works will be available for justification: so that Paul's argument is perfectly conclusive. He tells us that God made two covenants with men; one through Abraham, and another through Moses. The former, being founded on Christ, was free; and therefore the law, which came after, could not enable men to obtain salvation otherwise than by grace, for then, "it would make the promise of none effect." That this is the meaning appears clearly from what immediately follows.

18. *If the inheritance be of the law.* His opponents might still reply, that nothing was farther from their intention than to weaken or disannul God's covenant. To deprive them of every kind of subterfuge, he comes forward with the assertion, that salvation by the law, and salvation by the promise of God, are wholly inconsistent with each other. Who will dare to explain this as applying to ceremonies alone, while Paul comprehends under it whatever interferes with a free promise? Beyond all doubt, he excludes works of every description. "For," says he to the Romans,

"if they which are of the law be heirs, faith is made void,
and the promise made of none effect." (Ro 4:14.)

Why so? Because salvation would be suspended on the condition of satisfying the law; and so he immediately concludes:

"Therefore it is of faith, that it might be by grace, in order that the promise might be sure to all the seed." (Ro 4:16.)

Let us carefully remember the reason why, in comparing the promise with the law, the establishment of the one overturns the other. The reason is, that the promise has respect to faith, and the law to works. Faith receives what is freely given, but to works a reward is paid. And he immediately adds, *God gave it to Abraham,* not by requiring some sort of compensation on his part, but by free promise; for if you view it as conditional, the word *gave*, (κεχάρισται,) would be utterly inapplicable.

Galatians 3:19-22

19. Wherefore then *serveth* the law? It was added because of transgressions, till the seed should come to whom the promise was made; *and it was* ordained by angels in the hand of a mediator.

19. Quid igitur Lex? transgressionum causa adjuneta fuit, donee veniret semen, cui promissum fuerat, ordinata per angelos in manu mediatoris.

20. Now a mediator is not *a mediator* of one, but God is one.

20. Porro mediator unius non est; Deus autem unus est.

21. *Is* the law then against the promises of God? God forbid: for if there had been a law given which could have given life, verily righteousness should have been by the law.

21. Lexne igitur adversus promissiones Dei? absit; nam si data esset Lex, quae posset vivificare, vere ex Lege esset justitia.

22. But the scripture hath concluded all under sin, that the promise by faith of Jesus Christ might be given to them that believe.

22. Sed conclusit Scriptura omnia sub peccatum, ut promissio ex fide Iesu Christi daretur credentibus.

When we are told that the law has no influence in obtaining justification, various suggestions immediately arise, that it must be either useless, or opposed to God's covenant, or something of that sort. Nay, it might occur, why should we not say of the law, what Jeremiah says of the New Testament, (Jer 31:31,) that it was given at a later period, in order to supply the weakness of the former doctrine? Objections of this kind must be answered, if Paul wished to satisfy the Galatians. First, then, he inquires, — what is the use of the law? Having come after the promise, it appears to have been intended to supply its defects; and there was room at least for doubting, whether the promise would have been effectual, if it had not been aided by the law. Let it be observed, that Paul does not speak of the moral law only, but of everything connected with the office held by Moses. That office, which was peculiar to Moses, consisted in laying down a rule of life and ceremonies to be observed in the worship of God, and in afterwards adding promises and threatenings. Many promises, no doubt, relating to the free mercy of God and to Christ, are to be found in his writings; and these promises belong to faith. But this must be viewed as accidental, and altogether foreign to the inquiry, so far as a comparison is made between the law and the doctrine of grace. Let it be remembered, that the amount of the question is this: When a promise had been made, why did Moses afterwards add that new condition, "If a man do, he shall live in them;" and, "Cursed be he that confirmeth not all the words of this law to do them?" (Le 18:5; De 27:26.) Was it to produce something better and more perfect?

19. *Because of transgressions.* The law has manifold uses, but Paul confines himself to that which bears on his present subject. He did not propose to inquire in how many ways the law is of advantage to men. It is necessary to put readers on their guard on this point; for very many, I find, have fallen into the mistake of acknowledging no other advantage belonging to the law, but what is expressed in this passage. Paul himself elsewhere speaks of the precepts of the law as profitable for doctrine and exhortations. (2Ti 3:16.) The definition here given of the use of the law is not complete, and those who refuse to make any other acknowledgment in favor of the law do wrong. Now, what is the import of the phrase, *because of transgressions*? It agrees with the saying of philosophers, that "The law was made for restraining evil-doers," and with the old proverb, "From bad manners have sprung good laws." But Paul's meaning is more extensive than the words may seem to convey. He means that the law was published in order to make known transgressions, and in this way to compel men to acknowledge their guilt. As men naturally are too ready to excuse themselves, so, until they are roused by the law, their consciences are asleep.

"Until the law," says Paul, "sin was in the world:
but sin is not imputed where there is no law." (Ro 5:13.)

The law came and roused the sleepers, for this is the true preparation for Christ. "By the law is the knowledge of sin." (Ro 3:20.) Why?

"That Sin by the commandment might become exceeding sinful." (Ro 7:13.)

Thus, "the law was added because of transgressions," in order to reveal their true character, or, as he tells the Romans, that it might make them to abound. (Ro 5:20.)

This passage has tortured the ingenuity of Origen, but to no purpose. If God summon consciences to his tribunal, that those qualities in their transgression, which would otherwise give them pleasure, may humble them by a conviction of guilt, — if he shake off the listlessness which overwhelmed all dread of his judgment-seat, — if he drag to light; sin, which lurked like a thief in the den of hypocrisy, — what is there in all this that can be reckoned absurd? But it may be objected: "As the law is the rule of a devout and holy life, why is it said to be added 'because of transgressions,' rather than 'because of obedience?'" I answer, however much it may point out true righteousness, yet, owing to the corruption of our nature, its instruction tends only to increase transgressions, until the Spirit of regeneration come, who writes it on the heart; and that Spirit is not given by the law, but is received by faith. This saying of Paul, let the reader remember, is not of a philosophical or political character, but expresses a purpose of the law, with which the world had been always unacquainted.

Till the seed should come. If it has respect *to seed*, it must be to that on which the blessing has been pronounced, and therefore it does not interfere with the promise. The word till, (ἄχρις οὗ,) signifies *so long as* the seed is expected: and hence it follows, that it must have been intended to occupy not the highest, but a subordinate rank. It was given in order to rouse men to the expectation of Christ. But was it necessary that it should last only until the coming of Christ? For if so, it follows that it is now abolished. The whole of that administration, I reply, was temporal, and was given for the purpose of preserving among the ancient people an attachment to the faith of Christ. And yet I do not admit that, by the coming of Christ, the whole law was abolished. The apostle did not intend this, but merely that the mode of administration, which for a time had been introduced, must receive its accomplishment in Christ, who is the fulfillment of the promise. [60] But on this subject we shall have occasion to speak more fully afterwards.

Ordained by angels. The circumstance, that it was delivered through angels, tends to the commendation of the law. This is declared by Stephen (Ac 7:53) also, who says, that they had "received the law, (εἰς διαταγὰς ἀγγέλων,) into the dispositions of angels." The interpretation given by some, that Moses and Aaron, and the priests, are the angels here meant, is more ingenious than solid. Nor is it wonderful that angels, by whom God bestows on us some of the smallest of his blessings, should have been intrusted also with this office of attending as witnesses at the promulgation of the law.

In the hand of a Mediator Hand usually signifies ministration; but as angels were ministers in giving the law, I consider "the hand of the Mediator" to denote the highest rank of service. The Mediator was at the head of the embassy, and angels were united with him as his companions. Some apply this expression to Moses, as marking a comparison between Moses and Christ; but I agree rather with the ancient expositors, who apply it to Christ himself. [61] This view, it will be found, agrees better with the context, though I differ from the ancients likewise as to the meaning of the word. *Mediator* does not, as they imagine, signify here one who makes reconciliation, which it does in these words,

"There is one Mediator between God and men,
the man Christ Jesus," (1Ti 2:5,)
— but an ambassador employed in promulgating a law.

We are thus to understand, that, since the beginning of the world, God has held no intercourse with men, but through the agency of his eternal Wisdom or Son. Hence Peter says, that the holy prophets spake by the "Spirit of Christ," (1Pe 1:11,) and Paul makes him the leader of the people in the wilderness. (1Co 10:4.) And certainly the Angel who appeared to Moses, (Ex 3:2,) can be no other person; for he claims to himself the peculiar and essential name of God, which is never applied to creatures. As he is the Mediator of reconciliation, by whom we are accepted of God, — the Mediator of intercession, who opens up for us a way to "call on the Father," (1Pe 1:17,) — so he has always been the Mediator of all doctrine, because by him God has always revealed himself to men. And this he intended to state expressly, for the purpose of informing the Galatians, that he who is the foundation of the covenant of grace, held also the highest rank in the giving of the law.

20. *Now, a mediator is not a mediator of one.* Some are disposed to philosophize on this expression, and would make Paul's meaning to be, that the twofold nature of Christ is not one in essence. But that Paul is here speaking of the contracting parties, no man of sound judgment entertains a doubt. And so they commonly expound it, that there is no room for a Mediator, unless when one of the parties has a matter to transact with the other. But why that statement should have been introduced they leave undetermined, though the passage manifestly deserves the most careful attention. There may, perhaps, be an Anticipation (πρόληψις) of some wicked thought that might arise about a change of the divine purpose. Some one might say, "As men, when they change their mind about their covenants, are wont to retract them, so has it happened with the covenants of God." If you take this to be the meaning, then, in the former clause, Paul would acknowledge that men, who occupy one side of this contract, are unsteady and changeable, while God nevertheless remains the same, is consistent with himself, and partakes not of the unsteadiness of men.

But when I take a closer view of the whole subject, I rather think that it marks a difference between Jews and Gentiles. Christ is not the Mediator of one, because, in respect of outward character, there is a diversity of condition among those with whom, through his mediation, God enters into covenant. But Paul asserts that we have no right to judge in this manner of the covenant of God, as if it contradicted itself, or varied according to the diversities of men. The words are now clear. As Christ formerly reconciled God to the Jews in making a covenant, so now he is the Mediator of the Gentiles. The Jews differ widely from the Gentiles; for circumcision and ceremonies have erected "the middle wall of partition between them." (Eph 2:14.) They were "nigh" to God, (Eph 2:13,) while the Gentiles were "afar off;" but still God is consistent with himself. This becomes evident, when Christ brings those who formerly differed among themselves to one God, and makes them unite in one body. *God is one*, because he always continues to be like himself, and, with unvarying regularity, holds fixed and unalterable the purpose which he has once made. [62]

21. *Is the law then against the promises of God?* The certainty and steadiness of the divine purpose being admitted, we are bound equally to conclude that its results are not contrary to each other. Still there was a difficulty to be resolved, arising from the apparent contradiction between the Law and the covenant of grace. This is, perhaps, an exclamation. Dreading no farther contradiction, now that the point is settled, Paul concludes, that the former arguments have placed it beyond a doubt, and exclaims: "Who will now dare to imagine a disagreement between the law and the promises?" And yet this does not prevent Paul from proceeding to remove the difficulties that might still arise.

Before answering the question, he expresses, in his usual manner, a high disdain of such folly; thus intimating the strong abhorrence with which pious men must regard whatever brings reproach on the Divine character. But another instance of high address, which claims our notice, is found in this turn of expression. He charges his adversaries with the offense of making God contradict himself. For from him the Law and the promises have evidently proceeded: whoever then alleges any contradiction between them blasphemes against God: but they do contradict each other, if the Law justifies. Thus does Paul most dexterously retort upon his adversaries the charge which they falsely and calumniously brought against him.

For if there had been a law given. The reply is (what is called) indirect, and does not plainly assert an agreement between the law and the promises, but contains all that is necessary to remove the contradiction. At first sight, you would say that this sentence departs from the context, and has nothing to do with the solution of the question; but this is not the case. The law would be opposed to the promises, if it had the power of justifying; for there would be two opposite methods of justifying a man, two separate roads towards the attainment of righteousness. But Paul refuses to the law such a power; so that the contradiction is removed. I would admit, says he, that righteousness is obtained by the law, if salvation were found in it. But what?

22. *The Scripture hath concluded.* By the word Scripture is chiefly intended the law itself. It "hath concluded all under sin," and therefore, instead of giving, it takes away righteousness from all. The reasoning is most powerful. "You seek righteousness in the law: but the law itself, with the whole of Scripture, leaves nothing to men but condemnation; for all men, with their works, are pronounced to be unrighteous: who then shall live by the law?" He alludes to these words,

"He who shall do these things, shall live in them." (Le 18:5.)

Shut out by it, says he, from life through guilt, in vain should we seek salvation by the law. — The word translated *all* (τὰ πάντα) signifies *all things*, and conveys more than if he had said *all men*; for it embraces not only men, but every thing which they possess or can accomplish.

That the promise by faith. There is no remedy but to throw away the righteousness of works, and betake ourselves to the faith of Christ. The result is certain. If works come into judgment, we are all condemned; therefore we obtain, by the faith of Christ, a free righteousness. This sentence is full of the highest consolation. It tells us that, wherever we hear ourselves condemned in Scripture, there is help provided for us in Christ, if we betake ourselves to him. We are lost, though God were silent: why then does he so often pronounce that we are lost? It is that we may not perish by everlasting destruction, but, struck and confounded by such a dreadful sentence, may by faith seek Christ, through whom we "pass from death into life." (1Jo 3:14.) By a figure of speech, (μετωνυμία,) in which the thing containing is put for the thing contained, the *promise* denotes that which is promised.

Galatians 3:23-29

23. But before faith came, we were kept under the law, shut up unto the faith which should afterwards be revealed.

23. Antequam autem veniret fides, sub Lege custodiebamur, conclusi sub fidem, quae revelanda erat.

24. Wherefore the law was our schoolmaster *to bring us* unto Christ, that we might be justified by faith.

24. Itaque Lex paedagogus noster fuit in Christum, ut ex fide justificaremur.

25. But after that faith is come, we are no longer under a schoolmaster.

25. Adveniente autem fide, non amplius sub paedagogo sumus.

26. For ye are all the children of God by faith in Christ Jesus.

26. Nam omnes filii Dei estis per fidem in Christo Iesu.

27. For as many of you as have been baptized into Christ have put on Christ.

27. Siquidem quicunque in Christum baptizati estis, Christum induistis.

28. There is neither Jew nor Greek, there is neither bond nor free, there is neither male nor female: for ye are all one in Christ Jesus.

28. Non est Iudaeus neque Graecus, non est servus neque liber, non est masculus neque femina; onmes enim vos unus estis in Christo Iesu.

29. And if ye *be* Christ's, then are ye Abraham's seed, and heirs according to the promise.

29. Si autem vos Christi, ergo semen Abrahae estis, et secundum promissionem haeredes.

23. *Before faith came.* The question proposed is now more fully defined. He explains at great length the use of the law, and the reason why it was temporal; for otherwise it would have appeared to be always unreasonable that a law should be delivered to the Jews, from which the Gentiles were excluded. If there be but one church consisting of Jews and Gentiles, why is there a diversity in its government? Whence is this new liberty derived, and on what authority does it rest, since the fathers were under subjection to the law? He therefore informs us, that the distinction is such as not to interrupt the union and harmony of the church.

We must again remind the reader that Paul does not treat exclusively of ceremonies, or of the moral law, but embraces the whole economy by which the Lord governed his people under the Old Testament. It became a subject of dispute whether the form of government instituted by Moses had any influence in obtaining righteousness. Paul compares this law first to a *prison*, and next to a *schoolmaster*. Such was the nature of the law, as both comparisons plainly show, that it could not have been in force beyond a certain time.

Faith denotes the full revelation of those things which, during the darkness of the shadows of the law, were dimly seen; for he does not intend to say that the fathers, who lived under the law, did not possess faith. The faith of Abraham has already come under our notice, and other instances are quoted by the author of the Epistle to the Hebrews. (Heb 11.) The doctrine of faith, in short, is attested by Moses and all the prophets: but, as faith was not then clearly manifested, so the *time of faith* is an appellation here given, not in an absolute, but in a comparative sense, to the time of the New Testament. That this was his meaning is evident from what he immediately adds, that they were *shut up under the faith which should afterwards be revealed;* for this implies that those who were under the custody of the law were partakers of the same faith. The law did not restrain them from faith; but, that they might not wander from the fold of faith, it kept possession of themselves. There is an elegant allusion, too, to what he had formerly said, that "the scripture hath concluded all under sin." They were besieged on every hand by the curse, but this siege was counteracted by an imprisonment which protected them from the curse; so that the imprisonment by the law is here proved to have been highly generous in its character.

Faith was not yet *revealed*, not because the fathers wanted light, but because they had less light than we have. The ceremonies might be said to shadow out an absent Christ, but to us he is represented as actually present, and thus while they had the mirror, we have the substance. Whatever might be the amount of darkness under the law, the fathers were not ignorant of the road in which they ought to walk. Though the dawn is not equal to the splendor of noon, yet, as it is sufficient to direct a journey, travelers do not wait till the sun is fully risen. Their portion of light resembled the dawn, which was enough to preserve them from all error, and guide them to everlasting blessedness.

24. *Wherefore the law was our schoolmaster* This is the second comparison, which still more clearly expresses Paul's design. A schoolmaster is not appointed for the whole life, but only for childhood, as the etymology of the Greek word παιδαγωγός implies. [63] Besides, in training a child, the object is to prepare him, by the instructions of childhood, for maturer years. The comparison applies in both respects to the law, for its authority was limited to a particular age, and its whole object was to prepare its scholars in such a manner, that, when its elementary instructions were closed, they might make progress worthy of manhood. And so he adds, that it was our schoolmaster (εἰς Χριστὸν) *unto Christ.* The grammarian, when he has trained a boy, delivers him into the hands of another, who conducts him through the higher branches of a finished education. In like manner, the law was the grammar of theology, which, after carrying its scholars a short way, handed them over to *faith* to be completed. Thus, Paul compares the Jews to children, and us to advanced youth.

But a question arises, what was the instruction or education of this schoolmaster? First, the law, by displaying the justice of God, convinced them that in themselves they were unrighteous; for in the commandments of God, as in a mirror, they might see how far they were distant from true righteousness. They were thus reminded that righteousness must be sought in some other quarter. The promises of the law served the same purpose, and might lead to such reflections as these: "If you cannot obtain life by works but by fulfilling the law, some new and different method must be sought. Your weakness will never allow you to ascend so high; nay, though you desire and strive ever so much, you will fall far short of the object." The threatenings, on the other hand, pressed and entreated them to seek refuge from the wrath and curse of God, and gave them no rest till they were constrained to seek the grace of Christ.

Such too, was the tendency of all the ceremonies; for what end did sacrifices and washings serve but to keep the mind continually fixed on pollution and condemnation? When a man's uncleanness is placed before his eyes, when the unoffending animal is held forth as the image of his own death, how can he indulge in sleep? How can he but be roused to the earnest cry for deliverance? Beyond all doubt, ceremonies accomplished their object, not merely by alarming and humbling the conscience, but by exciting them to the faith of the coming Redeemer. In the imposing services of the Mosaic ritual, every thing that was presented to the eye bore an impress of Christ. The law, in short, was nothing else than an immense variety of exercises, in which the worshippers were led by the hand to Christ.

That we might be justified by faith. He has already said that the law is not perfect, when he compared it to the training of childhood; but it would make men perfect if it bestowed upon them righteousness. What remains but that faith shall take its place? And so it does, when we, who are destitute of a righteousness of our own, are clothed by it with the righteousness of Christ. Thus is the saying accomplished, "he hath filled the hungry with good things." (Lu 1:53.)

25. *But after that faith is come.* This phrase has been already considered. It denotes the brighter revelation of grace after that "the vail of the temple was rent in twain," (Mt 27:51,) which, we know, was effected by the manifestation of Christ. He affirms that, under the reign of Christ, there is no longer any childhood which needs to be placed under a schoolmaster, and that, consequently, the law has resigned its office, — which is another application of the comparison. There were two things which he had undertaken to prove, — that the law is a preparation for Christ, and that it is temporal. But here the question is again put, Is the law so abolished that we have nothing to do with it? I answer, the law, so far as it is a rule of life, a bridle to keep us in the fear of the Lord, a spur to correct the sluggishness of our flesh, — so far, in short, as it is

"profitable for doctrine, for reproof, for correction, for instruction in righteousness, that believers may be instructed in every good work," (2 Tim. 3: 16, 17,)

— is as much in force as ever, and remains untouched.

In what respect, then, is it abolished? Paul, we have said, looks at the law as possessing certain qualities, and those qualities we shall enumerate. It annexes to works a reward and a punishment; that is, it promises life to those who keep it, and curses all transgressors. Meanwhile, it requires from man the highest perfection and most exact obedience. It makes no abatement, gives no pardon, but calls to a severe reckoning the smallest offenses. It does not openly exhibit Christ and his grace, but points him out at a distance, and only when hidden by the covering of ceremonies. All such qualities of the law, Paul tells us, are abolished; so that the office of Moses is now at an end, so far as it differs in outward aspect from a covenant of grace.

26. *For ye are all the children of God.* It would be unjust, and in the highest degree unreasonable, that the law should hold believers in perpetual slavery. This is proved by the additional argument, that they are the children of God. It would not be enough to say that we are no longer children, unless it were added that we are freemen; for in slaves age makes no alteration. The fact of their being the children of God proves their freedom. How? *By faith in Christ Jesus;* for

"as many as received him, to them gave he power to become the sons of God, even to them that believe on his name."

(Joh 1:12.)

Since, then, by faith we have obtained adoption, by faith likewise we have obtained our freedom.

27. *As many of you as have been baptized.* The greater and loftier the privilege is of being the children of God, the farther is it removed from our senses, and the more difficult to obtain belief. He therefore explains, in a few words, what is implied in our being united, or rather, made one with the Son of God; so as to remove all doubt, that what belongs to him is communicated to us. He employs the metaphor of a garment, when he says that the Galatians *have put on Christ*; but he means that they are so closely united to him, that, in the presence of God, they bear the name and character of Christ, and are viewed in him rather than in themselves. This metaphor or similitude, taken from garments, occurs frequently, and has been treated by us in other places.

But the argument, that, because they have been baptized, they have put on Christ, appears weak; for how far is baptism from being efficacious in all? Is it reasonable that the grace of the Holy Spirit should be so closely linked to an external symbol? Does not the uniform doctrine of Scripture, as well as experience, appear to confute this statement? I answer, it is customary with Paul to treat of the sacraments in two points of view. When he is dealing with hypocrites, in whom the mere symbol awakens pride, he then proclaims loudly the emptiness and worthlessness of the outward symbol, and denounces, in strong terms, their foolish confidence. In such cases he contemplates not the ordinance of God, but the corruption of wicked men. When, on the other hand, he addresses believers, who make a proper use of the symbols, he then views them in connection with the truth — which they represent. In this case, he makes no boast of any false splendor as belonging to the sacraments, but calls our attention to the actual fact represented by the outward ceremony. Thus, agreeably to the Divine appointment, the truth comes to be associated with the symbols.

But perhaps some person will ask, Is it then possible that, through the fault of men, a sacrament shall cease to bear a figurative meaning? The reply is easy. Though wicked men may derive no advantage from the sacraments, they still retain undiminished their nature and force. The sacraments present, both to good and to bad men, the grace of God. No falsehood attaches to the promises which they exhibit of the grace of the Holy Spirit. Believers receive what is offered; and if wicked men, by rejecting it, render the offer unprofitable to themselves, their conduct cannot destroy the faithfulness of God, or the true meaning of the sacrament. [64] With strict propriety, then, does Paul, in addressing believers, say, that when they were baptized, they "put on Christ;" just as, in the Epistle to the Romans, he says,

"that we have been planted together into his death,
so as to be also partakers of his resurrection."
(Ro 6:5.)

In this way, the symbol and the Divine operation are kept distinct, and yet the meaning of the sacraments is manifest; so that they cannot be regarded as empty and trivial exhibitions; and we are reminded with what base ingratitude they are chargeable, who, by abusing the precious ordinances of God, not only render them unprofitable to themselves, but turn them to their own destruction!

28. *There is neither Jew nor Greek.* The meaning is, that there is no distinction of persons here, and therefore it is of no consequence to what nation or condition any one may belong: nor is circumcision any more regarded than sex or civil rank. And why? Because Christ makes them all one. Whatever may have been their former differences, Christ alone is able to unite them all. *Ye are one:* the distinction is now removed. The apostle's object is to shew that the grace of adoption, and the hope of salvation, do not depend on the law, but are contained in Christ alone, who therefore is all. Greek is here put, as usual, for Gentile, and one department for the whole class.

29. *Then are ye Abraham's seed.* This is not intended to convey the idea, that to be a child of Abraham is better than to be a member of Christ, — but to repress the pride of the Jews, who gloried in their privilege, as if they alone were the people of God. They reckoned no distinction higher than to belong to the race of Abraham; and this very distinction he makes to be common to all who believe in Christ. The conclusion rests on this argument, that Christ is the blessed seed, in whom, as we have said, all the children of Abraham are united. He proves this by the universal offer of the inheritance to them all, from which it follows, that the promise includes them among the children. It deserves notice, that, wherever faith is mentioned, it is always his relation to the promise.

Footnotes

54

"Βασκαίνειν, 'to enchant, to fascinate, to delude by magical charms,' — -rather an uncommon word, ἅπαξ λεγόμενον in the New Testament. It may amuse to notice the etumon of the word. Some grammarians have strangely thought it derived from φάεσι καίνειν, 'to kill with the eyes.' Its true etymology obviously is, βάω, βάσκω, βασκάω βασκαίνω. βάσκω (equivalent to φάσκω,), 'to say, to speak,' comes, in the form βασκαίνω, to signify κακολογεῖν, 'to calumniate,' then 'to deceive,' then 'to deceive by magical arts.'" — Brown.

55

Καὶ μὴν οὐκ ἐν τῶ Γαλατῶν χώρᾳ ἀλλ ' ἐν ἱεροσολύμοις ἐσταυρώθν. Πῶς οὖν φησιν, ἐν ὑμῖν; Τῶς πίστεως δεικνὺς τὴν ἰσχυν καὶ τὰ πόῤ ῥωθεν δυναμένης ὁρᾶν. Καὶ οὐκ εἶπεν, ἐσταυρώθη ἀλλὰ προεγράθη ἐσταυρωμένος δηλῶν ὅτι τοῖς τῶς πίστεως ὀφθαλμοῖς ἀκριβέστερον ἐθεώρησαν τῶν παρόντων ἐνίων καὶ τὰ γινόμενα θεωμένων "Yet it was not in the country of the Galatians, but in Jerusalem, that he was crucified. How, then, does he say, 'Among you?' To demonstrate the power of faith, which is able to see even distant objects, And he does not say, 'Was crucified,' but 'Was painted crucified,' shewing that by the eyes of faith they beheld more distinctly than some who were present and saw the transactions." — Chrysostom.

56

"Display the sufferings of Christ like one who was an eye-witness of those sufferings, and hold up the blood, the precious blood of atonement, as issuing warm from the cross." — Robert Hall.

57

"Did ye receive that Spirit which was the fullest evidence of your being justified, accepted, and received as the children and people of God, by conformity to the law of Moses, or by embracing the doctrine of the gospel? If by embracing the doctrine of the gospel, then you became justified by embracing that doctrine, and consequently need not conform to the law of Moses, in order to obtain justification." — Chandler.

58

"The scope of the passage shews that γινώσκετε is not the Indicative, but the Imperative. Paul does not presuppose that the Galatians acknowledge this principle; he is exerting himself to convince them of it." — Brown.

59

"La malediction de tous hommes."

60

"Qui est le parfait accomplissement de la promesse." "Who is the perfect accomplishment of the promise."

61

"Though some learned men have been of opinion that the mediator here mentioned is the Son of God, yet I think no reasonable doubt can be entertained as to its denoting Moses. Strictly speaking, Aaron, or rather the priesthood, was the mediator of the old covenant. It answers to the Great High-Priest, (ἀρχιερεύς,) Mediator, (μεσίτης,) and Surety, (ἔγγυος,) of the new covenant. But the reference seems here to the *giving* of the law: that was by Moses. 'The law was given by Moses.' (Joh 1:17.) God speaks to Moses, and Moses speaks to the people; and this arrangement was entered into by the express request of the people themselves. Moses himself says, 'I stood between the Lord and you at that time. (De 5:5.) Philo calls Moses μεσίτης." — Brown.

62

"This is confessedly one of the most obscure passages in the New Testament, and, perhaps, above all others, 'vexatus ab interpretibus,' (tortured by interpreters,) if it be true, as Winer affirms, that there are no less than 250 modes of explanation, most of which are stated and reviewed by Koppe, Berger, Keil, Bonitz, Weigand, and Scheft." — (Bloomfield.) Schott remarks, that the bare fact of upwards of 250 interpretations makes it impossible to deny that some obscurity attaches to the Apostle's language in this passage, arising chiefly from mere brevity of style, but judiciously adds, that, had there not been many commentators more eager to bring forward anything that has the appearance of novelty, than to investigate the ordinary meaning of the terms, the scope of the passage, and the doctrinal statements and reasonings contained in the writings of the Apostle Paul, the interpretations would never have swelled to so large an amount. — *Ed.*

63

"As the law was before compared to a *jailer*, so it is here likened to a παιδαγωγός, by which term is not to be understood a *schoolmaster*, (for that would have been διδάσκαλος,) but the paedagous or person (usually a freedman or slave) who conducted children to and from school, attended them out of school hours, formed their manners, superintended their moral conduct, and in various respects prepared them for the διδάσκαλος." — Bloomfield. Our author's observations on παιδαγωγός, in another passage, have brought out the full meaning of this word, and the classical authorities for the use of it, in the translator's notes. — Calvin on the Corinthians, vol. 1, p. 169. — *Ed*

64

"If any person receives nothing more than this bodily washing, which is perceived by the eyes of flesh, he has not put on the Lord Jesus Christ." — Jerome.

CHAPTER 4

Galatians 4:1-5

1. Now I say, *That* the heir, as long as he is a child, differeth nothing from a servant, though he be lord of all;

1. Dico antem: quamdiu haeres puer est, nihil differt a servo, quum tamen sit dominus onmium;

2. But is under tutors and governors, until the time appointed of the father.

2. Sed sub tutoribus et curatorbus est, usque ad tempus a patre definitum.

3. Even so we, when we were children, were in bondage under the elements of the world:

3. Sic et nos quum essemus pueri, sub elementis mundi in servitute eramus.

4. But when the fulness of the time was come, God sent forth his Son, made of a woman, made under the law,

4. Quando autem venit plenitudo temporis, misit Deus Filium suum, facturn ex muliere, redactum sub Legem;

5. To redeem them that were under the law, that we might receive the adoption of sons.

5. Ut eos, qui sub Lege erant, redimeter, ut adoptionem reciperemus.

1. *Now I say.* Whoever made the division into chapters has improperly separated this paragraph from the preceding, as it is nothing else than the concluding section, (ἐπεξεϱγασία,) in which Paul explains and illustrates the difference that exists between us and the ancient people. He does so by introducing a third comparison, drawn from the relation which a person under age bears to his tutor. The young man, though he is free, *though he is lord of all* his father's family, still resembles a slave; for he is under the government of tutors. [65] But the period of guardianship lasts only "until the time appointed by the father" after which he enjoys his freedom. In this respect the fathers under the Old Testament, being the sons of God, were free; but they were not in possession of freedom, while the law held the place of their tutor, and kept them under its yoke. That slavery of the law lasted as long as it pleased God, who put an end to it at the coming of Christ. Lawyers enumerate various methods by which the tutelage or guardianship is brought to a close; but of all these methods, the only one adapted to this comparison is that which Paul has selected, "the appointment of the father."

Let us now examine the separate clauses. Some apply the comparison in a different manner to the case of any man whatever, whereas Paul is speaking of two nations. What they say, I acknowledge, is true; but it has nothing to do with the present passage. The elect, though they are the children of God from the womb, yet, until by faith they come to the possession of freedom, remain like slaves under the law; but, from the time that they have known Christ, they no longer require this kind of tutelage. Granting all this, I deny that Paul here treats of individuals, or draws a distinction between the time of unbelief and the calling by faith. The matters in dispute were these. Since the church of God is one, how comes it that our condition is different from that of the Israelites? Since we are free by faith, how comes it that they, who had faith in common with us, were not partakers with us of the same freedom? Since we are all equally the children of God, how comes it that we at this day are exempt from a yoke which they were forced to bear? On these points the controversy turned, and not on the manner in which the law reigns over each of us before we are freed by faith from its slavery. Let this point be first of all settled, that Paul here compares the Israelitish church, which existed under the Old Testament, with the Christian church, that thus we may perceive in what points we agree and in what we differ. This comparison furnishes most abundant and most profitable instruction.

First, we learn from it that our hope at the present day, and that of the fathers under the Old Testament, have been directed to the same inheritance; for they were partakers of the same adoption. According to the dreams of some fanatics, and of Servetus among others, the fathers were divinely elected for the sole purpose of prefiguring to us a people of God. Paul, on the other hand, contends that they were elected in order to be together with us the children of God, and particularly attests that to them, not less than to us, belonged the spiritual blessing promised to Abraham.

Secondly, we learn that, notwithstanding their outward slavery, their consciences were still free. The obligation to keep the law did not hinder Moses and Daniel, all the pious kings, priests, and prophets, and the whole company of believers, from being free in spirit. They bore the yoke of the law upon their shoulders, but with a free spirit they worshipped God. More particularly, having been instructed concerning the free pardon of sin, their consciences were delivered from the tyranny of sin and death. Hence we ought to conclude that they held the same doctrine, were joined with us in the true unity of faith, placed reliance on the one Mediator, called on God as their Father, and were led by the same Spirit. All this leads to the conclusion, that the difference between us and the ancient fathers lies in accidents, not in substance. In all the leading characters of the Testament or Covenant we agree: the ceremonies and form of government, in which we differ, are mere additions. Besides, that period was the infancy of the church; but now that Christ is come, the church has arrived at the estate of manhood.

The meaning of Paul's words is clear, but has he not some appearance of contradicting himself? In the Epistle to the Ephesians he exhorts us to make daily progress

"till we come to a perfect man, to the measure of the stature of the fullness of Christ." (Eph 4:13.)

In the first Epistle to the Corinthians he says, (1Co 3:2,)

"I have fed you with milk, and not with meat: for hitherto ye were not able to bear it, neither yet now are ye able;"

and shortly after this he compares the Galatians to children. (Ga 4:19) In those passages, I reply, the apostle speaks of particular men, and of their faith as individuals; but here he speaks generally of two bodies without regard to persons. This reply will assist us in resolving a much greater difficulty. When we look at the matchless faith of Abraham, and the vast intelligence of the holy prophets, with what effrontery shall we dare to talk of such men as our inferiors? Were not they rather the heroes, and we the children? To say nothing of ourselves, who among the Galatians would have been found equal to any of those men?

But here, as I have already said, the apostle describes not particular persons, but the universal condition of both nations. Some men were endowed with extraordinary gifts; but they were few, and the whole body did not share with them. Besides, though they had been numerous, we must inquire not what they inwardly were, but what was that kind or government under which God had placed them; and that was manifestly a school, παιδαγωγία, a system of instruction for children. And what are we now? God has broken those chains, governs his church in a more indulgent manner, and lays not upon us such severe restraint. At the same time, we may remark in passing, that whatever amount of knowledge they might attain partook of the nature of the period; for a dark cloud continually rested on the revelation which they enjoyed. And hence that saying of our Savior,

"Blessed are the eyes which see the things that ye see: for I tell you that many prophets and kings have desired to see those things which ye see, and have not seen them; and to hear those things which ye hear, and have not heard them." (Luke 10:23, 24.)

We now understand in what respect we are preferred to those who were greatly our superiors; for the statements are not applied to persons, but relate entirely to the economy of the Divine administration.

This passage will prove a most powerful battery for destroying the pageantry of ceremonies, which constitutes the entire splendor of the Papal system. For what else is it that dazzles the eyes of simple people, so as to lead them to regard the dominion of the Pope, if not with admiration, at least with some degree of reverence, but the magnificent army of ceremonies, rites, gesticulations, and equipage of every description, contrived for the express purpose of amazing the ignorant? From this passage it appears that they are false disguises, by which the true beauty of the church is impaired. I do not now speak of greater and more frightful corruptions, such as, that they hold them out for divine worship, imagine them to possess the power of meriting salvation, and enforce with more rigid severity the observation of those trifles than the whole law of God. I only advert to the specious pretext under which our modern contrivers apologize for such a multitude of abominations. What though they object that the ignorance of the multitude prevails to a greater extent than it formerly did among the Israelites, and that many assistances are therefore required? They will never be able in this way to prove that the people must be placed under the discipline or a school similar to what existed among the people of Israel; for I shall always meet them with the declaration, that the appointment of God is totally different.

If they plead expediency, I ask, are they better judges of what is expedient than God himself? Let us entertain the firm conviction that the highest advantage, as well as the highest propriety, will be found in whatever God has determined. In aiding the ignorant, we must employ not those methods which the fancy of men may have been pleased to contrive, but those which had been fixed by God themself, who unquestionably has left out nothing that was fitted to assist their weakness. Let this shield suffice for repelling any objections: "God has judged otherwise, and his purpose supplies to us the place of all arguments; unless it be supposed that men are capable of devising better aids than those which God had provided, and which he afterwards threw aside as useless." Let it be carefully observed, Paul does not merely say that the yoke which had been laid upon the

Jews is removed from us, but expressly lays down a distinction in the government which God has commanded to be observed. I acknowledge that we are now at liberty as to all outward matters, but only on the condition that the church shall not be burdened with a multitude of ceremonies, nor Christianity confounded with Judaism. The reason of this we shall afterwards consider in the proper place.

3. *Under the elements of the world. Elements* may either mean, literally, outward and bodily things, or, metaphorically, rudiments. I prefer the latter interpretation. But why does he say that those things which had a spiritual signification were *of the world*? We did not, he says, enjoy the truth in a simple form, but involved in earthly figures; and consequently, what was outward must have been "of the world," though there was concealed under it a heavenly mystery.

4. *When the fullness of the time was come.* He proceeds with the comparison which he had adduced, and applies to his purpose the expression which has already occurred, "the time appointed by the Father," — but still shewing that the time which had been ordained by the providence of God was proper and seasonable. That season is the most fit, and that mode of acting is the most proper, which the providence of God directs. At what time it was expedient that the Son of God should be revealed to the world, it belonged to God alone to judge and determine. This consideration ought to restrain all curiosity. Let no man presume to be dissatisfied with the secret purpose of God, and raise a dispute why Christ did not appear sooner. If the reader desires more full information on this subject, he may consult what I have written on the conclusion of the Epistle to the Romans.

God sent forth his Son. These few words contain much instruction. The Son, who was sent, must have existed before he was sent; and this proves his eternal Godhead. Christ therefore is the Son of God, sent from heaven. Yet this same person was *made of a woman*, because he assumed our nature, which shews that he has two natures. Some copies read *natum* instead of *filium*; but the latter reading is more generally followed, and, in my opinion, is preferable. But the language was also expressly intended to distinguish Christ from other men, as having been formed of the substance of his mother, and not by ordinary generation. In any other sense, it would have been trifling, and foreign to the subject. The word *woman* is here put generally for the female sex.

Subjected under the law. The literal rendering is, *Made under the law*; but in my version I have preferred another word, which expresses more plainly the fact that he was placed in subjection to the law. Christ the Son of God, who might have claimed to be exempt from every kind of subjection, became subject to the law. Why? He did so in our room, that he might obtain freedom for us. A man who was free, by constituting himself a surety, redeems a slave: by putting on himself the chains, he takes them off from the other. So Christ chose to become liable to keep the law, that exemption from it might be obtained for us; otherwise it would have been to no purpose that he should come under the yoke of the law, for it certainly was not on his own account that he did so.

To redeem them that were under the law [66] We must here observe, the exemption from the law which Christ has procured for us does not imply that we no longer owe any obedience to the doctrine of the law, and may do whatever we please; for the law is the everlasting rule of a good and holy life. But Paul speaks of the law with all its appendages. From subjection to that law we are redeemed, because it is no longer what it once was. "The vail being rent," (Mt 27:51,) freedom is openly proclaimed, and this is what he immediately adds.

5. *That we might receive the adoption.* The fathers, under the Old Testament, were certain of their adoption, but did not so fully as yet enjoy their privilege. *Adoption*, like the phrase, "the redemption of our body," (Ro 8:23,) is here put for actual possession. As, at the last day, we receive the fruit of our redemption, so now we receive the fruit of adoption, of which the holy fathers did not partake before the coming of Christ; and therefore those who now burden the church with an excess of ceremonies, defraud her of the just right of adoption.

Galatians 4:6-11

6. And because ye are sons, God hath sent forth the Spirit of his Son into your hearts, crying, Abba, Father.

6. Quoniam autem estis filii, misit Deus Spiritum Filii sui in corda vestra, clamantem, Abba, Pater.

7. Wherefore thou art no more a servant, but a son; and if a son, then an heir of God through Christ.

7. Itaque non amplius es servus, sed filius; si antem filius, etiam haeres Dei per Christum.

8. Howbeit then, when ye knew not God, ye did service unto them which by nature are no gods.

8. At tunc quum nondum cognoveratis Deum, serviebatis eis qui natura non sunt dii.

9. But now, after that ye have known God, or rather are known of God, how turn ye again to the weak and beggarly elements, whereunto ye desire again to be in bondage?

9. Nunc autem postquam cognovistis Deum, vel potius cogniti fuistis a Deo; quomode convertimini rursus ad infirma et egena elementa, quibus rursus Deuteronomy integro servire vultis?

10. Ye observe days, and months, and times, and years.

10. Dies observatis, et menses, et tempera, et annos.

11. I am afraid of you, lest I have bestowed upon you labour in vain.

11. Timeo Deuteronomy vobis, ne forte in vobis frustra laboraverim.

6. *And because ye are sons.* The adoption which he had mentioned, is proved to belong to the Galatians by the following argument. This adoption must have preceded the testimony of adoption given by the Holy Spirit; but the effect is the sign of the cause. In venturing, he says, to call God your Father, you have the advice and direction of the Spirit of Christ; therefore it is certain that you are the sons of God. This agrees with what is elsewhere taught by him, that the Spirit is the earnest and pledge of our adoption, and gives to us a well-founded belief that God regards us with a father's love.

"Who hath also sealed us, and given the earnest of the Spirit in our hearts." (2Co 1:22.)

"Now he that hath wrought us for the self-same thing is God, who also hath given unto us the earnest of the Spirit." (2Co 5:5.)

But it will be objected, do not wicked men, too, carry their rashness so far as to proclaim that God is their Father? Do they not frequently, with greater confidence than others, utter their false boasts? I reply, Paul's language does not relate to idle boasting, or to the proud opinion of himself which any man may entertain, but to the testimony of a pious conscience which accompanies the new birth. This argument can have no weight but in the case of believers, for ungodly men have no experience of this certainty; as our Lord himself declares.

"The Spirit of truth," says he, "whom the world cannot receive, because it seeth him not, neither knoweth him."

(Joh 14:17.)

This is implied in Paul's words, *God hath sent forth the Spirit of his Son into your hearts.* It is not what the persons themselves, in the foolish judgment of the flesh, may venture to believe, but what God declares in their hearts by his Spirit. *The Spirit of his Son* is a title more strictly adapted to the present occasion than any other that could have been employed. We are the sons of God, because we have received the same Spirit as his only Son.

Let it be observed, that Paul ascribes this universally to all Christians; for where this pledge of the Divine love towards us is wanting, there is assuredly no faith. Hence it is evident what sort of Christianity belongs to Popery, since any man who says, that he has the Spirit of God, is charged by them with impious presumption. Neither the Spirit of God, nor certainty, belongs to their notion of faith. This single tenet held by them is a remarkable proof that, in all the schools of the Papists, the devil, the father of unbelief, reigns. I acknowledge, indeed, that the scholastic divines, when they enjoin upon the consciences of men the agitation of perpetual doubt, are in perfect agreement with what the natural feelings of mankind would dictate. It is the more necessary to fix in our minds this doctrine of Paul, that no man is a Christian who has not learned, by the teaching of the Holy Spirit, to call God his Father.

Crying. This participle, I think, is used in order to express greater boldness. Hesitation does not allow us to speak freely, but keeps the mouth nearly shut, while the half-broken words can hardly escape from a stammering tongue. "Crying," on the other hand, expresses firmness and unwavering confidence.

"For we have not received again the spirit of bondage to fear,

but of freedom to full confidence." (Ro 8:15.)

Abba, Father. The meaning of these words, I have no doubt, is, that calling upon God is common to all languages. It is a fact which bears directly on the present subject, that the name *Father* is given to God both by the Hebrews and by the Greeks; as had been predicted by Isaiah,

"Every tongue shall make confession to my name."

(Isa 45:23.)

The whole of this subject is handled by the apostle at greater length in his Epistle to the Romans. I judge it unnecessary to repeat here observations which I have already made in the exposition of that Epistle, and which the reader may consult. Since, therefore, Gentiles are reckoned among the sons of God, it is evident that adoption comes not by the merit of the law, but by the grace of faith.

7. *Wherefore thou art no more a servant.* In the Christian Church slavery no longer exists, but the condition of the children is free. In what respect the fathers under the law were slaves, we have already inquired; for their freedom was not yet revealed, but was hidden under the coverings and yoke of the law. Our attention is again directed to the distinction between the Old and New Testaments. The ancients were also sons of God, and heirs through Christ, but we hold the same character in a different manner; for we have Christ present with us, and in that manner enjoy his blessings.

8. *But when ye as yet knew not God.* This is not intended as an additional argument; and indeed he had already proved his point so fully, that no doubt remained, and the rebuke which was now to be administered could not be evaded. His object is to make their fall appear more criminal, by comparing it with past events. It is not wonderful, he says, that formerly *ye did service to them which by nature are no gods*; for, wherever ignorance of God exists, there must be dreadful blindness. You were then wandering in darkness, but how disgraceful is it that in the midst of light you should fall into such gross errors! The main inference is, that the Galatians were less excusable for corrupting the gospel than they had formerly been for idolatry. But here it ought to be observed, that, till we have been enlightened in the true knowledge of one God, we always serve idols, whatever pretext we may throw over the false religion. The lawful worship of God, therefore, must be preceded by just views of his character. *By nature*, that is, in reality, *they are no gods*. Every object of worship which men contrive is a creature of their own imagination. In the opinion of men idols may be gods, but in reality they are nothing.

9. *But now,* [67] *after that ye have known God.* No language can express the base ingratitude of departing from God, when he has once been known. What is it but to forsake, of our own accord, the light, the life, the fountain of all benefits, — "to forsake," as Jeremiah complains,

"the fountain of living waters, and hew out cisterns,
broken cisterns, that can hold no water!" (Jer 2:13.)

Still farther to heighten the blame, he corrects his language, and says, *or rather have been, known by God*; for the greater the grace of God is towards us, our guilt in despising it must be the heavier. Paul reminds the Galatians whence they had derived the knowledge of God. He affirms that they did not obtain it by their own exertions, by the acuteness or industry of their own minds, but because, when they were at the farthest possible remove from thinking of him, God visited them in his mercy. What is said of the Galatians may be extended to all; for in all are fulfilled the words of Isaiah,

"I am sought by them that asked not for me:
I am found by them that sought me not." (Isa 65:1.)

The origin of our calling is the free election of God, which predestinates us to life before we are born. On this depends our calling, our faith, our whole salvation.

How turn ye again? They could not turn *again* to ceremonies which they had never practiced. The expression is figurative, and merely denotes, that to fall again into wicked superstition, as if they had never received the truth of God, was the height of folly. When he calls the ceremonies *beggarly elements*, he views them as out of

Christ, and, what is more, as opposed to Christ. To the fathers they were not only profitable exercises and aids to piety, but efficacious means of grace. But then their whole value lay in Christ, and in the appointment of God. The false apostles, on the other hand, neglecting the promises, endeavored to oppose the ceremonies to Christ, as if Christ alone were not sufficient. That they should be regarded by Paul as worthless trifles, cannot excite surprise; but of this I have already spoken. The word *bondage* conveys a reproof for submitting to be slaves. [68]

10. *Ye observe days.* He adduces as an instance one description of "elements," the observance of days. No condemnation is here given to the observance of dates in the arrangements of civil society. The order of nature out of which this arises, is fixed and constant. How are months and years computed, but by the revolution of the sun and moon? What distinguishes summer from winter, or spring from harvest, but the appointment of God, — an appointment which was promised to continue to the end of the world? (Ge 8:22.) The civil observation of days contributes not only to agriculture and to matters of politics, and ordinary life, but is even extended to the government of the church. Of what nature, then, was the observation which Paul reproves? It was that which would bind the conscience, by religious considerations, as if it were necessary to the worship of God, and which, as he expresses it in the Epistle to the Romans, would make a distinction between one day and another. (Ro 14:5.)

When certain days are represented as holy in themselves, when one day is distinguished from another on religious grounds, when holy days are reckoned a part of divine worship, then days are improperly observed. The Jewish Sabbath, new moons, and other festivals, were earnestly pressed by the false apostles, because they had been appointed by the law. When we, in the present age, intake a distinction of days, we do not represent them as necessary, and thus lay a snare for the conscience; we do not reckon one day to be more holy than another; we do not make days to be the same thing with religion and the worship of God; but merely attend to the preservation of order and harmony. The observance of days among us is a free service, and void of all superstition.

11. *Lest I have bestowed upon you labor in vain.* The expression is harsh, and must have filled the Galatians with alarm; for what hope was left to them, if Paul's labor had been in vain? Some have expressed astonishment that Paul should be so powerfully affected by the observance of days, as almost to designate it a subversion of the whole gospel. But if we carefully weigh the whole, we shall see that there was just reason; and that the false apostles not only attempted to lay the yoke of Jewish bondage on the neck of the church, but filled their minds with wicked superstitions. To bring back Christianity to Judaism, was in itself no light evil; but far more serious mischief was done, when, in opposition to the grace of Christ, they set up holidays as meritorious performances, and pretended that this mode of worship would propitiate the divine favor. When such doctrines were received, the worship of God was corrupted, the grace of Christ made void, and the freedom of conscience oppressed.

Do we wonder that Paul should be afraid that he had labored in vain, that the gospel would henceforth be of no service? And since that very description of impiety is now supported by Popery, what sort of Christ or what sort of gospel does it retain? So far as respects the binding of consciences, they enforce the observance of days with not less severity than was done by Moses. They consider holidays, not less than the false apostles did, to be a part of the worship of God, and even connect with them the diabolical notion of merit. The Papists must therefore be held equally censurable with the false apostles; and with this addition in aggravation, that, while the former proposed to keep those days which had been appointed by the law of God, the latter enjoin days, rashly stamped with their own seal, to be observed as most holy.

Galatians 4:12-20

12. Brethren, I beseech you, be as I *am*; for I *am* as ye *are*: ye have not injured me at all.

12. Estote ut ego; quia ego quoque sum ut vos. Fratres, rogo vos; nihil mihi fecistis injuriae.

13. Ye know how through infirmity of the flesh I preached the gospel unto you at the first.

13. Novistis antem, quod per infirmitatem carnis evangelizaverim vobis prius;

14. And my temptation which was in my flesh ye despised not, nor rejected; but received me as an angel of God, *even* as Christ Jesus.

14. Et experimenturn mei, quod fuit in carne mea, non contempsistis, neque respuistis; sed tanquam angelum Dei suscepistis me, tanquam Christum Iesum.

15. Where is then the blessedness ye spake of? for I bear you record, that, if *it had been* possible, ye would have plucked out your own eyes, and have given them to me.

15. Ubi igitur beatitude vestra? testimonium enim reddo vobis, quod, si possibile fuisset, etiam oculos vestros effossos dedissetis mihi.

16. Am I therefore become your enemy, because I tell you the truth?

16. Ergdne vera loquendo inimicus sum vobis factus?

17. They zealously affect you, *but* not well; yea, they would exclude you, that ye might affect them.

17. AEmulantur vos, non bene; imo excludere vos volunt, ut ipsos aemulemini.

18. But *it is* good to be zealously affected always in *a* good *thing*, and not only when I am present with you.

18. Bonum autem est aemulari in bono semper, et non tanturn quum praesens sum apud vos.

19. My little children, of whom I travail in birth again until Christ be formed in you,

19. Filioli mei, quos iterum parturio, donec formetur in vobis Christus.

20. I desire to be present with you now, and to change my voice; for I stand in doubt of you.

20. Vellem autem nunc coram esse vobiscum, et routare vocem meam; quia anxius sum in vobis.

12. *Be as I am.* Having till now spoken roughly, he begins to adopt a milder strain. The former harshness had been more than justified by the heinousness of the offense; but as he wished to do good, he resolves to adopt a style of conciliation. It is the part of a wise pastor to consider, not what those who have wandered may justly deserve, but what may be the likeliest method of bringing them back to the right path. He must "be instant in season, out of season; reprove, rebuke, exhort, with all long-suffering and doctrine." (2Ti 4:2.) Following the method which he had recommended to Timothy, he leaves off chiding, and begins to use entreaties. *I beseech you*, he says, and calls them *brethren*, to assure them that no bitterness had mingled with his reproofs.

The words, *be as I am*, refer to the affection of the mind. As he endeavors to accommodate himself to them, so he wishes that they would do the like by him in return. *For I am as ye are.* "As I have no other object in view than to promote your benefit, so it is proper that you should be prevailed on to adopt moderate views, and to lend a willing, obedient ear to my instructions." And here again pastors are reminded of their duty to come down, as far as they can, to the people, and to study the various dispositions of those with whom they have to deal, if they wish to obtain compliance with their message. The proverb still holds: "to be loved, you must be lovely."

Ye have not injured me at all. This is intended to remove the suspicion which might have rendered his former reproofs more disagreeable. If we think that a person is speaking under a sense of injury, or revenging a private quarrel, we turn away our minds from him entirely, and are sure to torture whatever he says into an unfavourable interpretation. Paul therefore meets the rising prejudice by saying, "So far as respects myself, I have no cause to complain of you. It is not on my own account, nor from any hostility to you, that I feel warmly; and therefore, if I use strong language, it must arise from some other cause than hatred or anger."

13. *Ye know that, through infirmity of the flesh.* He recalls to their recollection the friendly and respectful manner in which they had received him, and he does so for two reasons. First, to let them know that he loved them, and thus to gain a ready ear to all that he says; and secondly, to encourage them, that, as they had begun well, they would go on in the same course. This mention of past occurrences, then, while it is an expression of his kind regards, is intended likewise as an exhortation to act in the same manner as they had done at an earlier period.

By *infirmity of the flesh* he means here, as in other places, what had a tendency to make him appear mean and despised. *Flesh* denotes his outward appearance, which the word infirmity describes to have been contemptible. Such was Paul when he came among them, without show, without pretense, without worldly honors or rank, without everything that could gain him respect or estimation in the eyes of men. Yet all this did not prevent the Galatians from giving him the most honorable reception. The narrative contributes powerfully to his argument, for what was there in Paul to awaken their esteem or veneration, but the power of the Holy Spirit alone? Under what pretext, then, will they now begin to despise that power? Next, they are charged with inconsistency, since no subsequent occurrence in the life of Paul could entitle them to esteem him less than before. But this he leaves to be considered by the Galatians, contenting himself with indirectly suggesting it as a subject of consideration.

14. *My temptation.* That is, "Though ye perceived me to be, in a worldly point of view, a contemptible person, yet ye did not reject me." He calls it a *temptation* or trial, because it was a thing not unknown or hidden, and he did not himself attempt to conceal it, as is usually done by ambitious men, who are ashamed of anything about them that may lower them in public estimation. It frequently happens that unworthy persons receive applause, before their true character has been discovered, and shortly afterwards are dismissed with shame and disgrace. But widely different was the case of Paul, who had used no disguise to impose on the Galatians, but had frankly told them what he was.

As an angel of God. In this light every true minister of Christ ought to be regarded. As God employs the services of angels for communicating to us his favors, so godly teachers are divinely raised up to administer to us the most excellent of all blessings, the doctrine of eternal salvation. Not without good reason are they, by whose hands God dispenses to us such a treasure, compared to angels: for they too are the messengers of God, by whose mouth God speaks to us. And this argument is used by Malachi.

"The priest's lips should keep knowledge, and they should seek the law at his mouth, *for he is the messenger of the Lord of hosts.*" (Mal 2:7.)

But the apostle rises still higher, and adds, *even as Christ Jesus*; for the Lord himself commands that his ministers shall be viewed in the same light as himself.

"He that heareth you heareth me,
and he that despiseth you despiseth me." (Lu 10:16.)

Nor is this wonderful; for it is in his name that they discharge their embassy, and thus they hold the rank of him in whose room they act. Such is the highly commendatory language which reveals to us at once the majesty of the gospel, and the honorable character of its ministry. If it be the command of Christ that his ministers shall be thus honored, it is certain that contempt of them proceeds from the instigation of the devil; and indeed they never can be despised so long as the word of God is esteemed. In vain do the Papists attempt to hold out this pretext for their own arrogant pretensions. As they are plainly the enemies of Christ, how absurd is it that they should assume the garb, and take to themselves the character, of Christ's servants! If they wish to obtain the honors of angels, let them perform the duty of angels: if they wish that we should listen to them as to Christ, let them convey to us faithfully his pure word.

15. *Where is there your blessedness?* Paul had made them happy, and he intimates that the pious affection with which they formerly regarded him was an expression of their happiness. But now, by allowing themselves to be deprived of the services of him to whom they ought to have attributed whatever knowledge they possessed of Christ, they gave evidence that they were unhappy. This hint was intended to produce keen reflection. "What? Shall all this be lost? Will you forfeit all the advantage of having once heard Christ speaking by my lips? Shall the foundation in the faith which you received from me be to no purpose? Shall your falling away now destroy the glory of your obedience in the presence of God?" In short, by despising the pure doctrine which they had embraced, they throw away, of their own accord, the *blessedness* which they had obtained, and draw down upon themselves the destruction in which their unhappy career must terminate.

For I bear you record. It is not enough that pastors be respected, if they are not also loved; for both are necessary to make the doctrine they preach be fully relished; and both, the apostle declares, had existed among the Galatians. He had already spoken of their respect for him, and he now speaks of their love. To be willing to *pluck out their own eyes*, if it had been necessary, was an evidence of very extraordinary love, stronger than the willingness to part with life.

16. *Am I therefore become your enemy?* He now returns to speak about himself. It was entirely their own fault, he says, that they had changed their minds. Though it is a common remark, that truth begets hatred, yet, except through the malice and wickedness of those who cannot endure to hear it, truth is never hateful. While he vindicates himself from any blame in the unhappy difference between them, he indirectly censures their ingratitude. Yet still his advice is friendly, not to reject, on rash or light grounds, the apostleship of one whom they had formerly considered to be worthy of their warmest love. What can be more unbecoming than that the hatred of truth should change enemies into friends? His aim then is, not so much to upbraid, as to move them to repentance.

17. *They are jealous of you.* He comes at length to the false apostles, and does more by silence to make them odious, than if he had given their names; for we usually abstain from naming those whose very names produce in us dislike and aversion. He mentions the immoderate ambition of those men, and warns the Galatians not to be led astray by their appearance of zeal. The comparison is borrowed from honorable love, as contrasted with those professions of regard which arise from unhallowed desires. Jealousy, on the part of the false apostles, ought not to impose upon them; for it proceeded not from right zeal, but from an improper desire of obtaining reputation, — a desire most unlike that holy jealousy of which Paul speaks to the Corinthians.

"For I am jealous over you with godly jealousy; for I have espoused you to one husband, that I may present you as a chaste virgin to Christ. But I fear lest by any means, as the serpent beguiled Eve through his subtlety, so your minds should be corrupted from the simplicity that is in Christ."

(2 Cor. 11:2, 3.)

To expose still more fully their base arts, he corrects his language. *Yea, they would exclude you* [69] They not only endeavor to gain your affections, but, as they cannot obtain possession of you by any other means, they endeavor to kindle strife between us. When you have been thrown as it were destitute, they expect that you will yield yourselves up to them; for they perceive that, so long as there shall be maintained between us a religious harmony, they can have no influence. This stratagem is frequently resorted to by all the ministers of Satan. By producing in the people a dislike of their pastor, they hope afterwards to draw them to themselves; and, having disposed of the rival, to obtain quiet possession. A careful and judicious examination of their conduct will discover that in this way they always begin.

18. *But it is good to be the object of jealousy.* It is hard to say whether this refers to himself or to the Galatians. Good ministers are exhorted to cherish holy jealousy in watching over the churches,

"that they may present them as a chaste virgin to Christ."

(2Co 11:2.)

If it refers to Paul, the meaning will be: "I confess that I also am jealous of you, but with a totally different design: and I do so as much when I am absent as when I am present, because I do not seek my own advantage." But I am rather inclined to view it as referring to the Galatians, though in this case it will admit of more than one interpretation. It may mean: "They indeed attempt to withdraw your affections from me, that, when you are thrown destitute, you may go over to them; but do you, who loved me while I was present, continue to cherish the same regard for me when I am absent." But a more correct explanation is suggested by the opposite senses which the word ζηλοῦσθαι bears. As, in the former verse, he had used the word *jealous* in a bad sense, denoting an improper way of accomplishing an object, so here he uses it in a good sense, denoting a zealous imitation of the good qualities of another. By condemning improper jealousy, he now exhorts the Galatians to engage in a different sort of competition, and that, too, while he was absent.

19. *My little children.* The word *children* is still softer and more affectionate than brethren; and the diminutive, *little children*, is an expression, not of contempt, but of endearment, though, at the same time, it suggests the tender years of those who ought now to have arrived at full age. (Heb 5:12.) The style is abrupt, which is usually the case with highly pathetic passages. Strong feeling, from the difficulty of finding adequate expression, breaks off our words when half uttered, while the powerful emotion chokes the utterance.

Of whom I travail in birth again. This phrase is added, to convey still more fully his vehement affection, which endured, on their account, the throes and pangs of a mother. It denotes likewise his anxiety; for

"a woman, when she is in travail, hath sorrow, because her hour is come; but as soon as she is delivered of the child, she remembereth no more the anguish, for joy that a man is born into the world." (Joh 16:21.)

The Galatians had already been conceived and brought forth; but, after their revolt, they must now be begotten a second time.

Until Christ be formed in you. By these words he soothes their anger; for he does not set aside the former birth, but says that they must be again nourished in the womb, as if they had not yet been fully formed. That Christ should be formed in us is the same thing with our being formed in Christ; for we are born so as to become new creatures in him; and he, on the other hand, is born in us, so that we live his life. Since the true image of Christ, through the superstitions introduced by the false apostles, had been defaced, Paul labors to restore that image in all its perfection and brightness. This is done by the ministers of the gospel, when they give

"milk to babes, and strong meat to them that are of full age," (Heb. 5:13, 14,)

and, in short, ought to be their employment during the whole course of their preaching. But Paul here compares himself to a woman in labor, because the Galatians were not yet completely born.

This is a remarkable passage for illustrating the efficacy of the Christian ministry. True, we are "born of God," (1Jo 3:9;) but, because he employs a minister and preaching as his instruments for that purpose, he is pleased to ascribe to them that work which Himself performs, through the power of his Spirit, in co-operation with the labors of man. Let us always attend to this distinction, that, when a minister is contrasted with God, he is nothing, and can do nothing, and is utterly useless; but, because the Holy Spirit works efficaciously by means of him, he comes to be regarded and praised as an agent. Still, it is not what he can do in himself, or apart from God, but what God does by him, that is there described. If ministers wish to do anything, let them labor to form Christ, not to form themselves, in their hearers. The writer is now so oppressed with grief, that he almost faints from exhaustion without completing his sentence.

20. *I would wish to be present with you now.* This is a most serious expostulation, the complaint of a father so perplexed by the misconduct of his sons, that he looks around him for advice, and knows not to what hand to turn. [70] He wishes to have an opportunity of personally addressing them, because we thus obtain a better idea of what is adapted to present circumstances; because, according as the hearer is affected, according as he is submissive or obstinate, we are enabled to regulate our discourse. But something more than this was meant by the desire to *change the voice* [71] He was prepared most cheerfully to assume a variety of forms, and even, if the case required it, to frame a new language. This is a course which pastors ought most carefully to follow. They must not be entirely guided by their own inclinations, or by the bent of their own genius, but must accommodate themselves, as far as the case will allow, to the capacity of the people, — with this reservation, however, that they are to proceed no farther than conscience shall dictate, [72] and that no departure from integrity shall be made, in order to gain the favor of the people.

Galatians 4:21-26

21. Tell me, ye that desire to be under the law, do ye not hear the law?

21. Dicite mihi, qui sub Lege vultis esse, Legem non auditis?

22. For it is written, that Abraham had two sons, the one by a bondmaid, the other by a freewoman.

22. Scriptum est enim, quod Abraham duos filios habuit; unum ex ancilla, alterum ex libera.

23. But he *who was* of the bondwoman was born after the flesh; but he of the freewoman *was* by promise.

23. Sed qui erat ex ancilla, secundum carnem erat genitus: qui vero ex libera, per promissionem.

24. Which things are an allegory: for these are the two covenants; the one from the mount Sinai, which gendereth to bondage, which is Agar.

24. Quae allegorica sunt; nam duae sunt pactiones, una quidem a monte Sina, quae in servitutem generat; ea est Agar.

25. For this Agar is mount Sinai in Arabia, and answereth to Jerusalem which now is, and is in bondage with her children.

25. Nam Agar, Sina mons est in Arabia; ex adverso autem respondet ei quae nunc est Ierusalem; servit enim cum liberis suis.

26. But Jerusalem which is above is free, which is the mother of us all.

26. Quae autem sursum est Ierusalem, libera est, quae mater est nostra omnium.

21. *Tell me.* Having given exhortations adapted to touch the feelings, he follows up his former doctrine by an illustration of great beauty. Viewed simply as an argument, it would not be very powerful; but, as a confirmation added to a most satisfactory chain of reasoning, it is not unworthy of attention.

To be under the law, signifies here, to come under the yoke of the law, on the condition that God will act toward you according to the covenant of the law, and that you, in return, bind yourself to keep the law. In any other sense than this, all believers are under the law; but the apostle treats, as we have already said, of the law with its appendages.

22. *For it is written.* No man who has a choice given him will be so mad as to despise freedom, and prefer slavery. But here the apostle teaches us, that they who are under the law are slaves. Unhappy men! who willingly choose this condition, when God desires to make them free. He gives a representation of this in the two sons of Abraham, one of whom, the son of a slave, held by his mother's condition; [73] while the other, the son of a free woman, obtained the inheritance. He afterwards applies the whole history to his purpose, and illustrates it in an elegant manner.

In the first place, as the other party armed themselves with the authority of the law, the apostle quotes the law on the other side. *The law* was the name usually given to the Five Books of Moses. Again, as the history which he quotes appeared to have no bearing on the question, he gives to it an allegorical interpretation. But as the apostle declares that these things are *allegorized*, (ἀλληγορούμενα,) Origen, and many others along with him, have seized the occasion of torturing Scripture, in every possible manner, away from the true sense. They concluded that the literal sense is too mean and poor, and that, under the outer bark of the letter, there lurk deeper mysteries, which cannot be extracted but by beating out allegories. And this they had no difficulty in accomplishing; for speculations which appear to be ingenious have always been preferred, and always will be preferred, by the world to solid doctrine.

With such approbation the licentious system gradually attained such a height, that he who handled Scripture for his own amusement not only was suffered to pass unpunished, but even obtained the highest applause. For many centuries no man was considered to be ingenious, who had not the skill and daring necessary for changing into a variety of curious shapes the sacred word of God. This was undoubtedly a contrivance of Satan to undermine the authority of Scripture, and to take away from the reading of it the true advantage. God visited this profanation by a just judgment, when he suffered the pure meaning of the Scripture to be buried under false interpretations.

Scripture, they say, is fertile, and thus produces a variety of meanings. [74] I acknowledge that Scripture is a most rich and inexhaustible fountain of all wisdom; but I deny that its fertility consists in the various meanings which any man, at his pleasure, may assign. Let us know, then, that the true meaning of Scripture is the natural and obvious meaning; and let us embrace and abide by it resolutely. Let us not only neglect as doubtful, but boldly set aside as deadly corruptions, those pretended expositions, which lead us away from the natural meaning.

But what reply shall we make to Paul's assertion, that these things *are allegorical?* Paul certainly does not mean that Moses wrote the history for the purpose of being turned into an allegory, but points out in what way the history may be made to answer the present subject. This is done by observing a figurative representation of the Church there delineated. And a mystical interpretation of this sort (ἀναγωγή) was not inconsistent with the true and literal meaning, when a comparison was drawn between the Church and the family of Abraham. As the house of Abraham was then a true Church, so it is beyond all doubt that the principal and most memorable events which happened in it are so many types to us. As in circumcision, in sacrifices, in the whole Levitical priesthood, there was an allegory, as there is an allegory at the present day in our sacraments, — so was there likewise in the house of Abraham; but this does not involve a departure from the literal meaning. In a word, Paul adduces the history, as containing a figurative representation of the two covenants in the two wives of Abraham, and of the two nations in his two sons. And Chrysostom, indeed, acknowledges that the word *allegory* points out the present application to be (κατάχρησις) [75] different from the natural meaning; which is perfectly true.

23. *But he who was of the bond woman.* Both were sons of Abraham according to the flesh; but in Isaac there was this peculiarity, that he had the promise of grace. In Ishmael there was nothing besides nature; in Isaac there was the election of God, signified in part by the manner of his birth, which was not in the ordinary course, but miraculous. Yet there is an indirect reference to the calling of the Gentiles, and the rejection of the Jews: for the latter boast of their ancestry, while the former, without any human interference, are become the spiritual offspring of Abraham.

24. *These are the two covenants.* I have thought it better to adopt this translation, in order not to lose sight of the beauty of the comparison; for Paul compares the two διαθῶκαι, to two mothers, and to employ *testamentum,* (a testament,) which is a neuter noun, for denoting a mother, would be harsh. The word *pactio* (a covenant) appears to be, on that account, more appropriate; and indeed the desire of obtaining perspicuity, as well as elegance, has led me to make this choice. [76]

The comparison is now formally introduced. As in the house of Abraham there were two mothers, so are there also in the Church of God. Doctrine is the mother of whom we are born, and is twofold, Legal and Evangelical. The legal mother, whom Hagar resembles, *gendereth to bondage.* Sarah again, represents the second, which gendereth to freedom; though Paul begins higher, and makes our first mother Sinai, and our second, Jerusalem. The two covenants, then, are the mothers, of whom children unlike one another are born; for the legal covenant makes slaves, and the evangelical covenant makes freemen.

But all this may, at first sight, appear absurd; for there are none of God's children who are not born to freedom, and therefore the comparison does not apply. I answer, what Paul says is true in two respects; for the law formerly brought forth its disciples, (among whom were included the holy prophets, and other believers,) to slavery, though not to permanent slavery, but because God placed them for a time under the law as "a schoolmaster." [77] (Ga 3:25.) Under the vail of ceremonies, and of the whole economy by which they were governed, their freedom was concealed: to the outward eye nothing but slavery appeared. "Ye have not," says Paul to the Romans, "received the spirit of bondage again to fear." (Ro 8:15.) Those holy fathers, though inwardly they were free in the sight of God, yet in outward appearance differed nothing from slaves, and thus resembled their mother's condition. But the doctrine of the gospel bestows upon its children perfect freedom as soon as they are born, and brings them up in a liberal manner.

Paul does not, I acknowledge, speak of that kind of children, as the context will show. By the children of Sinai, it will afterwards be explained, are meant hypocrites, who are at length expelled from the Church of God, and deprived of the inheritance. What, then, is the gendering to bondage, which forms the subject of the present dispute? It denotes those who make a wicked abuse of the law, by finding in it nothing but what tends to slavery. Not so the pious fathers, who lived under the Old Testament; for their slavish birth by the law did not hinder them from having Jerusalem for their mother in spirit. But those who adhere to the bare law, and do not acknowledge it to be "a schoolmaster to bring them to Christ," (Ga 3:24,) but rather make it a hinderance to prevent their coming to him, are the Ishmaelites born to slavery.

It will again be objected, why does the apostle say that such persons are born of God's covenant, and are considered to belong to the Church? I answer, strictly speaking, they are not God's children, but are degenerate and spurious, and are disclaimed by God, whom they falsely call their Father. They receive this name in the Church, not because they are members of it in reality, but because for a time they presume to occupy that place, and impose on men by the disguise which they wear. The apostle here views the Church, as it appears in this world: but on this subject we shall afterwards speak.

25. *For Agar is mount Sinai* [78] I shall not waste time in refuting the expositions of other writers; for Jerome's conjecture, that Mount Sinai had two names, is trifling; and the disquisitions of Chrysostom about the agreement of the names are equally unworthy of notice. Sinai is called Hagar, [79] because it is a type or figure, as the Passover was Christ. The situation of the mountain is mentioned by way of contempt. It lies in Arabia, beyond the limits of the holy land, by which the eternal inheritance was prefigured. The wonder is, that in so familiar a matter they erred so egregiously.

And answers, on the other hand. The Vulgate translates it, *is joined* (conjunctus est) to Jerusalem; and Erasmus makes it, *borders on* (confinis) Jerusalem; but I have adopted the phrase, *on the other hand,* (ex adverso,) in order to avoid obscurity. For the apostle certainly does not refer to nearness, or relative position, but to resemblance, as respects the present comparison. The word, σύστοιχα, which is translated *corresponding to*, denotes those things which are so arranged as to have a mutual relation to each other, and a similar word, συατοιχία, when applied to trees and other objects, conveys the idea of their following in regular order. Mount Sinai is said (συστοιχεῖν) *to correspond to* that which is now Jerusalem, in the same sense as Aristotle says that Rhetoric is (ἀντίστροφος) the *counterpart* to Logic, by a metaphor borrowed from lyric compositions, which were usually arranged in two parts, so adapted as to be sung in harmony. In short, the word, συστοιχεῖ, *corresponds*, means nothing more than that it belongs to the same class.

But why does Paul compare the present Jerusalem with Mount Sinai? Though I was once of a different opinion, yet I agree with Chrysostom and Ambrose, who explain it as referring to the earthly Jerusalem, and who interpret the words, *which now is*, τῷ νῦν ἱερουσαλὴμ, as marking the slavish doctrine and worship into which it had degenerated. It ought to have been a lively image of the new Jerusalem, and a representation of its character. But such as it now is, it is rather related to Mount Sinai. Though the two places may be widely distant from each other, they are perfectly alike in all their most important features. This is a heavy reproach against the Jews, whose real mother was not Sarah but the spurious Jerusalem, twin sister of Hagar; who were therefore slaves born of a slave, though they haughtily boasted that they were the sons of Abraham.

26. *But Jerusalem, which is above.* The Jerusalem which he calls *above*, or heavenly, is not contained in heaven; nor are we to seek for it out of this world; for the Church is spread over the whole world, and is a "stranger and pilgrim on the earth." (Heb 11:13.) Why then is it said to be from heaven? Because it originates in heavenly grace; for the sons of God are

"born, not of blood, nor of the will of the flesh,
nor of the will of man," (Joh 1:13,)

but by the power of the Holy Spirit. The heavenly Jerusalem, which derives its origin from heaven, and dwells above by faith, is the mother of believers. To the Church, under God, we owe it that we are

"born again, not of corruptible seed, but of incorruptible,"
(1Pe 1:23,)

and from her we obtain the milk and the food by which we are afterwards nourished.

Such are the reasons why the Church is called the mother of believers. And certainly he who refuses to be a son of the Church in vain desires to have God as his Father; for it is only through the instrumentality of the Church that we are "born of God," (1Jo 3:9,) and brought up through the various stages of childhood and youth, till we arrive at manhood. This designation, "the mother of us all," reflects the highest credit and the highest honor on the Church. But the Papists are fools and twice children, who expect to give us uneasiness by producing these words; for their mother is an adulteress, who brings forth to death the children of the devil; and how foolish is the demand, that the children of God should surrender themselves to her to be cruelly slain! Might not the synagogue of Jerusalem at that time have assumed such haughty pretensions, with far higher plausibility than Rome at the present day? and yet we see how Paul strips her of every honorable distinction, and consigns her to the lot of Hagar.

Galatians 4:27-31

27. For it is written, Rejoice, *thou* barren that bearest not; break forth and cry, thou that travailest not: for the desolate hath many more children than she which hath an husband.

27. Scriptum est enim: Exulta, sterilis, qum non paris; erumpe et elama, quae non parturis; quaE plures erunt liberi desertae quam habentis maritum. (Isa 54:1.)

28. Now we, brethren, as Isaac was, are the children of promise.

28. Nos autem, fratres, secundum Issac, promissionis sumus filii. (Ro 9:7.)

29. But as then he that was born after the flesh persecuted him *that was born* after the Spirit, even so *it is* now.

29. Sed quemadmodum tunc, qui secundum carnem erat genitus, persequebatur eum qui secundum Spiritum genitus erat; sic et nunc.

30. Nevertheless, what saith the scripture? Cast out the bondwoman and her son: for the son of the bondwoman shall not be heir with the son of the freewoman.

30. Sed quid dicit Scriptura? Ejice ancillam, et filium ejus; non enim haereditatem obtinebit filius ancillae cum filio liberae. (Ge 21:10.)

31. So then, brethren, we are not children of the bondwoman, but of the free.

31. Ergo, fratres, non sumus ancillae filii, sed liberae.

27. *For it is written.* The apostle proves, by a quotation from Isaiah, that the lawful sons of the Church are born according to the promise. The passage is in Isa 54 where the prophet speaks of the kingdom of Christ and the calling of the Gentiles, and promises to the barren wife and the widow a numerous offspring; for it is on this ground that he exhorts the Church to "sing" and "rejoice." The design of the apostle, let it be carefully remarked, is to deprive the Jews of all claim to that spiritual Jerusalem to which the prophecy relates. Isaiah proclaims, that her children shall be gathered out of all the nations of the earth, and not by any preparation of hers, but by the free grace and blessing of God.

He next concludes that we become the sons of God by promise, after the example (κατὰ 'Ισαὰκ) of Isaac, and that in no other way do we obtain this honor. To readers little skilled or practiced in the examination of Scripture, this reasoning may appear inconclusive; because they do not hold the most undoubted of all principles, that all the promises, being founded on the Messiah, are of free grace. It was because the apostle took this for granted, that he so fearlessly contrasted the promise with the law.

29. *As then, he that was born after the flesh.* He denounces the cruelty of the false apostles, who wantonly insulted pious persons that placed all their confidence in Christ. There was abundant need that the uneasiness of the oppressed should be soothed by consolation, and that the cruelty of their oppressors should be severely checked. It is not wonderful, he says, that the children of the law, at the present day, do what Ishmael their father at first did, who, trusting to his being the first-born, persecuted Isaac the true heir. With the same proud disdain do his posterity now, on account of outward ceremonies, circumcision, and the various services of the law, molest and vaunt over the lawful sons of God. *The Spirit* is again contrasted with the flesh, that is, the calling of God with human appearance. (1Sa 16:7.) So the disguise is admitted to be possessed by the followers of the Law and of works, but the reality is claimed for those who rely on the calling of God alone, and depend upon his grace.

Persecuted. But persecution is nowhere mentioned, only Moses says that Ishmael was מצחק, (*metzahek,*) *mocking*, (Ge 21:9;) and by this participle he intimates that Ishmael ridiculed his brother Isaac. The explanation offered by some Jews, that this was a simple smile, is entirely inadmissible; for what cruelty would it have argued, that a harmless smile should have been so fearfully revenged? There cannot then be a doubt that he maliciously endeavored to provoke the child Isaac by reproachful language.

But how widely distant is this from persecution? [80] And yet it is not idly or unguardedly that Paul enlarges on this point. No persecution ought to distress us so much as to see our calling attempted to be undermined by the reproaches of wicked men. Neither blows, nor scourging, nor nails, nor thorns, occasioned to our Lord such intense suffering as that blasphemy:

"He trusted in God; what availeth it to him? for he is deprived of all assistance." (Mt 27:43.)

There is more venom in this than in all persecutions; for how much more alarming is it that the grace of Divine adoption shall be made void, than that this frail life shall be taken from us? Ishmael did not persecute his brother with the sword; but, what is worse, he treated him with haughty disdain by trampling under foot the promise of God. All persecutions arise from this source, that wicked men despise and hate in the elect the grace of God; a memorable instance of which we have in the history of Cain and Abel. (Ge 4:8.)

This reminds us, that not only ought we to be filled with horror at outward persecutions, when the enemies of religion slay us with fire and sword; when they banish, imprison, torture, or scourge; but when they attempt, by their blasphemies, to make void our confidence, which rests on the promises of God; when they ridicule our salvation, when they wantonly laugh to scorn the whole gospel. Nothing ought to wound our minds so deeply as contempt of God, and reproaches cast upon His grace: nor is there any kind of persecution more deadly than when the salvation of the soul is assailed. We who have escaped from the tyranny of the Pope, are not called to encounter the swords of wicked men. But how blind must we be, if we are not affected by that spiritual persecution, in which they strive, by every method, to extinguish that doctrine, from which we draw the breath of life! — when they attack our faith by their blasphemies, and shake not a few of the less informed! For my own part, I am far more grieved by the fury of the Epicureans than of the Papists. They do not attack us by open violence; but, in proportion as the name of God is more dear to me than my own life, the diabolical conspiracy which I see in operation to extinguish all fear and worship of God, to root out the remembrance of Christ, or to abandon it to the jeers of the ungodly, cannot but rack my mind with greater anxiety, than if a whole country were burning in one conflagration:

30. *But what saith the Scripture?* There was some consolation in knowing that we do but share the lot of our father Isaac; but it is a still greater consolation, when he adds, that hypocrites, with all their boasting, can gain nothing more than to be *cast out* of the spiritual family of Abraham; and that, to whatever extent they may harass us for a time, the inheritance will certainly be ours. Let believers cheer themselves with this consolation, that the tyranny of the Ishmaelites will not last for ever. They appear to have reached the highest pre-eminence, and, proud of their birthright, look down upon us with contempt; but they will one day be declared to be the descendants of Hagar, the sons of a slave, and unworthy of the inheritance.

Let us be instructed by this beautiful passage,

"not to fret ourselves because of evil-doers,
neither be envious against the workers of iniquity,"
(Ps 37:1,)

when they hold a temporary habitation and rank in the Church, but patiently to look for the end which awaits them. There are many pretended Christians, or strangers, who hold a place in the Church, but who afterwards give evidence of their departure from the faith, as he who, proud of his birthright, at first reigned, was cast out like a foreigner with the posterity of Ishmael. Some censorious persons smile at Paul's simplicity, in comparing a woman's passion, arising out of a trifling quarrel, to a judgment of God. But they overlook the decree of God, which took effect in such a manner, as to make it manifest that the whole transaction was directed by a heavenly providence. That Abraham should have been commanded to humor his wife (Ge 21:12) entirely in the matter, is no doubt extraordinary, but proves that God employed the services of Sarah for confirming his own promise. In a word, the *casting out* of Ishmael was nothing else than the consequence and the accomplishment of that promise, "In Isaac shall thy seed be called," (Ge 21:12,) — not in Ishmael. Although, therefore, it was the revenging of a woman's quarrel, yet God did not the less make known his sentence by her mouth as a type of the Church.

31. *So then, brethren.* He now exhorts the Galatians to prefer the condition of the children of Sarah to that of the children of Hagar; and having reminded them that, by the grace of Christ, they were born to freedom, he desires them to continue in the same condition. If we shall call the Papists, Ishmaelites and Hagarites, and boast that we are the lawful children, they will smile at us; but if the two subjects in dispute be fairly compared, the most ignorant person will be at no loss to decide.

Footnotes

65

"Επίτροπος signifies both a child's guardian to take care of his person and estate, and his instructor and tutor, ἐπίτροπος καὶ τοῦ παιδὸς καὶ τῶν χρημάτων, 'the guardian both of the child and of his property.' (AElian, v. H. 1. 3. c. 26.) Here it properly signifies the latter, his preceptor or tutor. The next word, οἰκόνομος, which we render governor, here denotes his guardian, who is to take care of his person and estate; and to each of these the heirs to large inheritances are generally subject, even as servants are subject to their proper masters." — Chandler.

66

"So far was he from subjecting to the yoke of the law those to whom the law had not been given, that he came in order to emancipate even the Jews themselves." — Wetstein.

67

Μᾶλλον δὲ "The Greek writers make use of these two particles for the purpose of correcting what they have already said, and, as if it had not been enough, of adding something more. Thus, Ro 8:34, and in Polybius. Χρήσιμον εἴη μᾶλλον δ ' αηναγκαῖον. "It would be useful, it would even be necessary." Καὶ γὰρ ἄτοπον μᾶλλον δ ' ὡς εἰπεῖν ἀδύνατον, αδυνατον. "It would be absurd; it would even be impossible." — Raphelius.

68

"Par ce mot de *Servir*, il reprend la necessity, a laquelle ils s'astraignoyent d'observer les ceremonies." "By the word 'bondage,' he reproves them for the necessity to which they had reduced themselves to observe ceremonies."

69

Ἔστι γὰρ καὶ ζῶλος ἀγαθὸς ὅταν τις οὕτω ζηλοῖ ὥστε μιμήσασθαι τὴν ἀρετήν· ἔστι καὶ ζῶλος προνηρὸς ὥστε ἐκβάλλειν τῶς ἀρετῶς τὸν κατορθοῦντα· ὅ δὴ καὶ αὕτοὶ νῦν ἐπιχειροῦσι, τῶς μὲν τελείας γνώσεως ἐκβάλλειν θέλοντες, εἰς δὲ τὴν ἠκρωτηριασμένην ὑμᾶς δὲ τοὺς νῦν ὑψηλοτέρους αὐτῶν ὄντας, ἐν τάξει καταστήσωσι μαθητῶν· τοῦτο γὰρ ἐδήλωσεν εἰτὼν ἵνα αὐτοὺς ζηλοῦτε

"There is a good zeal, when one emulates in such a manner as to imitate virtue; and there is a bad zeal, which 'drives away' from virtue one who is acting right. And this is what they are now attempting to do, when they wish to 'drive away' from perfect knowledge, and to lead them to that which is mutilated and spurious, for no other reason than that they may occupy the ranks of teachers, and that you, who are higher than themselves, may be placed by them in the rank of scholars; for this is what he meant by saying, 'that ye may emulate them.'" — Chrysostom.

70

ἀποροῦμαι ἐν ὑμῖν. "By these words the apostle undoubtedly expresses more than that he was 'in doubt about' the Galatians, and was at a loss what he should say about them; for in the preceding verse he had given utterance to the vehement emotion of his mind. With very nearly the same kind of emphasis does this word occur in the Septuagint, at Ge 32:7, where it is said, 'And Jacob was greatly afraid, and was in deep anxiety.' The concluding words are translated καὶ ἠπορεῖτο " — Keuchenius.

71

"To speak sometimes gently, and sometimes harshly, as the case might demand." — Luther. Φωνή signifies not only a voice, but the thing that is spoken, (AElian, V. H., p. 347,) whether it be by word of mouth, or by letter. And therefore, when the apostle says that he 'desired to change his voice,' he means, that he should be glad to be present and converse with them personally, instead of writing to them at a distance; because then he could be more fully informed of their true state, and better able to know how to order his discourse to them." — Chandler.

72

"Seulement qu'ils regardent de ne faire chose contre l'honneur de Dieu et leur conscience." "Only let them beware of doing anything against the honour of God and their own conscience."

73

"La servile condition de sa mere." "His mother's condition as a slave."

74

"Et pour ceste cause elle engendre plusieurs sens et de diverses sortes." "And therefore it produces many meanings, and of various kinds."

75

"A cataehresis borrows the name of one thing to express another; which thing, though it has a name of its own, yet, under a borrowed name, surprises us with novelty, or infuses into our discourses a bold and daring energy. The Sacred Scriptures will furnish us with many instances of this trope. Le 26:30, — 'And I will cast your carcases upon the carcases of your idols;' that is, upon the ruins of your idols, which shall be as much destroyed as the body is when it is slain, and become a dead carcase. So De 32:14; Ps 80:5; Ho 14:2. But the boldest catachresis, perhaps, in all the Holy Scriptures, is in 1Co 1:25., Because the foolishness of God,' says the apostle, 'is wiser than men, and the weakness of God is stronger than men;' that is, what men are apt to account foolishness in God surpasses their wisdom, and what they may be ready to misconstrue as weakness in God, excels all their power. Gibbons's Rhetoric.

76

To a Latin scholar the author's meaning is obvious enough. But it may be proper to apprize the English reader, that *pactio* (a covenant) is a feminine noun, and, on that account, is pronounced to be more natural and graceful, in a metaphorical description of a mother, than *testamentum*, (a testament,) which, being a neuter noun, sounds harshly in this connection. In that point of view, the preference is little else than a matter of taste; but, on far higher grounds, "covenant" is a more faithful translation than "testament;" and a careful investigation of the meaning of διαθήκη would contribute greatly to elucidate many passages of Scripture. — Ed.

77

"C'est a dire, les conduisoit comme petits enfans." "That is, treated them like little children."

78

"Car Agar est la montagne de Sina en Arabie, et est correspondante a Ierusalem; ou, Sina est une montagne en Arabie, correspondante a Ierusalem." "For Agar is Mount Sinai in Arabia, and corresponds to Jerusalem; or, Sinai is a mountain in Arabia, which corresponds to Jerusalem."

79

"Several critics have thought it so extraordinary, that they have attempted to alter it from mere conjecture, as may be seen in Bowyer's 'Critical Conjectures.' But no man, who knew that the Arabic word 'Hagar' meant *a rock*, could think of making an alteration in this passage; for it is obvious that τὸ Ἄγαϱ, in the neuter gender, cannot signify the woman *Hagar*; and Paul has not been guilty of a grammatical error, since the passage must be translated, 'The word Hagar denotes Mount Sinai in Arabia.'" — Michaelis.

"That this was an appellation of Sinai among the people of the surrounding country, we have the testimony of Chrysostom and the ancient commentators, which is also confirmed by the accounts of modern travellers. And it might well have it, since הגר (*hagar*) in Arabia signifies a rock, or rocky mountain; and as Sinai is remarkably such, it might be κατ ' ἐξοχὴν, called τὸ Ἄγαϱ." — Bloomfield.

80

"The history tells us, that he laughed at, derided, and mocked him to scorn, which is real persecution; probably through pride, and the conceit of being Abraham's eldest son and heir." — Chandler. "Διώκω will here denote injurious treatment of every kind, both in deeds and words. And although the Mosaic history records only one instance of insulting treatment, — namely, on Ishmael mocking Sarah, when she weaned Isaac, (Gen. 21:9, 10,) yet when we consider the disappointment which both Hagar and Ishmael must have felt on the birth of Isaac, it was not unnatural for them to feel ill-will, and show it on every occasion, to the real heir of the promise. And many such are recorded, from tradition, in the Rabbinical writers." — Bloomfield.

CHAPTER 5

Galatians 5:1-6

1. Stand fast therefore in the liberty wherewith Christ hath made us free, and be not entangled again with the yoke of bondage.

1. In libertate igitur, qua Christus nos liberavit, state; et ne rursum jugo servitutis implicemini.

2. Behold, I Paul say unto you, that if ye be circumcised, Christ shall profit you nothing.

2. Ecee, ego Paulus denuncio vobis, quod, si circumcidamini, Christus vobis nihil proderit.

3. For I testify again to every man that is circumcised, that he is a debtor to do the whole law.

3. Testificor enim rursum cuivis homini, qui circumciditur, quod debitor sit totius Legis faciendae.

4. Christ is become of no effect unto you, whosoever of you are justified by the law; ye are fallen from grace.

4. Exinaniti estis a Christo, quicunque per Legem justificamini, a gratia excidistis.

5. For we through the Spirit wait for the hope of righteousness by faith.

5. Nos enim Spiritu, ex fide, spem justitiae expectamus.

6. For in Jesus Christ neither circumcision availeth any thing, nor uncircumcision; but faith which worketh by love.

6. Nam in Christo Iesu neque Circumcisio quicquam valet, neque Praeputium; sed fides per dilectionero operans.

1. *Stand fast therefore.* After having told them that they are the *children of the free woman,* he now reminds them that they ought not lightly to despise a freedom so precious. And certainly it is an invaluable blessing, in defense of which it is our duty to fight, even to death; since not only the highest temporal considerations, but our eternal interests also, animate us to the contest. [81] Many persons, having never viewed the subject in this light, charge us with excessive zeal, when they see us so warmly and earnestly contending for freedom of faith as to outward matters, in opposition to the tyranny of the Pope. Under this cloak, our adversaries raise a prejudice against us among ignorant people, as if the whole object of our pursuit were licentiousness, which is the relaxation of all discipline. But wise and skillful persons are aware that this is one of the most important doctrines connected with salvation. This is not a question whether you shall eat this or that food, — whether you shall observe or neglect a particular day, (which is the foolish notion entertained by many, and the slander uttered by some,) but what is your positive duty before God, what is necessary to salvation, and what cannot be omitted without sin. In short, the controversy relates to the liberty of conscience, when placed before the tribunal of God.

The *liberty* of which Paul speaks is exemption from the ceremonies of the law, the observance of which was demanded by the false apostles as necessary. But let the reader, at the same time, remember, that such liberty is only a part of that which Christ has procured for us: for how small a matter would it be, if he had only freed us from ceremonies? This is but a stream, which must be traced to a higher source. It is because

"Christ was made a curse, that he might redeem us from the curse of the law," (Ga 3:13;)

because he has revolted the power of the law" so far as it held us liable to the judgment of God under the penalty of eternal death; because, in a word, he has rescued us from the tyranny of sin, Satan, and death. Thus, under one department is included the whole class; but on this subject we shall speak more fully on the Epistle to the Colossians.

This *liberty* was procured for us by Christ on the cross: the fruit and possession of it are bestowed upon us through the Gospel. Well does Paul, then, warn the Galatians, *not to be entangled again with the yoke of bondage*, — that is, not to allow a snare to be laid for their consciences. For if men lay upon our shoulders an unjust burden, it may be borne; but if they endeavor to bring our consciences into bondage, we must resist valiantly, even to death. If men be permitted to bind our consciences, we shall be deprived of an invaluable blessing, and an insult will be, at the same time, offered to Christ, the Author of our freedom. But what is the force of the word *again*, in the exhortation, "and be not entangled *again* with the yoke of bondage?" for the Galatians had never lived under the law. It simply means that they were not to be entangled, as if they had not been redeemed by the grace of Christ. Although the law was given to Jews, not to Gentiles, yet, apart from Christ, neither the one nor the other enjoys any freedom, but absolute bondage.

2. *Behold, I Paul.* He could not have pronounced a severer threatening than that it would exclude them entirely from the grace of Christ. But what is the meaning of this, that Christ will *profit nothing* to all who are circumcised? Did Christ *profit nothing* to Abraham? Nay, it was in order that Christ might profit him that he received circumcision. If we say that it was in force till the coming of Christ, what reply shall we make to the case of Timothy? We must observe, that Paul's reasoning is directed not so properly against the outward rite or ceremony, as against the wicked doctrine of the false apostles, who pretended that it was a necessary part of the worship of God, and at the same time made it a ground of confidence as a meritorious work. These diabolical contrivances made Christ to *profit nothing*; not that the false apostles denied Christ, or wished him to be entirely set aside, but that they made such a division between his grace and the works of the law as to leave not more than the half of salvation due to Christ. The apostle contends that Christ cannot be divided in this way, and that he "profiteth nothing," unless he is wholly embraced.

And what else do our modern Papists but thrust upon us, in place of circumcision, trifles of their own invention? The tendency of their whole doctrine is to blend the grace of Christ with the merit of works, which is impossible. Whoever wishes to have the half of Christ, loses the whole. And yet the Papists think themselves exceedingly acute when they tell us that they ascribe nothing to works, except through the influence of the grace of Christ, as if this were a different error from what was charged on the Galatians. They did not believe that they had departed from Christ, or relinquished his grace; and yet they lost Christ entirely, when that important part of evangelical doctrine was corrupted.

The expression *Behold, I Paul,* is very emphatic; for he places himself before them, and gives his name, to remove all appearance of hesitation. And though his authority had begun to be less regarded among the Galatians, he asserts that it is sufficient to put down every adversary.

3. *For I testify again.* What he now advances is proved by the contradiction involved in the opposite statement. He who is *a debtor to do the whole law* [82] will never escape death, but will always continue to be held as guilty; for no man will ever be found who satisfies the law. [83] Such being the obligation, the man must unavoidably be condemned, and Christ can render him no service. We see then the contradictory nature of the two propositions, that we are partakers of the grace of Christ, and yet that we are bound to fulfill the whole law. But will it not then follow, that none of the fathers were saved? Will it not also follow that Timothy was ruined, since Paul caused him to be circumcised? (Ac 16:3.) Wo to us then, till we have been emancipated from the law, for subjection is inseparable from circumcision!

It ought to be observed that Paul is accustomed to view circumcision in two different aspects, as every person who has best, owed a moderate degree of attention on his writings will easily perceive. In the Epistle to the Romans, (Ro 4:11,) he calls it "a seal of the righteousness of faith;" and there, under circumcision, he includes Christ and the free promise of salvation. But here he contrasts it with Christ, and faith, and the gospel, and grace, — viewing it simply as a legal covenant, founded on the merit of works.

The consequence is, as we have already said, that he does not always speak about circumcision in the same way; but the reason of the difference must be taken into account. When he views circumcision in its own nature, he properly makes it to be a symbol of grace, because such was the appointment of God. But when he is dealing with the false apostles, who abused circumcision by making it an instrument for destroying the Gospel, he does not there consider the purpose for which it was appointed by the Lord, but attacks the corruption which has proceeded from men.

A very striking example occurs in this passage. When Abraham had received a promise concerning Christ, and justification by free grace, and eternal salvation, circumcision was added, in order to confirm the promise; and thus it became, by the appointment of God, a sacrament, which was subservient to faith. Next come the false apostles, who pretend that it is a meritorious work, and recommend the observance of the law, making a profession of obedience to it to be signified by circumcision as an initiatory rite. Paul makes no reference here to the appointment of God, but attacks the unscriptural views of the false apostles.

It will be objected, that the abuses, whatever they may be, which wicked men commit, do not at all impair the sacred ordinances of God. I reply, the Divine appointment of circumcision was only for a time. After the coming of Christ, it ceased to be a Divine institution, because baptism had suceeeded in its room. Why, then, was Timothy circumcised? Not certainly on his own account, but for the sake of weak brethren, to whom that point was yielded. To show more fully the agreement between the doctrine of the Papists and that which Paul opposes, it must be observed, that the sacraments, when we partake of them in a sincere manner, are not the works of men, but of God. In baptism or the Lord's supper, we do nothing but present ourselves to God, in order to receive his grace. Baptism, viewed in regard to us, is a passive work: we bring nothing to it but faith; and all that belongs to it is laid up in Christ. But what are the views of the Papists? They contrive the *opus operatum*, [84] by which men merit the grace of God; and what is this, but to extinguish utterly the truth of the sacrament? Baptism and the Lord's supper are retained by us, because it was the will of Christ that the use of them should be perpetual; but those wicked and foolish notions are rejected by us with the strong abhorrence which they deserve.

4. *Christ has become of no effect unto you.* "If ye seek any part of righteousness in the works of the law, Christ has no concern with you, and *ye are fallen from grace.*" They were not so grossly mistaken as to believe that by the observance of the law alone they were justified, but attempted to mix Christ with the law. In any other point of view, Paul's threatenings would have utterly failed to produce alarm. "What are you doing? You deprive yourselves of every advantage from Christ, and treat his grace as if it were of no value whatever." We see then that the smallest part of justification cannot be attributed to the law without renouncing Christ and his grace.

5. *For we through the Spirit.* He now anticipates an objection that, might readily occur. "Will circumcision then be of no use?" *In Jesus Christ,* he replies, it *availeth* nothing. *Righteousness,* therefore, depends on faith, and is obtained, through the Spirit, without ceremonies. To *wait for the hope of righteousness,* is to place our confidence in this or that object, or, to decide from what quarter righteousness is to be expected; though the words probably contain the exhortation, "Let us continue steadfastly in the hope of righteousness which we obtain by faith." When he says that we obtain righteousness by faith, this applies equally to us and to our fathers. All of them, as Scripture testifies, (Heb 11:5,) "pleased God;" but their faith was concealed by the veil of ceremonies, and therefore he distinguishes us from them by the word *Spirit,* which is contrasted with outward shadows. His meaning therefore is, that all that is now necessary for obtaining righteousness is a simple faith, which declines the aid of splendid ceremonies, and is satisfied with the spiritual worship of God.

6. *For in Jesus Christ.* The reason why believers now wait for the hope of righteousness through the Spirit is, that in Christ, that is, in the kingdom of Christ, or in the Christian church, circumcision with its appendages is abolished; for, by a figure of speech in which a part is taken for the whole, the word Circumcision is put for ceremonies. While he declares that they no longer possess any influence, he does not admit that they were always useless; for he does not maintain that they were repealed till after the revelation of Christ. This enables us to answer another question, Why does he here speak so contemptuously of circumcision, as if it had been of no advantage? The rank which circumcision once held as a sacrament is not now considered. The question is not what was its value before it had been abolished. But under the kingdom of Christ, he pronounces it to be on a level with uncircumcision, because the coming of Christ has put an end to legal ceremonies.

But faith, which worketh by love. The contrast here introduced, between ceremonies and the exercise of love, was intended to prevent the Jews from thinking too highly of themselves, and imagining that they were entitled to some superiority; for towards the close of the Epistle, instead of this clause, he uses the words, *a new creature*. (Ga 6:15.) As if he had said, Ceremonies are no longer enjoined by Divine authority; and, if we abound in the exercise of love, all is well. Meanwhile, this does not set aside our sacraments, which are aids to faith but is merely a short announcement of what he had formerly taught as to the spiritual worship of God.

There would be no difficulty in this passage, were it not for the dishonest manner in which it has been tortured by the Papists to uphold the righteousness of works. When they attempt to refute our doctrine, that we are justified by faith alone, they take this line of argument. If the faith which justifies us be that "which worketh by love," then faith alone does not justify. I answer, they do not comprehend their own silly talk; still less do they comprehend our statements. It is not our doctrine that the faith which justifies is alone; we maintain that it is invariably accompanied by good works; only we contend that faith alone is sufficient for justification. The Papists themselves are accustomed to tear faith after a murderous fashion, sometimes presenting it out of all shape and unaccompanied by love, and at other times, in its true character. We, again, refuse to admit that, in any case, faith can be separated from the Spirit of regeneration; but when the question comes to be in what manner we are justified, we then set aside all works.

With respect to the present passage, Paul enters into no dispute whether love cooperates with faith in justification; but, in order to avoid the appearance of representing Christians as idle and as resembling blocks of wood, he points out what are the true exercises of believers. When you are engaged in discussing the question of justification, beware of allowing any mention to be made of love or of works, but resolutely adhere to the exclusive particle. Paul does not here treat of justification, or assign any part of the praise of it to love. Had he done so, the same argument would prove that circumcision and ceremonies, at a former period, had some share in justifying a sinner. As in Christ Jesus he commends faith accompanied by love, so before the coming of Christ ceremonies were required. But this has nothing to do with obtaining righteousness, as the Papists themselves allow; and neither must it be supposed that love possesses any such influence.

Galatians 5:7-12

7. Ye did run well; who did hinder you that ye should not obey the truth?

7. Currebatis bene. Quis vos impedivit, ne obediretis veritati?

8. This persuasion *cometh* not of him that calleth you.

8. Persuasio non est ex eo qui vocavit vos.

9. A little leaven leaveneth the whole lump.

9. Modicum fermentum totam massam fermentat.

10. I have confidence in you through the Lord, that ye will be none otherwise minded: but he that troubleth you shall bear his judgment, whosoever he be.

10. Ego persuasus sum Deuteronomy vobis in Domino, quod non aliud sitis sensuri: qui autem turbat vos, portabit judicium, quisquis sit.

11. And I, brethren, if I yet preach circumcision, why do I yet suffer persecution? then is the offence of the cross ceased.

11. Ego autem, fratres, si circumcisionem adhuc praedicem, quid adhuc persequutionem patior? exinanitum est scandalurn crucis.

12. I would they were even cut off which trouble you.

12. Utinam etiam abscindantur, qui vos conturbant.

7. *Ye did run well.* The censure which the apostle administers for their present departure from the truth is mingled with approbation of their former course, for the express purpose that, by being brought to a sense of shame, they may return more speedily to the right path. The astonishment conveyed in the question, *who hindered you?* was intended to produce a blush. I have chosen to translate the Greek word πείθσθαι, *obey*, rather than *believe*, because, having once embraced the purity of the gospel, they had been led away from a course of obedience.

8. *This persuasion cometh not.* Having formerly combated them by arguments, he at length pronounces, with a voice of authority, that their *persuasion* came not from God. Such an admonition would not be entitled to much regard, were it not supported by the authority of the speaker. But Paul, to whom the Galatians had been indebted for the announcement of their Divine calling, was well entitled to address them in this confident language. This is the reason why he does not directly say, *from God*, but expresses it by a circumlocution, *him that hath called you* [85] As if he had said, "God is never inconsistent with himself, and he it is who by my preaching called you to salvation. This new persuasion then has come from some other quarter; and if you wish to have it thought that your calling is from God, beware of lending an ear to those who thrust upon you their new inventions." Though the Greek participle καλοῦντος, I acknowledge, is in the present tense, I have preferred translating, *who hath called you*, in order to remove the ambiguity.

9. *A little leaven.* This refers, I think, to doctrine, not to men. It guards them against the mischievous consequences which arise from corruption of doctrine, and warns them not to consider it, as is commonly done, to be a matter attended by little or no danger. Satan's stratagem is, that he does not attempt an avowed destruction of the whole gospel, but he taints its purity by introducing false and corrupt opinions. Many persons are thus led to overlook the seriousness of the injury done, and therefore make a less determined resistance. The apostle proclaims aloud that, after the truth of God has been corrupted, we are no longer safe. He employs the metaphor of *leaven*, which, however small in quantity, communicates its sourness to the whole mass. We must exercise the utmost caution lest we allow any counterfeit to be substituted for the pure doctrine of the gospel.

10. *I have confidence in you.* All his fierceness is again directed against the false apostles. To them the evil is traced, and on them the punishment is threatened. Good hopes are expressed regarding the Galatians, that they will quickly and readily return to a sincere belief. It gives us courage to learn that good hopes are entertained about us; for we reckon it shameful to disappoint those whose feelings towards us are kind and friendly. But to bring back the Galatians to the pure doctrine of faith, from which they had turned aside, was the work of God. The apostle says that he has confidence in them, ἐν Κυϱίω, *through the Lord*, by which he reminds them that repentance is a heavenly gift, and that they must ask it from God.

He that troubleth you [86] The sentiment which he had just delivered is confirmed by thus indirectly imputing the greater part of the blame to those impostors by whom the Galatians had been deceived. From the punishment denounced against *them*, the Galatians are very nearly exempted. Let all who introduce confusion into churches, who break the unity of faith, who destroy their harmony, lend an ear to this; and if they have any right feeling, let them tremble at this word. God declares, by the mouth of Paul, that none "through whom such offenses come" (Lu 17:1) will pass unpunished. The phrase, *whosoever he be*, is emphatic; for the high sounding language of the false apostles had terrified the ignorant multitude. It became necessary for Paul to defend his doctrine with corresponding warmth and energy, and not to spare any one who dared to raise his voice against it, however eminent or however distinguished.

11. *And I, brethren.* This argument, is drawn from the final cause. "It would be completely in my power," he says, "to avoid the displeasure of men, and every kind of danger and persecution, were I only to mix ceremonies with Christ. The earnestness with which I oppose them is not on my own account, nor for my own advantage." But does it therefore follow that his doctrine is true? I answer, proper feelings and pure conscience, when manifested by a teacher, have no small share in obtaining confidence. Besides, it cannot be believed that any man would be so mad as to take measures, of his own accord, for bringing distress upon himself. Lastly, he throws upon his adversaries the suspicion, that, in preaching circumcision, they were more disposed to consult their own ease than to be faithful in the service of Christ. In short, Paul was at the farthest remove from ambition, covetousness, or regard to personal interest, since he despised favor and applause, and exposed himself to the persecutions and fury of the multitude rather than swerve a hair's-breadth from the purity of the gospel.

Then is the offense of the cross ceased. Willingly does Paul, in speaking of the gospel, call it the cross, or the preaching of the cross, when he wishes to bring its poor, simple style, into contrast with the "great swelling words" (Jude 1:16) of human wisdom or righteousness. For the Jews, puffed up with an ill-founded confidence in their righteousness, and the Greeks, with a foolish belief of their wisdom, despised the meanness of the gospel. When therefore he says that now, If the preaching of circumcision be admitted, the offense of the cross will no longer exist, he means that the gospel will meet with no annoyance from the Jews, but will be taught with their entire concurrence. And why? Because they will no longer take offense at a pretended and spurious gospel, gathered out of Moses and out of Christ, but will look with greater indulgence on that mixture which will leave them in possession of their former superiority.

12. *Would that they were even cut off.* His indignation proceeds still farther, and he prays for destruction on those impostors by whom the Galatians had been deceived. The word, "cut off," appears to be employed in allusion to the circumcision which they pressed. "They tear the church for the sake of circumcision: I wish they were entirely cut off." Chrysostom favors this opinion. But how can such an imprecation be reconciled with the mildness of an apostle, who ought to wish that all should be saved, and that not a single person should perish? So far as men are concerned, I admit the force of this argument; for it is the will of God that we should seek the salvation of all men without exception, as

Christ suffered for the sins of the whole world. But devout minds are sometimes carried beyond the consideration of men, and led to fix their eye on the glory of God, and the kingdom of Christ. The glory of God, which is in itself more excellent than the salvation of men, ought to receive from us a higher degree of esteem and regard. Believers earnestly desirous that the glory of God should be promoted, forget men, and forget the world, and would rather choose that the whole world should perish, than that the smallest portion of the glory of God should be withdrawn.

Let us remember, however, that such a prayer as this proceeds from leaving men wholly out of view, and fixing our attention on God alone. Paul cannot be accused of cruelty, as if he were opposed to the law of love. Besides, if a single man or a few persons be brought into comparison, how immensely must the church preponderate! It is a cruel kind of mercy which prefers a single man to the whole church. "On one side, I see the flock of God in danger; on the other, I see a wolf "seeking," like Satan, "whom he may devour." (1Pe 5:8.) Ought not my care of the church to swallow up all my thoughts, and lead me to desire that its salvation should be purchased by the destruction of the wolf? And yet I would not wish that a single individual should perish in this way; but my love of the church and my anxiety about her interests carry me away into a sort of ecstasy, so that I can think of nothing else." With such zeal as this, every true pastor of the church will burn. The Greek word translated "who *trouble* you," signifies to remove from a certain rank or station. By using the word καὶ, *even*, he expresses more strongly his desire that the impostors should not merely be degraded, but entirely separated and cut off. [87]

Galatians 5:13-18

13. For, brethren, ye have been called unto liberty; only *use* not liberty for an occasion to the flesh, but by love serve one another.

13. Vos enim in libertatem vocati estis, fratres; tantum ne libertatem in occasionem detis carni, sed per charitatem servite vobis invicem.

14. For all the law is fulfilled in one word, *even* in this, Thou shalt love thy neighbour as thyself.

14. Nam tota Lex in uno verbo completur, nempe hoc: Diliges proximum tuum sicut to ipsum.

15. But if ye bite and devour one another, take heed that ye be not consumed one of another.

15. Quodsi alius alium vicissim mordetis et devoratis, videte, ne vicissim alius ab alio consumamini.

16. *This* I say then, Walk in the Spirit, and ye shall not fulfil the lust of the flesh.

16. Dico autem: Spiritu ambulate; et concupiscentiam carnis non perficietis.

17. For the flesh lusteth against the Spirit, and the Spirit against the flesh: and these are contrary the one to the other: so that ye cannot do the things that ye would.

17. Nam care concupiscit adversus Spiritum; Spiritus antem adversus carnem; haec mutuo inter se adversantur; ut non, qnaecunqne volueritis, eadem faciails.

18. But if ye be led by the Spirit, ye are not under the law.

18. Quod si Spiritu ducimini, non estis sub Lege.

13. *Ye have been called to liberty.* He now proceeds to show in what way liberty must be used. In the course of expounding the First Epistle to the Corinthians, we have pointed out that liberty is one thing, and that the use of it is another thing. Liberty lies in the conscience, and looks to God; the use of it lies in outward matters, and deals not with God only, but with men. Having exhorted the Galatians to suffer no diminution of their liberty, he now enjoins them to be moderate in the use of it, and lays down as a rule for the lawful use, that it shall not be turned into pretext or occasion for licentiousness. Liberty is not granted to the flesh, which ought rather to be held captive under the yoke, but is a spiritual benefit, which none but pious minds are capable of enjoying.

But by love. The method here explained of restraining liberty from breaking out into wide and licentious abuse is, to have it regulated *by love.* Let us always remember that the present question is not, in what manner we are free before God, but in what manner we may use our liberty in our intercourse with men. A good conscience submits to no slavery; but to practice outward slavery, or to abstain from the use of liberty, is attended by no danger. In a word, if "by love we serve one another," we shall always have regard to edification, so that we shall not grow wanton, but use the grace of God for his honor and the salvation of our neighbors.

14. *For all the law.* There is a contrast in this verse, though not plainly stated, yet evidently to be understood, between Paul's exhortation and the doctrine of the false apostles. While they insisted on ceremonies alone, Paul takes a passing glance of the actual duties and exercises of Christians. The present commendation of love is intended to inform the Galatians, that love forms the chief part of Christian perfection. But we must inquire in to the reason why all the precepts of the law are included under *love.* The law consists of two tables, the first of which instructs us concerning the worship of God and the duties of piety, and the second instructs us concerning the love of our neighbor; for it is ridiculous to make a part the same with the whole. Some avoid this difficulty by reminding us that the first table contains nothing more than to love God with our whole heart. But Paul makes express mention of love to our neighbor, and therefore a more satisfactory solution must be sought.

Piety to God, I acknowledge, ranks higher than love of the brethren; and therefore the observance of the first table is more valuable in the sight of God than the observance of the second. But as God himself is invisible, so piety is a thing hidden from the eyes of men; and, though the manifestation of it was the purpose for which ceremonies were appointed, they are not certain proofs of its existence. It frequently happens, that none are more zealous and regular in observing ceremonies than hypocrites. God therefore chooses to make trial of our love to himself by that love of our brother, which he enjoins us to cultivate. This is the reason why, not here only, but in the Epistle to the Romans, (Rom. 8:8, Rom. 13:10,) love is called "the fulfilling of the law;" not that it excels, but that it proves the worship of God to be real. God, I have said, is invisible; but he represents himself to us in the brethren, and in their persons demands what is due to himself. Love to men springs only from the fear and love of God; and therefore we need not wonder if, by a figure of speech, in which a part is taken for the whole, the effect include under it the cause of which it is the sign. But it would be wrong in any person to attempt to separate our love of God from our love of men.

Thou shalt love thy neighbor. He who loves will render to every man his right, will do injury or harm to no man, will do good, as far as lies in his power, to all; for what else is included in the whole of the second table? This, too, is the argument employed by Paul in his Epistle to the Romans (Ro 13:10.) The word, *neighbor*, includes all men living; for we are linked together by a common nature, as Isaiah reminds us, "that thou hide not thyself from thine own flesh" (Isa 58:7.) The image of God ought to be particularly regarded as a sacred bond of union; but, for that very reason, no distinction is here made between friend and foe, nor can the wickedness of men set aside the right of nature.

"*Thou shalt love thy neighbor as thyself*". The love which men naturally cherish toward themselves ought to regulate our love of our neighbor. All the doctors of the Sorbonne [88] are in the habit of arguing that, as the rule is superior to what it directs, the love of ourselves must always hold the first rank. This is not to interpret, but to subvert our Lord's words. They are asses, and have not even a spark of the love of their neighhour; for if the love of ourselves were the rule, it would follow that it is proper and holy, and is the object of the divine approbation. But we shall never love our neighbors with sincerity, according to our Lord's intention, till we have corrected the love of ourselves. The two affections are opposite and contradictory; for the love of ourselves leads us to neglect and despise others, — produces cruelty, covetousness, violence, deceit, and all kindred vices, — drives us to impatience, and arms us with the desire of revenge. Our Lord therefore enjoins that it be changed into the love of our neighbor.

15. *But if ye bite and devour one another.* From the nature of the subject, as well as from the language employed, we may conjecture that the Galatians had disputes among themselves; for they differed about doctrine. The apostle now demonstrates, from the result, how destructive such proceedings in the church must ultimately prove to be. False doctrine was probably a judgment from heaven upon their ambition, pride, and other offenses. This may be concluded from what frequently happens in the divine dispensations, as well as from an express declaration by the hand of Moses.

"Thou shalt not hearken unto the words of that prophet, or that dreamer of dreams; for the Lord your God proveth you, to know whether ye love the Lord your God with all your heart, and with all your soul." (De 13:3.)

By *biting and devouring* [89] he means, I think, slanders, accusations, reproaches, and every other kind of offensive language, as well as acts of injustice arising either from fraud or violence. And what is the end of them? To be *consumed*, while the tendency of brotherly love is to produce mutual protection and kindness. I wish we could always remember, when the devil tempts us to disputes, that the disagreement of members within the church can lead to nothing else than the ruin and consumption of the whole body. How distressing, how mad is it, that we, who are members of the same body, should be leagued together, of our own accord, for mutual destruction!

16. *This I say then.* Now follows the remedy. The ruin of the church is no light evil, and whatever threatens it must be opposed with the most determined resistance. But how is this to be accomplished? By not permitting the flesh to rule in us, and by yielding ourselves to the direction of the Spirit of God. The Galatians are indirectly told, that they are carnal, destitute of the Spirit of God, and that the life which they lead is unworthy of Christians; for whence did their violent conduct towards each other proceed, but from their being guided by the lust of the flesh? This, he tells them, is an evidence that they do not walk according to the Spirit.

Ye shall not fulfill. We ought to mark the word *fulfill*; by which he means, that, though the sons of God, so long as they groan under the burden of the flesh, are liable to commit sin, they are not its subjects or slaves, but make habitual opposition to its power. The spiritual man may be frequently assaulted by the lusts of the flesh, but *fulfill* them, — he does not permit them to reign over him. — On this subject, it will be proper to consult Ro 8

17. *For the flesh lusteth.* The spiritual life maintained without a struggle. We are here informed of the nature of the difficulty, which arises from our natural inclinations being opposed to the Spirit. The word *flesh*, as we had occasion to observe, in expounding the Epistle to the Romans, denotes the nature of man; for the limited application of it, which the sophists make to the lower senses, as they are called, is refuted by various passages; and the contrast between the two words puts an end to all doubt. *The Spirit* denotes the renewed nature, or the grace of regeneration; and what else does the *flesh* mean, but "the old man?" (Ro 6:6 Eph 4:22 Col 3:9.) Disobedience and rebellion against the Spirit of God pervade the whole nature of man. If we would obey the Spirit, we must labor, and fight, and apply our utmost energy; and we must begin with self-denial. The compliment paid by our Lord to the natural inclinations of men, amounts to this, — that there is no greater agreement between them and righteousness, than between fire and water. Where, then, shall we find a drop of goodness in man's free will? unless we pronounce that to be good which is contrary to the Spirit of God;

"because the carnal mind is enmity against God, for it is not subject to the law of God, neither indeed can be."

(Ro 8:7.)

All the thoughts of the flesh are acts of enmity against God.

So that ye cannot do the things that ye would. This refers, unquestionably, to the regenerate. Carnal men have no battle with depraved lusts, no proper desire to attain to the righteousness of God. Paul is addressing believers. *The things that ye would* must mean, not our natural inclinations, but the holy affections which God bestows upon us by his grace. Paul therefore declares, that believers, so long as they are in this life, whatever may be the earnestness of their endeavors, do not obtain such a measure of success as to serve God in a perfect manner. The highest result does not correspond to their wishes and desires. I must again refer the reader, for a more extended view of my sentiments on this subject, to the Exposition of the Epistle to the Romans, (See Calvin on Ro 7:15.)

18. *But if ye be led by the Spirit.* In the way of the Lord believers are apt to stumble. But let them not be discouraged, because they are unable to satisfy the demands of the law. Let them listen to the consolatory declaration of the apostle, which is also found in other parts of his writings, (Ro 6:14,) *ye are not under the law.* Hence it follows, that the performance of their duties is not rejected on account of their present defects, but is accepted in the sight of God, as if it had been in every respect perfect and complete. Paul is still pursuing the controversy about freedom.

The Spirit is elsewhere (Ro 8:15) denominated by him, "the Spirit of adoption;" and when the Spirit makes men free, he emancipates them from the yoke of the law. As if he had said, "Is it your desire instantly to terminate the controversies in which you are now engaged? Walk according to the Spirit. You will then be free from the dominion of the law, which will act only in the capacity of a kind adviser, and will no longer lay a restraint upon your consciences." Besides, when the condemnation of the law is removed, freedom from ceremonies follows as a necessary consequence; for ceremonies mark the condition of a slave.

Galatians 5:19-21

19. Now the works of the flesh are manifest, which are *these*; Adultery, fornication, uncleanness, lasciviousness,

19. Manifesta vero sunt opera carnis, quae sunt adulterium, scortatio, immunditia, lascivia,

20. Idolatry, witchcraft, hatred, variance, emulations, wrath, strife, seditions, heresies,

20. Idololatria, veneficium, inimicitiae, contentio, aemulationes, irae, concertationes, seditiones, haereses,

21. Envyings, murders, drunkenness, revellings, and such like: of the which I tell you before, as I have also told *you* in time past, that they which do such things shall not inherit the kingdom of God.

21. Invidiae, homicidia, ebrietates, comissationes, et his similia; Deuteronomy quibus praedico vobis, quemadmodum et praedixi, quod qui talia agunt regnum Dei haereditate non possidebunt.

19. *Now the works of the flesh are manifest.* To obey the spirit and to oppose the flesh, are two great objects which have been set before Christians, and for the attainment of which they have been urged to make the most strenuous exertions. In accordance with these views, he now draws a picture both of the flesh and of the spirit. If men knew themselves, they would not need this inspired declaration, for they are nothing but flesh; but such is the hypocrisy belonging to our natural state, we never perceive our depravity till the tree has been fully made known by its fruits. (Mt 7:16; Lu 6:44.)

The apostle therefore now points out to us those sins against which we must fight, in order that we may not live according to the flesh. He does not indeed enumerate them all, and so he himself states at the conclusion of the list; but from those brought forward, the character of the remainder may be easily ascertained. *Adultery* and *fornication* are placed first, and next follows *uncleanness*, which extends to every species of unchastity. *Lasciviousness* appears to be a subsidiary term, for the Greek word ασέλγεια, which is thus translated, is applied to those who lead wanton and dissolute lives. These four denote sins forbidden by the seventh commandment. The next mentioned is *idolatry*, which is here employed as a general term for services grossly superstitious and openly practiced.

Seven classes which immediately follow, are closely allied, and another two are afterwards added. *Anger* and *hatred* differ chiefly in this, that anger is short, and hatred is lasting. *Emulations* and *envyings* are the occasions of hatred; and the following distinction between them is stated by Aristotle, in his second book on Rhetoric: — He who *emulates* is grieved that another should excel him, not because the virtue or worth of that person, in itself considered, gives him uneasiness, but because he would wish to be superior. The *envious* man has no desire to excel, but is grieved at the excellence of other men. None, therefore, he tells us, but low and mean persons indulge in envy, while emulation dwells in lofty and heroic minds. Paul declares both to be diseases of the *flesh*. From anger and hatred arise *variance, strife, seditions*; and he even traces the consequences so far as to mention *murders* and *witchcraft* [90] By revellings, [91] he means a dissolute life, and every kind of intemperance in the gratification of the palate. It deserves notice, that heresies are enumerated among the works of the flesh; for it shows clearly that the word *flesh* is not confined, as the sophists imagine, to sensuality. What produces heresies but ambition, which deals not with the lower senses, but with the highest faculties of the mind? He says that these works are *manifest*, so that no man may think that he will gain anything by evading the question; [92] for what avails it to deny that the flesh reigns in us, if the fruit betrays the quality of the tree?

21. *Of which I tell you before.* By this awful threatening he intended not only to alarm the Galatians, but likewise to glance indirectly at the false apostles, who had laid aside the far more valuable instruction, and spent their time in disputing about ceremonies. He instructs us, by his example, to press those exhortations and threatenings, agreeably to the words of the prophet,

"Cry aloud, spare not; proclaim to my people their sins."

(Isa 58:1)

What can be conceived more dreadful than that men should walk after the flesh, and shut themselves out from the kingdom of God? Who will dare to treat lightly the "abominable things which God hates?" (Jer 44:4.)

But in this way, we shall be told, all are cut off from the hope of salvation; for who is there that is not chargeable with some of those sins? I reply, Paul does not threaten that all who have sinned, but that all who remain impenitent, shall be excluded from the kingdom of God. The saints themselves often fall into grievous sins, but they return to the path of righteousness, "that which they do they allow not," (Ro 7:15,) and therefore they are not included in this catalogue. All threatenings of the judgments of God call us to repentance. They are accompanied by a promise that those who repent will obtain forgiveness; but if we continue obstinate, they remain as a testimony from heaven against us.

They who do such things shall not inherit the kingdom of God. The word κληρονομεῖν signifies to possess by hereditary right; for by no right but that of adoption, as we have seen in other passages, do we obtain eternal life.

Galatians 5:22-26

22. But the fruit of the Spirit is love, joy, peace, longsuffering, gentleness, goodness, faith,

22. Fructus vero Spiritus est charitas, gaudium, pax, tolerantia, comitas, benignitas, fides,

23. Meekness, temperance: against such there is no law.

23. Mansuetudo, temperantia: adversus ejusmodi non est Lex.

24. And they that are Christ's have crucified the flesh with the affections and lusts.

24. Qui autem Christi sunt carnem crucifixerunt cum affectibus et concupiscentiis.

25. If we live in the Spirit, let us also walk in the Spirit.

25. Si vivimus Spiritu, etiam Spiritu ambulemus.

26. Let us not be desirous of vain glory, provoking one another, envying one another.

26. Ne sinms inanis gloriae cupidi, invicem provocantes, invicem invidentes.

22. *But the fruit* [93] *of the Spirit.* In the former part of the description he condemned the whole nature of man as producing nothing but evil and worthless fruits. He now informs us that all virtues, all proper and well regulated affections, proceed from the Spirit, that is, from the grace of God, and the renewed nature which we derive from Christ. As if he had said, "Nothing but what is evil comes from man; nothing good comes but from the Holy Spirit." There have often appeared in unrenewed men remarkable instances of gentleness, integrity, temperance, and generosity; but it is certain that all were but specious disguises. Curius and Fabrieius were distinguished for courage, Cato for temperance, Scipio for kindness and generosity, Fabius for patience; but it was only in the sight of men, and as members of civil society, that they were so distinguished. In the sight of God nothing is pure but what proceeds from the fountain of all purity.

Joy does not here, I think, denote that "joy in the Holy Ghost" (Ro 14:17,) of which he speaks elsewhere, but that cheerful behavior towards our fellow-men which is the opposite of moroseness. *Faith* means truth, and is contrasted with cunning, deceit, and falsehood, as *peace* is with quarrels and contentions. *Long-suffering* is gentleness of mind, which disposes us to take everything in good part, and not to be easily offended. The other terms require no explanation, for the dispositions of the mind must be learned from the outward conduct.

But if spiritual men are known by their works, what judgment, it will be asked, shall we form of wicked men and idolaters, who exhibited an illustrious resemblance of all the virtues? for it is evident from their works that they were spiritual. I reply, as all the works of the flesh do not appear openly in a carnal man, but his carnaltry is discovered by one or another vice, so a single virtue will not entitle us to conclude that a man is spiritual. Sometimes it will be made evident, by other vices, that sin reigns in him; and this observation may be easily applied to all the cases which I have enumerated.

23. *Against such there is no law.* Some understand these words as meaning simply that the law is not directed against good works, "from evil manners have sprung good laws." But Paul's real meaning is deeper and less obvious; namely, that, where the Spirit reigns, the law has no longer any dominion. By moulding our hearts to his own righteousness, the Lord delivers us from the severity of the law, so that our intercourse with himself is not regulated by its covenant, nor our consciences bound by its sentence of condemnation. Yet the law continues to teach and exhort, and thus performs its own office; but our subjection to it is withdrawn by the Spirit of adoption. He thus ridicules the false apostles, who, while they enforced subjection to the law, were not less eager to release themselves from its yoke. The only way, he tells us, in which this is accomplished, is, when the Spirit of God obtains dominion, from which we are led to conclude that they had no proper regard to spiritual righteousness.

24. *And they that are Christ's.* He adds this, in order to show that all Christians have renounced the flesh, and therefore enjoy freedom. While he makes this statement, the apostle reminds the Galatians what true Christianity is, so far as relates to the life, and thus guards them against a false profession of Christianity. The word *crucified* is employed to point out that the mortification of the flesh is the effect of the cross of Christ. This work does not belong to man. By the grace of Christ

"we have been planted together in the likeness of his death" (Ro 6:5,)

that we no longer might live unto ourselves. If we are buried with Christ, by true self-denial, and by the destruction of the old man, we shall then enjoy the privilege of the sons of God. The flesh is not yet indeed entirely destroyed; but it has no right to exercise dominion, and ought to yield to the Spirit. The *flesh* and its *lusts* are a figure of speech of exactly the same import with the *tree* and its *fruits.* The *flesh* itself is the depravity of corrupt nature, from which all evil actions proceed. (Mt 15:19; Mr 7:21.) Hence it follows, that the members of Christ have cause to complain, if they are still held to be in bondage to the law, from which all who have been regenerated by his Spirit are set free.

25. *If we live in the Spirit.* According to his usual custom, the apostle draws from the doctrine a practical exhortation. The death of the flesh is the life of the Spirit. If the Spirit of God lives in us, let him govern our actions. There will always be many persons daring enough to make a false boast of living in the Spirit, but the apostle challenges them to a proof of the fact. As the soul does not remain idle in the body, but gives motion and rigour to every member and part, so the Spirit of God cannot dwell in us without manifesting himself by the outward effects. By the *life* is here meant the inward power, and by the *walk* the outward actions. The metaphorical use of the word *walk*, which frequently occurs, describes works as evidences of the spiritual life.

26. *Let us not be desirous of vain-glory,* The special exhortations which were addressed to the Galatians were not more necessary for them than they are adapted to our own time. Of many evils existing in society at large, and particularly in the church, ambition is the mother. Paul therefore directs us to guard against it, for the *vain-glory* (κενοδοξία) of which he speaks is nothing else than *ambition,* (filimia,) or the desire of honor, by which every one desires to excel all others. The heathen philosophers do not condemn every desire of glory; but among Christians, whoever is desirous of glory departs from true glory, and therefore is justly charged with idle and foolish ambition. It is not lawful for us to glow but in God alone. Every other kind of glorying is pure vanity. Mutual *provocations* and *envyings* are the daughters of ambition. He who aspires to the highest rank must of necessity envy all others, and disrespectful, biting, stinging language is the unavoidable consequence.

Footnotes

81

"Car il n'est pas yci seulement question du monde et des eommoditez de ceste vie, mais aussi des choses sainctes et qui eoncernent le service de Dieu." "For the present subject comprehends not merely the world and the benefits of this life, but also holy things, and those which relate to the worship of God."

82

"If Judaism is the road to salvation, the whole of Judaism must be observed. You must not cull and throw away whatever part of it you think fit." — Grotius.

83

"Car il ne s'en trouvera jamais un seul, qui satisfait entierement a la Loy." "For never will there be found a single individual who entirely satisfies the law."

84

'Thus the Council of Trent has decreed: "If any man shall say that the sacraments of the new law do not contain the grace which they signify, or do not confer grace upon those who do not oppose an obstacle to it, as if external signs of grace or righteousness received by faith, let him be accursed." — Sessio 7. *De Sacramentis in genere*, Canon vi. Again, "If any man shall say, that grace is not confered by the sacraments of the new law themselves, *ex opere operato*, but that faith alone in the divine promise is sufficient to obtain grace, let him be accursed. — Sessio vii. *De Sacramentis in genere*, Canon viii. The translator subjoins a few observations, by the late Rev. Dr. Dick, on a phrase which appears to defy translation. "This barbarous phrase *opus operatum*, which is utterly unintelligible without an explanation, signifies the external celebration of the sacraments. It has been defined by Popish writers to be the performance of the external work without any internal motion; and sacraments have been said to confer grace *ex opere operato*, because, besides the exhibition and application of the sign, no good motion is necessary in the receiver. All that is required is, that no obstacle shall be opposed to the reception of grace, and the only obstacle is mortal sin." — Lectares on Theology, volume 4.

85

"The apostle's statement seems to be, 'This persuasion to which you have yielded is not from Christ. It comes from a very different quarter. The men who have employed it are not moved by *his* spirit. They have no divine authority; and you ought not to yield to them, no, not for an hour.'" — Brown.

86

"However, he 'that troubleth you,' or rather, 'perplexes and unsettles you;' as if this was *all* he could do, — not *teach* them. So Galen, cited by Wetstein; ταράττοντες μόνον τοὺς μανθάνοντας, διδάσκοντες δὲ οὐδέν, 'only troubling the scholars, and teaching them nothing.' The use of the singular will not prove that there was no more than *one* false teacher; since it may be used collectively. Yet the apostle seems to glance at one, the principal of them; and by ὅστις ἄν ᾖ, 'whosoever he be,' we may infer that he was a person of some consequence." — Bloomfield.

87

"But I am so far from inculcating on you the necessity of circumcision, I would even wish that all those, without exception, who endeavour thus to subvert your faith, were wholly cut off from the communion of the Christian church. — I wish that, instead of having hearkened to these seducing teachers, they had been cut off by you, excluded from the church, and disowned as brethren.' (See 1 Cor. 5:7, 11.) And where he here expresses his wish, that the troublers of the Galatians were cut off, it is only putting them in mind what would have been both their prudence and their duty to have done; not to have hearkened to them, but to have disowned, and refused society with them as Christians. This being the plain and natural sense of the apostle's words, they cannot be charged with any ill-natured or unfriendly wish." — Chandler.

88

The College of the *Sorbonne*, in Paris, takes its name from *Robert de Serbonne*, who founded it in the middle of the thirteenth century. Its reputation for theological learning, philosophy, classical literature, and all that formerly constituted a liberal education, was deservedly high. In the Doctors of the Sorbonne the Reformation found powerful adversaries. The very name of this university, to which the greatest scholars in Europe were accustomed to pay deference, would be regarded by the multitude with blind veneration. If such men as Calvin, Beza, Melanchthon, and Luther, were prepared by talents and acquirements of the first order to brave the terrors of that name, they must have frequently lamented its influence on many of their hearers. Yet our author meets undaunted this formidable array, and enters the field with the full assurance of victory. Despising, as we naturally do, the weak superstitions and absurd tenets held by the Church of Rome, we are apt to underrate our obligations to the early champions of the Reformed faith, who encountered, with success, those veteran warriors, and 'contended earnestly for the faith which was once delivered to the saints.' (Jude 1:3.)" — *Ed.*

89

Ταῖς λέξεσι δὲ ἐμφαντικῶς ἐχρήσατο· Οὐ γὰρ εἶπε δάκνετε, μόνον ὅπερ ἐστὶ φυμονμένου ἀλλὰ καὶ κατεσθίετε ὅπερ ἔστιν ἐμμένοντος τῶ πονηρίᾳ· ὁ μὲν γὰρ δάκνων ὀργῶς ἐπλήρωσε πάθος ὁ δὲ κατεσθίων θηριωδίας ἐσχάτης παρέσχεν ἀπόδειξιν·. "These words are used by him emphatically; for he did not merely say 'Bite,' which denotes an angry person, but likewise, 'Devour,' which denotes one who persists in wickedness. He who 'bites' has exhausted his angry passion, but he who 'devours' has given a demonstration of extreme cruelty." — Chrysostom.

90

"The original word φαρμακεία sometimes denotes 'poisonings,' which were frequently practised among the heathens. Sometimes it signifies incantations or magic arts, or witchcraft, by which impostors and cheats endeavoured to impose on ignorant and credulous people, and which were carried on by poisonous intoxicating draughts and ointments, by which they did great mischief to the bodies of men. As it is here immediately placed after idolatry, I should imagine that the apostle intended those cursed arts of incantations and charms, those various methods of imposture and cheats, which were made use of by the heathen priests, to promote the idolatrous reverence and worship of their false gods. (See Re 18:23.)" — Chandler.

91

By κῶμοι are denoted those nocturnal revellings usually attendant on an evening of debauchery, consisting of licentious singing, dancing, and parading the streets with drunken riotings." — Bloomfield.

92

"En volant nier, et usant de tergiversation." "By wishing to deny it, and by shuffling."

93

"In the service of *sin* the toil is so great that, in comparison thereof, the benefit is as nothing; in the service of *God* the benefit is so great that, in comparison thereof, the labour is as nothing. Where the flesh rules all, the 'work' exceeds the 'fruit;' and therefore, without even mentioning the 'work,' it is called the 'fruit' of the Spirit. (See Eph. 5:9, 11.)" — Bishop Sanderson.

CHAPTER 6

Galatians 6:1-5

1. Brethren, if a man be overtaken in a fault, ye which are spiritual, restore such an one in the spirit of meekness; considering thyself, lest thou also be tempted.

1. Fratres, etiamsi praeoccupatus fuerit homo in aliquo lapsu, vos, qui spirituales estis, instaurate ejusmodi hominem spiritu lenitatis; considerans to ipsum, ne tu quoque tenteris.

2. Bear ye one another's burdens, and so fulfil the law of Christ.

2. Alii aliorum onera portate, et sic adimplete legem Christi.

3. For if a man think himself to be something, when he is nothing, he deceiveth himself.

3. Nam si quis putat se esse aliquid, quum nihil sit, se ipsum decipit.

4. But let every man prove his own worth, and then shall he have rejoicing in himself alone, and not in another.

4. Opus antem suum probet unusquisque; et tunc in se ipso solo gloriam habebit, non antem in alio.

5. For every man shall bear his own burden.

5. Quisque enim proprium onus portabit.

1. *Brethren, if a man be overtaken in any fault* [94] Ambition is a serious and alarming evil. But hardly less injury is frequently done by unseasonable and excessive severity, which, under the plausible name of zeal, springs in many instances from pride, and from dislike and contempt of the brethren. Most men seize on the faults of brethren as an occasion of insulting them, and of using reproachful and cruel language. Were the pleasure they take in upbraiding equalled by their desire to produce amendment, they would act in a different manner. Reproof, and often sharp and severe reproof, must be administered to offenders. But while we must not shrink from a faithful testimony against sin, neither must we omit to mix oil with the vinegar.

We are here taught to correct the faults of brethren in a mild manner, and to consider no rebukes as partaking a religious and Christian character which do not breathe the spirit of meekness. To gain this object, he explains the design of pious reproofs, which is, *to restore him who is fallen,* to place him in his former condition. That design will never be accomplished by violence, or by a disposition to accuse, or by fierceness of manner or language; and consequently, we must display a gentle and meek spirit, if we intend to heal our brother. And lest any man should satisfy himself with assuming the outward form, he demands *the spirit of meekness*; for no man is prepared for chastising a brother till he has succeeded in acquiring a gentle spirit. [95]

Another argument for gentleness in correcting brethren is contained in the expression, "if a man be *overtaken.*" If he has been carried away through want of consideration, or through the cunning arts of a deceiver, it would be cruel to treat such a man with harshness. Now, we know that the devil is always lying in wait, and has a thousand ways of leading us astray. When we perceive a brother to have transgressed, let us consider that he has fallen into the snares of Satan; let us be moved with compassion, and prepare our minds to exercise forgiveness. But offenses and falls of this description must undoubtedly be distinguished from deep seated crimes, accompanied by deliberate and obstinate disregard of the authority of God. Such a display of wicked and perverse disobedience to God must be visited with greater severity, for what advantage would be gained by gentle treatment? The particle *if also*, (ἐα ν καὶ,) implies that not only the weak who have been tempted, but those who have yielded to temptation, shall receive forbearance.

Ye who are spiritual. This is not spoken in irony; for, however spiritual they might be, still they were not wholly filled with the Spirit. It belongs to such persons to raise up the fallen. To what better purpose can their superior attainments be applied than to promote the salvation of the brethren? The more eminently any man is endowed with Divine grace, the more strongly is he bound to consult the edification of those who have been less favored. But such is our folly, that in our best duties we are apt to fail, and therefore need the exhortation which the apostle gives to guard against the influence of carnal views.

Considering thyself. It is not without reason that the apostle passes from the plural to the singular number. He gives weight to his admonition, when he addresses each person individually, and bids him look carefully into himself. "Whoever thou art that takest upon thee the office of reproving others, look to thyself." Nothing is more difficult than to bring us to acknowledge or examine our own weakness. Whatever may be our acuteness in detecting the faults of others, we do not see, as the saying is, "the wallet that hangs behind our own back;" [96] and therefore, to arouse us to greater activity, he employs the singular number.

These words may admit of two senses. As we acknowledge that we are liable to sin, we more willingly grant that forgiveness to others which, in our turn, we expect will be extended to us. Some interpret them in this manner: "Thou who art a sinner, and needest the compassion of thy brethren, oughtest not to show thyself fierce and implacable to others." [97] But I would rather choose to expound them as a warning given by Paul, that, in correcting others, we should not ourselves commit sin. There is a danger here which deserves our most careful attention, and against which it is difficult to guard; for nothing is more easy than to exceed the proper limits. The word *tempt*, however, may very properly be taken in this passage as extended to the whole life. Whenever we have occasion to pronounce censure, let us begin with ourselves, and, remembering our own weakness, let us be indulgent to others.

2. *Bear ye one another's burdens.* The weaknesses or sins, under which we groan, are called *burdens.* This phrase is singularly appropriate in an exhortation to kind behavior, for nature dictates to us that those who bend under a burden ought to be relieved. He enjoins us to *bear* the burdens. We must not indulge or overlook the sins by which our brethren are pressed down, but relieve them, — which can only be done by mild and friendly correction. There are many adulterers and thieves, many wicked and abandoned characters of every description, who would willingly make Christ an accomplice in their crimes. All would choose to lay upon believers the task of bearing their burdens. But as the apostle had immediately before exhorted us to *restore* a brother, the manner in which Christians are required to *bear one another's burdens* cannot be mistaken.

And so fulfill the law of Christ. The word *law*, when applied here to Christ, serves the place of an argument. There is an implied contrast between the law of Christ and the law of Moses. "If you are very desirous to keep a law, Christ enjoins on you a law which you are bound to prefer to all others, and that is, to cherish kindness towards each other. He who has not this has nothing. On the other hand, he tells us, that, when every one compassionately assists his neighbor, the law of Christ is *fulfilled*; by which he intimates that every thing which does not proceed from love is superfluous; for the composition of the Greek word ἀναπληρώσατε, conveys the idea of what is absolutely perfect. But as no man performs in every respect what Paul requires, we are still at a distance from perfection. He who comes the nearest to it with regard to others, is yet far distant with respect to God.

3. *For if a man think himself.* There is an ambiguity in the construction, but Paul's meaning is clear. The phrase, *When he is nothing*, appears at first view to mean, "if any person, who is in reality nothing, claims to be something;" as there are many men of no real worth who are elated by a foolish admiration of themselves. But the meaning is more general, and may be thus expressed: "Since all men are nothing, he who wishes to appear something, and persuades himself that he is somebody, deceives himself." First, then, he declares that we are nothing, by which he means, that we have nothing of our own of which we have a right to boast, but are destitute of every thing good: so that all our glorying is mere vanity. Secondly, he infers that they who claim something as their own deceive themselves. Now, since nothing excites our indignation more than that others should impose upon us, it argues the height of folly that we should willingly impose upon ourselves. This consideration will render us much more candid to others. Whence proceeds fierce insult or haughty sternness, but from this, that every one exalts himself in his own estimation, and proudly despises others? Let arrogance be removed, and we shall all discover the greatest modesty in our conduct towards each other.

4. *But let every man prove his own work.* By a powerful blow, Paul has already struck down the pride of man. But it frequently happens that, by comparing ourselves with others, the low opinion which we form of them leads us to entertain a high opinion of ourselves. Paul declares that no such comparison ought to be allowed. Let no man, he says, measure himself by the standard of another, or please himself with the thought, that others appear to him less worthy of approbation. Let him lay aside all regard to other men, examine his own conscience, and inquire what is *his own work*. It is not what we gain by detracting from others, but what we have without any comparison, that can be regarded as true praise.

Some consider Paul to be speaking in irony. "Thou flatterest thyself by a comparison with the faults of others; but if thou wilt consider who thou art, thou wilt then enjoy the praise which is justly due to thee." In other words, no praise whatever shall be thine; because there is no man by whom the smallest portion of praise is really deserved. In conformity with this view, the words that follow, *every man shall bear his own burden*, are supposed to mean, that it is usual for every man to bear his own burden. But the plain and direct sense of the words agrees better with the apostle's reasoning. "With respect to thyself alone, and not by comparison with others, thou wilt have praise." I am well aware that the next sentence, which annihilates all the glory of man, has been regarded as justifying the ironical interpretation. But the glorying of which this passage treats, is that of a good conscience, in which the Lord allows his people to indulge, and which Paul elsewhere expresses in very animated language.

"Paul earnestly beholding the council, said, Men and brethren, I have lived in all good conscience before God until this day."

(Ac 23:1.)

This is nothing more than an acknowledgment of Divine grace, which reflects no praise whatever on man, but excites him to give God the glory. Such a reason for glorying do the godly find in themselves; and they ascribe it, not to their own merits, but to the riches of the grace of God.

"For our rejoicing is this, the testimony of a good conscience, that in simplicity and godly sincerity, not with fleshly wisdom, but by the grace of God, we have had our conversation in the world."

(2Co 1:12.)

Our Lord himself instructs us:

"But thou, when thou prayest, enter into thy closet; and when thou hast shut thy door, pray to thy Father who is in secret; and thy Father, who seeth in secret, shall reward thee openly."

(Mt 6:6.)

Strictly speaking, he makes no assertion, but leads us to conclude, that, when a man is valued for his own worth, and not for the baseness of others, the praise is just and substantial. The statement is therefore conditional, and imports that none are entitled to be regarded as good men, who are not found to be so, apart from the consideration of others.

5. *For every man shall bear his own burdens.* To destroy sloth and pride, he brings before us the judgment of God, in which every individual for himself, and without a comparison with others, will give an account of his life. It is thus that we are deceived; for, if a man who has but one eye is placed among the blind, he considers his vision to be perfect; and a tawny person among negroes thinks himself white. The apostle affirms that the false conclusions to which we are thus conducted will find no place in the judgment of God; because there every one will bear his own burden, and none will stand acquitted by others from their own sins. This is the true meaning of the words.

Galatians 6:6-10

6. Let him that is taught in the word communicate unto him that teacheth in all good things.

6. Coremunicet is, qui instituitur in sermone, cum doctore, in omnibus bonis.

7. Be not deceived; God is not mocked: for whatsoever a man soweth, that shall he also reap.

7. Ne erretis: Deus non subsannatur; quod enim seminaverit homo, hoc etiam metet.

8. For he that soweth to his flesh shall of the flesh reap corruption; but he that soweth to the Spirit shall of the Spirit reap life everlasting.

8. Nam qui seminat carni suae, ex carne metet corruptionem; qui autem seminat Spiritui, ex Spiritu metet vitam aeternam.

9. And let us not be weary in well doing: for in due season we shall reap, if we faint not.

9. Bonum antem faciendo ne defatigemur; nam si non defecerimus, metemus opportuno tempore.

10. As we have therefore opportunity, let us do good unto all *men*, especially unto them who are of the household of faith..

10. Ergo ubi tempus habemus, benefaciamus erga omnes, praesertim vero erga domesticos fidel.

6. *Let him that is taught in the word.* It is probable that the teachers and ministers of the word were at that time neglected. This shewed the basest ingratitude. How disgraceful is it to defraud of their temporal support those by whom our souls are fed! — to refuse an earthly recompense to those from whom we receive heavenly benefits! But it is, and always has been, the disposition of the world, freely to bestow on the ministers of Satan every luxury, and hardly to supply godly pastors with necessary food. Though it does not become us to indulge too much in complaint, or to be too tenacious of our rights, yet Paul found himself called upon to exhort the Galatians to perform this part of their duty. He was the more ready to do so, because he had no private interest in the matter, but consulted the universal benefit of the Church, without any regard to his own advantage. He saw that the ministers of the word were neglected, because the word itself was despised; for if the word be truly esteemed, its ministers will always receive kind and honorable treatment. It is one of the tricks of Satan to defraud godly ministers of support, that the Church may be deprived of such ministers. [98] An earnest desire to preserve a gospel ministry, led to Paul's recommendation that proper attention should be paid to good and faithful pastors.

The word is here put, by way of eminence, (κατ ' ἐξοχὴν,) for the doctrine of godliness. Support is declared to be due to those by whom we *are taught in the word.* Under this designation the Papal system supports idle bellies of dumb men, and fierce wild beasts, who have nothing in common with the doctrine of Christ. *In all good things.* He does not propose that no limit should be set to their worldly enjoyments, or that they should revel in superfluous abundance, but merely that none of the necessary supports of life should be withheld. Ministers ought to be satisfied with moderate fare, and the danger which attends pomp and luxury ought to be prevented. To supply their real necessities, let believers cheerfully devote any part of their property that may be required for the services of devout and holy teachers. What return will they make for the invaluable treasure of eternal life, which is communicated to them by the preaching of those men?

7. *God is not mocked.* The design of this observation is to reply to the dishonest excuses which are frequently pleaded. One alleges that he has a family to support, and another asserts that he has no superfluity of wealth to spend in liberality or profusion. The consequence is, that, while such multitudes withhold their aid, the few persons who do their duty are generally unable to contribute the necessary support. These apologies Paul utterly rejects, for a reason which the world little considers, that this transaction is with God. The supply of a man's bodily wants is not the sole question, but involves the degree of our regard for Christ and his gospel. This passage contains evidence that the custom of treating faithful ministers with scorn did not originate in the present day; but their wicked taunts will not pass unpunished.

For whatsoever a man soweth. Our liberality is restrained by the supposition, that whatever passes into the hands of another is lost to ourselves, and by the alarm we feel about our own prospects in life. Paul meets these views by a comparison drawn from seed-time, which, he tells us, is a fit representation of acts of beneficence. On this subject we had occasion to speak, in expounding the Second Epistle to the Corinthians, where the same metaphor was employed. Happy would it be for us, if this truth were deeply impressed upon our minds. How "very gladly" would we "spend and be spent" (2Co 12:15) for the good of our neighbours, encouraged by the hope of the coming harvest! No operation is more cheerfully performed by husbandmen than throwing the seed into the ground. They are enabled to wait with patience during nine months of the year, by the expectation of reaping a corruptible harvest, while our minds are not properly affected by the hope of a blessed immortality.

8. *For he that soweth to his flesh.* Having stated the general sentiment, he now divides it into parts. To *sow to the flesh*, is to look forward to the wants of the present life, without any regard to a future life. They who do this will gather fruit corresponding to the seed which they have sown, — will heap up that which shall miserably perish. *To sow in the flesh*, (*seminare in carne*,) is supposed by some to mean indulgence in the lusts of the flesh, and corruption to mean destruction; but the former exposition agrees better with the context. In departing from the old translation and from Erasmus, I have not acted rashly. The Greek words, ὁ σπείρων εἰς τὴν σάρκα ἑαυτοῦ, literally signify, *he that soweth into his flesh.* And what else does this mean, but to be so entirely devoted to the flesh, as to direct all our thoughts to its interests or convenience?

But he that soweth to the spirit. By *the spirit* I understand the spiritual life, to which they are said to sow whose views are directed more to heaven than to earth, and whose life is regulated by the desire of reaching the kingdom of God. From their spiritual employments they will reap in heaven incorruptible fruit. Those employments are denominated spiritual on account of their end, though in some respects they are external and relate to the body, as in the very case now under consideration of supporting pastors. If the Papists shall endeavor, in their usual manner, to build upon these words the righteousness of works, we have already shewn how easily their absurdities may be exposed. Though eternal life is a reward, it does not follow either that we are justified by works, or that works are meritorious of salvation. The undeserved kindness of God appears in the very act of honoring the works which his grace has enabled us to perform, by promising to them a reward to which they are not entitled.

Is a more complete solution of the question demanded?

1. We have no good works which God rewards but those which we derive from his grace.

2. The good works which we perform by the guidance and direction of the Holy Spirit, are the fruits of that adoption which is an act of free grace.

3. They are not only unworthy of the smallest and most inconsiderable reward, but deserve to be wholly condemned, because they are always stained by many blemishes; and what have pollutions to do with the presence of God?

4. Though a reward had been a thousand times promised to works, yet it is not due but by fulfilling the condition of obeying the law perfectly; and how widely distant are we all from that perfection!

Let Papists now go and attempt to force their way into heaven by the merit of works. We cheerfully concur with Paul and with the whole Bible in acknowledging, that we are unable to do anything but by the free grace of God, and yet that the benefits resulting from our works receive the name of a reward.

9. *Let us not be weary in well-doing. Well-doing* (καλὸν) does not simply mean doing our duty, but the performance of acts of kindness, and has a reference to men. We are instructed *not to be weary* in assisting our neighbours, in performing good offices, and in exercising generosity. This precept is highly necessary; for we are naturally reluctant to discharge the duties of brotherly love, and many unpleasant occurrences arise by which the ardor of the best disposed persons is apt to be cooled. We meet with many unworthy and many ungrateful persons. The vast number of necessitous cases overwhelms us, and the applications which crowd upon us from every quarter exhaust our patience. Our warmth is abated by the coolness of other men. In short, the world presents innumerable hinderances, which tend to lead us aside from the right path. Most properly, therefore, does Paul admonish us not to relax through weariness.

If we faint not. That is, we shall reap the fruit which God promises, if we "persevere to the end." (Mt 10:22.) Those who do not persevere resemble indolent husbandmen, who, after ploughing and sowing, leave the work unfinished, and neglect to take the necessary precautions for protecting the seed from being devoured by birds, or scorched by the sun, or destroyed by cold. It is to no purpose that we begin to do good, if we do not press forward to the goal.

In due season [99] Let no man, from a wish to gather the fruit in this life, or before its *proper time*, deprive himself of the spiritual harvest. The desires of believers must be both supported and restrained by the exercise of hope and patience.

10. *While we have opportunity.* The metaphor is still pursued. Every season is not adapted to tillage and sowing. Active and prudent husbandmen will observe the proper season, and will not indolently allow it to pass unimproved. Since, therefore, God has set apart the whole of the present life for ploughing and sowing, let us avail ourselves of the season, lest, through our negligence, it may be taken out of our power. Beginning with liberality to ministers of the gospel, Paul now makes a wider application of his doctrine, and exhorts us to *do good to all men*, but recommends to our particular regard *the household of faith*, or believers, because they belong to the same family with ourselves. This similitude is intended to excite us to that kind of communication which ought to be maintained among the members of one family. There are duties which we owe to all men arising out of a common nature; but the tie of a more sacred relationship, established by God himself, binds us to believers.

Galatians 6:11-13

11. Ye see how large a letter I have written unto you with mine own hand.
11. Videtis, qualibus literis vobis scripserim mea manu.

12. As many as desire to make a fair shew in the flesh, they constrain you to be circumcised; only lest they should suffer persecution for the cross of Christ.

12. Quicunque volunt placere juxta faciem in carne, hi cogunt vos circumcidi; tantum ut ne persequutionem sustineant cruce Christi.

13. For neither they themselves who are circumcised keep the law; but desire to have you circumcised, that they may glory in your flesh.

13. Neque enim qui circumciduntur, ipsi Legera servant; sed volunt vos circumcidi, ut in carne vestra glorientur.

11. *Ye see.* The meaning of the Greek verb ἴδετε, is so far doubtful that it may be taken either in the imperative or indicative mood; but the force of the passage is little if at all affected. To convince the Galatians more fully of his anxiety about them, and at the same time to ensure their careful perusal, he mentions that this long Epistle had been written with his own hand. The greater the toil to which he had submitted on their account, the stronger were their inducements to read it, not in a superficial manner, but with the closest attention.

12. *As many as desire to make a fair shew in the flesh.* Such men pay no regard to edification, but are guided by an ambitious desire to hunt after popular applause. The Greek verb εὐπροσωπῶσαι, [100] is highly expressive, and denotes the kind looks and address which were assumed for the purpose of pleasing. He charges the false apostles with ambition. As if he had said, "When those men lay circumcision upon you as a necessary burden, do you wish to know what sort of persons they are, what are the objects of their regard or pursuit? You are mistaken if you imagine that they are at all influenced by godly zeal. To gain or preserve the favor of men is the object they have in view in offering this bribe." It was because they were Jews that they adopted this method of retaining the good-will, or at least allaying the resentment, of their own nation. It is the usual practice of ambitious men meanly to fawn on those from whose favor they hope to derive advantage, and to insinuate themselves into their good graces, that, when better men have been displaced, they may enjoy the undivided power. This wicked design he lays open to the Galatians, in order to put them on their guard.

Only lest they should suffer persecution. The pure preaching of the gospel is again designated the cross of Christ. But there is likewise an allusion to their favourite scheme of resolving to preach Christ without the cross. The deadly rage by which the Jews were animated against Paul, arose from their being unable to endure a neglect of ceremonies. To avoid persecution, those men flattered the Jews. Yet after all, if they had themselves kept the law, their conduct might have been suffered. On the contrary, they disturbed the whole church for the sake of their personal ease, and scrupled not to lay a tyrannical yoke on the consciences of men, that they might be entirely freed from bodily uneasiness. A dread of the cross led them to corrupt the true preaching of the cross.

13. *For neither they who hold by circumcision keep the law.* The old version and Erasmus translate thus: *who are circumcised.* But Paul appears to me to refer to teachers only; and for this reason I would prefer to render the words, *those who hold by circumcision,* which would not include all circumcised persons, and thus would avoid ambiguity. The meaning is, "It is not from a strong attachment to the law that they bind you with the yoke of ceremonies; for, even with their own circumcision, they do not keep the law. It is no doubt under the pretext of the law that they require you to be circumcised; but, though they have themselves been circumcised, they do not perform what they enjoin upon others." When he says, indeed, that they do not *keep the law*, it is doubtful whether he refers to the whole law, or to ceremonies. Some understand him as saying that the law is an intolerable burden, and therefore they do not satisfy its demands. But he rather insinuates against them a charge of insincerity, because, except when it suited their own designs, they found themselves at liberty to despise the law.

Even now this disease rages everywhere with virulence. You will find many who are prompted more by ambition than by conscience to defend the tyranny of the papal system. I speak of our courtly apostles, who are attracted by the smell of a kitchen, and who pronounce, with an air of authority, that the decrees of the holy Church of Rome must be observed with reverence. And what is their own practice all the while! They pay no more regard to any decisions of the Roman see than to the braying of an ass, but they take care to avoid personal risk. In short, Paul had the same kind of controversy with those impostors as we now have with hypocritical professors of the gospel, who hold out to us a monstrous union between Christ and the Pope. Paul therefore declares that they are not acting the part of honest men, and that they have no other object in enjoining circumcision than to boast to the Jews of the converts they have made. Such is the import of the words, *that they may glory in your flesh.* "They wish to triumph over you, and to gratify their own desire of applause, by offering up your mutilated flesh to the false zealots of the law, as a token of peace and harmony."

Galatians 6:14-18

14. But God forbid that I should glory, save in the cross of our Lord Jesus Christ, by whom the world is crucified unto me, and I unto the world.

14. Mihi antem absit gloriari, nisi in truce Domini nostri Iesu Christi, per quam mundus mihi crucifixus est, et ego mundo.

15. For in Christ Jesus neither circumcision availeth any thing, nor uncircumcision, but a new creature.

15. Nam in Christo neque circumcisio quicquam valet, neque praeputium; sed nova creatura.

16. And as many as walk according to this rule, peace *be* on them, and mercy, and upon the Israel of God.

16. Et quicunque hac regula ambulabunt, pax super eos et misericordia, et super Israelem Dei.

17. From henceforth let no man trouble me: for I bear in my body the marks of the Lord Jesus.

17. In reliquis nemo facessat mihi molestiam; ego enim stigmata Domini Iesu in corpore meo porto.

18. Brethren, the grace of our Lord Jesus Christ *be* with your spirit. Amen.

18. Gratia Domini nostri Iesu Christi cum spiritu vestro, fratres. Amen.

To the Galatians written from Rome.

Ad Galatas missa fuit e Roma.

14. *But God forbid that I should glory.* The designs of the false apostles are here contrasted with his own sincerity. As if he had said, "To avoid being compelled to bear a cross, they deny the cross of Christ, purchase with your flesh the applause of men, and end by triumphing over you. But my triumph and my glory are in the cross of the Son of God." If the Galatians had not been utterly destitute of common sense, ought they not to have held in abhorrence the men whom they beheld making sport of their dangerous condition.

To glory in the cross of Christ, is to glory in Christ crucified. But something more is implied. In that death, — so full of disgrace and ignominy, which God himself has pronounced to be accursed, and which men are wont to view with abhorrence and shame, — in that death he will glory, because he obtains in it perfect happiness. Where man's highest good exists, there is his glory. But why does not Paul seek it elsewhere? Though salvation is held out to us in the cross of Christ, what does he think of his resurrection? I answer, in the cross redemption in all its parts is found, but the resurrection of Christ does not lead us away from the cross. And let it be carefully observed, that every other kind of glorying is rejected by him as nothing short of a capital offense. "May God protect us from such a fearful calamity!" Such is the import of the phrase which Paul constantly employs, *God forbid*

BY WHICH *the world is crucified.* As the Greek word for *cross*, σταυρὸς, is masculine, the relative pronoun may be either rendered *by whom*, or *by which*, according as we refer it to Christ or to the cross. In my opinion, however, it is more proper to apply it to the cross; for by it strictly we die to the world. But what is the meaning of *the world*? It is unquestionably contrasted with the *new creature.* Whatever is opposed to the spiritual kingdom of Christ is the world, because it belongs to the old man; or, in a word, *the world* is the object and aim of the old man.

The world is crucified to me. This exactly agrees with the language which he employs on another occasion.

"But what things were gain to me, those I counted loss for Christ; yea doubtless, and I count all things but loss for the excellency of the knowledge of Christ Jesus my Lord; for whom I have suffered the loss of all things, and do count them but dung, that I may win Christ" (Phil. 3:7, 8.)

To crucify the world is to treat it with contempt and disdain.

He adds, *and I unto the world.* By this he means that he regarded himself as unworthy to be taken into the account, and indeed as utterly annihilated; because this was a matter with which a dead man had nothing to do. At all events, he means, that by the mortification of the old man he had renounced the world. Some take his meaning to be, "If the world looks upon me as abhorred and excommunicated, I consider the world to be condemned and accursed." This appears to me to be overstrained, but I leave my readers to judge.

15. *For in Christ Jesus.* The reason why he is crucified to the world, and the world to him, is, that in Christ, to whom he is spiritually united, nothing but a new creature is of any avail. Everything else must be dismissed, must perish. I refer to those things which hinder the renewing of the Spirit. "If any man be in Christ" says he, "let him be a new creature." (2Co 5:17.) That is, if any man wishes to be considered as belonging to the kingdom of Christ, let him be created anew by the Spirit of God; let him not live any longer to himself or to the world, but let him be raised up to "newness of life." (Ro 6:4.) His reasons for concluding that neither circumcision nor uncircumcision is of any importance, have been already considered. The truth of the gospel swallows up, and brings to nought, all the shadows of the law.

16. *And as many as walk according to this rule.* "May they enjoy all prosperity and happiness!" This is not merely a prayer in their behalf, but a token of approbation. His meaning therefore is, that those who teach this doctrine are worthy of all esteem and regard, and those who reject it do not deserve to be heard. The word *rule* denotes the regular and habitual course which all godly ministers of the gospel ought to pursue. Architects employ a model in the erection of buildings, to assist them in preserving the proper form and just proportions. Such a *model* (κανόνα) does the apostle prescribe to the ministers of the word, who are to build the church "according to the pattern shewn to them." (Heb 8:5.)

Faithful and upright teachers, and all who allow themselves to conform to this rule, must derive singular encouragement from this passage, in which God, by the mouth of Paul, pronounces on them a blessing. We have no cause to dread the thunders of the Pope, if God promises to us from heaven *peace* and *mercy*. The word *walk* may apply both to a minister and to his people, though it refers chiefly to ministers. The future tense of the verb, (ὅσοι στοιχήσουσιν,) as many as *shall walk*, is intended to express perseverance.

And upon the Israel of God [101] This is an indirect ridicule of the vain boasting of the false apostles, who vaunted of being the descendants of Abraham according to the flesh. There are two classes who bear this name, a pretended Israel, which appears to be so in the sight of men, — and the Israel of God. Circumcision was a disguise before men, but regeneration is a truth before God. In a word, he gives the appellation of the *Israel of God* to those whom he formerly denominated the children of Abraham by faith, (Ga 3:29,) and thus includes all believers, whether Jews or Gentiles, who were united into one church. On the contrary, the name and lineage are the sole boast of Israel according to the flesh; and this led the apostle to argue in the Epistle to the Romans, that "they are not all Israel which are of Israel, neither because they are the seed of Abraham, are they all children." (Rom. 9:6, 7.)

17. *Let no man trouble me.* He now speaks with the voice of authority for restraining his adversaries, and employs language which his high rank fully authorized. "Let them cease to throw hinderances in the course of my preaching." He was prepared, for the sake of the church, to encounter difficulties, but does not choose to be interrupted by contradiction. *Let no man trouble me.* Let no man make opposition to obstruct the progress of my work.

As to everything else, (τοῦ λοιποῦ,) that is, as to everything besides the *new creature.* "This one thing is enough for me. Other matters are of no importance, and give me no concern. Let no man question me about them." He thus places himself above all men, and allows to none the power of attacking his ministry. Literally, the phrase signifies, as to *the rest* or *the remainder*, which Erasmus, in my opinion, has improperly applied to time.

For I bear [102] *in my body the marks of the Lord Jesus.* This accounts for his bold, authoritative language. And what were those marks? Imprisonment, chains, scourging, blows, stoning, and every kind of injurious treatment which he had incurred in bearing testimony to the gospel. Earthly warfare has its honors, in conferring which a general holds out to public view the bravery of a soldier. So

Christ our leader has his own marks, of which he makes abundant use, for conferring on some of his followers a high distinction. These marks, however, differ from the other in one important respect, that they partake of the nature of the cross, and in the sight of the world are disgraceful. This is suggested by the word translated *marks*, (στίγματα,) for it literally denotes the *marks* with which barbarian slaves, or fugitives, or malefactors, were usually branded. Paul, therefore, can hardly be said to use a figure, when he boasts of shining in those marks with which Christ is accustomed to honor his most distinguished soldiers, [103] which in the eye of the world were attended by shame and disgrace, but which before God and the angels surpass all the honors of the world. [104]

18. *The grace* [105] *of our Lord Jesus Christ be with your spirit.* His prayer is not only that God may bestow upon them his grace in large measure, but that they may have a proper feeling of it in their hearts. Then only is it truly enjoyed by us, when it comes to our *spirit.* We ought therefore to entreat that God would prepare in our souls a habitation for his grace. Amen.

Footnotes

94

"In the original it is ἔν τινι παραπτώματι, 'in any fault.' The expression is general, though it seems to refer to those works of the flesh of which he had made mention in the 19th and following verses of the foregoing chapter. 'If in any of these faults any person should happen to be overtaken;' the last word seems to denote somewhat of a surprise, by which a man might be drawn into a sin, without any previous deliberate purpose or design; a sin committed through some extraordinary and sudden temptation. The last words of the verse, 'lest thou also be tempted,' seem plainly to intimate that this was the apostle's meaning." — Chandler.

95

"I observe an agreement in a somewhat peculiar rule of Christian conduct, as laid down in this epistle, and as exemplified in the Second Epistle to the Corinthians. It is not the repetition of the same general precept, which would have been a coincidence of little value; but it is the general precept in one place, and the application of that precept to an actual occurrence in the other. (See 2Co 2:6-8.) I have little doubt but that it was the same mind which dictated these two passages." Paley's Horae Paulinae.

96

Catullus.

97

"Even in those who do not need forbearance, nothing is more becoming than gentleness; and I reckon him to be the best and most blameless man who pardons others, as if he were daily sinning, and yet abstains from sin, as if he pardoned nobody." — Plin. Ep.

98

"De tels serviteurs." "Of such servants."

99

᾿Εγενήσαν ἀμφότεροι κατὰ τοὺς ἰδίους καιροὺς τύραννοι Συρακουσῶν. "Both at their onwn time became tyrants of Syracuse" — Polybius. Xenophon and other classical writers employ the phrase ἐν καιρῷ in the general sense of "seasonably," and sometimes very nearly in the same sense as when the adjective ἴδιος is added. Κυρ. Παιδ.. 8:5. 5. — *Ed*

100

"The word we render, 'to make a fair shew,' properly signifies to be handsome and lovely. Hence it is used to signify anything that recommends itself by its specious appearance, [Thus ἀπολογία εὐπροσῶπος, Lucian.] Now this was the case of these Judaising teachers. Their great care was to avoid persecution: and, in order to this, they made it their study εὐπροσωπῶσαι, to keep fair with the Jews, ἐν σαρκὶ, by means of the flesh, that is, not only by boasting of their own circumcision, but by making it a point of merit with them, that they had pressed the necessity of circumcision upon others." — Chandler.

101

Ισραηλιτικὸν γὰρ τὸ ἀληθινὸν πνευματικὸν καὶ Ἰακὼβ καὶ Ἰσαὰκ καὶ ᾿Αβραὰμ τοῦ ἐν ἀκροβυστίᾳ ἐπὶ τῶ πίστει μερτυρηθέντος ὑπὸ τοῦ Θεοῦ καὶ εὐλογηθέντος καὶ πατρὸς πολλῶν κληθέντος ἡμεῖς ἐσμεν, οἱ διὰ τούτου σταυρωθέντος Χριστοῦ τῷ Θεῷ προσαχθῶντες. "We, who have been brought to God by this crucified Christ are the true spiritual Israel, and the seed of Judah, and of Jacob, and of Isaac, and of Abraham, whose faith was attested, and who was blessed by God, and called the father of many nations, while he was in circumcision" — Justin Martyr.

102

Οὐκ εἶπε δὲ ἔχω ἀλλὰ βαστάζω ὥσπερ τι τρόπαιον ἢ σημεῖον βασιλικὸν καὶ τούτοις ἐναβρύνομαι. "He does not say, I have, but, I bear, as some trophy or royal symbol; and I deck myself with them." — Theophylact

103

"There is no warlike weapon, οὗγε οὐκ ἴχνη ἐν ἐμαυτῷ φέρω, of which I do not bear the marks upon me." — Arrian.

104

"So far am I from being liable to be torn away from the truth of the gospel, by any reproaches or afflictions, that the disgrace inflicted on me for Christ's sake, and the imprisonment, and scourging, and bonds, and stonings, and other distresses which I have endured for the name of Christ, shall be carried about with me, in my body, wherever I go, as marks and tokens of my Lord Jesus Christ. I will exhibit them as so many trophies, and will reckon it to be my glory, that I am counted worthy to imitate, in any manner, the cross of Christ which I preach."-Erasmus's Paraphrase.

105

"It is of little moment whether, by the 'grace,' we understand that free love and favour, which He always bears in his heart to all that believe in his name, or all that kindness — all those heavenly and spiritual blessings — in the communication of which He manifests this love, this free favour." — Brown.

COMMENTARIES ON THE EPISTLE OF PAUL TO THE EPHESIANS.

THE ARGUMENT

Ephesus, which is familiarly known in history under a great variety of names, [106] was a very celebrated city of Lesser Asia. The remarkable events connected with the work of God in "forming there a people for himself," (Isa 43:21,) through the labors of Paul, together with the commencement and progress of that church, are related by Luke in the Acts of the Apostles. At present, I shall do nothing more than glance at what bears directly on the argument of the Epistle. The Ephesians had been instructed by Paul in the pure doctrine of the gospel. At a later period, while he was a prisoner at Rome, and perceiving that they needed confirmation, he wrote to them, on that account, the present Epistle.

The first three chapters are chiefly occupied with commending the grace of God. Immediately after the salutation in the commencement of the first chapter, he treats of God's free election. This affords him an opportunity of stating that they were now called into the kingdom of God, because they had been appointed to life before they were born. And here occurs a striking display of God's wonderful mercy, when the salvation of men is traced to its true and native source, the free act of adoption. But as the minds of men are ill fitted to receive so sublime a mystery, he betakes himself to prayer, that God would enlighten the Ephesians in the full knowledge of Christ.

In the second chapter, by drawing two comparisons, he places in a strong light the riches of divine grace. **1.** He reminds them how wretched they were before they were called to Christ. We never become duly sensible of our obligations to Christ, nor estimate aright his kindness towards us, till we have been led to view, on the other side, the unhappy condition in which we formerly were "without Christ." (Eph 2:12.) **2.** The Gentiles were "aliens" from the promises of eternal life, which God had been pleased to bestow on the Jews alone.

In the third chapter, he declares that he had been appointed to be, in a peculiar manner, the Apostle of the Gentiles, because, for a long period, they were "strangers and foreigners," (Eph 2:19,) but are now included among the people of God. As this was an unusual event, and as its very novelty produced uneasiness in many minds, he calls it a

"mystery which in other ages was not made known
to the sons of men," (Eph. 3:4, 5,)

but "the dispensation" (Eph 3:2) of which had been intrusted to himself.

Towards the close of the chapter, he again prays that God would grant to the Ephesians such an intimate knowledge of Christ, that they would have no desire to know anything else. His object in doing so is not merely to lead them to gratitude to God for so many favors, and to the expression of that gratitude by entire devotion to his service, but still more to remove all doubt about his own calling. Paul was probably afraid that the false apostles would shake their faith by insinuating that they had been only half-instructed. They had been Gentiles, and, when they embraced pure Christianity, had been told nothing about ceremonies or circumcision. But all who enjoined on Christians the observance of the law were loud in the avowal, that those who have not been introduced into the church of God by circumcision must be held as profane persons. This was their ordinary song, that no man who is not circumcised is entitled to be reckoned among the people of God, and that all the rites prescribed by Moses ought to be observed. Accordingly, they brought it as a charge against Paul, that he exhibited Christ as equally the Savior of Gentiles and of Jews. They asserted that his apostleship was a profanation of the heavenly doctrine, because it threw open to wicked men, without discrimination, a share in the covenant of grace.

That the Ephesians, when assailed by these calumnies, might not give way, he resolved to meet them. While he argues so earnestly that they were called to the gospel because they had been chosen before the creation of the world, he charges them, on the other hand, not to imagine that the gospel had been accidentally brought to them by the will of men, or that it flew to them by chance; [107] for the preaching of Christ among them was nothing else than the announcement of that eternal decree. While he lays before them the unhappy condition of their former life, he at the same time reminds them that the singular and astonishing mercy of God appeared in rescuing them from so deep a gulf. While he sets before their eyes his own commission as the apostle of the Gentiles, he confirms them in the faith which they had once received, because they had been divinely admitted into the communion of the church. And yet each of the sentences to which we have now referred must be viewed as an exhortation fitted to excite the Ephesians to gratitude.

In the fourth chapter, he describes the manner in which the Lord governs and protects his church, which is, by the gospel preached by men. Hence it follows, that in no other way can its integrity be preserved, and that the object at which it aims is true perfection. The apostle's design is, to commend to the Ephesians the ministry by which God reigns amongst us. He afterwards details the fruits of this preaching, — a holy life and all the duties of piety. Nor does he satisfy himself with describing in general terms how Christians ought to live, but lays down particular exhortations adapted to the various relations of society.

Footnotes

106

See Rosenmuller's Biblical Geography, volume 27, page 26, Biblical Cabinet.

107

"Ou, qu'il ait prins sa volee vers eux." "Or, that it took its flight towards them."

CHAPTER 1

Ephesians 1:1-6

1. Paul, an apostle of Jesus Christ by the will of God, to the saints which are at Ephesus, and to the faithful in Christ Jesus:

1. Paulus Apostolus Iesu Christi per voluntatem Dei, sanctis omnibus qui sunt Ephesi, et fidelibus in Christo Iesu,

2. Grace *be* to you, and peace, from God our Father, and *from* the Lord Jesus Christ.

2. Gratia vobis et pax a Deo Patre nostro, et Domino Iesu Christo,

3. Blessed *be* the God and Father of our Lord Jesus Christ, who hath blessed us with all spiritual blessings in heavenly *places* in Christ;

3. Benedictus Deus et Pater Domini nostri Iesu Christi, qui benedixit nos in omni benedictione spirituali, in coelestibus Christo;

4. According as he hath chosen us in him before the foundation of the world, that we should be holy and without blame before him in love:

4. Quemadmodum elegit nos in ipso ante mundi creationem, ut simus sancti et inculpati in conspectu suo per charitatem;

5. Having predestinated us unto the adoption of children by Jesus Christ to himself, according to the good pleasure of his will,

5. Qui praedestinavit nos in adoptionem per Iesum Christum in seipso, secundum beneplacitum voluntatis suae,

6. To the praise of the glory of his grace, wherein he hath made us accepted in the beloved.

6. In laudem gloriae gratiae suae, qua nos gratos habuit in dilecto.

1. *Paul, an apostle.* As the same form of salutation, or at least very little varied, is found in all the Epistles, it would be superfluous to repeat here the observations which we have formerly made. He calls himself "an apostle of Jesus Christ;" for all to whom has been given the ministry of reconciliation are his ambassadors. The word Apostle, indeed, carries something more; for it is not every minister of the gospel, as we shall afterwards see, (Eph 4:11,) that can be called an apostle. But this subject has been explained more fully in my remarks on the Epistle to the Galatians. (See Calvin on "Ga 1:1")

He adds, *by the will of God;* for "no man ought to take this honor unto himself," (Heb 5:4,) but every man ought to wait for the calling of God, which alone makes lawful ministers. He thus meets the jeers of wicked men by holding out the authority of God, and removes every occasion of inconsiderate strife.

To all the saints. He gives the name of *saints* to those whom he afterwards denominates *faithful in Christ Jesus.* No man, therefore, is a believer who is not also a saint; and, on the other hand, no man is a saint who is not a believer. Most of the Greek copies want the word *all;* but I was unwilling to strike it out, because it must, at all events, be understood.

3. *Blessed* [108] *be the God and Father of our Lord Jesus Christ.* The lofty terms in which he extolls the grace of God toward the Ephesians, are intended to rouse their hearts to gratitude, to set them all on flame, to fill them even to overflowing with this thought. They who perceive in themselves discoveries of the Divine goodness, so full and absolutely perfect, and who make them the subject of earnest meditation, will never embrace new doctrines, by which the very grace which they feel so powerfully in themselves is thrown into the shade. The design of the apostle, therefore, in asserting the riches of divine grace toward the Ephesians, was to protect them against having their faith shaken by the false apostles, as if their calling were doubtful, or salvation were to be sought in some other way. He shews, at the same time, that the full certainty of future happiness rests on the revelation of his love to us in Christ, which God makes in the gospel. But to confirm the matter more fully, he rises to the first cause, to the fountain, — the eternal election of God, by which, ere we are born, (Ro 9:11,) we are adopted as sons. This makes it evident that their salvation was accomplished, not by any accidental or unlooked-for occurrence, but by the eternal and unchangeable decree of God.

The word *bless* is here used in more than one sense, as referring to God, and as referring to men. I find in Scripture four different significations of this word. **1.** We are said to bless God when we offer praise to him for his goodness. **2.** God is said to bless us, when he crowns our undertakings with success, and, in the exercise of his goodness, bestows upon us happiness and prosperity; and the reason is, that our enjoyments depend entirely upon his pleasure. Our attention is here called to the singular efficacy which dwells in the very word of God, and which Paul expresses in beautiful language. **3.** Men bless each other by prayer. **4.** The priest's blessing is not simply a prayer, but is likewise a testimony and pledge of the Divine blessing; for the priests received a commission to bless in the name of the Lord. Paul therefore blesses God, because *he hath blessed us,* that is, hath enriched us with all blessing and grace.

With all spiritual blessings. I have no objection to Chrysostom's remark, that the word *spiritual* conveys an implied contrast between the blessing of Moses and of Christ. The law had its blessings; but in Christ only is perfection found, because he gives us a perfect revelation of the kingdom of God, which leads us directly to heaven. When the body itself is presented to us, figures are no longer needed.

In heavenly. Whether we understand the meaning to be, in heavenly Places, or in heavenly Benefits, is of little consequence. All that was intended to be expressed is the superiority of that grace which we receive through Christ. The happiness which it bestows is not in this world, but in heaven and everlasting life. In the Christian religion, indeed, as we are elsewhere taught, (1Ti 4:8,) is contained the "promise of the life that now is, and of that which is to come;" but its aim is spiritual happiness, for the kingdom of Christ is spiritual. A contrast is drawn between Christ and all the Jewish emblems, by which the blessing under the law was conveyed; for where Christ is, all those things are superfluous.

4. *According as he hath chosen us.* The foundation and first cause, both of our calling and of all the benefits which we receive from God, is here declared to be his eternal election. If the reason is asked, why God has called us to enjoy the gospel, why he daily bestows upon us so many blessings, why he opens to us the gate of heaven, — the answer will be constantly found in this principle, that *he hath chosen us before the foundation of the world.* The very time when the election took place proves it to be free; for what could we have deserved, or what merit did we possess, before the world was made? How childish is the attempt to meet this argument by the following sophism! "We were chosen because we were worthy, and because God foresaw that we would be worthy." We were all lost in Adam; and therefore, had not God, through his own election, rescued us from perishing, there was nothing to be foreseen. The same argument is used in the Epistle to the Romans, where, speaking of Jacob and Esau, he says,

"For the children being not yet born, neither having done any good or evil, that the purpose of God according to election might stand, not of works, but of him that calleth." (Ro 9:11.)

But though they had not yet acted, might a sophist of the *Sorbonne* reply, God foresaw that they would act. This objection has no force when applied to the depraved natures of men, in whom nothing can be seen but materials for destruction.

In Christ. This is the second proof that the election is free; for if we are chosen *in* Christ, it is *not of* ourselves. It is not from a perception of anything that we deserve, but because our heavenly Father has introduced us, through the privilege of adoption, into the body of Christ. In short, the name of Christ excludes all merit, and everything which men have of their own; for when he says that we are *chosen in Christ,* it follows that in ourselves we are unworthy.

That we should be holy. This is the immediate, but not the chief design; for there is no absurdity in supposing that the same thing may gain two objects. The design of building is, that there should be a house. This is the immediate design, but the convenience of dwelling in it is the ultimate design. It was necessary to mention this in passing; for we shall immediately find that Paul mentions another design, the glory of God. But there is no contradiction here; for the glory of God is the highest end, to which our sanctification is subordinate.

This leads us to conclude, that holiness, purity, and every excellence that is found among men, are the fruit of election; so that once more Paul expressly puts aside every consideration of merit. If God had foreseen in us anything worthy of election, it would have been stated in language the very opposite of what is here employed, and which plainly means that all our holiness and purity of life flow from the election of God. How comes it then that some men are religious, and live in the fear of God, while others give themselves up without reserve to all manner of wickedness? If Paul may be believed, the only reason is, that the latter retain their natural disposition, and the former have been chosen to holiness. The cause, certainly, is not later than the effect. Election, therefore, does not depend on the righteousness of works, of which Paul here declares that it is the cause.

We learn also from these words, that election gives no occasion to licentiousness, or to the blasphemy of wicked men who say, "Let us live in any manner we please; for, if we have been elected, we cannot perish." Paul tells them plainly, that they have no right to separate holiness of life from the grace of election; for

"whom he did predestinate, them he also called, and whom he called, them he also justified." (Ro 8:30.)

The inference, too, which the Catharists, Celestines, and Donatists drew from these words, that we may attain perfection in this life, is without foundation. This is the goal to which the whole course of our life must be directed, and we shall not reach it till we have finished our course. Where are the men who dread and avoid the doctrine of predestination as an inextricable labyrinth, who believe it to be useless and almost dangerous? No doctrine is more useful, provided it be handled in the proper and cautious manner, of which Paul gives us an example, when he presents it as an illustration of the infinite goodness of God, and employs it as an excitement to gratitude. This is the true fountain from which we must draw our knowledge of the divine mercy. If men should evade every other argument, election shuts their mouth, so that they dare not and cannot claim anything for themselves. But let us remember the purpose for which Paul reasons about predestination, lest, by reasoning with any other view, we fall into dangerous errors.

Before him it love. Holiness *before God* (κατενώπιον αὐτοῦ) is that of a pure conscience; for God is not deceived, as men are, by outward pretense, but looks to faith, or, which means the same thing, the truth of the heart. If we view the word *love* as applied to God, the meaning will be, that the only reason why he chose us, was his love to men. But I prefer connecting it with the latter part of the verse, as denoting that the perfection of believers consists in love; not that God requires love alone, but that it is an evidence of the fear of God, and of obedience to the whole law.

5. *Who hath predestinated us.* What follows is intended still further to heighten the commendation of divine grace. The reason why Paul inculcated so earnestly on the Ephesians the doctrines of free adoption through Christ, and of the eternal election which preceded it, has been already considered. But as the mercy of God is nowhere acknowledged in more elevated language, this passage will deserve our careful attention. Three causes of our salvation are here mentioned, and a fourth is shortly afterwards added. The efficient cause is *the good pleasure of the will* of God, the material cause is, *Jesus Christ,* and the final cause is, *the praise of the glory of his grace.* Let us now see what he says respecting each.

To the first belongs the whole of the following statement *God hath predestinated us in himself, according to the good pleasure of his will, unto the adoption of sons, and hath made us accepted by his grace.* In the word *predestinate* we must again attend to the order. We were not then in existence, and therefore there was no merit of ours. The cause of our salvation did not proceed from us, but from God alone. Yet Paul, not satisfied with these statements, adds *in himself.* The Greek phrase is, εἰς αὐτὸν, and has the same meaning with ἐν αὐτῷ. By this he means that God did not seek a cause out of himself, but predestinated us, because such was his will.

But this is made still more clear by what follows, *according to the good pleasure of his will.* The word *will* was enough, for Paul very frequently contrasts it with all outward causes by which men are apt to imagine that the mind of God is influenced. But that no doubt may remain, he employs the word *good pleasure,* which expressly sets aside all merit. In adopting us, therefore, God does not inquire what we are, and is not reconciled to us by any personal worth. His single motive is the eternal good pleasure, by which he predestinated us. [109] Why, then, are the sophists not ashamed to mingle with them other considerations, when Paul so strongly forbids us to look at anything else than the good pleasure of God?

Lest anything should still be wanting, he adds, ἐχαρίτωσεν ἐν χάριτι [110] This intimates, that, in the freest manner, and on no mercenary grounds, does God bestow upon us his love and favor, just as, when we were not yet born, and when he was prompted by nothing but his own will, he fixed upon us his choice. [111]

The material cause both of eternal election, and of the love which is now revealed, is *Christ, the Beloved.* This name is given, to remind us that by him the love of God is communicated to us. Thus he is the well-beloved, in order that we may be reconciled by him. The highest and last end is immediately added, the glorious praise of such abundant grace. Every man, therefore, who hides this glory, is endeavoring to overturn the everlasting purpose of God. Such is the doctrine of the sophists, which entirely overturns the doctrine of Christ, lest the whole glory of our salvation should be ascribed undividedly to God alone.

Ephesians 1:7-12

7. In whom we have redemption through his blood, the forgiveness of sins, according to the riches of his grace;

7. In quo habemus redemptionem per sangiunem ejus, remissionem peccatorum, secundum divitias gratiae ejus;

8. Wherein he hath abounded toward us in all wisdom and prudence;

8. Qua exundavit in nos in omni sapientia et prudentia;

9. Having made known unto us the mystery of his will, according to his good pleasure, which he hath purposed in himself:

9. Patefacto nobis arcano voluntatis suae, secundum beneplacitum suum, quod in seipso proposuerat.

10. That, in the dispensation of the fullness of times, he might gather together in one all things in Christ, both which are in heaven, and which are on earth, *even* in him:

10. In dispensationem plenitudinis temporum; ut recolligeret omnia in Christo, tam quae in coelis sunt, quam quae super terram, in ipso.

11. In whom also we have obtained an inheritance, being predestinated according to the purpose of him who worketh all things after the counsel of his own will;

11. Per quem etiam in sortem adsciti sumus, praedestinati secundum propositum ejus, qui omnia efficit secundum consilium voluntatis suae;

12. That we should be to the praise of his glory, who first trusted in Christ.

12. Ut simus in laudem gloriae ipsius, nos qui ante speravimus in Christo.

7. *In whom we have redemption.* The apostle is still illustrating the material cause, — the manner in which we are reconciled to God through Christ. By his death he has restored us to favor with the Father; and therefore we ought always to direct our minds to the blood of Christ, as the means by which we obtain divine grace. After mentioning that, through the blood of Christ, we obtain redemption, he immediately styles it *the forgiveness of sins,* — to intimate that we are redeemed, because our sins are not imputed to us. Hence it follows, that we obtain by free grace that righteousness by which we are accepted of God, and freed from the chains of the devil and of death. The close connection which is here preserved, between our redemption itself and the manner in which it is obtained, deserves our notice; for, so long as we remain exposed to the judgment of God, we are bound by miserable chains, and therefore our exemption from guilt, becomes an invaluable freedom.

According to the riches of his grace. He now returns to the efficient cause, — the largeness of the divine kindness, which has given Christ to us as our Redeemer. *Riches,* and the corresponding word *overflow,* in the following verse, are intended to give us large views of divine grace. The apostle feels himself unable to celebrate, in a proper manner, the goodness of God, and desires that the contemplation of it would occupy the minds of men till they are entirely lost in admiration. How desirable is it that men were deeply impressed with "the riches of that grace" which is here commended! No place would any longer be found for pretended satisfactions, or for those trifles by which the world vainly imagines that it can redeem itself; as if the blood of Christ, when unsupported by additional aid, had lost all its efficacy. [112]

8. *In all wisdom.* He now comes to the formal cause, the preaching of the gospel, by which the goodness of God *overflows upon us.* [113] It is through faith that we receive Christ, by whom we come to God, and by whom we enjoy the privilege of adoption. Paul gives to the gospel the magnificent appellations of *wisdom and prudence,* for the purpose of leading the Ephesians to despise all contrary doctrines. The false apostles insinuated themselves, under the pretense of imparting views more elevated than the elementary instructions which Paul conveyed. And the devil, in order to undermine our faith, labors, as far as he can, to disparage the gospel. Paul, on the other hand, builds up the authority of the gospel, that believers may rest upon it with unshaken confidence. *All wisdom* means — full or perfect wisdom.

9. *Having made known to us the mystery of his will.* Some were alarmed at the novelty of his doctrine. With a view to such persons, he very properly denominates it a *mystery of the divine will,* and yet a mystery which God has now been pleased to reveal. As he formerly ascribed their election, so he now ascribes their calling, to the good pleasure of God. The Ephesians are thus led to consider that Christ has been made known, and the gospel preached to them, not because they deserved any such thing, but because it pleased God.

Which he hath purposed in himself. All is wisely and properly arranged. What can be more just than that his purposes, with which men are unacquainted, should be known to God alone, so long as he is pleased to conceal them, — or, again, that it should be in his own will and power to fix the time when they shall be communicated to men? The decree to adopt the Gentiles is declared to have been till now hidden in the mind of God, but so hidden, that God reserved it in his own power until the time of the revelation. Does any one now complain of it as a new and unprecedented occurrence, that those who were formerly "without God in the world," (Eph 2:12,) should be received into the church? Will he have the hardihood to deny that the knowledge of God is greater than that of men?

10. *That in the dispensation of the fullness of times.* That no man may inquire, why one time rather than another was selected, the apostle anticipates such curiosity, by calling the appointed period *the fullness of times,* the fit and proper season, as he also did in a former epistle. (Ga 4:4) Let human presumption restrain itself, and, in judging of the succession of events, let it bow to the providence of God. The same lesson is taught by the word *dispensation,* for by the judgment of God the lawful administration of all events is regulated.

That he might gather together in one. In the old translation it is rendered *(instaurare) restore;* to which Erasmus has added *(summatim) comprehensively.* I have chosen to abide closely by the meaning of the Greek word, ἀνακεφαλαιώσασθαι, [114] because it is more agreeable to the context. The meaning appears to me to be, that out of Christ all things were disordered, and that through him they have been restored to order. And truly, out of Christ, what can we perceive in the world but mere ruins? We are alienated from God by sin, and how can we but present a broken and shattered aspect? The proper condition of creatures is to keep close to God. Such a *gathering together* (ἀνακεφαλαίωσις) as might bring us back to regular order, the apostle tells us, has been made in Christ. Formed into one body, we are united to God, and closely connected with each other. Without Christ, on the other hand, the whole world is a shapeless chaos and frightful confusion. We are brought into actual unity by Christ alone.

But why are heavenly beings included in the number? The angels were never separated from God, and cannot be said to have been scattered. Some explain it in this manner. Angels are said to be *gathered together,* because men have become members of the same society, are admitted equally with them to fellowship with God, and enjoy happiness in common with them by means of this blessed unity. The mode of expression is supposed to resemble one frequently used, when we speak of a whole building as repaired, many parts of which were ruinous or decayed, though some parts remained entire.

This is no doubt true; but what hinders us from saying that the angels also have been *gathered together?* Not that they were ever scattered, but their attachment to the service of God is now perfect, and their state is eternal. What comparison is there between a creature and the Creator, without the interposition of a Mediator? So far as they are creatures, had it not been for the benefit which they derived from Christ, they would have been liable to change and to sin, and consequently their happiness would not have been eternal. Who then will deny that both angels and men have been brought back to a fixed order by the grace of Christ? Men had been lost, and angels were not beyond the reach of danger. By *gathering* both into his own body, Christ hath united them to God the Father, and established actual harmony between heaven and earth.

11. *Through whom also we have obtained an inheritance.* Hitherto he has spoken generally of all the elect; he now begins to take notice of separate classes. When he says, *WE have obtained,* he speaks of himself and of the Jews, or, perhaps more correctly, of all who were the first fruits of Christianity; and afterwards he comes to the Ephesians. It tended not a little to confirm the faith of the Ephesian converts, that he associated them with himself and the other believers, who might be said to be the first-born in the church. As if he had said, "The condition of all godly persons is the same with yours; for we who were first called by God owe our acceptance to his eternal election." Thus, he shews, that, from first to last, all have obtained salvation by free grace, because they have been freely adopted according to eternal election.

Who worketh all things. The circumlocution employed in describing the Supreme Being deserves attention. He speaks of Him as the sole agent, and as doing everything according to His own will, so as to leave nothing to be done by man. In no respect, therefore, are men admitted to share in this praise, as if they brought anything of their own. God looks at nothing out of himself to move him to elect them, for *the counsel of his own will* is the only and actual cause of their election. This may enable us to refute the error, or rather the madness, of those who, whenever they are unable to discover the reason of God's works, exclaim loudly against his design.

12. *That we should be to the praise of his glory.* Here again he mentions the *final* cause of salvation; for we must eventually become illustrations of the glory of God, if we are nothing but vessels of his mercy. The word *glory,* by way of eminence, (κατ ' ἐξοχὴν) denotes, in a peculiar manner, that which shines in the goodness of God; for there is nothing that is more peculiarly his own, or in which he desires more to be glorified, than goodness.

Ephesians 1:13-14

13. In whom ye also *trusted,* after that ye heard the word of truth, the gospel of your salvation: in whom also, after that ye believed, ye were sealed with that Holy Spirit of promise,

13. In quo vos etiam, audito sermone veritatis, Evangelio salutis vestrae; in quo etiam, postquam credidistis, obsignati estis Spiritu promissionis sancto,

14. Which is the earnest of our inheritance, until the redemption of the purchased possession, unto the praise of his glory.

14. Qui est arrhabo haereditatis nostrae, in redemptionem acquisitae possessionis, in laudem gloriae ejus.

13. *In whom ye also.* He associates the Ephesians with himself, and with the rest of those who were the first fruits; for he says that they, in like manner, trusted in Christ. His object is, to shew that both had the same faith; and therefore we must supply the word *trusted* from the twelfth verse. He afterwards states that they were brought to that hope by the preaching of the gospel.

Two epithets are here applied to the gospel, — *the word of truth,* and *the gospel of your salvation.* Both deserve our careful attention. Nothing is more earnestly attempted by Satan than to lead us either to doubt or to despise the gospel. Paul therefore furnishes us with two shields, by which we may repel both temptations. In opposition to every doubt, let us learn to bring forward this testimony, that the gospel is not only certain truth, which cannot deceive, but is, by way of eminence, (κατ ' ἐξοχὴν,) *the word of truth,* as if, strictly speaking, there were no truth but itself. If the temptation be to contempt or dislike of the gospel, let us remember that its power and efficacy have been manifested in bringing to us salvation. The apostle had formerly declared that

"it is the power of God to salvation to every one that believeth," (Ro 1:16;)

but here he expresses more, for he reminds the Ephesians that, having been made partakers of salvation, they had learned this by their own experience. Unhappy they who weary themselves, as the world generally does, in wandering through many winding paths, neglecting the gospel, and pleasing themselves with wild romances, —

"ever learning and never able to come to the knowledge of the truth," (2Ti 3:7)

or to find life! But happy they who have embraced the gospel, and whose attachment to it is steadfast; for this, beyond all doubt, is truth and life.

In whom also, after that ye believed. Having maintained that the gospel is certain, he now comes to the proof. And what higher surety can be found than the Holy Spirit? "Having denominated the gospel *the word of truth,* I will not prove it by the authority of men; for you have the testimony of the Spirit of God himself, who seals the truth of it in your hearts." This elegant comparison is taken from Seals, which among men have the effect of removing doubt. Seals give validity both to charters and to testaments; anciently, they were the principal means by which the writer of a letter could be known; and, in short, a seal distinguishes what is true and certain, from what is false and spurious. This office the apostle ascribes to the Holy Spirit, not only here, but in another part of this Epistle, (Eph 4:30,) and in the Second Epistle to the Corinthians, (2Co 1:22.) Our minds never become so firmly established in the truth of God as to resist all the temptations of Satan, until we have been confirmed in it by the Holy Spirit. The true conviction which believers have of the word of God, of their own salvation, and of religion in general, does not spring from the judgment of the flesh, or from human and philosophical arguments, but from the sealing of the Spirit, who imparts to their consciences such certainty as to remove all doubt. The foundation of faith would be frail and unsteady, if it rested on human wisdom; and therefore, as preaching is the instrument of faith, so the Holy Spirit makes preaching efficacious.

But is it not the faith itself which is here said to be sealed by the Holy Spirit? If so, faith goes before the sealing. I answer, there are two operations of the Spirit in faith, corresponding to the two parts of which faith consists, as it enlightens, and as it establishes the mind. The commencement of faith is knowledge: the completion of it is a firm and steady conviction, which admits of no opposing doubt. Both, I have said, are the work of the Spirit. No wonder, then, if Paul should declare that the Ephesians, who received by faith the truth of the gospel, were confirmed in that faith by the seal of the Holy Spirit.

With that Holy Spirit of promise. This title is derived from the effect produced; for to him we owe it that the promise of salvation is not made to us in vain. As God promises in his word, "that he will be to us a Father," (2Co 6:18,) so he gives to us the evidence of having adopted us by the Holy Spirit.

14. *Which is the earnest* [115] *of our inheritance.* This phrase is twice used by Paul in another Epistle. (2 Cor. 1:22, 2 Cor. 5:5.) The metaphor is taken from bargains, in which, when a pledge has been given and accepted, the whole is confirmed, and no room is left for a change of mind. Thus, when we have received the Spirit of God, his promises are confirmed to us, and no dread is felt that they will be revoked. In themselves, indeed, the promises of God are not weak; but, until we are supported by the testimony of the Spirit, we never rest upon them with unshaken confidence. The Spirit, then, is *the earnest of our inheritance* of eternal life, *until the redemption,* that is, until the day of complete redemption is arrived. So long as we are in this world, our warfare is sustained by hope, and therefore this earnest is necessary; but when the possession itself shall have been obtained, the necessity and use of the earnest will then cease.

The significance of a pledge lasts no longer than till both parties have fulfilled the bargain; and, accordingly, he afterwards adds, *ye are sealed to the day of redemption,* (Eph 4:30,) which means the day of judgment. Though we are now redeemed by the blood of Christ, the fruit of that redemption does not yet appear; for "every creature groaneth, desiring to be delivered from the bondage of corruption. And not only they, but ourselves also, who have the first-fruits of the Spirit, even we ourselves groan within ourselves, waiting for the adoption, to wit, *the redemption* of our body;" for we have not yet obtained it, but by hope. (Ro 8:21-23.) But we shall obtain it in reality, when Christ shall appear to judgment. Such is the meaning of the word *redemption* in the passage now quoted from the Epistle to the Romans, and in a saying of our Lord,

"Look up, and lift up your heads, for your redemption draweth nigh." (Lu 21:28.)

Περιποίησις, which we translate *the possession obtained,* is not the kingdom of heaven, or a blessed immortality, but the Church itself. This is added for their consolation, that they might not think it hard to cherish their hope till the day of Christ's coming, or be displeased that they have not yet obtained the promised inheritance; for such is the common lot of the whole Church.

To the praise of his glory. The word *praise,* as in the twelfth verse, Eph 1:12 signifies "making known." [116] The glory of God may sometimes be concealed, or imperfectly exhibited. But in the Ephesians God had given proofs of his goodness, that his glory might be celebrated and openly proclaimed. Those persons, therefore, who slighted the calling of the Ephesians, might be charged with envying and slighting the glory of God.

The frequent mention of the glory of God ought not to be regarded as superfluous, for what is infinite cannot be too strongly expressed. This is particularly true in commendations of the Divine mercy, for which every godly person will always feel himself unable to find adequate language. He will be more ready to utter, than other men will be to hear, the expression of praise; for the eloquence both of men and angels, after being strained to the utmost, falls immeasurably below the vastness of this subject. We may likewise observe, that there is not a more effectual method of shutting the mouths of wicked men, than by shewing that our views tend to illustrate, and theirs to obscure, the glory of God.

Ephesians 1:15-19

15. Wherefore I also, after I heard of your faith in the Lord Jesus, and love unto all the saints,

15. Quapropter ego etiam, audita fide quae apud vos est in Domino Iesu, et charitate erga omnes sanctos,

16. Cease not to give thanks for you, making mention of you in my prayers;

16. Non cesso gratias agere pro vobis, memoriam vestri faciens in orationibus meis;

17. That the God of our Lord Jesus Christ, the Father of glory, may give unto you the spirit of wisdom and revelation in the knowledge of him:

17. Ut Deus Domini nostri Iesu Christi, Pater gloriae, det vobis Spiritum sapientiae et revelationis, in agnitione ipsius,

18. The eyes of your understanding being enlightened; that ye may know what is the hope of his calling, and what the riches of the glory of his inheritance in the saints,

18. Illuminatos oculos mentis vestrae, ut sciatis quae sit spes vocationis ipsius, et quae divitiae gloriae haereditatis ejus in sanctis,

19. And what *is* the exceeding greatness of his power to us-ward who believe, according to the working of his mighty power.

19. Et quae superexcellens magnitudo potentiae ejus erga nos, qui credidimus secundum efficaciam potentiae roboris ejus.

15. *Wherefore I also.* This thanksgiving was not simply an expression of his ardent love to the Ephesians. He congratulated them before God, that the opinion which he had formed respecting them was highly favorable. Observe here, that under *faith and love* Paul includes generally the whole excellence of Christian character. He uses the expression, *faith in the Lord Jesus,* [117] because Christ is the aim and object of faith. *Love* ought to embrace all men, but here the *saints* are particularly mentioned; because love, when properly regulated, begins with them, and is afterwards extended to all others. If our love must have a view to God, the nearer any man approaches to God, the stronger unquestionably must be his claims to our love.

16. *Making mention of you.* To thanksgiving, as his custom is, he adds prayer, in order to excite them to additional progress. It was necessary that the Ephesians should understand that they had entered upon the proper course. But it was equally necessary that they should not turn aside to any new scheme of doctrine, or become indifferent about proceeding farther; for nothing is more dangerous than to be satisfied with that measure of spiritual benefits which has been already obtained. Whatever, then, may be the height of our attainments, let them be always accompanied by the desire of something higher.

17. *That the God of our Lord Jesus Christ.* But what does Paul wish for the Ephesians? *The spirit of wisdom,* and *the eyes of their understanding being enlightened.* And did they not possess these? Yes; but at the same time they needed increase, that, being endowed with a larger measure of the Spirit, and being more and more enlightened, they might more clearly and fully hold their present views. The knowledge of the godly is never so pure, but that some dimness or obscurity hangs over their spiritual vision. But let us examine the words in detail.

The God of our Lord Jesus Christ. The Son of God became man in such a manner, that God was his God as well as ours.

"I ascend," says he, "to my Father, and your Father; and to my God, and your God." (Joh 20:17)

And the reason why he is our God, is, that he is the God of Christ, whose members we are. Let us remember, however, that this relates to his human nature; so that his subjection takes nothing away from his eternal godhead.

The Father of glory. This title springs from the former; for God's glory, as a Father, consists in subjecting his Son to our condition, that, through him, he might be our God. *The Father of glory* is a well-known Hebrew idiom for *The glorious Father.* There is a mode of pointing and reading this passage, which I do not disapprove, and which connects the two clauses in this manner: *That God, the glorious Father of our Lord Jesus Christ, may give to you.*

The Spirit of wisdom and revelation is here put, by a figure of speech, (metonymy,) for the grace which the Lord bestows upon us by his own Spirit. But let it be observed, that the gifts of the Spirit are not the gifts of nature. Till the Lord opens them, *the eyes of our heart* are blind. Till the Spirit has become our instructor, all that we know is folly and ignorance. Till the Spirit of God has made it known to us by a secret revelation, the knowledge of our Divine calling exceeds the capacity of our own minds.

In the knowledge of him. This might also be read, *In the knowledge of himself.* Both renderings agree well with the context, for he that knows the Son knows also the Father; but I prefer the former as more natively suggested by the Greek pronoun, ἐν ἐπιγνώσει αὐτοῦ

18. *The eyes of your understanding being enlightened. The eyes of your heart* is the rendering of the Vulgate, which is supported by some Greek manuscripts. The difference is immaterial, for the Hebrews frequently employ it to denote the rational powers of the soul, though more strictly, being the seat of the affections, it means the will or desire; but I have preferred the ordinary translation.

And what the riches. A comparison, suggested by its excellence, reminds us how unfit we are to receive this elevated knowledge; for the power of God is no small matter. This great power, he tells us, had been exerted, and in a very extraordinary manner, towards the Ephesians, who were thus laid under constant obligations to follow his calling. By thus extolling the grace of God toward themselves, he intended to check every tendency to despise or dislike the duties of the Christian life. But the splendid encomiums which he pronounces on faith convey to us also this instruction, that it is so admirable a work and gift of God, that no language can do justice to its excellence. Paul is not in the habit of throwing out hyperboles without discrimination; but when he comes to treat of a matter which lies so far beyond this world as faith does, he raises our minds to the admiration of heavenly power.

19. *According to the working.* Some consider this clause as referring solely to the word *believe*, which comes immediately before it; but I rather view it as an additional statement, tending to heighten the greatness of the power, as a demonstration, or, if you prefer it, an instance and evidence of the efficacy of the power. The repetition of the word *power,* (δυνάμεως) has the appearance of being superfluous; but in the former case it is restricted to one class, — in the next, it has a general application. Paul, we find, never thinks that he can say enough in his descriptions of the Christian calling. And certainly the power of God is wonderfully displayed, when we are brought from death to life, and when, from being the children of hell, we become the children of God and heirs of eternal life.

Foolish men imagine that this language is absurdly hyperbolical; but godly persons, who are engaged in daily struggles with inward corruption, have no difficulty in perceiving that not a word is here used beyond what is perfectly just. As the importance of the subject cannot be too strongly expressed, so our unbelief and ingratitude led Paul to employ this glowing language. We never form adequate conceptions of the treasure revealed to us in the gospel; or, if we do, we cannot persuade ourselves that it is possible for us to do so, because we perceive nothing in us that corresponds to it, but everything the reverse. Paul's object, therefore, was not only to impress the Ephesians with a deep sense of the value of Divine grace, but also to give them exalted views of the glory of Christ's kingdom. That they might not be cast down by a view of their own unworthiness, he exhorts them to consider the power of God; as if he had said, that their regeneration was no ordinary work of God, but was an astonishing exhibition of his power.

According to the efficacy of the power of his strength. There are three words here, on which we may make a passing remark. We may view *strength* as the root, — *power* as the tree, — and *efficacy* as the fruit, or the stretching out of the Divine arm which terminates in action.

Ephesians 1:20-23

20. Which he wrought in Christ, when he raised him from the dead, and set *him* at his own right hand in the heavenly *places*,

20. Quam exeruit in Christo, dum illum excitavit a mortuis, et sedere fecit in dextera sua, in coelestibus;

21. Far above all principality, and power, and might, and dominion, and every name that is named, not only in this world, but also in that which is to come;

21. Super omnem principatum, et potestatem, et virtutem, et dominationem, et omne nomen quod nominatur, non tantum in seculo hoc, sed etiam in futuro;

22. And hath put all *things* under his feet, and gave him *to be* the head over all *things* to the church,

22. Et omnia subjecit pedibus ejus, et ipsum posuit caput super omnia Ecclesiae,

23. Which is his body, the fullness of him that filleth all in all.

23. Quae est corpus ejus et complementum ejus, qui omnia in omnibus adimplet.

20. *Which he wrought in Christ.* The Greek verb is ἐνέργησεν, from which ἐνέργεια is derived. It might run thus, *According to the efficacy which he effected.* But the translation which I have given conveys the same meaning, and is less harsh.

With the greatest propriety does he enjoin us to contemplate this power in Christ; for in us it is hitherto concealed. "My strength," says he, "is made perfect in weakness." (2Co 12:9.) In what do we excel the children of the world but in this, that our condition appears to be somewhat worse than theirs? Though sin does not reign, it continues to dwell in us, and death is still strong. Our blessedness, which lies in hope, is not perceived by the world. The power of the Spirit is a thing unknown to flesh and blood. A thousand distresses, to which we are daily liable, render us more despised than other men.

Christ alone, therefore, is the mirror in which we can contemplate that which the weakness of the cross hinders from being clearly seen in ourselves. When our minds rise to a confident anticipation of righteousness, salvation, and glory, let us learn to turn them to Christ. We still lie under the power of death; but he, raised from the dead by heavenly power, has the dominion of life. We labor under the bondage of sin, and, surrounded by endless vexations, are engaged in a hard warfare, (1Ti 1:18;) but he, sitting at the right hand of the Father, exercises the highest government in heaven and earth, and triumphs gloriously over the enemies whom he has subdued and vanquished. We lie here mean and despised; but to him has been "given a name" (Php 2:9,) which angels and men regard with reverence, and devils and wicked men with dread. We are pressed down here by the scantiness of all our comforts: but he has been appointed by the Father to be the sole dispenser of all blessings. For these reasons, we shall find our advantage in directing our views to Christ, that in him, as in a mirror, we may see the glorious treasures of Divine grace, and the unmeasurable greatness of that power, which has not yet been manifested in ourselves.

And set him at his own right hand. This passage shews plainly, if any one does, what is meant by *the right hand of God.* It does not mean any particular place, but the power which the Father has bestowed on Christ, that he may administer in his name the government of heaven and earth. It is idle, therefore, to inquire why Stephen *saw him standing,* (Ac 7:55,) while Paul describes him as *sitting* at God's right hand. The expression does not refer to any bodily posture, but denotes the highest royal power with which Christ has been invested. This is intimated by what immediately follows, *far above all principality and power:* for the whole of this description is added for the purpose of explaining what is meant by *the right hand.*

God the Father is said to have raised Christ to "his right hand," because he has made him to share in his government, because by him he exerts all his power; the metaphor being borrowed from earthly princes, who confer the honor of sitting along with themselves on those whom they have clothed with the highest authority. As the right hand of God fills heaven and earth, it follows that the kingdom and power of Christ are equally extensive. It is in vain, therefore, to attempt to prove that, because Christ sitteth at the right hand of God, he dwells in heaven alone. His human nature, it is true, resides in heaven, and not in earth; but that argument is foreign to the purpose. The expression which follows, *in heavenly places,* does not at all imply that the right hand of God is confined to heaven, but directs us to contemplate the heavenly glory amidst which our Lord Jesus dwells, the blessed immortality which he enjoys, and the dominion over angels to which he has been exalted.

21. *Far above all principality, and power, and might, and dominion.* All these names, there can be no doubt, are applied to angels, who are so denominated, because, by means of them, God exercises his power, and might, and dominion. He permits them to share, as far as is competent to creatures, what belongs to himself, and even gives to them his own name; for we find that they are called םיהלא, (*elohim,*) *gods.* From the diversity of names we conclude that there are various orders of angels; but to attempt to settle these with exactness, to fix their number, or determine their ranks, would not merely discover foolish curiosity, but would be rash, wicked, and dangerous.

But why did he not simply call them Angels? I answer, it was to convey exalted views of the glory of Christ that Paul employed those lofty titles. As if he had said, "There is nothing so elevated or excellent, by whatever name it may be named, that is not subject to the majesty of Christ." There was an ancient superstition, prevalent both among Jews and Gentiles, falsely attributing to angels many things, in order to draw away their minds from God himself, and from the true Mediator. Paul constantly labors to prevent this imaginary lustre of angels from dazzling the eyes of men, or obscuring the brightness of Christ; and yet his utmost exertions could not prevent "the wiles of the devil"(Eph 6:11) from succeeding in this matter. Thus we see how the world, through a superstitious dread of angels, departed from Christ. It was indeed the unavoidable consequence of the false opinions entertained respecting angels, that the pure knowledge of Christ disappeared.

Above every name that is named. Name is here taken for largeness, or excellence; and *to be named* means to enjoy celebrity and praise. *The age that is to come* is expressly mentioned, to point out that the exalted rank of Christ is not temporal, but eternal; and that it is not limited to this world, but shines illustriously in the kingdom of God. For this reason, too, Isaiah calls him, (Isa 9:6,) *The Father of the future age*. In short, the glories of men and angels are made to hold an inferior place, that the glory of Christ, unequalled and unapproached, may shine above them all.

22. *And gave him to be the head.* He was made the head of the Church, on the condition that he should have the administration of all things. The apostle shews that it was not a mere honorary title, but was accompanied by the entire command and government of the universe. The metaphor of a *head* denotes the highest authority. I am unwilling to dispute about a name, but we are driven to it by the base conduct of those who flatter the Romish idol. Since Christ alone is called "the head," all others, whether angels or men, must rank as members; so that he who holds the highest place among his fellows is still one of the members of the same body. And yet they are not ashamed to make an open avowal that the Church will be ἀκέφαλον, *without a head*, if it has not another head on earth besides Christ. So small is the respect which they pay to Christ, that, if he obtain undivided that honor which his Father has bestowed upon him, the Church is supposed to be disfigured. This is the basest sacrilege. But let us listen to the Apostle, who declares that the Church is His body, and, consequently, that those who refuse to submit to Him are unworthy of its communion; for on Him alone the unity of the Church depends.

23. *The fullness of him that filleth all in all.* This is the highest honor of the Church, that, until He is united to us, the Son of God reckons himself in some measure imperfect. What consolation is it for us to learn, that, not until we are along with him, does he possess all his parts, or wish to be regarded as complete! Hence, in the First Epistle to the Corinthians, [1Co 12:12-31] when the apostle discusses largely the metaphor of a human body, he includes under the single name of Christ the whole Church.

That filleth all in all. This is added to guard against the supposition that any real defect would exist in Christ, if he were separated from us. His wish to be filled, and, in some respects, made perfect in us, arises from no want or necessity; for all that is good in ourselves, or in any of the creatures, is the gift of his hand; and his goodness appears the more remarkably in raising us out of nothing, that he, in like manner, may dwell and live in us. There is no impropriety in limiting the word *all* to its application to this passage; for, though all things are regulated by the will and power of Christ, yet the subject of which Paul particularly speaks is the spiritual government of the Church. There is nothing, indeed, to hinder us from viewing it as referring to the universal government of the world; but to limit it to the case in hand is the more probable interpretation.

Footnotes

108

"As to the accumulation of cognate terms in εὐλογητὸς εὐλογήσας and εὐλογία, it may be observed, that in composition such was by the ancients, especially the early writers, rather sought after as a beauty than avoided as a blemish." — Bloomfield.

109

"This could not have been obtained by our own strength, had he not by his eternal decree, adopted us into the right and privilege of children, and that by Jesus Christ, to whom he hath so closely united us by faith and love, that we have become his members, and are one with him, and obtain (by communication with him) what was not due to our own merits." — Erasmus.

110

"Il nous a rendu agreables." "He hath made us acceptable."

111

"The original word, ἐχαρίτωσεν, 'he hath made us accepted,' is not used by any profane authors; however, the sense of it is plain. It is used in the angel's salutation to the Virgin Mary, 'Hail, thou that art highly favored;' and that the word there is rightly rendered, is plain from the reason which the angel himself gives, 'Thou hast found favor with God.' (Luke 1:28, 30) So that the plain meaning of the word, and the true rendering of it in the place before us, is, not as we have translated it, 'made us accepted,' but 'highly favored us.'" — Chandler.

112

"Comme si le sang de Christ sechoit et perdoit sa vigueur." "As if the blood of Christ were dried up, and lost its force."

113

ἧς ἐπερίσσευσεν — "ἧς for ᾗ, (by a common Grecism, in which the relative is attracted by the antecedent,) if, at least, we take ἐπερίσσευσεν, with many modern expositors, in a *neuter* sense, 'in which he hath renewed his abundant goodness to us;' but if, with the ancient and some modern ones, in an active sense, 'to make to abound,' (as in 2 Cor. 4:15, 2 Cor. 9:8,) the ἧς will be for ἥν, meaning, 'which he has bountifully bestowed upon us.'" — Bloomfield.

114

"Ἀνακεφαλαιώσασθαι "I have compared this word with συγκεφαλαιοῦσθαι in the writings of Xenophon, so as to bring out this sense, that 'to Christ, as the Head, all things are subject.' I am confirmed in this opinion by Chrysostom, who explains it in this manner: μίαν κεφαλὴν ἅπασιν ἐπέθηκε τὸ κατὰ σάρκα Χριστόν, 'he hath given to all one head, Christ according to the flesh.' Polybius. also uses συγκεφαλαιοῦσθαι, instead of ἀνακεφαλαιοῦσθαι. So that it is evident that those two words are employed indiscriminately." — Raphelius.

115

"The original word ἀρ᾽ῥαβών, seems properly to denote the first part of the price that is paid in any contract, as an earnest and security of the remainder, and which, therefore, is not taken back, but kept till the residue is paid to complete the whole sum. And thus it differs from a pledge, which is somewhat given for the security of a contract, but redeemed and restored, when the contract is completed;

but it must be owned that the word is used to denote both an earnest and a pledge, and in either sense it is very properly applied to the Holy Spirit of promise." — Chandler.

116

"*Louange* yci se prend comme ci devant pour la publication et manifestation." "Here, as formerly, 'praise' denotes proclamation and manifestation."

117

"'Having heard of your faith in the Lord Jesus.' It is wrong to argue from this expression, with Olshausen and De Wette, that the apostle had no personal knowledge of the persons whom he addressed. This was an early surmise, for it is referred to by Theodoret. Some, says he, have supposed that the apostle wrote to the Ephesians, ὡς μηδέπω θεασάμενος αὐτοὺς, (as having never seen them.) But some years had elapsed since the apostle had visited Ephesus, and seen the Ephesian Church; and might he not refer to reports of their Christian steadfastness which had reached him? Nay, his use of the word may signify that such intelligence had been repeatedly brought to him." — Eadie.

CHAPTER 2

Ephesians 2:1-3

1. And you *hath he quickened*, who were dead in trespasses and sins;

1. Et vos, quum essetis mortui delictis et peccatis vestris;

2. Wherein in time past ye walked according to the course of this world, according to the prince of the power of the air, the spirit that now worketh in the children of disobedience:

2. In quibus aliquando ambulastis secundum saeculum mundi hujus, secundum principem potestatis aeris, spiritus scilicet, qui nunc operatur in filiis inobedientiae;

3. Among whom also we all had our conversation in times past in the lusts of our flesh, fulfilling the desires of the flesh and of the mind; and were by nature the children of wrath, even as others.

3. Inter quos nos quoque omnes aliquando conversati sumus in concupiscentiis carnis nostrae, facientes quae carni libebant, et menti; et eramus natura filii irae, sicut et caeteri.

1. *And you who were dead.* This is an ἐπεξεργασία of the former statements, that is, an exposition accompanied by an illustration. [118] To bring home more effectually to the Ephesians the general doctrine of Divine grace, he reminds them of their former condition. This application consists of two parts. "Ye were formerly lost; but now God, by his grace, has rescued you from destruction." And here we must observe, that, in laboring to give an impressive view of both of these parts, the apostle makes a break in the style by (ὑπερβατὸν) a transposition. There is some perplexity in the language; but, if we attend carefully to what the apostle says about those two parts, the meaning is clear. As to the first, he says that they *were dead;* and states, at the same time, the cause of the death — *trespasses and sins.* [119] He does not mean simply that they were in danger of death; but he declares that it was a real and present death under which they labored. As spiritual death is nothing else than the alienation of the soul from God, we are all born as dead men, and we live as dead men, until we are made partakers of the life of Christ, — agreeably to the words of our Lord,

"The hour is coming, and now is, when the dead shall hear the voice of the Son of God, and they that hear shall live." (Joh 5:25)

The Papists, who are eager to seize every opportunity of undervaluing the grace of God, say, that while we are out of Christ, we are half dead. But we are not at liberty to set aside the declarations of our Lord and of the Apostle Paul, that, while we remain in Adam, we are entirely devoid of life; and that regeneration is a new life of the soul, by which it rises from the dead. Some kind of life, I acknowledge, does remain in us, while we are still at a distance from Christ; for unbelief does not altogether destroy the outward senses, or the will, or the other faculties of the soul. But what has this to do with the kingdom of God? What has it to do with a happy life, so long as every sentiment of the mind, and every act of the will, is death? Let this, then, be held as a fixed principle, that the union of our soul with God is the true and only life; and that out of Christ we are altogether dead, because sin, the cause of death, reigns in us.

2. *In which for some time ye walked.* From the effects or fruits, he draws a proof that sin formerly reigned in them; for, until sin displays itself in outward acts, men are not sufficiently aware of its power. When he adds, *according to the course of this world,* [120] he intimates that the death which he had mentioned rages in the nature of man, and is a universal disease. He does not mean that course of the world which God has ordained, nor the elements, such as the heaven, and earth, and air, — but the depravity with which we are all infected; so that sin is not peculiar to a few, but pervades the whole world.

According to the prince of the power of the air. He now proceeds farther, and explains the cause of our corruption to be the dominion which the devil exercises over us. A more severe condemnation of mankind could not have been pronounced. What does he leave to us, when he declares us to be the slaves of Satan, and subject to his will, so long as we live out of the kingdom of Christ? Our condition, therefore, though many treat it with ridicule, or, at least, with little disapprobation, may well excite our horror. Where is now the free-will, the guidance of reason, the moral virtue, about which Papists babble to much? What will they find that is pure or holy under the tyranny of the devil? On this subject, indeed, they are extremely cautious, and denounce this doctrine of Paul as a grievous heresy. I maintain, on the contrary, that there is no obscurity in the apostle's language; and that all men who live *according to the world,* that is, according to the inclinations of their flesh, are here declared to fight under the reign of Satan.

In accordance with the practice of the inspired writers, the Devil is mentioned in the singular number. As the children of God have one head, so have the wicked; for each of the classes forms a distinct body. By assigning to him the dominion over all wicked beings, ungodliness is represented as an unbroken mass. As to his attributing to the devil power over the air, that will be considered when we come to the sixth chapter. At present, we shall merely advert to the strange absurdity of the Manicheans, in endeavoring to prove from this passage the existence of two principles, as if Satan could do anything without the Divine permission. Paul does not allow him the highest authority, which belongs to the will of God alone, but merely a tyranny which God permits him to exercise. What is Satan but God's executioner to punish man's ingratitude? This is implied in Paul's language, when he represents the success of Satan as confined to unbelievers; for the children of God are thus exempted from his power. If this be true, it follows that Satan does nothing but under the control of a superior: and that he is not (αὐτοκϱάτωϱ) an unlimited monarch.

We may now draw from it also this inference, that ungodly men have no excuse in being driven by Satan to commit all sorts of crimes. Whence comes it that they are subject to his tyranny, but because they are rebels against God? If none are the slaves of Satan, but those who have renounced the service, and refuse to yield to the authority, of God, let them blame themselves, for having so cruel a master.

By *the children of disobedience,* according to a Hebrew idiom, are meant obstinate persons. Unbelief is always accompanied by disobedience; so that it is the source — the *mother* of all stubbornness.

3. *Among whom also we all had our conversation.* Lest it should be supposed that what he had now said was a slanderous reproach against the former character of the Ephesians, or that Jewish pride had led him to treat the Gentiles as an inferior race, he associates himself and his countrymen along with them in the general accusation. This is not done in hypocrisy, but in a sincere ascription of glory to God. It may excite wonder, indeed, that he should speak of himself as having walked "in the lusts of the flesh," while, on other occasions, he boasts that his life had been throughout irreproachable.

"Touching the righteousness which is in the law, blameless." (Php 3:6.)

And again,

"Ye are witnesses, and God also, how holily, and justly, and unblamably, we behaved ourselves among you that believe."

(1Th 2:10)

I reply, the statement applies to all who have not been regenerated by the Spirit of Christ. However praiseworthy, in appearance, the life of some may be, because their lusts do not break out in the sight of men, there is nothing pure or holy which does not proceed from the fountain of all purity.

Fulfilling the desires of the flesh and of the mind. To fulfill these desires, is to live according to the guidance of our natural disposition and of our mind. *The flesh* means here the disposition, or, what is called, the inclination of the nature; and the next expression (τῶν διανοιῶν) means what proceeds from the mind. Now, *the mind* includes reason, such as it exists in men by nature; so that *lusts* do not refer exclusively to the lower appetites, or what is called the sensual part of man, but extend to the whole.

And were by nature [121] *children of wrath.* All men without exception, whether Jews or Gentiles, (Gal. 2:15, 16,) are here pronounced to be guilty, until they are redeemed by Christ; so that out of Christ there is no righteousness, no salvation, and, in short, no excellence. *Children of wrath* are those who are lost, and who deserve eternal death. *Wrath* means the judgment of God; so that *the children of wrath* are those who are condemned before God. Such, the apostle tells us, had been the Jews, — such had been all the excellent men that were now in the Church; and they were so *by nature,* that is, from their very commencement, and from their mother's womb.

This is a remarkable passage, in opposition to the views of the Pelagians, and of all who deny original sin. What dwells naturally in all is certainly original; but Paul declares that we are all naturally liable to condemnation; therefore sin dwells naturally in us, for God does not condemn the innocent. Pelagians were wont to object, that sin spread from Adam to the whole human race, not by descent, but by imitation. But Paul affirms that we are born with sin, as serpents bring their venom from the womb. Others who think that it is not in reality sin, are not less at variance with Paul's language; for where condemnation is, there must unquestionably be sin. It is not with blameless men, but with sin, that God is offended. Nor is it wonderful that the depravity which we inherit from our parents is reckoned as sin before God; for the seeds of sin, before they have been openly displayed, are perceived and condemned.

But one question here arises. Why does Paul represent the Jews, equally with others, as subject to wrath and curse, while they were the blessed seed? I answer, they have a common nature. Jews differ from Gentiles in nothing but this, that, through the grace of the promise, God delivers them from destruction; but that is a remedy which came after the disease. Another question is, since God is the Author of nature, how comes it that no blame attaches to God, if we are lost by nature? I answer, there is a twofold nature: the one was produced by God, and the other is the corruption of it. This condemnation therefore which Paul mentions does not proceed from God, but from a depraved nature: for we are not born such as Adam was at first created, we are not

"wholly a right seed, but are turned into the degenerate"

(Jer 2:21)

offspring of a degenerate and sinful man.

Ephesians 2:4-7

4. But God, who is rich in mercy, for his great love wherewith he loved us,

4. Deus autem, qui dives est in misericordia, propter multam suam dilectionem, qua nos dilexit,

5. Even when we were dead in sins, hath quickened us together with Christ; (by grace ye are saved;)

5. Etiam quum essemus mortui peccatis, convivificavit cum Christo; (Gratia estis salvati;)

6. And hath raised *us* up together, and made *us* sit together in heavenly places in Christ Jesus;

6. Et simul excitavit, et sedere fecit in coelestibus in Christo Iesu,

7. That in the ages to come he might shew the exceeding riches of his grace, in *his* kindness toward us through Christ Jesus.

7. Ut demonstraret in saeculis supervenientibus exsuperantes divitias gratiae suae, in benignitate erga nos in Christo Iesu.

4. *But God, who is rich in mercy.* [122] Now follows the second member of the sentence, the substance of which is, that God had delivered the Ephesians from the destruction to which they were formerly liable; but the words which he employs are different. *God, who is rich in mercy, hath quickened you together with Christ.* The meaning is, that, there is no other life than that which is breathed into us by Christ: so that we begin to live only when we are ingrafted into him, and enjoy the same life with himself. This enables us to see what the apostle formerly meant by death, for that death and this resurrection are brought into contrast. To be made partakers of the life of the Son of God, — to be quickened by one Spirit, is an inestimable privilege.

On this ground he praises the *mercy* of God, meaning by its *riches,* that it had been poured out in a singularly large and abundant manner. The whole of our salvation is here ascribed to the mercy of God. But he presently adds, *for his great love wherewith he loved us.* [123] This is a still more express declaration, that all was owing to undeserved goodness; for he declares that God was moved by this single consideration. "Herein," says John, "is love, not that we loved God, but that he loved us. — We love him because he first loved us." (1 John 4:10, 19.)

5. *Even when we were dead in sin.* These words have the same emphasis as similar expressions in another Epistle.

"For *when we were yet without strength,* in due time Christ died, for the ungodly. — But God commendeth his love toward us, in that, *while we were yet sinners,* Christ died for us."

(Rom. 5:6, 8.)

Whether the words, *by grace ye are saved,* have been inserted by another hand, I know not; but, as they are perfectly agreeable to the context, I am quite willing to receive them as written by Paul. They show us that he always feels as if he had not sufficiently proclaimed the riches of Divine grace, and accordingly expresses, by a variety of terms, the same truth, that everything connected with our salvation ought to be ascribed to God as its author. And certainly he who duly weighs the ingratitude of men will not complain that this parenthesis is superfluous.

6. *And hath raised us up together.* The resurrection and sitting in heaven, which are here mentioned, are not yet seen by mortal eyes. Yet, as if those blessings were presently in our possession, he states that we have received them; and illustrates the change which has taken place in our condition, when we were led from Adam to Christ. It is as if we had been brought from the deepest hell to heaven itself. And certainly, although, as respects ourselves, our salvation is still the object of hope, yet in Christ we already possess a blessed immortality and glory; and therefore, he adds, *in Christ Jesus.* Hitherto it does not appear in the members, but only in the head; yet, in consequence of the secret union, it belongs truly to the members. Some render it, *through Christ;* but, for the reason which has been mentioned, it is better to retain the usual rendering, *in Christ.* We are thus furnished with the richest consolation. Of everything which we now want, we have a sure pledge and foretaste in the person of Christ.

7. *That in the ages to come.* The final and true cause — the glory of God — is again mentioned, that the Ephesians, by making it the subject of earnest study, might be more fully assured of their salvation. He likewise adds, that it was the design of God to hallow, in all ages, the remembrance of so great goodness. This exhibits still more strongly the hateful character of those by whom the free calling of the Gentiles was attacked; for they were endeavoring instantly to crush that scheme which was destined to be remembered through all ages. But we, too, are instructed by it, that the mercy of God, who was pleased to admit our fathers into the number of his own people, deserves to be held in everlasting remembrance. The calling of the Gentiles is an astonishing work of divine goodness, which ought to be handed down by parents to children, and to their children's children, that it may never be forgotten or unacknowledged by the sons of men.

The riches of his grace in his kindness. The love of God to us in Christ is here proved, or again declared, to have had its origin in mercy. *That he might shew,* says he, *the exceeding riches of his grace.* How? *In his kindness towards us,* as the tree is known by its fruit. Not only, therefore, does he declare, that the love of God was free, but likewise that God displayed in it the riches, — the extraordinary pre-eminent riches of his grace. It deserves notice, also, that the name of *Christ* is repeated; for no grace, no love, must be expected by us from God, except through his mediation.

Ephesians 2:8-10

8. For by grace are ye saved through faith; and that not of yourselves: *it is* the gift of God:

8. Gratia enim estis salvati per fidem; idque non ex vobis: Dei donum est.

9. Not of works, lest any man should boast.

9. Non ex operibus; ne quis glorietur.

10. For we are his workmanship, created in Christ Jesus unto good works, which God hath before ordained that we should walk in them.

10. Ipsius enim opus sumus, creati in Christo Iesu ad opera bona, quae praeparavit Deus, ut in illis ambulemus.

8. *For by grace are ye saved.* This is an inference from the former statements. Having treated of election and of effectual calling, he arrives at this general conclusion, that they had obtained salvation by faith alone. First, he asserts, that the salvation of the Ephesians was entirely the work, the gracious work of God. But then they had obtained this grace by faith. On one side, we must look at God; and, on the other, at man. God declares, that he owes us nothing; so that salvation is not a reward or recompense, but unmixed grace. The next question is, in what way do men receive that salvation which is offered to them by the hand of God? The answer is, *by faith;* and hence he concludes that nothing connected with it is our own. If, on the part of God, it is grace alone, and if we bring nothing but faith, which strips us of all commendation, it follows that salvation does not come from us.

Ought we not then to be silent about free-will, and good intentions, and fancied preparations, and merits, and satisfactions? There is none of these which does not claim a share of praise in the salvation of men; so that the praise of grace would not, as Paul shews, remain undiminished. When, on the part of man, the act of receiving salvation is made to consist in faith alone, all other means, on which men are accustomed to rely, are discarded. Faith, then, brings a man empty to God, that he may be filled with the blessings of Christ. And so he adds, *not of yourselves;* that claiming nothing for themselves, they may acknowledge God alone as the author of their salvation.

9. *Not of works.* Instead of what he had said, that their salvation is of grace, he now affirms, that "it is the gift of God." [124] Instead of what he had said, "Not of yourselves," he now says, "Not of works." Hence we see, that the apostle leaves nothing to men in procuring salvation. In these three phrases, — *not of yourselves,* — *it is the gift of God,* — *not of works,* — he embraces the substance of his long argument in the Epistles to the Romans and to the Galatians, that righteousness comes to us from the mercy of God alone, — is offered to us in Christ by the gospel, — and is received by faith alone, without the merit of works.

This passage affords an easy refutation of the idle cavil by which Papists attempt to evade the argument, that we are justified without works. Paul, they tell us, is speaking about ceremonies. But the present question is not confined to one class of works. Nothing can be more clear than this. The whole righteousness of man, which consists in works, — nay, the whole man, and everything that he can call his own, is set aside. We must attend to the contrast between God and man, —

between grace and works. Why should God be contrasted with man, if the controversy related to nothing more than ceremonies?

Papists themselves are compelled to own that Paul ascribes to the grace of God the whole glory of our salvation, but endeavor to do away with this admission by another contrivance. This mode of expression, they tell us, is employed, because God bestows the first grace. It is really foolish to imagine that they can succeed in this way, since Paul excludes man and his utmost ability, — not only from the commencement, but throughout, — from the whole work of obtaining salvation.

But it is still more absurd to overlook the apostle's inference, *lest any man should boast.* Some room must always remain for man's boasting, so long as, independently of grace, merits are of any avail. Paul's doctrine is overthrown, unless the whole praise is rendered to God alone and to his mercy. And here we must advert to a very common error in the interpretation of this passage. Many persons restrict the word *gift* to faith alone. But Paul is only repeating in other words the former sentiment. His meaning is, not that faith is the gift of God, but that salvation is given to us by God, or, that we obtain it by the gift of God.

10. *For we are his work.* By setting aside the contrary supposition, he proves his statement, that *by grace we are saved,* — that we have no remaining works by which we can merit salvation; for all the good works which we possess are the fruit of regeneration. Hence it follows, that works themselves are a part of grace.

When he says, that "we are the work of God," this does not refer to ordinary creation, by which we are made men. We are declared to be new creatures, because, not by our own power, but by the Spirit of Christ, we have been formed to righteousness. This applies to none but believers. As the descendants of Adam, they were wicked and depraved; but by the grace of Christ, they are spiritually renewed, and become new men. Everything in us, therefore, that is good, is the supernatural gift of God. The context explains his meaning. *We are his work,* because we have been *created,* — not in Adam, but *in Christ Jesus,* — not to every kind of life, but to *good works.*

What remains now for free-will, if all the good works which proceed from us are acknowledged to have been the gifts of the Spirit of God? Let godly readers weigh carefully the apostle's words. He does not say that we are assisted by God. He does not say that the will is prepared, and is then left to run by its own strength. He does not say that the power of choosing aright is bestowed upon us, and that we are afterwards left to make our own choice. Such is the idle talk in which those persons who do their utmost to undervalue the grace of God are accustomed to indulge. But the apostle affirms that we are God's work, and that everything good in us is his creation; by which he means that the whole man is formed by his hand to be good. It is not the mere power of choosing aright, or some indescribable kind of preparation, or even assistance, but the right will itself, which is his workmanship; otherwise Paul's argument would have no force. He means to prove that man does not in any way procure salvation for himself, but obtains it as a free gift from God. The proof is, that man is nothing but by divine grace. Whoever, then, makes the very smallest claim for man, apart from the grace of God, allows him, to that extent, ability to procure salvation.

Created to good works. They err widely from Paul's intention, who torture this passage for the purpose of injuring the righteousness of faith. Ashamed to affirm in plain terms, and aware that they could gain nothing by affirming, that we are not justified by faith, they shelter themselves under this kind of subterfuge. "We are justified by faith, because faith, by which we receive the grace of God, is the commencement of righteousness; but we are made righteous by regeneration, because, being renewed by the Spirit of God, we walk in good works." In this manner they make faith the door by which we enter into righteousness, but imagine that we obtain it by our works, or, at least, they define righteousness to be that uprightness by which a man is formed anew to a holy life. I care not how old this error may be; but they err egregiously who endeavor to support it by this passage.

We must look to Paul's design. He intends to shew that we have brought nothing to God, by which he might be laid under obligations to us; and he shews that even the good works which we perform have come from God. Hence it follows, that we are nothing, except through the pure exercise of his kindness. Those men, on the other hand, infer that the half of our justification arises from works. But what has this to do with Paul's intention, or with the subject which he handles? It is one thing to inquire in what righteousness consists, and another thing to follow up the doctrine, that it is not from ourselves, by this argument, that we have no right to claim good works as our own, but have been formed by the Spirit of God, through the grace of Christ, to all that is good. When Paul lays down the cause of justification, he dwells chiefly on this point, that our consciences will never enjoy peace till they rely on the propitiation for sins. Nothing of this sort is even alluded to in the present instance. His whole object is to prove, that,

"by the grace of God, we are all that we are."

(1Co 15:10)

Which God hath prepared Beware of applying this, as the Pelagians do, to the instruction of the law; as if Paul's meaning were, that God commands what is just, and lays down a proper rule of life. Instead of this, he follows up the doctrine which he had begun to illustrate, that salvation does not proceed from ourselves. He says, that, before we were born, the good works were prepared by God; meaning, that in our own strength we are not able to lead a holy life, but only so far as we are formed and adapted by the hand of God. Now, if the grace of God came before our performances, all ground of boasting has been taken away. Let us carefully observe the word *prepared.* On the simple ground of the order of events, Paul rests the proof that, with respect to good works, God owes us nothing. How so? Because they were drawn out of his treasures, in which they had long before been laid up; for whom he called, them he justifies and regenerates.

Ephesians 2:11-13

11. Wherefore remember, that ye *being* in time past Gentiles in the flesh, who are called Uncircumcision by that which is called the Circumcision in the flesh made by hands;

11. Quamobrem memores estote, quod aliquando vos Gentes in carne, qui dicebamini Praeputium ab ea, quae vocatur Circumcisio, in carne manu facta;

12. That at that time ye were without Christ, being aliens from the commonwealth of Israel, and strangers from the covenants of promise, having no hope, and without God in the world:

12. Illo tempore eratis absque Christo, alienati a republica Israelis, hospites tabularum promissionis, spem non habentes, et sine Deo in mundo.

13. But now, in Christ Jesus, ye who sometimes were far off are made nigh by the blood of Christ.

13. Nunc autem in Christo Iesu vos, qui quondam eratis procul, facti estis propinqui per Christi sanguinem.

11. *Wherefore remember.* The apostle never once loses sight of his subject, marks it out clearly, and pursues it with increasing earnestness. He again exhorts the Ephesians to remember what their character had been before they were called. This consideration was fitted to convince them that they had no reason to be proud. He afterwards points out the method of reconciliation, that they might rest with perfect satisfaction on Christ alone, and not imagine that other aids were necessary. The first clause may be thus summed up: "Remember that, when ye were uncircumcised, ye were aliens from Christ, from the hope of salvation, and from the Church and kingdom of God; so that ye had no friendly intercourse with God." The second may run thus: "But now ingrafted into Christ, ye are at the same time reconciled to God." What is implied in both parts of the description, and what effect the remembrance of it was fitted to produce on their minds, has been already considered.

Gentiles in the flesh. He first mentions that they had wanted the marks of God's people. *Circumcision* was a token by which the people of God were marked out and distinguished from other men: *Uncircumcision* was the mark of a profane person. Since, therefore, God usually connects his grace with the sacraments, their want of the sacraments is taken as an evidence that neither were they partakers of his grace. The argument, indeed, does not hold universally, though it does hold as to God's ordinary dispensations. Hence we find the following language:

"And the Lord God said, Behold, the man is become as one of us, to know good and evil: and now, lest he put forth his hand, and take also of the tree of life, and eat, and live for ever: therefore the Lord God sent him forth from the garden of Eden, to till the ground from whence he was taken. So he drove out the man." (Gen. 3:22, 23)

Though he had devoured the whole tree, he would not, by merely eating it, have recovered the possession of life; but, by taking away the sign, the Lord took from him also life itself. Uncircumcision is thus held out to the Ephesians as a mark of pollution. By taking from the Ephesians the token of sanctification, he deprives them also of the thing signified.

Some are of opinion, that all these observations are intended to throw contempt on outward circumcision; but this is a mistake. At the same time, I acknowledge, that the qualifying clause, *the Circumcision in the flesh made by hands,* points out a twofold circumcision. The Jews were thus taught that they should no longer indulge in foolish boasting about the literal circumcision. The Ephesians, on the other hand, were instructed to abstain from all scruples on their own account, since the most important privilege—nay, the whole truth expressed by the outward sign—was in their possession. He calls it, *Uncircumcision in the flesh,* because they bore the mark of their pollution; but, at the same time, he suggests that their uncircumcision was no hinderance to their being spiritually circumcised by Christ.

The words may likewise be read in one clause, *Circumcision in the flesh made by hands,* or in two clauses: *Circumcision in the flesh,* meaning that it was carnal; *made by hands,* meaning that it was done by the hand of man. This kind of circumcision is contrasted with that of the Spirit, or *of the heart,* (Ro 2:29,) which is also called *the circumcision of Christ.* (Col 2:11)

By that which is called. Circumcision may be viewed here either as a collective noun for the Jews themselves, or literally for the thing itself; and then the meaning would be, that the Gentiles were called *Uncircumcision,* because they wanted the sacred symbol, that is, by way of distinction. This latter sense is countenanced by the qualifying phrase; but the substance of the argument is little affected.

12. *That at that time ye were without Christ.* He now declares that the Ephesians had been excluded, not only from the outward badge, but from everything necessary to the salvation and happiness of men. As Christ is the foundation of hope and of all the promises, he mentions, first of all, that they *were without Christ.* But for him that is without Christ, there remains nothing but destruction. On Him *the commonwealth of Israel* was founded; and in whom, but in Himself, could the people of God be collected into one holy society?

A similar observation might be made as to *the tables of the promise* On one great promise made to Abraham all the others hang, and without it they lose all their value:

"In thy seed shall all the nations of the earth be blessed."

(Ge 22:18.)

Hence our apostle says elsewhere,

"All the promises of God in him are yea, and in him Amen."

(2Co 1:20.)

Take away the covenant of salvation, and there remains no hope. I have translated τῶν διαθηκῶν by *the tables,* or, in ordinary legal phrase, the *instruments.* By solemn ritual did God sanction His covenant with Abraham and his posterity, that he would be their God for ever and ever. (Ge 15:9.) *Tables* of this covenant were ratified by the hand of Moses, and intrusted, as a peculiar treasure, to the people of Israel, to whom, and not to the Gentiles, "pertain the covenants." (Ro 9:4.)

And without God in the world. But at no period were the Ephesians, or any other Gentiles, destitute of all religion. Why, then, are they styled (ἄθεοι) *Atheists?* for (ἄθεος) an *Atheist,* strictly speaking, is one who does not believe, and who absolutely ridicules, the being of a God. That appellation, certainly, is not usually given to superstitious persons, but to those who have no feeling of religion, and who desire to see it utterly destroyed. I answer, Paul was right in giving them this name, for he treated all the notions entertained respecting false gods as nothing; and with the utmost propriety do godly persons regard all idols as "nothing in the world." (1Co 8:4.) Those who do not worship the true God, whatever may be the variety of their worship, or the multitude of laborious ceremonies which they perform, are without God: they adore what they know not. (Ac 17:23.) Let it be carefully observed, that the Ephesians are not charged with (ἀθεϊσμὸς) *Atheism,* in the same degree as Diagoras, and others of the same stamp, who were subjected to that reproach. Persons who imagined themselves to be very religious are charged with that crime; for an idol is a forgery, an imposition, not a Divinity.

From what has been said, the conclusion will be easily drawn, that out of Christ there are none but idols. Those who were formerly declared to be *without Christ,* are now declared to be *without God;* [125] as John says,

"Whosoever hath not the Son, hath not the Father," (1Jo 2:23;)

and again,

"Whosoever transgresseth, and abideth not in the doctrine of Christ, hath not God."

(2Jo 1:9.)

Let us know, therefore, that all who do not keep this way wander from the true God. We shall next be asked, Did God never reveal himself to any of the Gentiles? I answer, no manifestation of God without Christ was ever made among the Gentiles, any more than among the Jews. It is not to one age only, or to one nation, that the saying of our Lord applies,

"I am the way;" for he adds, "no man cometh
unto the Father but by me." (Joh 14:6.)

13. *But now in Christ Jesus.* We must either supply the verb, *now that ye have been received in Christ Jesus,* or connect the word *now* with the conclusion of the verse, *now through the blood of Christ,* — which will be a still clearer exposition. In either case, the meaning is, that the Ephesians, *who were far off* from God and from salvation, had been reconciled to God through Christ, and *made nigh by his blood;* for the blood of Christ has taken away *the enmity* which existed between them and God, and from being enemies hath made them sons.

Ephesians 2:14-16

14. For he is our peace, who hath made both one, and hath broken down the middle wall of partition *between us*;

14. Ipse enim est pax nostra, qui fecit utraque unum, et interstitium maceriae solvens, inimicitias in carne sua;

15. Having abolished in his flesh the enmity, *even* the law of commandments *contained* in ordinances; for to make in himself of twain one new man, *so* making peace;

15. Legem mandatorum in decretis positam abolens, ut duos conderet in se ipso, in unum novum hominem, faciens pacem;

16. And that he might reconcile both unto God in one body by the cross, having slain the enmity thereby.

16. Ut reconciliaret ambos in uno corpore Deo per crucem, inimicitias in ipsa interimens.

14. *For he is our peace.* He now includes Jews in the privilege of reconciliation, and shows that, through one Messiah, all are united to God. This consideration was fitted to repress the false confidence of the Jews, who, despising the grace of Christ, boasted that they were the holy people, and chosen inheritance, of God. If Christ *is our peace,* all who are out of him must be at variance with God. What a beautiful title is this which Christ possesses, — the peace between God and men! Let no one who dwells in Christ entertain a doubt that he is reconciled to God.

Who hath made both one. This distinction was necessary. [126] All intercourse with the Gentiles was held to be inconsistent with their own superior claims. [127] To subdue this pride, he tells them that they and the Gentiles have been united into one body. Put all these things together, and you will frame the following syllogism: If the Jews wish to enjoy peace with God, they must have Christ as their Mediator. But Christ will not be their peace in any other way than by making them one body with the Gentiles. Therefore, unless the Jews admit the Gentiles to fellowship with them, they have no friendship with God.

And breaking down the middle wall of partition. To understand this passage, two things must be observed. The Jews were separated, for a certain time, from the Gentiles, by the appointment of God; and ceremonial observances were the open and avowed symbols of that separation. Passing by the Gentiles, God had chosen the Jews to be a peculiar people to himself. A wide distinction was thus made, when the one class were "fellow-citizens and of the household" (Eph 2:19) of the Church, and the other were foreigners. This is stated in the Song of Moses:

"When the Most High divided to the nations their inheritance, when he separated the sons of Adam, he set the bounds of the people according to the number of the children of Israel: for the Lord's portion is his people, Jacob is the lot of his inheritance." (Deut. 32:8, 9)

Bounds were thus fixed by God to separate one people from the rest; and hence arose *the enmity* which is here mentioned. A separation is thus made. The Gentiles are set aside. God is pleased to choose and sanctify the Jewish people, by freeing them from the ordinary pollution of mankind. Ceremonial observances were afterwards added, which, like walls, enclosed the inheritance of God, prevented it from being open to all or mixed with other possessions, and thus excluded the Gentiles from the kingdom of God.

But now, the apostle, says, the *enmity* is removed, and the wall is broken down. By extending the privilege of adoption beyond the limits of Judea, Christ has now made us all to be brethren. And so is fulfilled the prophecy,

"God shall enlarge Japheth,
and he shall dwell in the tents of Shem." (Ge 9:27)

15. *Having abolished in his flesh the enmity.* The meaning of Paul's words is now clear. *The middle wall of partition* hindered Christ from forming Jews and Gentiles into one body, and therefore the wall has been *broken down.* The reason why it is broken down is now added — *to abolish the enmity,* by the flesh of Christ. The Son of God, by assuming a nature common to all, has formed in his own body a perfect unity.

Even the law of commandments contained in ordinances. What had been metaphorically understood by the word *wall* is now more plainly expressed. The ceremonies, by which the distinction was declared, have been abolished through Christ. What were circumcision, sacrifices, washings, and abstaining from certain kinds of food, but symbols of sanctification, reminding the Jews that their lot was different from that of other nations; just as the white and the red cross distinguish the French of the present day from the inhabitants of Burgundy. Paul declares not only that the Gentiles are equally with the Jews admitted to the fellowship of grace, so that they no longer differ from each other, but that the mark of difference has been taken away; for ceremonies have been abolished. If two contending nations were brought under the dominion of one prince, he would not only desire that they should live in harmony, but would remove the badges and marks of their former enmity. When an obligation is discharged, the *handwriting* is destroyed, — a metaphor which Paul employs on this very subject in another Epistle. [128] (Col 2:14.)

Some interpreters, [129] — though, in my opinion, erroneously, — connect the words, *in ordinances,* with *abolished,* making the *ordinances* to be the act of abolishing the ceremonies. This is Paul's ordinary phrase for describing the ceremonial law, in which the Lord not only enjoined upon the Jews a simple rule of life, but also bound them by various statutes. It is evident, too, that Paul is here treating exclusively of the ceremonial law; for the moral law is not a wall of partition separating us from the Jews, but lays down instructions in which the Jews were not less deeply concerned than ourselves. This passage affords the means of refuting an erroneous view held by some, that circumcision and all the ancient rites, though they are not binding on the Gentiles, are in force at the present day upon the Jews. On this principle there would still be a middle wall of partition between us, which is proved to be false.

That he might make in himself. When the apostle says, *in himself,* he turns away the Ephesians from viewing the diversity of men, and bids them look for unity nowhere but in Christ. To whatever extent the two might differ in their former condition, in Christ they are become one man. But he emphatically adds, *one new man,* intimating (what he explains at greater length on another occasion) that

"neither circumcision, nor uncircumcision, availeth anything," (Ga 6:15,)

but that "a new creature" holds the first and the last place. The principle which cements them is spiritual regeneration. If then we are all renewed by Christ, let the Jews no longer congratulate themselves on their ancient condition, but let them be ready to admit that, both in themselves and in others, Christ is all.

16. *And that he might reconcile both.* The reconciliation between ourselves which has now been described is not the only advantage which we derive from Christ. We have been brought back into favor with God. The Jews are thus led to consider that they have not less need of a Mediator than the Gentiles. Without this, neither the Law, nor ceremonies, nor their descent from Abraham, nor all their dazzling prerogatives, would be of any avail. We are all sinners; and forgiveness of sins cannot be obtained but through the grace of Christ. He adds, *in one body,* to inform the Jews, that to cultivate union with the Gentiles will be well-pleasing in the sight of God.

By the cross. The word *cross* is added, to point out the propitiatory sacrifice. Sin is the cause of enmity between God and us; and, until it is removed, we shall not be restored to the Divine favor. It has been blotted out by the death of Christ, in which he offered himself to the Father as an expiatory victim. There is another reason, indeed, why the cross is mentioned here, as it is through the cross that all ceremonies have been abolished. Accordingly, he adds, *slaying the enmity thereby.* These words, which unquestionably relate to the cross, may admit of two senses, — either that Christ, by his death, has turned away from us the Father's anger, or that, having redeemed both Jews and Gentiles, he has brought them back into one flock. The latter appears to be the more probable interpretation, as it agrees with a former clause, *abolishing in his flesh the enmity.* (Eph 2:15.)

17. And came and preached peace to you which were afar off, and to them that were nigh.

17. Et veniens evangelizavit pacem vobis, qui eratis procul, et pacem iis qui propinqui erant;

18. For through him we both have access by one Spirit unto the Father.

18. Quoniam per ipsum habemus accessum ambo in uno spiritu ad Patrem.

19. Now therefore ye are no more strangers and foreigners, but fellow-citizens with the saints, and of the household of God;

19. Ergo non amplius estis hospites et inquilini; sed cives sanctorum et domestici Dei,

20. And are built upon the foundation of the apostles and prophets, Jesus Christ himself being the chief corner-*stone*;

20. Superaedificati fundamento Apostolorum et Prophetarum, cujus lapis summus angularis est ipse Christus;

21. In whom all the building, fitly framed together, groweth unto an holy temple in the Lord:

21. In quo totum aedificium coagmentatum crescit in templum sanctum in Domino;

22. In whom ye also are builded together for an habitation of God through the Spirit.

22. In quo et vos coaedificamini in habitaculum Dei in Spiritu.

17. *And came and preached peace.* All that Christ had done towards effecting a reconciliation would have been of no service, if it had not been proclaimed by the gospel; and therefore he adds, that the fruit of this peace has now been offered both to Jews and to Gentiles. Hence it follows, that to save Gentiles as well as Jews was the design of our Savior's coming, as the preaching of the gospel, which is addressed indiscriminately to both, makes abundantly manifest. The same order is followed in the second Epistle to the Corinthians.

"He hath committed to us the word of reconciliation. Now, then, we are ambassadors for Christ. For he hath made him to be sin for us who knew no sin." (2Co 5:18-21.)

Salvation through the death of Christ is first announced, and a description is afterwards given of the manner in which Christ communicates to us himself and the benefit of his death. But here Paul dwells chiefly on this circumstance, that Gentiles are united with Jews in the Kingdom of God. Having already represented Christ as a Savior common to both, he now speaks of them as companions in the gospel. The Jews, though they possessed the law, needed the gospel also; and God had bestowed upon the Gentiles equal grace. Those therefore whom

"God hath joined together, let no man put asunder."

(Mt 19:6.)

No reference to distance of place is conveyed by the words *afar off* and *nigh*. The Jews, in respect of the covenant, were *nigh* to God. The Gentiles, so long as they had no promise of salvation, were *afar off*— were banished from the kingdom of God.

And preached peace; not indeed by his own lips, but by the apostles. It was necessary that Christ should rise from the dead, before the Gentiles were called to the fellowship of grace. Hence that saying of our Lord,

"I am not sent but to the lost sheep of the house of Israel."

(Mt 15:24.)

The apostles were forbidden, while he was still in the world, to carry their first embassy to the Gentiles

"Go not into the way of the Gentiles, and into any city of the Samaritans, enter ye not. But go rather to the lost sheep of the house of Israel." (Matt. 10:5, 6,)

His apostles were afterwards employed as trumpets for proclaiming the gospel to the Gentiles. What they did, not only in his name, and by his command, but as it were in his own person, is justly ascribed to none other than himself. We too speak as if Christ himself exhorted you by us. (2Co 5:20) The faith of the gospel would be weak indeed, were we to look no higher than to men. Its whole authority is derived from viewing men as God's instruments, and hearing Christ speak to us by their mouth. Observe here, the gospel is the message of *peace,* by which God declares himself to be reconciled to us, and makes known his paternal love. Take away the gospel, and war and enmity continue to subsist between God and men; and, on the other hand, the native tendency of the gospel is, to give peace and calmness to the conscience, which would otherwise be tormented by distressing alarm.

18. *For through him we both have access.* This is an argument from the fact, that we are permitted to draw near to God. But it may be viewed also as an announcement of peace; for wicked men, lulled into a profound sleep, sometimes deceive themselves by false notions of peace, but are never at rest, except when they have learned to forget the Divine judgment, and to keep themselves at the greatest possible distance from God. It was necessary, therefore, to explain the true nature of evangelical peace, which is widely different from a stupefied conscience, from false confidence, from proud boasting, from ignorance of our own wretchedness. It is a settled composure, which leads us not to dread, but to desire and seek, the face of God. Now, it is Christ who opens the door to us, yea, who is himself *the door.* (Joh 10:9.) As this is a double door thrown open for the admission both of Jews and Gentiles, we are led to view God as exhibiting to both his fatherly kindness. He adds, *by one Spirit;* who leads and guides us to Christ, and "by whom we cry, Abba, Father," (Ro 8:15,) for hence arises the boldness of approach. Jews had various means of drawing near to God; now all have but one way, to be led by the Spirit of God.

19. *Now therefore ye are no more strangers.* The Ephesians are now exclusively addressed. They were formerly *strangers from the covenants of promise,* but their condition was now changed. They were *foreigners,* but God had made them *citizens* of his church. The high value of that honor which God had been pleased to bestow upon them, is expressed in a variety of language. They are first called *fellow-citizens with the saints,* — next, *of the household of God,* — and lastly, stones properly fitted into the building of the temple of the Lord. The first appellation is taken from the comparison of the church to a state, which occurs very frequently in Scripture. Those who were formerly profane, and utterly unworthy to associate with godly persons, have been raised to distinguished honor in being admitted to be members of the same community with Abraham, — with all the holy patriarchs, and prophets, and kings, — nay, with the angels themselves. To be *of the household of God,* which is the second comparison, suggests equally exalted views of their present condition. God has admitted them into his own family; for the church is God's house.

20. *And are built.* The third comparison illustrates the manner in which the Ephesians, and all other Christians are admitted to the honor of being *fellow-citizens with the saints and of the household of God.* They are *built on the foundation,* — they are founded on the doctrine, *of the apostles and prophets.* We are thus enabled to distinguish between a true and a false church. This is of the greatest importance; for the tendency to error is always strong, and the consequences of mistake are dangerous in the extreme. No churches boast more loudly of the name than those which bear a false and empty title; as may be seen in our own times. To guard us against mistake, the mark of a true church is pointed out.

Foundation, in this passage, unquestionably means doctrine; for no mention is made of patriarchs or pious kings, but only of those who held the office of teachers, and whom God had appointed to superintend the edification of his church. It is laid down by Paul, that the faith of the church ought to be founded on this doctrine. What opinion, then, must we form of those who rest entirely on the contrivances of men, and yet accuse us of revolt, because we embrace the pure doctrine of God? But the manner in which it is founded deserves inquiry; for, in the strict sense of the term, Christ is the only foundation. He alone supports the whole church. He alone is the rule and standard of faith. But Christ is actually the foundation on which the church is built by the preaching of doctrine; and, on this account, the prophets and apostles are called builders. (1Co 3:10.) Nothing else, Paul tells us, was ever intended by the prophets and apostles, than to found a church on Christ.

We shall find this to be true, if we begin with Moses; for "Christ is the end of the law," (Ro 10:4,) and the sum of the gospel. Let us remember, therefore, that if we wish to be reckoned among believers, we must place our reliance on no other: if we wish to make sure progress in the knowledge of the Scriptures, to him our whole attention must be directed. The same lesson is taught, when we consult the word of God as contained in the writings of the prophets and apostles. To shew us how we ought to combine them, their harmony is pointed out; for they have a common foundation, and labor jointly in building the temple of God. Though the apostles have become our teachers, the instruction of the prophets has not been rendered superfluous; but one and the same object is promoted by both.

I have been led to make this remark by the conduct of the Marcionites in ancient times, who expunged the word *prophets* from this passage; and by that of certain fanatics in the present day, who, following their footsteps, exclaim loudly that we have nothing to do with the law and the prophets, because the gospel has put an end to their authority. The Holy Spirit everywhere declares, that he has spoken to us by the mouth of the prophets, and demands that we shall listen to him in their writings. This is of no small consequence for maintaining the authority of our faith. All the servants of God, from first to last, are so perfectly agreed, that their harmony is in itself a clear demonstration that it is one God who speaks in them all. The commencement of our religion must be traced to the creation of the world. In vain do Papists, Mahometans, and other sects, boast of their antiquity, while they are mere counterfeits of the true, the pure religion.

Jesus Christ, himself is the chief corner-stone [130] Those who transfer this honor to Peter, and maintain that on him the church is founded, are so void of shame, as to attempt to justify their error by quoting this passage. They hold out that Christ is called *the chief corner-stone,* by comparison with others; and that there are many stones on which the church is founded. But this difficulty is easily solved. Various metaphors are employed by the apostles according to the diversity of circumstances, but still with the same meaning. In writing to the Corinthians, Paul lays down an incontestable proposition, that "no other foundation can be laid." (1Co 3:11.) He does not therefore mean, that Christ is merely a corner, or a part of the foundation; for then he would contradict himself. What then? He means that Jews and Gentiles were two separate walls, but are formed into one spiritual building. Christ is placed in the middle of the corner for the purpose of uniting both, and this is the force of the metaphor. What is immediately added shews sufficiently that he is very far from limiting Christ to any one part of the building.

21. *In whom all the building groweth.* If this be true, what will become of Peter? When Paul, in writing to the Corinthians, speaks of Christ as a "Foundation," he does not mean that the church is begun by him and completed by others, but draws a distinction arising out of a comparison of his own labors with those of other men. It had been his duty to found the church at Corinth, and to leave to his successors the completion of the building.

"According to the grace of God which is given to me, as a wise master-builder, I have laid the foundation, and another buildeth on it." (1Co 3:10.)

With respect to the present passage, he conveys the instruction, that all who are *fitly framed together in Christ* are the temple of the Lord. There is first required a fitting together, that believers may embrace and accommodate themselves to each other by mutual intercourse; otherwise there would not be a building, but a confused mass. The chief part of the symmetry consists in unity of faith. Next follows progress, or increase. Those who are not united in faith and love, so as to *grow in the Lord,* belong to a profane building, which has nothing in common with the temple of the Lord.

Groweth unto an holy temple. Individual believers are at other times called "temples of the Holy Ghost," (1Co 6:19; 2Co 6:16,) but here all are said to constitute one temple. In both cases the metaphor is just and appropriate. When God dwells in each of us, it is his will that we should embrace all in holy unity, and that thus he should form one temple out of many. Each person, when viewed separately, is a temple, but, when joined to others, becomes a stone of a temple; and this view is given for the sake of recommending the unity of the church.

22. *In whom ye also are builded together,* or *in whom also* Be Ye Builded *together.* The termination of the Greek verb, συνοικοδομεῖσθε, like that of the Latin, *cooedificamini,* does not enable us to determine whether it is in the imperative or indicative mood. The context will admit either, but I prefer the latter sense. It is, I think, an exhortation to the Ephesians to grow more and more in the faith of Christ, after having been once founded in it, and thus to form a part of that new temple of God, the building of which through the gospel was then in progress in every part of the world.

Through the Spirit. This is again repeated for two reasons: first, to remind them that all human exertions are of no avail without the operation of the Spirit; and secondly, to point out the superiority of the spiritual building to all Jewish and outward services.

Footnotes

118
"Il expose et esclarcit ce qu'il avoit dit ci-dessus." "He explains and illustrates what he had formerly said."
119
Classical writers employ the same metaphor, to denote not spiritual death, with which they were unacquainted, but the absence of moral principle, or utter ignorance of right and wrong. Thus Epictetus says, νεκρὸς μὲν ὁ παιδευτὴς νεκροὶ δ ' ὑμεῖς ὅτε χορτασθῶτε σήμερον, καθῶσθε κλαίοντες περὶ τῶς αὔριον πόθεν φάγητε. "The instructor is dead, and you are dead. When you are satiated to-day, you sit down and weep about to-morrow, what you shall have to eat." — *Ed.*
120
"The Greek word αἰών, and likewise the Latin word AEvum, both signify the 'lip of man' and from thence, by an easy figure, 'the manner and custom' of a person's living; and therefore it denotes here the corrupt principles and morals, and particularly the idolatrous practices of the Heathen world, with which the Ephesians were as truly chargeable as the rest of mankind, before their conversion to the faith of Christ." — Chandler.
121
"Φύσις, 'nature,' in such an idiom, signifies what is essential as opposed to what is accidental, what is innate in contrast with what is acquired. This is its general sense, whatever its specific application. Thus, Φαρμάκου φύσις is the nature of a drug, its color, growth, and potency. Φύσις τοῦ Αἰγύπτου is the nature of the land of Egypt — a phrase referring to no artificial peculiarity, but to results which follow from its physical conformation." — Eadie.
122
"That is, exceedingly bountiful and liberal in the exercise of mercy. And in this metaphorical sense, the words 'rich' and 'riches' are used by the best writers. Lucian speaks of πλοῦτος φιλοσοφίας, 'the riches of philosophy.' The Roman orator frequently speaks of the 'riches of the mind,' by which he means those excellencies of understanding and virtue which are the peculiar ornaments and riches of it. De Orat. I. So the apostle means here the infinite benignity of the Divine Nature, and his unchangeable disposition to be merciful." — Chandler.
123
"'Loving with love,' increaseth the emphasis and force of the expression. Cicero hath an expression exactly parallel: 'Cura ut me ames amore illo tuo singulari.' — Ep. Fam. 'Be sure you love me with your singular and peculiar love.' An allowed beauty in a profane author should not be censured as a tautology in a sacred one." — Chandler.

124

"Καὶ τοῦτο οὐκ ἐξ ὑμῶν. It has been not a little debated, among both ancient and modern commentators, to what noun τοῦτο should be referred. Some say, to πίστωες; others, to χάριτι; though on the sense of πίστις they differ in their views. The reference seems, however, to be neither to the one nor to the other, but to the subject of the foregoing *clause,* salvation by grace, through faith in Christ and his gospel; a view, I find, adopted by Dr. Chandler, Dean Tucker, Dr. Macknight, and Dr. A. Clarke. And to show that this interpretation is not a mere novelty, I need only refer the reader to Theophylact, who thus explains: Οὐ τὴν πίστιν λέγει δῶρον Θεοῦ ἀλλὰ τὸ διὰ πίστεως σωθῆναι τοῦτο δῶρόν ἐστι Θεοῦ. 'He does not say that faith is the gift of God; but to be saved by faith, this is the gift of God.' Such also is the view adopted by Chrysostom and Theodoret." — Bloomfield.

125

"They either knew him not, or did not worship him as God; they had not avouched, or solemnly owned, or taken him for their God; and, in consequence, were not avouched, were not owned, and blessed, and accepted by him as his peculiar people. This was their condition as Gentiles born." — Chandler.

126

"Il estoit necessaire que l'Apostre distinguast ainsi les hommes en deux bandes." "It was necessary that the apostle should separate men into two classes."

127

"Les Juifs estans enflez du privilege que Dieu leur avoit fait, tenoyent les Gentils pour indignes de communiquer avec eux en sorte quelconque." "The Jews, puffed up with the privilege which God had conferred upon them, reckoned the Gentiles to be unworthy of being admitted to any intercourse whatever."

128

᾿Εν δόγμασι — "Δόγμα is equivalent to the participial form — τὸ δεδογμένον, and has its apparent origin in the common phrases which prefaced a proclamation or statute— ἔδοξε τῷ λαῷ καὶ τῷ βουλῷ. In the New Testament it signifies decree, and is applied (Lu 2:1) to the edict of Caesar, and in Ac 17:7, it occurs with a similar reference. But not only does it signify imperial statutes; it is also the name given to the decrees of the ecclesiastical council in Jerusalem. (Ac 16:4.) It is found, too, in the parallel passage in Col 2:14. In the Septuagint its meaning is the same; and in the sense first quoted, that of royal mandate, it is frequently used in the book of Daniel." — Eadie.

129

Theodoret, Theophylact, and others.

130

According to that ancient prophecy, (Ps 118:22,) 'the stone, which the builders refused, is become the head-stone of the corner.' The strength of buildings lies in their angles; and the corner-stone is that which unites and compacts the different sides of them; the chief cornerstone is that which is laid at the foundation, upon which the whole angle of the building rests, and which therefore is the principal support and tie of the whole edifice." — Chandler.

CHAPTER 3

Ephesians 3:1-6

1. For this cause, I Paul, the prisoner of Jesus Christ for you Gentiles,
1. Hujus rei gratia ego Paulus, vinctus Iesu Christi, pro vobis Gentibus legatione fungor;
2. (If ye have heard of the dispensation of the grace of God which is given me to you-ward:
2. Siquidem audistis dispensationem gratiae Dei, mihi erga vos datae,
3. How that by revelation he made known unto me the mystery; as I wrote afore in few words;
3. Quod per revelationem mihi patefecerit arcanum, quemadmodum scripsi paulo ante.
4. Whereby, when ye read, ye may understand my knowledge in the mystery of Christ,
4. Ad quod potestis attendentes intelligere cognitionem meam in mysterio Christi,
5. Which in other ages was not made known unto the sons of men, as it is now revealed unto his holy apostles and prophets by the Spirit;
5. Quod aliis saeculis non innotuit filiis hominum, quemadmodum nunc revelatum est sanctis Apostolis ejus et Prophetis per Spiritum,
6. That the Gentiles should be fellow-heirs, and of the same body, and partakers of his promise in Christ by the gospel.
6. Gentes esse cohaeredes, et concorporeas, et consortes promissionis ejus in Christo per Evangelium.

1. *For this cause.* Paul's imprisonment, which ought to have been held as a confirmation of his apostleship, was undoubtedly presented by his adversaries in an opposite light. He therefore points out to the Ephesians that his chains served to prove and to declare his calling; and that the only reason why he had been imprisoned was, that he had preached the gospel to the Gentiles. His unshaken firmness was no small additional proof that he had discharged his office in a proper manner.

The prisoner of Jesus Christ. [131] To strengthen his authority still more, he speaks in lofty terms of his prison. In the presence of the world and of wicked men, this might have appeared to be foolish boasting; but, in addressing godly persons, it was a dignified and faithful manner. The glory of Christ not only overcomes the ignominy of the chains, but converts what was in itself a reproach into the highest honor. If he had merely said, "I am a prisoner," this would not have conveyed the idea of his being an ambassador. Imprisonment alone has no claim to this honor, being usually the mark of wickedness and crime. But the crowns and sceptres of kings, to say nothing of the imposing splendor of an ambassador, are less honorable than the chains of a prisoner of Jesus Christ. Men might think otherwise, but it is our duty to judge of the reasons. So highly ought the name of Christ to be revered by us, that what men consider to be the greatest reproach, ought to be viewed by us as the greatest honour.

For you Gentiles. Another circumstance greatly fitted to interest the Ephesians was, that the persecutions of Paul were endured for the Gentiles, — that his troubles and dangers were on their account.

2. *If ye have heard.* There is reason to believe, that, while Paul was at Ephesus, he had said nothing on these subjects, no necessity for doing so having arisen; for no controversy had taken place among them about the calling of the Gentiles. If he had made any mention of them in his discourses, he would have reminded the Ephesians of his former statements, instead of referring generally, as he now does, to common report and to his own Epistle. He did not, of his own accord, raise unnecessary disputes. It was only when the wickedness of his adversaries made it necessary, that he reluctantly undertook the defense of his ministry. *Dispensation* (οικονομια) means here a divine order or command, or, as it is generally expressed, a *commission*

3. *That by revelation.* Some might imagine, that, in attempting to discharge the office of an apostle, he had acted rashly, and was now paying the penalty of his rashness. It was this that made him so earnest in pleading the Divine authority for all his transactions. The present instance, on account of its novelty, had few supporters; and therefore he calls it a *mystery.* By this name he endeavors to remove the prejudice which the general displeasure at the event was fitted to excite. His own personal interest in the matter was less regarded than that of the Ephesians, who were deeply concerned in the information, that, through the settled purpose of God, they had been called by Paul's ministry. Lest what is little known should forthwith become the object of suspicion, the word *mystery* places it in opposition to the perverse judgments and opinions which were then prevalent in the world.

By revelation he made known to me the mystery. Paul draws the line of distinction between himself and those fanatics, who ascribe to God and to the Holy Spirit their own idle dreams. The false apostles boast of revelations, but it is a false boast. Paul was persuaded that his revelation was true, could prove it to others, and speaks of it as a fact of which no doubt could be entertained.

As I wrote a little before. This refers either to a rapid glance at the same subject in the second chapter, or — which appears to be the general opinion — to another Epistle. If the former exposition be adopted, it will be proper to translate, *as I wrote before in few words;* for the subject had received nothing more than a passing notice; but the latter being, as I have said, the prevailing opinion, I prefer translating, *as I wrote a little before.* The phrase, (ἐν ὀλίγῳ,) which Erasmus has translated *in a few words,* appears rather to refer to time. On this supposition there would be an implied comparison between the present and the former writings. But nothing would be more unlike the fact, than to contrast them on the score of brevity; for a more concise mode of expression than this passing glance can hardly be imagined. The phrase, *a little before,* seems purposely to be used as an appeal to their remembrance of a recent occurrence, though I do not insist on this point. There is more difficulty in the next verse.

4. *By attending to which, ye may understand,* πρὸς ὃ δύνασθε ἀναγινώσκοντες νοῶσαι. Erasmus renders it, "from which things, when ye read, ye may understand." But to translate ἀναγινώσκειν τι as signifying *to read* is, I think, at variance with Greek syntax. I leave it as a subject of consideration, whether it does not rather signify *to attend.* The participle would then be connected with the preposition πρὸς, in the commencement of the verse, and the clause would run thus, *to which when ye attend, ye may understand* If, however, by viewing the verb ἀναγινώσκοντες, as disjoined from the preposition, you make it signify *reading,* the meaning will still be, "by reading you may understand according to what I have written;" taking the phrase πρὸς ὃ, *to which,* as equivalent to καθ ' ὃ, *according to which;* but I suggest this merely as a doubtful conjecture.

If we adopt the view which is almost universally approved, that the apostle had formerly written to the Ephesians, this is not the only Epistle which we have lost. And yet there is no room for the sneers of the ungodly, as if the Scriptures had been mutilated, or in any part had become imperfect. If we duly consider Paul's earnestness, — his watchfulness and care, — his zeal and fervor, — his kindness and readiness in assisting brethren, — we shall be led to regard it as highly probable that he would write many epistles, both of a public and private nature, to various places. Those which the Lord judged to be necessary for his church have been selected by his providence for everlasting remembrance. Let us rest assured, that what is left is enough for us, and that the smallness of the remaining number is not the result of accident; but that the body of Scripture, which is in our possession, has been adjusted by the wonderful counsel of God.

My knowledge. The frequent mention of this point shews the necessity that the calling of ministers should be firmly believed both by themselves and by their people. But Paul looks more to others than to himself. He had everywhere indeed given great offense by preaching the gospel indiscriminately to Jews and Gentiles, but his solicitude was not chiefly on his own account. There were not a few who, overwhelmed by the slanders of wicked men, began to doubt of his apostleship, and whose faith was consequently shaken. It was this that induced him so frequently to remind the Ephesians that he knew the will and command of God who called him to the office. — *In the mystery of Christ,*

5. *Which in other ages was not made known.* He had simply called it a *mystery,* but now calls it *a mystery of Christ,* because it was necessary that it should remain hidden, until it was revealed by his coming; just as the appellation of "prophecies of Christ" may be given to those which relate to his kingdom. We must first explain the word *mystery,* and then inquire why it is said to have remained unknown in all ages. The *mystery* was,

"that the Gentiles should be fellow-heirs, and of the same body, and partakers of his promise in Christ by the gospel."

(Eph 3:6.)

When this name is given to the gospel, it has other meanings, which do not apply to the present passage. The calling of the Gentiles, then, was a "mystery of Christ;" that is, it was to be fulfilled under the reign of Christ.

But why does he affirm that it was not known, when it had been the subject of so many predictions? The prophets everywhere declare, that people shall come from every nation in the world, to worship God; that an altar shall be erected both in Assyria and in Egypt, and that all alike shall speak the language of Canaan. (Isa 19:18.) It is intimated by these words, that the worship of the true God, and the same profession of faith, will be everywhere diffused. Of the Messiah it is predicted, that he shall have dominion from east to west, and that all nations shall serve him. (Ps. 72:8, 11.) We see also, that many passages to this purpose are quoted by the apostles, not only from the later prophets, but from Moses. How could that be hidden which had been proclaimed by so many heralds? Why are all without exception pronounced to have been in ignorance? Shall we say, that the prophets spake what they did not understand, and uttered sounds without meaning?

I answer, the words of Paul must not be understood to mean that there had been no knowledge at all on these subjects. There had always been some of the Jewish nation who acknowledged that, at the advent of the Messiah, the grace of God would be proclaimed throughout the whole world, and who looked forward to the renovation of the human race. The prophets themselves, though they spoke with the certainty of revelation, left the time and manner undetermined. They knew that some communication of the grace of God would be made to the Gentiles, but at what time, in what manner, and by what means it should be accomplished, they had no information whatever. This ignorance was exemplified in a remarkable way by the apostles. They had not only been instructed by the predictions of the prophets, but had heard the distinct statement of their Master, (Joh 10:16,)

"Other sheep I have which are not of this fold: them also I must bring, and they shall hear my voice: and there shall be one fold and one shepherd;"

and yet the novelty of the subject prevented them from understanding it fully. Nay, after they had received the injunction,

"Go ye into all the world, and preach the gospel to every creature," (Mr 16:15,)

and,

"Ye shall be witnesses to me both in Jerusalem, and in all Judea, and in Samaria, and to the uttermost part of the earth," (Ac 1:8,)

they dreaded and recoiled from the calling of the Gentiles as a proposal absolutely monstrous, because the manner of its accomplishment was still unknown. Before the actual event arrived, they had dark and confused apprehensions of our Savior's words; for ceremonies were

"a vail over their face, that they could not steadfastly look to the end of that which is abolished." (2Co 3:13.)

With unquestionable propriety, therefore, does Paul call this a *mystery,* and say, that it had been hidden; for the repeal of the ceremonial law, which admitted them within the vail, was not understood.

As it is now revealed. To lay claim to information which none of the patriarchs, prophets, or holy kings, had possessed, might wear the aspect of arrogance. To guard against this imputation, Paul reminds them, first, that in this respect he was not alone, but shared the *revelation* with the most eminent teachers of the church; and, secondly, that it was the gift of the Holy Spirit, who has a right to bestow it on whom he pleases; for there is no other limit of our knowledge but that which he assigns to us.

These few words, *as it is now revealed,* throw additional light on the admission of the Gentiles to be the people of God. It is on the condition that they shall be placed on a level with the Jews, and form one body. That the novelty might give no offense, he states that this must be accomplished *by the gospel.* (Eph 3:6.) Now, the gospel was itself a novelty; for it had never till now been heard of, and yet was acknowledged by all the godly to have come from heaven. Where, then, was the wonder, if, in renewing the world, God should follow an unwonted method?

Ephesians 3:7-13

7. Whereof I was made a minister, according to the gift of the grace of God given unto me by the effectual working of his power.

7. Cujus factus sum minister, secundum donum gratiae Dei, quod mihi datum est secundum efficaciam potentiae ejus.

8. Unto me, who am less than the least of all saints, is this grace given, that I should preach among the Gentiles the unsearchable riches of Christ;

8. Mihi omnium sanctorum minimo data est gratia haec, ut evangelizem in Gentibus impervestigabiles divitias Christi;

9. And to make all *men* see what *is* the fellowship of the mystery, which from the beginning of the world hath been hid in God, who created all things by Jesus Christ:

9. Et omnibus conspicuum faciam, quae sit communio mysterii, quod absconditum fuit a saeculis in Deo, qui omnia creavit per Iesum Christum;

10. To the intent that now, unto the principalities and powers in heavenly *places*, might be known by the church the manifold wisdom of God,

10. Ut nunc patefieret principatibus et potestatibus in coelestibus per ecclesiam varie multiplex sapientia Dei,

11. According to the eternal purpose which he purposed in Christ Jesus our Lord:

11. Secundum propositum aeternum, quod statuit in Christo Iesu Domino nostro,

12. In whom we have boldness and access with confidence by the faith of him.

12. Perquem habemus audaciam, et aditum in fiducia, per fidem ejus.

13. Wherefore I desire that ye faint not at my tribulations for you, which is your glory.

13. Quare peto, ne deficiatis in afflictionibus meis pro vobis, quae est gloria vestra.

7. *Of which I was made a minister.* Having declared the gospel to be the instrument employed in communicating grace to the Gentiles, he now adds, that he *was made a minister* of the Gospel; and thus applies to himself the general statements which had been made. But, to avoid claiming for himself more than is proper, he affirms that it is *the gift of the grace of God,* and that this gift was an exhibition of divine *power.* As if he had said, "Inquire not what I have deserved; for in the free exercise of kindness, the Lord made me an apostle of the Gentiles, not for any excellence of mine, but by his own grace. Inquire not what I formerly was; for it is the Lord's prerogative to 'exalt them of low degree.'" (Lu 1:52.) To produce something great out of nothing, shews *the effectual working of his power.*

8. *To me, who am the least.* He labors to exhibit himself, and everything that belongs to him, in as humiliating a light as possible, in order that the grace of God may be the more highly exalted. But this acknowledgment had the additional effect of anticipating the objections which his adversaries might bring against him. "Who is this man that God should have raised him above all his brethren? What superior excellence did he possess that he should be chosen in preference to all the others?" All such comparisons of personal worth are set aside by the confession, that he was *the least of all the saints.*

This is no hypocritical declaration. Most men are ready enough to make professions of feigned humility, while their minds are swelled with pride, and in words to acknowledge themselves inferior to every one else, while they wish to be regarded with the highest esteem, and think themselves entitled to the highest honor. Paul is perfectly sincere in admitting his unworthiness; nay, at other times he speaks of himself in far more degrading language.

"For I am the least of the apostles, and am not worthy to be called an apostle, because I persecuted the church of God."

(1Co 15:9.)

"Christ Jesus came into the world to save *sinners, of whom I am chief*"

(1Ti 1:15.)

But let us observe, that, when he speaks of himself as the meanest of all, he confines his attention to what he was in himself, apart from the grace of God. As if he had said, that his own worthlessness did not prevent him from being appointed, while others were passed by, to be the apostle of the Gentiles. *The grace of God given to me* is the expression used by him, to intimate that it was a peculiar gift, as compared with what had been bestowed on others. Not that he alone had been elected to discharge that office, but that he held the highest rank among "the teachers of the Gentiles," — a title which he employs on another occasion as peculiar to himself.

"I am ordained a preacher, and an apostle, (I speak the truth in Christ, and lie not,) a teacher of the Gentiles in faith and truth."

(1Ti 2:7.)

By *the unsearchable riches of Christ* are meant the astonishing and boundless treasures of grace, which God had suddenly and unexpectedly bestowed on the Gentiles. The Ephesians are thus reminded how eagerly the gospel ought to be embraced, and how highly it ought to be esteemed. This subject has been treated in the Exposition of the Epistle to the Galatians, (Gal. 1:15, 16, Gal. 2:7, 9.) And certainly, while Paul held the office of apostleship in common with others, it was an honor peculiar to himself to be appointed apostle of the Gentiles.

9. *What is the fellowship of the mystery.* The publication of the gospel is called a *fellowship,* because it is the will of God that his purpose, which had formerly been hidden, shall now be shared by men. There is an appropriate metaphor in the words φωτίσαι πάντας, *to enlighten all men,* — conveying the thought, that, in his apostleship, the grace of God shines with the brightness of noon-day.

Which hath been hid in God. This is intended, as before, to obviate the prejudice of novelty, — to oppose the rashness of men, who think it improper that they should remain in ignorance of anything whatever. Who will question the right which God has to keep his own purposes concealed, until he shall be pleased to communicate them to men? What presumption, — yea, what madness is it, not to admit that God is wiser than we! Let us remember, therefore, that our rashness ought to receive a check, whenever the boundless height of the Divine foreknowledge is presented to our view. This, too, is the reason why he calls them *the unsearchable riches of Christ;* intimating that this subject, though it exceeds our capacity, ought to be contemplated with reverence and admiration.

Who created all things by Jesus Christ. This cannot so properly be understood of the first creation as of the spiritual renewal. It is, no doubt, true, and is frequently declared in Scripture, that by the Word of God all things were created; but the connection of the passage lays us under the necessity of understanding by it that renewal which is comprehended in the blessing of redemption. But it may, perhaps, be thought that the apostle is illustrating this renewal, by an argument drawn from the creation. "By Christ, as God, the Father created (Joh 1:3) all things; and why, then, should we wonder, if by Christ, as Mediator, all the Gentiles are now brought back to one body?" I have no objection to this view. A similar argument is used by him in another Epistle.

"For God, who commanded the light to shine out of darkness, is the same who hath shined in our hearts, to give the light of the knowledge of the glory of God in the face of Jesus Christ."

(2Co 4:6.)

From the creation of the world he concludes, that it is the work of God to enlighten the darkness; but what was visible in the former case is ascribed to the Spirit, when he comes to speak of the kingdom of Christ.

10. *That now to the principalities and powers.* Some are of opinion that these words cannot apply to angels, because such ignorance, as is here supposed, could not be found in those who are permitted to behold the brightness of God's countenance. They choose rather to refer them to devils, but without due reflection; for what could have been regarded as extraordinary in the assertion, that, by the preaching of the gospel and the calling of the Gentiles, information was, for the first time, conveyed to devils? There can be no doubt that the apostle labors to place in the strongest light the mercy of God toward the Gentiles, and the high value of the gospel. For this purpose he declares, that the preaching of the gospel exhibits the manifold grace of God, with which, till now, the heavenly angels themselves were unacquainted. The wisdom of God, therefore, which was manifested by uniting Jews and Gentiles in the fellowship of the gospel, ought to be regarded by men with the highest admiration.

He calls it πολυποίκιλον σοφίαν, *manifold wisdom,* because men are accustomed to try it by a false standard, confining their view to a particular department, and thus forming a most inadequate conception of the whole. The Jews thought, for example, that the dispensation under the law, with which they were acquainted and familiar, was the only form in which the wisdom of God could be seen. But, by making the gospel to be proclaimed to all men without exception, God has brought forth to view another instance and proof of his wisdom. Not that it was new wisdom, but that it was so large and *manifold,* [132] as to transcend our limited capacity. Let us rest assured that the knowledge, whatever it may be, which we have acquired, is, after all, but a slender proportion. And if the calling of the Gentiles draws the attention, and excites the reverence, of angels in heaven, how shameful that it should be slighted or disdained by men upon earth!

The inference which some draw from this passage, that angels are present in our assemblies, and make progress along with ourselves in knowledge, is a groundless speculation. We must always keep in view the purposes for which God appointed the ministry of his word. If angels, who are permitted to see the face of God, do not walk in faith, neither do they need the outward administration of the word. The preaching of the gospel, therefore, is of no service but to human beings, among whom alone the practice exists. Paul's meaning is this: "The church, composed both of Jews and Gentiles, is a mirror, in which angels behold the astonishing wisdom of God displayed in a manner unknown to them before. They see a work which is new to them, and the reason of which was hid in God. In this manner, and not by learning anything from the lips of men, do they make progress."

11. *According to the eternal purpose.* How carefully does he guard against the objection, that the purpose of God has been changed! A third time, he repeats that the decree was eternal and unchangeable, but must be carried into effect by *Christ Jesus our Lord,* because in him it was made. Thus he declares, that the proper time for publishing this decree belongs to the kingdom of Christ. Literally the words run, "according to the eternal purpose (ἣν ἐποίησεν) *which he made.*" But I consider the meaning to be, *which he purposed;* because the present discussion does not relate solely to the execution of the decree, but to the appointment itself, which, though it took place before all ages, was known to God only — till the manifestation of Christ.

12. *Through whom we have boldness.* The honor of reconciling the Father to the whole world must be given to Christ. From the effects of this grace its excellence is demonstrated; for *faith,* which is possessed by Gentiles in common with Jews, admits them into the presence of God. When the words, *through Christ* and *by the faith of him,* are used by Paul, in connection with the name of God, there is always an implied contrast, which shuts up every other approach, — which excludes every other method of obtaining Divine fellowship. Most important and valuable instruction is here conveyed. The true nature and power of faith, and the confidence which is necessary for calling upon God, are beautifully expressed. That the consequences of faith, and the duties which it performs, should be the subject of much controversy between us and the Papists, is not surprising. They do not properly understand the meaning of the word *Faith,* which they might learn from this passage, if they were not blinded by prejudice.

First, Paul denominates it *the faith of Christ;* by which he intimates, that everything which faith ought to contemplate is exhibited to us in Christ. Hence it follows, that an empty and confused knowledge of Christ must not be mistaken for Faith, but that knowledge which is directed to Christ, in order to seek God in Christ; and this can only be done when the power and offices of Christ are understood. *Faith* produces *confidence,* which again, in its turn, produces *boldness.* There are three stages in our progress. First, we believe the promises of God; next, by relying on them, we obtain that *confidence,* which is accompanied by holiness and peace of mind; and, last of all, comes *boldness,* which enables us to banish fear, and to come with firmness and steadiness into the presence of God.

To separate *faith* from *confidence* would be an attempt to take away heat and light from the sun. I acknowledge, indeed, that, in proportion to the measure of faith, confidence is small in some and greater in others; but faith will never be found unaccompanied by these effects or fruits. A trembling, hesitating, doubting conscience, will always be a sure evidence of unbelief; but a firm, steady faith, will prove to be invincible against the gates of hell. To trust in Christ as Mediator, and to entertain a firm conviction of our heavenly Father's love, — to venture boldly to promise to ourselves eternal life, and not to tremble at death or hell, — is, to use a common phrase, a holy presumption.

Observe the expression, *access with confidence.* Wicked men seek rest in forgetfulness of God, and are never at ease but when they remove to the greatest possible distance from God. His own children differ from them in this respect, that they "have peace with God," (Ro 5:1,) and approach to him with cheerfulness and delight. We infer, likewise, from this passage, that, in order to call on God in a proper manner, *confidence* is necessary, and thus becomes the key that opens to us the gate of heaven. Those who doubt and hesitate will never be heard.

"Let him ask in faith," says James, "nothing wavering: for he that wavereth is like a wave of the sea driven with the wind and tossed. For let not that man think that he shall receive anything of the Lord." (Jas. 1:6, 7)

The sophists of the *Sorbonne,* [133] when they enjoin men to hesitate, know not what it is to call upon God.

13. *Wherefore I desire.* His reason for alluding formerly to his imprisonment is now manifest. It was to prevent them from being discouraged when they heard of his persecution. [134] O heroic breast, which drew from a prison, and from death itself, comfort to those who were not in danger! He says that, he endured *tribulations for* the Ephesians, because they tended to promote the edification of all the godly. How powerfully is the faith of the people confirmed, when a pastor does not hesitate to seal his doctrine by the surrender of his life! And accordingly he adds, *which is your glory.* Such lustre was thrown around his instructions, that all the churches among whom he had labored, had good reason to glory, when they beheld their faith ratified by the best of all pledges.

Ephesians 3:14-19

14. For this cause I bow my knees unto the Father of our Lord Jesus Christ,

14. Hujus rei gratia flecto genua ad Patrem Domini nostri Iesu Christi,

15. Of whom the whole family in heaven and earth is named,

15. Ex quo omnis cognatio in coelis et super terram nominatur,

16. That he would grant you, according to the riches of his glory, to be strengthened with might by his Spirit in the inner man;

16. Ut det vobis secundum divitias gloriae suae, potentia roborari per Spiritum suum in hominem interiorem,

17. That Christ may dwell in your hearts by faith; that ye, being rooted and grounded in love,

17. Ut inhabitet Christus per fidem in cordibus vestris, ut sitis in charitate radicati atque fundati,

18. May be able to comprehend with all saints what *is* the breadth, and length, and depth, and height;

18. Quo valeatis comprehendere cum omnibus sanctis, quae sit latitudo, et longitudo, et profunditas, et altitudo;

19. And to know the love of Christ, which passeth knowledge, that ye might be filled with all the fulness of God.

19. Cognoscere, inquam, dilectionem Christi, quae cognitionem exsuperat, ut completi sitis in omnem plenitudinem Dei.

14. *For this cause.* His prayers for them are mentioned, not only to testify his regard for them, but likewise to excite them to pray in the same manner; for the seed of the word is scattered in vain, unless the Lord render it fruitful by his blessing. Let pastors learn from Paul's example, not only to admonish and exhort their people, but to entreat the Lord to bless their labors, that they may not be unfruitful. Nothing will be gained by their industry and toil, — all their study and application will be to no purpose, except so far as the Lord bestows his blessing. This ought not to be regarded by them as an encouragement to sloth. It is their duty, on the contrary, to labor earnestly in sowing and watering, provided they, at the same time, ask and expect the increase from the Lord.

We are thus enabled to refute the slanders of the Pelagians and Papists, who argue, that, if the grace of the Holy Spirit performs the whole work of enlightening our minds, and forming our hearts to obedience, all instruction will be superfluous. The only effect of the enlightening and renewing influences of the Holy Spirit is, to give to instruction its proper weight and efficacy, that we may not be blind to the light of heaven, or deaf to the strains of truth. While the Lord alone acts upon us, he acts by his own instruments. It is therefore the duty of pastors diligently to teach, — of the people, earnestly to receive instruction, — and of both, not to weary themselves in unprofitable exertions, but to look up for Divine aid.

I bow my knees. The bodily attitude is here put for the religious exercise itself. Not that prayer, in all cases, requires the bending of the knees, but because this expression of reverence is commonly employed, especially where it is not an incidental petition, but a continued prayer.

15. *Of whom the whole family.* [135] The relative, ἐξ οὗ, *of whom,* may apply equally to the Father and to the Son. Erasmus restricts it entirely to the Father. I do not approve of this; for readers ought to have been allowed a liberty of choice; nay, the other interpretation appears to be far more probable. The apostle alludes to that relationship which the Jews had with each other, through their father Abraham, to whom they trace their lineage. He proposes, on the contrary, to remove the distinction between Jews and Gentiles; and tells them, not only that all men have been brought into one family and one race through Christ, but that they are enabled to claim kindred even with angels.

To apply it to God the Father would not be equally defensible, being liable to this obvious exception, that God formerly passed by the Gentiles, and adopted the Jews as his peculiar people. But when we apply it to Christ, the whole of Paul's statement agrees with the facts; for all come and blend together, as one family, and, related to one God the Father, are mutually brethren. Let us therefore understand that, through the mediation of Christ, a relationship has been constituted between Jews and Gentiles, because, by reconciling us to the Father, he has made us all one. Jews have no longer any reason to boast that they are the posterity of Abraham, or that they belong to this or that tribe, — to despise others as profane, and claim the exclusive honor of being a holy people. There is but one relationship which ought to be reckoned, both in heaven and on earth, both among angels and among men

— a union to the body of Christ. Out of him all will be found scattered. He alone is the bond by which we are united.

16. *That he would give to you.* Paul wishes that the Ephesians should be *strengthened;* and yet he had already bestowed on their piety no mean commendation. But believers have never advanced so far as not to need farther growth. The highest perfection of the godly in this life is an earnest desire to make progress. This *strengthening,* he tells us, is the work of the *Spirit;* so that it does not proceed from man's own ability. The increase, as well as the commencement, of everything good in us, comes from the Holy Spirit. That it is the gift of Divine grace, is evident from the expression used, *that he would give to you* This the Papists utterly deny. They maintain that the *second* grace is bestowed upon us, according as we have individually deserved it, by making a proper use of the *first* grace. But let us unite with Paul in acknowledging that it is the "gift" of the grace of God, not only that we have begun to run well, but that we advance; not only that we have been born again, but that we grow from day to day.

According to the riches of his glory. These words are intended to express still more strongly the doctrine of Divine grace. They may be explained in two ways: either, *according to his glorious riches,* making the genitive, agreeably to the Hebrew idiom, supply the place of an adjective, — or, *according to his rich and abundant glory.* The word *glory* will thus be put for *mercy,* in accordance with an expression which he had formerly used, "to the praise of the glory of his grace." (Eph 1:6) I prefer the latter view.

In the inner man. By *the inner man,* Paul means the soul, and whatever relates to the spiritual life of the soul; as the *outward* man denotes the body, with everything that belongs to it, — health, honors, riches, vigor, beauty, and everything of that nature. "Though our outward man perish, yet our inward man is renewed day by day;" that is, if in worldly matters we decay, our spiritual life becomes more and more vigorous. (2Co 4:16) The prayer of Paul, that the saints may be *strengthened,* does not mean that they may be eminent and flourishing in the world, but that, with respect to the kingdom of God, their minds may be made strong by Divine power.

17. *That Christ may dwell.* He explains what is meant by "the strength of the inner man." As

"it pleased the Father that in him should all fullness dwell," (Col 1:19,)

so he who has Christ dwelling in him can want nothing. It is a mistake to imagine that the Spirit can be obtained without obtaining Christ; and it is equally foolish and absurd to dream that we can receive Christ without the Spirit. Both doctrines must be believed. We are partakers of the Holy Spirit, in proportion to the intercourse which we maintain with Christ; for the Spirit will be found nowhere but in Christ, on whom he is said, on that account, to have rested; for he himself says, by the prophet Isaiah, "The Spirit of the Lord God is upon me." (Isa 61:1; Lu 4:18.) But neither can Christ be separated from his Spirit; for then he would be said to be dead, and to have lost all his power.

Justly, therefore, does Paul affirm that the persons who are endowed by God with spiritual vigor are those in whom *Christ dwells.* He points to that part in which Christ peculiarly dwells, *in your hearts,* — to show that it is not enough if the knowledge of Christ dwell on the tongue or flutter in the brain.

May dwell through faith. The method by which so great a benefit is obtained is also expressed. What a remarkable commendation is here bestowed on *faith,* that, by means of it, the Son of God becomes our own, and "makes his abode with us!" (Joh 14:23.) By faith we not only acknowledge that Christ suffered and rose from the dead on our account, but, accepting the offers which he makes of himself, we possess and enjoy him as our Savior. This deserves our careful attention. Most people consider fellowship with Christ, and believing in Christ, to be the same thing; but the fellowship which we have with Christ is the consequence of faith. In a word, faith is not a distant view, but a warm embrace, of Christ, by which he dwells in us, and we are filled with the Divine Spirit.

That ye may be rooted and grounded in love. Among the fruits of Christ's dwelling in us the apostle enumerates love and gratitude for the Divine grace and kindness exhibited to us in Christ. Hence it follows, that this is true and solid excellence; so that, whenever he treats of the perfection of the saints, he views it as consisting of these two parts. The firmness and constancy which our love ought to possess are pointed out by two metaphors. There are many persons not wholly destitute of love; but it is easily removed or shaken, because its roots are not deep. Paul desires that it should be *rooted* [136] *and grounded,* — thoroughly fixed in our minds, so as to resemble a well-founded building or deeply-planted tree. The true meaning is, that our roots ought to be so deeply planted, and our foundation so firmly laid in love, that nothing will be able to shake us. It is idle to infer from these words, that love is the foundation and root of our salvation. Paul does not inquire here, as any one may perceive, on what our salvation is founded, but with what firmness and constancy we ought to continue in the exercise of love.

18. *May be able to comprehend.* The second fruit is, that the Ephesians should perceive the greatness of Christ's love to men. Such an apprehension or knowledge springs from faith. By desiring that they should comprehend it *with all saints,* he shows that it is the most excellent blessing which they can obtain in the present life; that it is the highest wisdom, to which all the children of God aspire. What follows is sufficiently clear in itself, but has hitherto been darkened by a variety of interpretations. Augustine is quite delighted with his own acuteness, which throws no light on the subject. Endeavouring to discover some kind of mysterious allusion to the figure of the cross, he makes the *breadth* to be love, — the *height,* hope, — the *length,* patience, and the *depth,* humility. This is very ingenious and entertaining: but what has it to do with Paul's meaning? Not more, certainly, than the opinion of Ambrose, that the allusion is to the figure of a sphere. Laying aside the views of others, I shall state what will be universally acknowledged to be the simple and true meaning.

19. *And to know the love of Christ.* By those dimensions Paul means nothing else than the love of Christ, of which he speaks afterwards. The meaning is, that he who *knows* it fully and perfectly is in every respect a wise man. As if he had said, "In whatever direction men may look, they will find nothing in the doctrine of salvation that does not bear some relation to this subject." The love of Christ contains within itself the whole of wisdom, so that the words may run thus: *that ye may be able to comprehend the love of Christ, which is the length and breadth, and depth, and height,* that is, the complete perfection of all wisdom. The metaphor is borrowed from mathematicians, taking the parts as expressive of the whole. Almost all men are infected with the disease of desiring to obtain useless knowledge. It is of great importance that we should be told what is necessary for us to know, and what the Lord desires us to contemplate, above and below, on the right hand and on the left, before and behind. The love of Christ is held out to us as the subject which ought to occupy our daily and nightly meditations, and in which we ought to be wholly plunged. He who is in possession of this alone has enough. Beyond it there is nothing solid, nothing useful, — nothing, in short, that is proper or sound. Though you survey the heaven and earth and sea, you will never go beyond this without overstepping the lawful boundary of wisdom.

Which surpasseth knowledge. A similar expression occurs in another Epistle:

"the peace of God, which surpasseth all understanding, shall keep your hearts and minds through Christ Jesus."

(Php 4:7)

No man can approach to God without being raised above himself and above the world. On this ground the sophists refuse to admit that we can know with certainty that we enjoy the grace of God; for they measure faith by the perception of the bodily senses. But Paul justly contends that this wisdom exceeds all knowledge; for, if the faculties of man could reach it, the prayer of Paul that God would bestow it must have been unnecessary. Let us remember, therefore, that the certainty of faith is knowledge, but is acquired by the teaching of the Holy Spirit, not by the acuteness of our own intellect. If the reader desire a more full discussion of this subject, he may consult the "Institutes of the Christian Religion."

That ye may be filled. Paul now expresses in one word what he meant by the various dimensions. He who has Christ has everything necessary for being made perfect in God; for this is the meaning of the phrase, *the fullness of God.* Men do certainly imagine that they have entire completeness in themselves, but it is only when their pride is swelled with empty trifles. It is a foolish and wicked dream, that by *the fullness of God* is meant the full Godhead, as if men were raised to an equality with God.

Ephesians 3:20-21

20. Now unto him that is able to do exceeding abundantly above all that we ask or think, according to the power that worketh in us,

20. Ei autem, qui potest cumulate super omnia facere, quae petimus aut cogitamus, secundum potentiam in nobis agentem,

21. Unto him *be* glory in the church by Christ Jesus throughout all ages, world without end. Amen.

21. Sit gloria in Ecclesia per Iesum Christum, in omnes aetates seculi seculorum. Amen.

20. *Now to him.* He now breaks out into thanksgiving, which serves the additional purpose of exhorting the Ephesians to maintain "good hope through grace," (2Th 2:16,) and to endeavor constantly to obtain more and more adequate conceptions of the value of the grace of God.

Who is able. [137] This refers to the future, and agrees with what we are taught concerning hope; and indeed we cannot offer to God proper or sincere thanksgivings for favors received, unless we are convinced that his goodness to us will be without end. When he says that God is *able,* he does not mean power viewed apart, as the phrase is, from the act, but power which is exerted, and which we actually feel. Believers ought always to connect it with the work, when the promises made to them, and their own salvation, form the subject of inquiry. Whatever God can do, he unquestionably will do, if he has promised it. This the apostle proves both by former instances, and by the efficacy of the Spirit, which was at this very time exerted on their own minds.

According to the power that worketh in us, — according to what we feel within ourselves; for every benefit which God bestows upon us is a manifestation of his grace, and love, and power, in consequence of which we ought to cherish a stronger confidence for the future. *Exceeding abundantly above all that we ask or think,* is a remarkable expression, and bids us entertain no fear lest faith of a proper kind should go to excess. Whatever expectations we form of Divine blessings, the infinite goodness of God will exceed all our wishes and all our thoughts.

Footnotes

131

"Know that for no other reason am I, Paul, loaded with these chains. It was for no evil action, but for the love which I bear to the Lord Jesus Christ." — Erasmus.

132

"His manifold wisdom, which regulates all things by amazing plans, through death bestowing life, through ignominy conducting to glory, through abasement displaying the majesty of God." — Erasmus.

133

See note, page 160.

134

"The original word ἐκκακεῖν signifies 'to behave like a coward, and through fear to desert the post of battle.'" — Chandler.

135

"This seems to me plainly to allude, and to be urged in opposition to Diana of Ephesus, who was the common goddess of the Asiatic cities, in whose worship they were united, and by whose common contributions her temple was built, which was the common temple of those incorporated cities, so that all Asia (as we have it, Ac 19:27) 'worshipped her;' which was therefore strictly and properly her family, over which she presided as the common mother and patroness; and there are models and ancient inscriptions remaining to this day, that abundantly prove it. Now the apostle tells these Ephesians, that, as Christians, they belonged to a nobler family, which took its denomination from, and was immediately subject to, God as a common Father; of whom the whole family in heaven and earth is named." — Chandler.

136

"Meaning (by a continuation of the same architectural metaphor) that 'the love should be deep and sincere;' and though ἐϱ᾽ῥιζωμένοι be properly applicable to *trees,* yet it was sometimes used of the foundations of massy edifices; in which case, however, it is in the classical writers almost always accompanied with some word which has reference to buildings.". — Bloomfield.

137

"Blessed are they that hunger and thirst for righteousness, for they shall be satisfied. He that hungereth, let him hunger more; and he that desireth, let him still more abundantly desire; for all that he can desire he shall fully obtain." — Bernard.

CHAPTER 4

Ephesians 4:1-6

1. I therefore, the prisoner of the Lord,) beseech you, that ye walk worthy of the vocation wherewith ye are called,

1. Obsecro itaque vos, ego vinctus in Domino, ut digne ambuletis vocatione, ad quam vocati estis,

2. With all lowliness and meekness, with long-suffering, forbearing one another in love;

2. Cum omni humilitate et mansuetudine, cum tolerantia sufferentes vos invicem in dilectione,

3. Endeavouring to keep the unity of the Spirit in the bond of peace.

3. Studentes servare unitatem Spiritus, in vinculo pacis.

4. *There is* one body, and one Spirit, even as ye are called in one hope of your calling;

4. Unum corpus et unus spiritus; quemadmodum vocati estis in una spe vocationis vestrae.

5. One Lord, one faith, one baptism,

5. Unus Dominus, una fides, unum baptisma.

6. One God and Father of all, who *is* above all, and through all, and in you all.

6. Unus Deus et Pater omnium, qui est super omnia, et per omnia, (*vel, super omnes et per omnes,*) et in omnibus vobis.

The three remaining chapters consist entirely of practical exhortations. Mutual agreement is the first subject, in the course of which a discussion is introduced respecting the government of the church, as having been framed by our Lord for the purpose of maintaining unity among Christians.

1. *I therefore, the prisoner of the Lord.* His imprisonment, which might have been supposed more likely to render him despised, is appealed to, as we have already seen, for a confirmation of his authority. It was the seal of that embassy with which he had been honored. Whatever belongs to Christ, though in the eyes of men it may be attended by ignominy, ought to be viewed by us with the highest regard. The apostle's prison is more truly venerable than the splendid retinue or triumphal chariot of kings.

That ye may walk worthy. This is a general sentiment, a sort of preface, on which all the following statements are founded. He had formerly illustrated *the calling with which they were called,* [138] and now reminds them that they must live in obedience to God, in order that they may not be unworthy of such distinguished grace.

2. *With all humility.* He now descends to particulars, and first of all he mentions *humility* The reason is, that he was about to enter on the subject of Unity, to which humility is the first step. This again produces *meekness,* which disposes us to bear with our brethren, and thus to preserve that unity which would otherwise be broken a hundred times in a day. Let us remember, therefore, that, in cultivating brotherly kindness, we must begin with humility. Whence come rudeness, pride, and disdainful language towards brethren? Whence come quarrels, insults, and reproaches? Come they not from this, that every one carries his love of himself, and his regard to his own interests, to excess? By laying aside haughtiness and a desire of pleasing ourselves, we shall become meek and gentle, and acquire that moderation of temper which will overlook and forgive many things in the conduct of our brethren. Let us carefully observe the order and arrangement of these exhortations. It will be to no purpose that we inculcate forbearance till the natural fierceness has been subdued, and mildness acquired; and it will be equally vain to discourse of *meekness,* till we have begun with *humility.*

Forbearing one another in love. This agrees with what is elsewhere taught, that "love suffereth long and is kind." (1Co 13:4.) Where love is strong and prevalent, we shall perform many acts of mutual forbearance.

3. *Endeavoring to keep the unity of the Spirit.* With good reason does he recommend forbearance, as tending to promote the unity of the Spirit. Innumerable offenses arise daily, which might produce quarrels, particularly when we consider the extreme bitterness of man's natural temper. Some consider *the unity of the Spirit* to mean that spiritual unity which is produced in us by the Spirit of God. There can be no doubt that He alone makes us "of one accord, of one mind," (Php 2:2,) and thus makes us one; but I think it more natural to understand the words as denoting harmony of views. This unity, he tells us, is maintained by *the bond of peace;* for disputes frequently give rise to hatred and resentment. We must live at peace, if we would wish that brotherly kindness should be permanent amongst us.

4. *There is one body.* [139] He proceeds to show more fully in how complete a manner Christians ought to be united. The union ought to be such that we shall form *one body and one soul.* These words denote the whole man. We ought to be united, not in part only, but in body and soul. He supports this by a powerful argument, *as ye have been called in one hope of your calling.* We are called to one inheritance and one life; and hence it follows, that we cannot obtain eternal life without living in mutual harmony in this world. One Divine invitation being addressed to all, they ought to be united in the same profession of faith, and to render every kind of assistance to each other. Oh, were this thought deeply impressed upon our minds, that we are subject to a law which no more permits the children of God to differ among themselves than the kingdom of heaven to be divided, how earnestly should we cultivate brotherly kindness! How should we dread every kind of animosity, if we duly reflected that all who separate us from brethren, estrange us from the kingdom of God! And yet, strangely enough, while we forget the duties which brethren owe to each other, we go on boasting that we are the sons of God. Let us learn from Paul, that none are at all fit for that inheritance who are not one body and one spirit.

5. *One Lord.* In the first Epistle to the Corinthians, he employs the word *Lord,* to denote simply the government of God.

"There are differences of administration, but the same Lord."

(1Co 12:5)

In the present instance, as he shortly afterwards makes express mention of the Father, he gives this appellation strictly to Christ, who has been appointed by the Father to be *our Lord,* and to whose government we cannot be subject, unless we are of one mind. The frequent repetition of the word *one* is emphatic. *Christ* cannot be divided. *Faith* cannot be rent. There are not various *baptisms,* but one which is common to all. *God* cannot cease to be *one,* and unchangeable. It cannot but be our duty to cherish holy unity, which is bound by so many ties. Faith, and baptism, and God the Father, and Christ, ought to unite us, so as almost to become one man. All these arguments for unity deserve to be pondered, but cannot be fully explained. I reckon it enough to take a rapid glance at the apostle's meaning, leaving the full illustration of it to the preachers of the gospel. The unity of *faith,* which is here mentioned, depends on the one, eternal truth of God, on which it is founded.

One baptism, This does not mean that Christian baptism is not to be administered more than once, but that one baptism is common to all; so that, by means of it, we begin to form one body and one soul. But if that argument has any force, a much stronger one will be founded on the truth, that the Father, and Son, and Spirit, are one God; for it is one baptism, which is celebrated in the name of the Three Persons. What reply will the Arians or Sabellians make to this argument? Baptism possesses such force as to make us one; and in baptism, the name of the Father, and of the Son, and of the Spirit, is invoked. Will they deny that one Godhead is the foundation of this holy and mysterious unity? We are compelled to acknowledge, that the ordinance of baptism proves the existence of Three Persons in one Divine essence.

6. *One God and Father of all.* This is the main argument, from which all the rest flow. How comes it that we are united by faith, by baptism, or even by the government of Christ, but because God the Father, extending to each of us his gracious presence, employs these means for gathering us to himself? The two phrases, ἐπὶ πάντων καὶ διὰ πάντων, may either mean, *above all and through all* Things, or *above all and through all* Men. Either meaning will apply sufficiently well, or rather, in both cases, the meaning will be the same. Although God by his power upholds, and maintains, and rules, all things, yet Paul is not now speaking of the universal, but of the spiritual government which belongs to the church. By the Spirit of sanctification, God spreads himself through all the members of the church, embraces all in his government, and dwells in all; but God is not inconsistent with himself, and therefore we cannot but be united to him into one body.

This spiritual unity is mentioned by our Lord.

"Holy Father, keep through thine own name those whom thou hast, given me, that they may be one as we are."

(Joh 17:11)

This is true indeed, in a general sense, not only of all men but of all creatures. "In him we live, and move, and have our being." (Ac 17:28.) And again, "Do not I fill heaven and earth, saith the Lord?" (Jer 23:24.) But we must attend to the connection in which this passage stands. Paul is now illustrating the mutual relation of believers, which has nothing in common either with wicked men or with inferior animals. To this relation we must limit what is said about God's government and presence. It is for this reason, also, that the apostle uses the word *Father,* which applies only to the members of Christ.

Ephesians 4:7-10

7. But unto every one of us is given grace according to the measure of the gift of Christ.

7. Unicuique autem nostrum data est gratia; secundum mensuram donationis Christi.

8. Wherefore he saith, When he ascended up on high, he led captivity captive, and gave gifts unto men.

8. Propterea dicit: Postquam ascendit in altum, captivam duxit captivitatem, et dedit dona hominibus. (Ps 68:19.)

9. (Now that he ascended, what is it but that he also descended first into the lower parts of the earth?

9. Illud autem Ascendit, quid est, nisi quod etiam descenderat prius in inferiores partes terrae?

10. He that descended is the same also that ascended up far above all heavens, that he might fill all things.)

10. Qui descendit, ipse est etiam qui ascendit super omnes coelos, ut impleret omnia.

7. *But to every one.* He now describes the manner in which God establishes and preserves among us a mutual relation. No member of the body of Christ is endowed with such perfection as to be able, without the assistance of others, to supply his own necessities. A certain proportion is allotted to each; and it is only by communicating with each other, that all enjoy what is sufficient for maintaining their respective places in the body. The diversity of gifts is discussed in another Epistle, and very nearly with the same object.

"There are diversities of gifts, but the same Spirit"

(1Co 12:4.)

Such a diversity, we are there taught, is so far from injuring, that it tends to promote and strengthen, the harmony of believers.

The meaning of this verse may be thus summed up. "On no one has God bestowed all things. Each has received a certain measure. Being thus dependent on each other, they find it necessary to throw their individual gifts into the common stock, and thus to render mutual aid." The words *grace* and *gift* remind us that, whatever may be our attainments, we ought not to be proud of them, because they lay us under deeper obligations to God. These blessings are said to be *the gift of Christ;* for, as the apostle, first of all, mentioned the Father, so his aim, as we shall see, is to represent all that we are, and all that we have, as gathered together in Christ.

8. *Therefore he saith.* To serve the purpose of his argument, Paul has departed not a little from the true meaning of this quotation. Wicked men charge him with having made an unfair use of Scripture. The Jews go still farther, and, for the sake of giving to their accusations a greater air of plausibility, maliciously pervert the natural meaning of this passage. What is said of God, is applied by them to David or to the people. "David, or the people," they say, "ascended on high, when, in consequence of many victories, they rose superior to their enemies." But a careful examination of the Psalm will convince any reader that the words, *he ascended up on high,* are applied strictly to God alone.

The whole Psalm may be regarded as an ἐπίνικιον, a song of triumph, which David sings to God on account of the victories which he had obtained; but, taking occasion from the narrative of his own exploits, he makes a passing survey of the astonishing deliverances which the Lord had formerly wrought for his people. His object is to shew, that we ought to contemplate in the history of the Church the glorious power and goodness of God; and among other things he says, *Thou hast ascended on high.* (Ps 68:18.) The flesh is apt to imagine that God remains idle and asleep, when he does not openly execute his judgments. To the view of men, when the Church is oppressed, God is in some manner humbled; but, when he stretches out his avenging arm for her deliverance, he then appears to rouse himself, and to ascend his throne of judgment.

"Then the Lord awaked as one out of sleep, and like a mighty man that shouteth by reason of wine. And he smote his enemies in the hinder parts; he put them to a perpetual reproach."

(Ps. 78:65, 66.)

This mode of expression is sufficiently common and familiar; and, in short, the deliverance of the Church is here called the *ascension* of God.

Perceiving that it is a song of triumph, in which David celebrates all the victories which God had wrought for the salvation of his Church, Paul very properly quoted the account given of God's ascension, and applied it to the person of Christ. The noblest triumph which God ever gained was when Christ, after subduing sin, conquering death, and putting Satan to flight, rose majestically to heaven, that he might exercise his glorious reign over the Church. Hitherto there is no ground for the objection, that Paul has applied this quotation in a manner inconsistent with the design of the Psalmist. The continued existence of the Church is represented by David to be a manifestation of the Divine glory. But no ascension of God more triumphant or memorable will ever occur, than that which took place when Christ was carried up to the right hand of the Father, that he might rule over all authorities and powers, and might become the everlasting guardian and protector of his people.

He led captivity captive. Captivity is a collective noun for *captive enemies;* and the plain meaning is, that God reduced his enemies to subjection, which was more fully accomplished in Christ than in any other way. He has not only gained a complete victory over the devil, and sin, and death, and all the power of hell, — but out of rebels he forms every day "a willing people," (Ps 110:3,) when he subdues by his word the obstinacy of our flesh. On the other hand, his enemies — to which class all wicked men belong — are held bound by chains of iron, and are restrained by his power from exerting their fury beyond the limits which he shall assign.

And gave gifts to men. There is rather more difficulty in this clause; for the words of the Psalm are, "thou hast *received* gifts for men," while the apostle changes this expression into *gave gifts,* and thus appears to exhibit an opposite meaning. Still there is no absurdity here; for Paul does not always quote the exact words of Scripture, but, after referring to the passage, satisfies himself with conveying the substance of it in his own language. Now, it is clear that the *gifts* which David mentions were not *received* by God for himself, but for his people; and accordingly we are told, in an earlier part of the Psalm, that "the spoil" had been "divided" among the families of Israel. (Ps 68:12.) Since therefore the intention of *receiving* was to *give* gifts, Paul can hardly be said to have departed from the substance, whatever alteration there may be in the words.

At the same time, I am inclined to a different opinion, that Paul purposely changed the word, and employed it, not as taken out of the Psalm, but as an expression of his own, adapted to the present occasion. Having quoted from the Psalm a few words descriptive of Christ's ascension, he adds, in his own language, *and gave gifts,* — for the purpose of drawing a comparison between the greater and the less. Paul intends to shew, that this ascension of God in the person of Christ was far more illustrious than the ancient triumphs of the Church; because it is a more honorable distinction for a conqueror to dispense his bounty largely to all classes, than to gather spoils from the vanquished.

The interpretation given by some, that Christ received from the Father what he would distribute to us, is forced, and utterly at variance with the apostle's purpose. No solution of the difficulty, in my opinion, is more natural than this. Having made a brief quotation from the Psalm, Paul took the liberty of adding a statement, which, though not contained in the Psalm, is true in reference to Christ — a statement, too, by which the ascension of Christ is proved to be more illustrious, and more worthy of admiration, than those ancient manifestations of the Divine glory which David enumerates.

9. *Now that he ascended.* Here again the slanderers exclaim, that Paul's reasoning is trifling and childish. "Why does he attempt to make those words apply to a real ascension of Christ, which were figuratively spoken about a manifestation of the Divine glory? Who does not know that the word *ascend* is metaphorical? The conclusion, *that he also descended first,* has therefore no weight."

I answer, Paul does not here reason in the manner of a logician, as to what necessarily follows, or may be inferred, from the words of the prophet. He knew that what David spake about God's ascension was metaphorical. But neither can it be denied, that the expression bears a reference to some kind of humiliation on the part of God which had previously existed. It is this humiliation which Paul justly infers from the declaration that God had ascended. And at what time did God descend lower than when Christ *emptied himself?* ('Αλλ ' ἑαυτὸν ἐκένωσε, Php 2:7.) If ever there was a time when, after appearing to lay aside the brightness of his power, God ascended gloriously, it was when Christ was raised from our lowest condition on earth, and received into heavenly glory.

Besides, it is not necessary to inquire very carefully into the literal exposition of the Psalm, since Paul merely alludes to the prophet's words, in the same manner as, on another occasion, he accommodates to his own subject a passage taken from the writings of Moses. "The righteousness which is of faith speaketh in this manner, Say not in thine heart, who shall ascend into heaven? (that is, to bring Christ down from above;) or, who shall descend into the deep (that is, to bring up Christ again from the dead.") (Rom. 10:6, 7 De 30:12.) But the appropriateness of the application which Paul makes of the passage to the person of Christ is not the only ground on which it must be defended. Sufficient evidence is afforded by the Psalm itself, that this ascription of praise relates to Christ's kingdom. Not to mention other reasons which might be urged, it contains a distinct prophecy of the calling of the Gentiles.

Into the lower parts of the earth. [140] These words mean nothing more than the condition of the present life. To torture them so as to make them mean purgatory or hell, is exceedingly foolish. The argument taken from the comparative degree, "the *lower* parts," is quite untenable. A comparison is drawn, not between one part of the earth and another, but between the whole earth and heaven; as if he had said, that from that lofty habitation Christ descended into our deep gulf.

10. *That ascended up far above all heavens;* that is, beyond this created world. When Christ is said to be in heaven, we must not view him as dwelling among the spheres and numbering the stars. Heaven denotes a place higher than all the spheres, which was assigned to the Son of God after his resurrection. [141] Not that it is literally a place beyond the world, but we cannot speak of the kingdom of God without using our ordinary language. Others, again, considering that the expressions, *above all heavens,* and *ascension into heaven,* are of the same import, conclude that Christ is not separated from us by distance of place. But one point they have overlooked. When Christ is placed above the heavens, or in the heavens, all that surrounds the earth — all that lies beneath the sun and stars, beneath the whole frame of the visible world — is excluded.

That he might fill all things. To fill often signifies to Finish, and it might have that meaning here; for, by his ascension into heaven, Christ entered into the possession of the authority given to him by the Father, that he might rule and govern all things. But a more beautiful view, in my opinion, will be obtained by connecting two meanings which, though apparently contradictory, are perfectly consistent. When we hear of the ascension of Christ, it instantly strikes our minds that he is removed to a great distance from us; and so he actually is, with respect to his body and human presence. But Paul reminds us, that, while he is removed from us in bodily presence, he *fills all things* by the power of his Spirit. Wherever the right hand of God, which embraces heaven and earth, is displayed, Christ is spiritually present by his boundless power; although, as respects his body, the saying of Peter holds true, that

"the heaven must receive him until the times of restitution of all things, which God hath spoken by the mouth of all his holy prophets since the world began." (Ac 3:21.)

By alluding to the seeming contradiction, the apostle has added not a little beauty to his language. *He ascended;* but it was that he, who was formerly bounded by a little space, *might fill all things* But did he not fill them before? In his divine nature, I own, he did; but the power of his Spirit was not so exerted, nor his presence so manifested, as after he had entered into the possession of his kingdom.

"The Holy Ghost was not yet given,
because Jesus was not yet glorified." (Joh 7:39.)

And again,

"It is expedient for you that I go away; for, if I go not away, the Comforter will not come to you." (Joh 16:7.)

In a word, when he began to sit at the right hand of the Father, he began also to fill all things. [142]

Ephesians 4:11-14

11. And he gave some, apostles; and some, prophets; and some, evangelists; and some, pastors and teachers;

11. Et ipse dedit alios quidem apostolos, alios autem prophetas, alios vero evangelistas, alios pastores et doctores,

12. For the perfecting of the saints, for the work of the ministry, for the edifying of the body of Christ:

12. Ad instaurationem sanctorum, in opus ministerii, in aedificationem corporis Christi,

13. Till we all come in the unity of the faith, and of the knowledge of the Son of God, unto a perfect man, unto the measure of the stature of the fullness of Christ:

13. Usquedum occurramus omnes in unitatem fidei, et cognitionis Filii Dei, in virum perfectum, in mensuram aetatis plenitudinis Christi;

14. That we *henceforth* be no more children, tossed to and fro, and carried about with every wind of doctrine, by the sleight of men, *and* cunning craftiness, whereby they lie in wait to deceive.

14. Ne amplius simus pueri, qui fluctuemur, et circumferamur quovis vento doctrinae, per aestum hominum, per versutiam ad circumventionem imposturae.

He returns to explain the distribution of gifts, and illustrates at greater length what he had slightly hinted, that out of this variety arises unity in the church, as the various tones in music produce sweet melody. The meaning may be thus summed up. "The external ministry of the word is also commended, on account of the advantages which it yields. Certain men appointed to that office, are employed in preaching the gospel. This is the arrangement by which the Lord is pleased to govern his church, to maintain its existence, and ultimately to secure its highest perfection."

It may excite surprise, that, when the gifts of the Holy Spirit form the subject of discussion, Paul should enumerate offices instead of gifts. I reply, when men are called by God, gifts are necessarily connected with offices. God does not confer on men the mere name of Apostles or Pastors, but also endows them with gifts, without which they cannot properly discharge their office. He whom God has appointed to be an apostle does not bear an empty and useless title; for the divine command, and the ability to perform it, go together. Let us now examine the words in detail.

11. *And he gave.* The government of the church, by the preaching of the word, is first of all declared to be no human contrivance, but a most sacred ordinance of Christ. The apostles did not appoint themselves, but were chosen by Christ; and, at the present day, true pastors do not rashly thrust themselves forward by their own judgment, but are raised up by the Lord. In short, the government of the church, by the ministry of the word, is not a contrivance of men, but an appointment made by the Son of God. As his own unalterable law, it demands our assent. They who reject or despise this ministry offer insult and rebellion to Christ its Author. It is himself who *gave* them; for, if he does not raise them up, there will be none. Another inference is, that no man will be fit or qualified for so distinguished an office who has not been formed and moulded by the hand of Christ himself. To

Christ we owe it that we have ministers of the gospel, that they abound in necessary qualifications, that they execute the trust committed to them. All, all is his *gift.*

Some, apostles. The different names and offices assigned to different persons take their rise from that diversity of the members which goes to form the completeness of the whole body, — every ground of emulation, and envy, and ambition, being thus removed. If every person shall display a selfish character, shall strive to outshine his neighbor, and shall disregard all concerns but his own, — or, if more eminent persons shall be the object of envy to those who occupy a lower place, — in each, and in all of these cases, gifts are not applied to their proper use. He therefore reminds them, that the gifts bestowed on individuals are intended, not to be held for their personal and separate interests, but to be employed for the benefit of the whole. Of the offices which are here enumerated, we have already spoken at considerable length, [143] and shall now say nothing more than the exposition of the passage seems to demand. Five classes of office-bearers are mentioned, though on this point, I am aware, there is a diversity of opinion; for some consider the two last to make but one office. Leaving out of view the opinions of others, I shall proceed to state my own.

I take the word *apostles* not in that general sense which the derivation of the term might warrant, but in its own peculiar signification, for those highly favored persons whom Christ exalted to the highest honor. Such were the twelve, to whose number Paul was afterwards added. Their office was to spread the doctrine of the gospel throughout the whole world, to plant churches, and to erect the kingdom of Christ. They had not churches of their own committed to them; but the injunction given to all of them was, to preach the gospel wherever they went.

Next to them come the *Evangelists,* who were closely allied in the nature of their office, but held an inferior rank. To this class belonged Timothy and others; for, while Paul mentions them along with himself in the salutations of his epistles, he does not speak of them as his companions in the apostleship, but claims this name as peculiarly his own. The services in which the Lord employed them were auxiliary to those of the apostles, to whom they were next in rank.

To these two classes the apostle adds *Prophets.* By this name some understand those persons who possessed the gift of predicting future events, among whom was Agabus. (Acts 11:28, Acts 21:10.) But, for my own part, as doctrine is the present subject, I would rather define the word *prophets,* as on a former occasion, [144] to mean distinguished interpreters of prophecies, who, by a remarkable gift of revelation, applied them to the subjects which they had occasion to handle; not excluding, however, the gift of prophecy, by which their doctrinal instruction was usually accompanied.

Pastors and Teachers are supposed by some to denote one office, because the apostle does not, as in the other parts of the verse, say, *and some, pastors; and some, teachers;* but, τοὺς δὲ, ποιμένας καὶ διδασκάλους, *and some, pastors and teachers* Chrysostom and Augustine are of this opinion; not to mention the commentaries of Ambrose, whose observations on the subject are truly childish and unworthy of himself. I partly agree with them, that Paul speaks indiscriminately of pastors and teachers as belonging to one and the same class, and that the name *teacher* does, to some extent, apply to all *pastors.* But this does not appear to me a sufficient reason why two offices, which I find to differ from each other, should be confounded.

Teaching is, no doubt, the duty of all pastors; but to maintain sound doctrine requires a talent for interpreting Scripture, and a man may be a *teacher* who is not qualified to preach.

Pastors, in my opinion, are those who have the charge of a particular flock; though I have no objection to their receiving the name of *teachers,* if it be understood that there is a distinct class of *teachers,* who preside both in the education of pastors and in the instruction of the whole church. It may sometimes happen, that the same person is both a pastor and a teacher, but the duties to be performed are entirely different.

It deserves attention, also, that, of the five offices which are here enumerated, not more than the last two are intended to be perpetual. Apostles, Evangelists, and Prophets were bestowed on the church for a limited time only, — except in those cases where religion has fallen into decay, and evangelists are raised up in an extraordinary manner, to restore the pure doctrine which had been lost. But without Pastors and Teachers there can be no government of the church.

Papists have some reason to complain, that their primacy, of which they boast so much, is openly insulted in this passage. The subject of discussion is the unity of the church. Paul inquires into the means by which its continuance is secured, and the outward expressions by which it is promoted, and comes at length to the government of the church. If he knew a primacy which had a fixed residence, was it not his duty, for the benefit of the whole church, to exhibit one ministerial head placed over all the members, under whose government we are collected into one body? We must either charge Paul with inexcusable neglect and foolishness, in leaving out the most appropriate and powerful argument, or we must acknowledge that this primacy is at variance with the appointment of Christ. In truth, he plainly rejects it as without foundation, when he ascribes superiority to Christ alone, and represents the apostles, and all the pastors, as indeed inferior to Him, but associated on an equal level with each other. There is no passage of Scripture by which that tyrannical hierarchy, regulated by one earthly head, is more completely overturned. Paul has been followed by Cyprian, who gives a short and clear definition of what forms the only lawful monarchy in the church. There is, he says, one *bishoprick,* which unites the various parts into one whole. This *bishoprick* he claims for Christ alone, leaving the administration of it to individuals, but in a united capacity, no one being permitted to exalt himself above others.

12. *For the renewing of the saints.* In this version I follow Erasmus, not because I prefer his view, but to allow the reader an opportunity of comparing his version with the Vulgate and with mine, and then choosing for himself. The old translation was, (*ad consummationem,*) *for the completeness.* The Greek word employed by Paul is καταρτισμός, which signifies literally the *adaptation* of things possessing symmetry and proportion; just as, in the human body, the members are united in a proper and regular manner; so that the word comes to signify *perfection.* But as Paul intended to express here a just and orderly arrangement, I prefer the word (*constitutio*) *settlement* or *constitution,* taking it in that sense in which a commonwealth, or kingdom, or province, is said to be *settled,* when confusion gives place to the regular administration of law.

For the work of the ministry. God might himself have performed this work, if he had chosen; but he has committed it to the *ministry* of men. This is intended to anticipate an objection. "Cannot the church be constituted and properly arranged, without the instrumentality of men?" Paul asserts that a *ministry* is required, because such is the will of God.

For the edifying of the body of Christ. This is the same thing with what he had formerly denominated the *settlement* or *perfecting of the saints*. Our true completeness and perfection consist in our being united in the one body of Christ. No language more highly commendatory of the ministry of the word could have been employed, than to ascribe to it this effect. What is more excellent than to produce the true and complete perfection of the church? And yet this work, so admirable and divine, is here declared by the apostle to be accomplished by the external ministry of the word. That those who neglect this instrument should hope to become perfect in Christ is utter madness. Yet such are the fanatics, on the one hand, who pretend to be favored with secret revelations of the Spirit, — and proud men, on the other, who imagine that to them the private reading of the Scriptures is enough, and that they have no need of the ordinary ministry of the church.

If the edification of the church proceeds from Christ alone, he has surely a right to prescribe in what manner it shall be edified. But Paul expressly states, that, according to the command of Christ, no real union or perfection is attained, but by the outward preaching. We must allow ourselves to be ruled and taught by men. This is the universal rule, which extends equally to the highest and to the lowest. The church is the common mother of all the godly, which bears, nourishes, and brings up children to God, kings and peasants alike; and this is done by the ministry. Those who neglect or despise this order choose to be wiser than Christ. Woe to the pride of such men! It is, no doubt, a thing in itself possible that divine influence alone should make us perfect without human assistance. But the present inquiry is not what the power of God can accomplish, but what is the will of God and the appointment of Christ. In employing human instruments for accomplishing their salvation, God has conferred on men no ordinary favor. Nor can any exercise be found better adapted to promote unity than to gather around the common doctrine — the standard of our General.

13. *Till we all come.* Paul had already said, that by the ministry of men the church is regulated and governed, so as to attain the highest perfection. But his commendation of the ministry is now carried farther. The necessity for which he had pleaded is not confined to a single day, but continues to the end. Or, to speak more plainly, he reminds his readers that the use of the ministry is not temporal, like that of a school for children, (παιδαγωγία, Ga 3:24,) but constant, so long as we remain in the world. Enthusiasts dream that the use of the ministry ceases as soon as we have been led to Christ. Proud men, who carry their desire of knowledge beyond what is proper, look down with contempt on the elementary instruction of childhood. But Paul maintains that we must persevere in this course till all our deficiencies are supplied; that we must make progress till death, under the teaching of Christ alone; and that we must not be ashamed to be the scholars of the church, to which Christ has committed our education.

In the unity of the faith. But ought not the unity of the faith to reign among us from the very commencement? It does reign, I acknowledge, among the sons of God, but not so perfectly as to make them *come together*. Such is the weakness of our nature, that it is enough if every day brings some nearer to others, and all nearer to

Christ. The expression, *coming together*, denotes that closest union to which we still aspire, and which we shall never reach, until this garment of the flesh, which is always accompanied by some remains of ignorance and weakness, shall have been laid aside.

And of the knowledge of the Son of God. This clause appears to be added for the sake of explanation. It was the apostle's intention to explain what is the nature of true faith, and in what it consists; that is, when the Son of God is known. To the Son of God alone faith ought to look; on him it relies; in him it rests and terminates. If it proceed farther, it will disappear, and will no longer be faith, but a delusion. Let us remember, that true faith confines its view so entirely to Christ, that it neither knows, nor desires to know, anything else.

Into a perfect man. This must be read in immediate connection with what goes before; as if he had said, "What is the highest perfection of Christians? How is that perfection attained?" Full manhood is found in Christ; for foolish men do not, in a proper manner, seek their perfection in Christ. It ought to be held as a fixed principle among us, that all that is out of Christ is hurtful and destructive. Whoever is a man in Christ, is, in every respect, a perfect man.

The AGE of fullness means — full or mature age. No mention is made of old age, for in the Christian progress no place for it is found. Whatever becomes old has a tendency to decay; but the vigor of this spiritual life is continually advancing.

14. *That we may be no more children.* Having spoken of that perfect manhood, towards which we are proceeding throughout the whole course of our life, he reminds us that, during such a progress, we ought not to resemble children. An intervening period is thus pointed out between childhood and man's estate. Those are "children" who have not yet advanced a step in the way of the Lord, but who still hesitate, — who have not yet determined what road they ought to choose, but move sometimes in one direction and sometimes in another, always doubtful, always wavering. Those, again, who are thoroughly founded in the doctrine of Christ, though not yet perfect, have so much wisdom and vigor as to choose properly, and proceed steadily, in the right course. Thus we find that the life of believers, marked by a constant desire and progress towards those attainments which they shall ultimately reach, bears a resemblance to youth. At no period of this life are we men. But let not such a statement be carried to the other extreme, as if there were no progress beyond childhood. After being born to Christ, we ought to grow, so as "not to be children in understanding." (1Co 14:20.) Hence it appears what kind of Christianity the Popish system must be, when the pastors labor, to the utmost of their power, to keep the people in absolute infancy.

Tossed to and fro, and carried about. The distressing hesitation of those who do not place absolute reliance on the word of the Lord, is illustrated by two striking metaphors. The first is taken from small ships, exposed to the fury of the billows in the open sea, holding no fixed course, guided neither by skill nor design, but hurried along by the violence of the tempest. The next is taken from straws, or other light substances, which are carried hither and thither as the wind drives them, and often in opposite directions. Such must be the changeable and unsteady character of all who do not rest on the foundation of God's eternal truth. It is their just punishment for looking, not to God, but to men. Paul declares, on the other hand, that faith, which rests on the word of God, stands unshaken against all the attacks of Satan.

By every wind of doctrine. By a beautiful metaphor, all the doctrines of men, by which we are drawn away from the simplicity of the gospel, are called *winds* God gave us his word, by which we might have placed ourselves beyond the possibility of being moved; but, giving way to the contrivances of men, we are carried about in all directions.

By the cunning of men. There will always be impostors, who make insidious attacks upon our faith; but, if we are fortified by the truth of God, their efforts will be unavailing. Both parts of this statement deserve our careful attention. When new sects, or wicked tenets, spring up, many persons become alarmed. But the attempts of Satan to darken, by his falsehoods, the pure doctrine of Christ, are at no time interrupted; and it is the will of God that these struggles should be the trial of our faith. When we are informed, on the other hand, that the best and readiest defense against every kind of error is to bring forward that doctrine which we have learned from Christ and his apostles, this surely is no ordinary consolation.

With what awful wickedness, then, are Papists chargeable, who take away from the word of God everything like certainty, and maintain that there is no steadiness of faith, but what depends on the authority of men! If a man entertain any doubt, it is in vain to bid him consult the word of God: he must abide by their decrees. But we have embraced the law, the prophets, and the gospel. Let us therefore confidently expect that we shall reap the advantage which is here promised, — that all the impostures of men will do us no harm. They will attack us, indeed, but they will not prevail. We are entitled, I acknowledge, to look for the dispensation of sound doctrine from the church, for God has committed it to her charge; but when Papists avail themselves of the disguise of the church for burying doctrine, they give sufficient proof that they have a diabolical synagogue.

The Greek word κυβεία, which I have translated *cunning,* is taken from players at dice, who are accustomed to practice many arts of deception. The words, ἐν πανουργία, *by craftiness,* intimate that the ministers of Satan are deeply skilled in imposture; and it is added, that they keep watch, in order to insnare, (πρὸς τὴν μεθοδείαν τῶς πλάνης.) All this should rouse and sharpen our minds to profit by the word of God. If we neglect to do so, we may fall into the snares of our enemies, and endure the severe punishment of our sloth.

Ephesians 4:15-16

15. But, speaking the truth in love, may grow up into him in all things, which is the head, *even* Christ:

15. Veritatem autem sectantes in charitate, crescamus in eum per omnia, qui est caput, nempe Christum;

16. From whom the whole body fitly joined together and compacted by that which every joint supplieth, according to the effectual working in the measure of every part, maketh increase of the body, unto the edifying of itself in love.

16. Ex quo totum corpus compositum et compactum per omnem juncturam subministrationis, secundum efficaciam in mensura uniuscujusque partis, incrementum corporis facit in aedificationem sui, in charitate.

15. *But, speaking the truth.* Having already said that we ought not to be children, destitute of reason and judgment, he now enjoins us to *grow up in the truth.* [145] Though we have not arrived at man's estate, we ought at least, as we have already said, to be advanced children. The truth of God ought to have such a firm hold of us, that all the contrivances and attacks of Satan shall not draw us from our course; and yet, as we have not hitherto attained full and complete strength, we must make progress until death.

He points out the design of this progress, that Christ may be *the head,* "that in all things he may have the pre-eminence," (Col 1:18,) and that in him alone we may grow in vigor or in stature. Again, we see that no man is excepted; all are enjoined to be subject, and to take their own places in the body.

What aspect then does Popery present, but that of a crooked, deformed person? Is not the whole symmetry of the church destroyed, when one man, acting in opposition to the head, refuses to be reckoned one of the members? The Papists deny this, and allege that the Pope is nothing more than a ministerial head. But such cavils do them no service. The tyranny of their idol must be acknowledged to be altogether inconsistent with that order which Paul here recommends. In a word, a healthful condition of the church requires that Christ alone "must increase," and all others "must decrease." (Joh 3:30.) Whatever increase we obtain must be regulated in such a manner, that we shall remain in our own place, and contribute to exalt the head.

When he bids us give heed to the truth *in love,* he uses the preposition *in,* (ἐν,) like the corresponding Hebrew preposition ב, (*beth,*) as signifying *with,* — *speaking the truth With love* [146] If each individual, instead of attending exclusively to his own concerns, shall desire mutual intercourse, there will be agreeable and general progress. Such, the Apostle assures us, must be the nature of this harmony, that men shall not be suffered to forget the claims of truth, or, disregarding them, to frame an agreement according to their own views. This proves the wickedness of the Papists, who lay aside the word of God, and labor to force our compliance with their decisions.

16. *From whom the whole body.* All our increase should tend to exalt more highly the glory of Christ. This is now proved by the best possible reason. It is he who supplies all our wants, and without whose protection we cannot be safe. As the root conveys sap to the whole tree, so all the vigor which we possess must flow to us from Christ. There are three things here which deserve our attention. The first is what has now been stated. All the life or health which is diffused through the members flows from the head; so that the members occupy a subordinate rank. The second is, that, by the distribution made, the limited share of each renders the communication between all the members absolutely necessary. The third is, that, without mutual love, the health of the body cannot be maintained. Through the members, as canals, is conveyed from the head all that is necessary for the nourishment of the body. While this connection is upheld, the body is alive and healthy. Each member, too, has its own proper share, — *according to the effectual working in the measure of every part.*

Lastly, he shows that by love the church is edified, — *to the edifying of itself in love.* This means that no increase is advantageous, which does not bear a just proportion to the whole body. That man is mistaken who desires his own separate growth. If a leg or arm should grow to a prodigious size, or the mouth be more fully distended, would the undue enlargement of those parts be otherwise than injurious to the whole frame? In like manner, if we wish to be considered members of Christ, let no man be anything for himself, but let us all be whatever we are for the benefit of each other. This is accomplished by love; and where it does not reign, there is no "edification," but an absolute scattering of the church.

Ephesians 4:17-19

17. This I say therefore, and testify in the Lord, that ye henceforth walk not as other Gentiles walk, in the vanity of their mind;

17. Hoc ergo dico et testificor in Domino, ne ambuletis amplius, quemadmodum et gentes reliquae ambulant,

18. Having the understanding darkened, being alienated from the life of God through the ignorance that is in them, because of the blindness of their heart:

18. In vanitate mentis suae, excaecatae in intelligentia, alienatae a vita Dei propter ignorantiam, quae in illis est, propter caecitatem cordis earum;

19. Who, being past feeling, have given themselves over unto lasciviousness, to work all uncleanness with greediness.

19. Quae postquam dolore tangi desierunt, seipsas tradiderunt lasciviae, ad perpetrandam omnem immunditiam cum aviditate.

17. *This I say therefore.* That government which Christ has appointed for the edification of his church has now been considered. He next inquires what fruits the doctrine of the gospel ought to yield in the lives of Christians; or, if you prefer it, he begins to explain minutely the nature of that edification by which doctrine ought to be followed.

That ye henceforth walk not in vanity. He first exhorts them to renounce the *vanity* of unbelievers, arguing from its inconsistency with their present views. That those who have been taught in the school of Christ, and enlightened by the doctrine of salvation, should follow vanity, and in no respect differ from those unbelieving and blind nations on whom no light of truth has ever shone, would be singularly foolish. On this ground he very properly calls upon them to demonstrate, by their life, that they had gained some advantage by becoming the disciples of Christ. To impart to his exhortation the greater earnestness, he beseeches them by the name of God, — *this I say and testify in the Lord,* [147] — reminding them, that, if they despised this instruction, they must one day give an account.

As other Gentiles walk. He means those who had not yet been converted to Christ. But, at the same time, he reminds the Ephesians how necessary it was that they should repent, since by nature they resembled lost and condemned men. The miserable and shocking condition of other nations is held out as the motive to a change of disposition. He asserts that believers differ from unbelievers; and points out, as we shall see, the causes of this difference. With regard to the former, he accuses their mind of *vanity:* and let us remember, that he speaks generally of all who have not been renewed by the Spirit of Christ.

In the vanity of their mind. Now, *the mind* holds the highest rank in the human constitution, is the seat of reason, presides over the will, and restrains sinful desires; so that our theologians of the *Sorbonne* are in the habit of calling her the Queen. But, Paul makes the *mind* to consist of nothing else than vanity; and, as if he had not expressed his meaning strongly enough, he gives no better title to her daughter, *the understanding.* Such is my interpretation of the word διανοία; for, though it signifies the thought, yet, as it is in the singular number, it refers to the thinking faculty. Plato, about the close of his Sixth Book on a Republic, assigns to διανοία an intermediate place between νόησις and πίστις but his observations are so entirely confined to geometrical subjects, as not to admit of application to this passage. Having formerly asserted that men see nothing, Paul now adds, that they are blind in reasoning, even on the most important subjects.

Let men now go and be proud of free-will, whose guidance is here marked by so deep disgrace. But experience, we shall be told, is openly at variance with this opinion; for men are not so blind as to be incapable of seeing anything, nor so vain as to be incapable of forming any judgment. I answer, with respect to the kingdom of God, and all that relates to the spiritual life, the light of human reason differs little from darkness; for, before it has pointed out the road, it is extinguished; and its power of perception is little else than blindness, for ere it has reached the fruit, it is gone. The true principles held by the human mind resemble sparks; [148] but these are choked by the depravity of our nature, before they have been applied to their proper use. All men know, for instance, that there is a God, and that it is our duty to worship him; but such is the power of sin and ignorance, that from this confused knowledge we pass all at once to an idol, and worship it in the place of God. And even in the worship of God, it leads to great errors, particularly in the first table of the law.

As to the second objection, our judgment does indeed agree with the law of God in regard to the mere outward actions; but sinful desire, which is the source of everything evil, escapes our notice. Besides, Paul does not speak merely of the natural blindness which we brought with us from the womb, but refers also to a still grosser blindness, by which, as we shall afterwards see, God punishes former transgressions. We conclude with observing, that the reason and understanding which men naturally possess, make them in the sight of God without excuse; but, so long as they allow themselves to live according to their natural disposition, they can only wander, and fall, and stumble in their purposes and actions. Hence it appears in what estimation and value false worship must appear in the sight of God, when it proceeds from the gulf of vanity and the maze of ignorance.

18. *Being alienated from the life of God. The life of God* may either mean what is accounted life in the sight of God, as in that passage,

"they loved the praise of men more than *the praise of God,*"

(Joh 12:43,)

or, that life which God bestows on his elect by the Spirit of regeneration. In both cases the meaning is the same. Our ordinary life, as men, is nothing more than an empty image of life, not only because it quickly passes, but also because, while we live, our souls, not keeping close to God, are dead. There are three kinds of life in this world. The first is animal life, which consists only of motion and the bodily senses, and which we have in common with the brutes; the second is human life, which we have as the children of Adam; and the third is that supernatural life, which believers alone obtain. And all of them are from God, so that each of them may be called *the life of God.* As to the first, Paul, in his sermon at Athens, says, (Ac 17:28,) "In him we live, and move, and have our being;" and the Psalmist says,

"Send forth thy Spirit, and they shall be created; and thou wilt renew the face of the earth." (Ps 104:30.)

Of the second Job says,

"Thou hast granted me life, and thy visitation hath preserved my spirit." (Job 10:12.)

But the regeneration of believers is here called, by way of eminence, *the life of God,* because then does God truly live in us, and we enjoy his life, when he governs us by his Spirit. Of this life all men who are not new creatures in Christ are declared by Paul to be destitute. So long, then, as we remain in the flesh, that is, in ourselves, how wretched must be our condition! We may now form a judgment of all the moral virtues, as they are called; for what sort of actions will that life produce which, Paul affirms, is not the life of God? Before anything good can begin to proceed from us, we must first be renewed by the grace of Christ. This will be the commencement of a true, and, as the phrase is, a *vital* life.

On account of the ignorance that is in them. We ought to attend to the reason which is here assigned; for, as the knowledge of God is the true life of the soul, so, on the contrary, ignorance is the death of it. And lest we should adopt the opinion of philosophers, that ignorance, which leads us into mistakes, is only an incidental evil, Paul shews that it has its root *in the blindness of their heart,* by which he intimates that it dwells in their very nature. The first blindness, therefore, which covers the minds of men, is the punishment of original sin; because Adam, after his revolt, was deprived of the true light of God, in the absence of which there is nothing but fearful darkness.

19. *Who being past feeling.* The account which had been given of natural depravity is followed by a description of the worst of all evils, brought upon men by their own sinful conduct. Having destroyed the sensibilities of the heart, and allayed the stings of remorse, they abandon themselves to all manner of iniquity. We are by nature corrupt and prone to evil; nay, we are wholly inclined to evil. Those who are destitute of the Spirit of Christ give loose reins to self-indulgence, till fresh offenses, producing others in constant succession, bring down upon them the wrath of God. The voice of God, proclaimed by an accusing conscience, still continues to be heard; but, instead of producing its proper effects, appears rather to harden them against all admonition. On account of such obstinacy, they deserve to be altogether forsaken by God.

The usual symptom of their having been thus forsaken is — the insensibility to pain, which is here described — *being past feeling.* Unmoved by the approaching judgment of God, whom they offend, they go on at their ease, and fearlessly indulge without restraint in the pleasures of sin. No shame is felt, no regard to character is maintained. The gnawing of a guilty conscience, tormented by the dread of the Divine judgment, may be compared to the porch of hell; but such hardened security as this — is a whirlpool which swallows up and destroys. As Solomon says,

"When the wicked is come to the deep, he despiseth it."
(Pr 18:3.)

Most properly, therefore, does Paul exhibit that dreadful example of Divine vengeance, in which men forsaken by God — having laid conscience to sleep, and destroyed all fear of the Divine judgment, — in a word, *being past feeling,* — surrender themselves with brutal violence to all wickedness. This is not universally the case. Many even of the reprobate are restrained by God, whose infinite goodness prevents the absolute confusion in which the world would otherwise be involved. The consequence is, that such open lust, such unrestrained intemperance, does not appear in all. It is enough that the lives of some present such a mirror, fitted to awaken our alarm lest anything similar should happen to ourselves.

Lasciviousness (ἀσελγεία) appears to me to denote that wantonness with which the flesh indulges in intemperance and licentiousness, when not restrained by the Spirit of God. *Uncleanness* is put for scandalous enormities of every description. It is added, *with greediness.* The Greek word πλεονεξία, which is so translated, often signifies covetousness, (Lu 12:15; 2Pe 2:14,) and is so explained by some in this passage; but I cannot adopt that view. Depraved and wicked desires being insatiable, Paul represents them as attended and followed by *greediness*, which is the contrary of moderation.

Ephesians 4:20-24

20. But ye have not so learned Christ;

20. Vos autem non ita didicistis Christum;

21. If so be that ye have heard him, and have been taught by him, as the truth is in Jesus:

21. Si quidem ipsum audistis, et in ipso estis edocti, quemadmodum est veritas in Iesu;

22. That ye put off, concerning the former conversation, the old man, which is corrupt according to the deceitful lusts;

22. Ut deponatis, secundum pristinam conversationem, Veterem hominem, qui corrumpitur secundum concupiscentias erroris;

23. And be renewed in the spirit of your mind;

23. Renovemini autem spiritu mentis vestrae,

24. And that ye put on the new man, which after God is created in righteousness and true holiness.

24. Et induatis Novum hominem, qui secundum Deum creatus est, in justitia et sanctitate veritatis.

20. *But ye have not.* He now draws a contrast of a Christian life, so as to make it evident how utterly inconsistent it is with the character of a godly man to defile himself regardlessly with the abominations of the Gentiles. Because the Gentiles walk in darkness, therefore they do not distinguish between right and wrong; but those on whom the truth of God shines ought to live in a different manner. That those to whom the vanity of the senses is a rule of life, should yield themselves up to base lusts, is not surprising; but the doctrine of Christ teaches us to renounce our natural dispositions. He whose life differs not from that of unbelievers, has learned nothing of Christ; for the knowledge of Christ cannot be separated from the mortification of the flesh.

21. *If ye have heard him.* To excite their attention and earnestness the more, he not only tells them that they had *heard Christ,* but employs a still stronger expression, *ye have been taught in him,* as if he had said, that this doctrine had not been slightly pointed out, but faithfully delivered and explained.

As the truth is in Jesus. This contains a reproof of that superficial knowledge of the gospel, by which many are elated, who are wholly unacquainted with newness of life. They think that they are exceedingly wise, but the apostle pronounces it to be a false and mistaken opinion. There is a twofold knowledge of Christ, — one, which is true and genuine, — and another, which is counterfeit and spurious. Not that, strictly speaking, there are two kinds; but most men falsely imagine that they know Christ, while they know nothing but what is carnal. In another Epistle he says,

"If any man be in Christ, let him be a new creature."

(2Co 5:17.)

So here he affirms that any knowledge of Christ, which is not accompanied by mortification of the flesh, is not true and sincere.

22. *That ye put off.* He demands from a Christian man repentance, or a new life, which he makes to consist of self-denial and the regeneration of the Holy Spirit. Beginning with the first, he enjoins us to lay aside, or *put off* the old man, employing the metaphor of garments, which we have already had occasion to explain. *The old man,* — as we have repeatedly stated, in expounding the sixth chapter of the Epistle to the Romans, and other passages where it occurs, — means the natural disposition which we bring with us from our mother's womb. In two persons, Adam and Christ, he describes to us what may be called two natures. As we are first born of Adam, the depravity of nature which we derive from him is called the *Old* man; and as we are born again in Christ, the amendment of this sinful nature is called the *New* man. In a word, he who desires to put off the old man must renounce his nature. To suppose that the words *Old* and *New* contain an allusion to the Old and New Testaments, is exceedingly unphilosophical.

Concerning the former conversation. To make it more evident that this exhortation to the Ephesians was not unnecessary, he reminds them of their former life. "Before Christ revealed himself to your minds, the old man reigned in you; and therefore, if you desire to lay him aside, you must renounce your former life." *Which is corrupted.* He describes the old man from the fruits, that is, from the wicked desires, which allure men to destruction; for the word, *corrupt,* alludes to old age, which is closely allied to corruption. Let us beware of considering *the deceitful lusts,* as the Papists do, to mean nothing more than the gross and visible lusts, which are generally acknowledged to be base. The word includes also those dispositions which, instead of being censured, are sometimes applauded, — such as ambition, cunning, and everything that proceeds either from self-love or from want of confidence in God.

23. *And be renewed.* The second part of the rule for a devout and holy life is to live, not in our own spirit, but in the Spirit of Christ. But what is meant by — *the spirit of your mind?* I understand it simply to mean, — *Be renewed,* not only with respect to the inferior appetites or desires, which are manifestly sinful, but with respect also to that part of the soul which is reckoned most noble and excellent.

And here again, he brings forward to view that Queen which philosophers are accustomed almost to adore. There is an implied contrast between *the spirit of our mind* and the Divine and heavenly Spirit, who produces in us another and a new mind. How much there is in us that is sound or uncorrupted may be easily gathered from this passage, which enjoins us to correct chiefly the reason or *mind,* in which we are apt to imagine that there is nothing but what is virtuous and deserves commendation.

24. *And that ye put on the new man.* All that is meant is, "Be renewed in the spirit, or, be renewed *within* or *completely,* — beginning with the mind, which appears to be the part most free from all taint of sin." What is added about the creation, may refer either to the first creation of man, or to the second creation, which is effected by the grace of Christ. Both expositions will be true. Adam was at first created after the image of God, and reflected, as in a mirror, the Divine righteousness; but that image, having been defaced by sin, must now be restored in Christ. The regeneration of the godly is indeed — as we have formerly explained [149] — nothing else than the formation anew of the image of God in them. There is, no doubt, a far more rich and powerful manifestation of Divine grace in this second creation than in the first; but our highest perfection is uniformly represented in Scripture as consisting in our conformity and resemblance to God. Adam lost the image which he had originally received, and therefore it becomes necessary that it shall be restored to us by Christ. The design contemplated by regeneration is to recall us from our wanderings to that end for which we were created.

In righteousness. If *righteousness* be taken as a general term for uprightness, *holiness* will be something higher, or that purity which lies in being devoted to the service of God. I am rather inclined to consider *holiness* as referring to the first table, and *righteousness* to the second table, of the law, as in the song of Zacharias,

"That we may serve him in *holiness and righteousness*, all the days of our life." (Luke 1:74, 75.)

Plato lays down the distinction correctly, that *holiness* (ὁσιότης) lies in the worship of God, and that the other part, *righteousness,* (δικαιοσύνη,) bears a reference to men. The genitive, *of truth*, (τῶς αληθείας,) is put in the place of an adjective, and refers to both terms; so that, while it literally runs, *in righteousness and holiness of truth,* the meaning is, *in true righteousness and holiness.* He warns us that both ought to be sincere; because we have to do with God, whom it is impossible to deceive.

Ephesians 4:25-28

25. Wherefore, putting away lying, speak every man truth with his neighbor: for we are members one of another.

25. Quare, deposito mendacio, loquimini veritatem unusquisque cum proximo suo; quia sumus vicissim inter nos membra.

26. Be ye angry, and sin not: let not the sun go down upon your wrath:

26. Irascimini, et ne peccetis. (Ps 4:5.) Sol non occidat super iracundiam vestram:

27. Neither give place to the devil.

27. Et ne detis locum diabolo.

28. Let him that stole steal no more: but rather let him labor, working with *his* hands the thing which is good, that he may have to give to him that needeth.

28. Qui furabatur, jam non furetur; magis autem laboret, operando quod bonum est manibus, ut habeat quod eroget opus habenti.

25. *Wherefore, putting away lying.* From this head of doctrine, that is, from the righteousness of the new man, all godly exhortations flow, like streams from a fountain; for if all the precepts which relate to life were collected, yet, without this principle, they would be of little value. Philosophers take a different method; but, in the doctrine of godliness, there is no other way than this for regulating the life. Now, therefore, he comes to lay down particular exhortations, drawn from the general doctrine. Having concluded from the truth of the gospel, that righteousness and holiness ought to be true, he now argues from the general statement to a particular instance, that *every man should speak truth with his neighbour. Lying* is here put for every kind of deceit, hypocrisy, or cunning; and *truth* for honest dealing. He demands that every kind of communication between them shall be sincere; and enforces it by this consideration, *for we are members one of another.* That *members* should not agree among themselves, — that they should act in a deceitful manner towards each other, is prodigious wickedness.

26. *Be ye angry, and sin not.* Whether or not the apostle had in his eye a part of the fourth Psalm is uncertain. The words used by him (Ὀργίζεσθε καὶ μὴ ἁμαρτάνετε) occur in the Greek translation, though the word ὀργίζεσθε, which is translated, *be ye angry,* is considered by some to mean *tremble.* [150] The Hebrew verb רגז (*ragaz*) signifies either to be agitated by anger, or, to tremble. As to the passage of the Psalm, the idea of *trembling* will be quite appropriate. "Do not choose to resemble madmen, who rush fearlessly in any direction, but let the dread of being accounted foolhardy keep you in awe." The word sometimes signifies to *strive* or *quarrel,* as, in that instance, (Ge 45:24,) "See that ye *fall not out* by the way;" and accordingly, the Psalmist adds, "Commune with your own heart, and be still," — abstain from furious encounters.

In my opinion, Paul merely alludes to the passage with the following view. There are three faults by which we offend God in being angry. The first is, when our anger arises from slight causes, and often from no cause whatever, or at least from private injuries or offenses. The second is, when we go beyond the proper bounds, and are hurried into intemperate excesses. The third is, when our anger, which ought to have been directed against ourselves or against sins, is turned against our brethren. Most appropriately, therefore, did Paul, when he wished to describe the proper limitation of anger, employ the well-known passage, *Be ye angry, and sin not.* We comply with this injunction, if the objects of our anger are sought, not in others, but in ourselves, — if we pour out our indignation against our own faults. With respect to others, we ought to be angry, not at their persons, but at their faults; nor ought we to be excited to anger by private offenses, but by zeal for the glory of the Lord. Lastly, our anger, after a reasonable time, ought to be allowed to subside, without mixing itself with the violence of carnal passions.

Let not the sun go down. It is scarcely possible, however, but that we shall sometimes give way to improper and sinful passion, — so strong is the tendency of the human mind to what is evil. Paul therefore suggests a second remedy, that we shall quickly suppress our anger, and not suffer it to gather strength by continuance. The first remedy was, *Be ye angry, and sin not;* but, as the great weakness of human nature renders this exceedingly difficult, the next is — not to cherish wrath too long in our minds, or allow it sufficient time to become strong. He enjoins accordingly, *let not the sun go down upon your wrath.* If at any time we happen to be angry, let us endeavor to be appeased before the sun has set.

27. *Neither give place* (τῷ διαβόλῳ) *to the devil.* I am aware of the interpretation which some give of this passage. Erasmus, who translates it, "neither give place to the Slanderer," (*calumniatori,*) shews plainly that he understood it as referring to malicious men. But I have no doubt, Paul's intention was, to guard us against allowing Satan to take possession of our minds, and, by keeping in his hands this citadel, to do whatever he pleases. We feel every day how impossible, or, at least, how difficult it is to cure long-continued hatred. What is the cause of this, but that, instead of resisting the devil, we yield up to him the possession of our heart? Before the poison of hatred has found its way into the heart, anger must be thoroughly dislodged.

28. *Let him that stole steal no more.* This includes not merely the grosser thefts which are punished by human laws, but those of a more concealed nature, which do not fall under the cognizance of men, — every kind of depredation by which we seize the property of others. But he does not simply forbid us to take that property in an unjust or unlawful manner. He enjoins us to assist our brethren, as far as lies in our power.

That he may have to give to him that needeth. "Thou who formerly stolest must not only obtain thy subsistence by lawful and harmless toil, but must give assistance to others." He is first required *to labor, working with his hands,* that he may not supply his wants at the expense of his brethren, but may support life by honorable labor. But the love which we owe to our neighbor carries us much farther. No one must live to himself alone, and neglect others. All must labor to supply each other's necessities.

But a question arises, does Paul oblige all men to labor with their hands? This would be excessively hard. I reply, the meaning is plain, if it be duly considered. Every man is forbidden to steal. But many people are in the habit of pleading want, and that excuse is obviated by enjoining them *rather to labor* (μᾶλλον δε κοπιάτω) with their hands. As if he had said, "No condition, however hard or disagreeable, can entitle any man to do injury to another, or even to refrain from contributing to the necessities of his brethren.

The thing which is good. This latter clause, which contains an argument from the greater to the less, gives no small additional strength to the exhortation. As there are many occupations which do little to promote the lawful enjoyments of men, he recommends to them to choose those employments which yield the greatest advantage to their neighbors. We need not wonder at this. If those trades which can have no other effect than to lead men into immorality, were denounced by heathens — and Cicero among the number — as highly disgraceful, would an apostle of Christ reckon them among the lawful callings of God?

Ephesians 4:29-31

29. Let no corrupt communication proceed out of your mouth, but that which is good to the use of edifying, that it may minister grace unto the hearers.

29. Omnis sermo spurcus ex ore vestro non procedat; sed si quis est bonus ad edificationem usus, ut det gratiam audientibus.

30. And grieve not the Holy Spirit of God, whereby ye are sealed unto the day of redemption.

30. Et ne contristetis Spiritum Sanctum Dei, quo obsignati estis in diem redemptionis.

31. Let all bitterness, and wrath, and anger, and clamor, and evil-speaking, be put away from you, with all malice.

31. Omnis amarulentia, et indignatio, et ira, et clamor, et maledicentia, removeatur a vobis cum omni malitia.

29. *No filthy speech.* He first forbids believers to use any *filthy* language, including under this name all those expressions which are wont to be employed for the purpose of inflaming lust. Not satisfied with the removal of the vice, he enjoins them to frame their discourse for edification. In another Epistle he says, "Let your speech be seasoned with salt." (Col 4:6.) Here a different phrase is employed, *if any* (speech) *be good to the use of edifying,* which means simply, *if it be useful.* The genitive, *of use,* may no doubt be viewed, according to the Hebrew idiom, as put for an adjective, so that *for the edification of use* (πρὸς οἰκοδομὴν τῶς χρείας) may mean *for useful edification;* but when I consider how frequently, and in how extensive a meaning, the metaphor of *edifying* occurs in Paul's writings, I prefer the former exposition. *The edification of use* will thus mean the progress of our edification, for to edify is to carry forward. To explain the manner in which this is done, he adds, *that it may impart grace to the hearers,* meaning by the word *grace,* comfort, advice, and everything that aids the salvation of the soul.

30. *And grieve not.* As the Holy Spirit dwells in us, to him every part of our soul and of our body ought to be devoted. But if we give ourselves up to aught that is impure, we may be said to drive him away from making his abode with us; and, to express this still more familiarly, human affections, such as joy and grief, are ascribed to the Holy Spirit. [151] Endeavour that the Holy Spirit may dwell cheerfully with you, as in a pleasant and joyful dwelling, and give him no occasion for grief. Some take a different view of it, that we grieve the Holy Spirit in others, when we offend by filthy language, or, in any other way, godly brethren, who are led by the Spirit of God. (Ro 8:14.) Whatever is contrary to godliness is not only disrelished by godly ears, but is no sooner heard than it produces in them deep grief and pain. But that Paul's meaning was different appears from what follows.

By whom ye are sealed. As God has sealed us by his Spirit, we grieve him when we do not follow his guidance, but pollute ourselves by wicked passions. No language can adequately express this solemn truth, that the Holy Spirit rejoices and is glad on our account, when we are obedient to him in all things, and neither think nor speak anything, but what is pure and holy; and, on the other hand, is grieved, when we admit anything into our minds that is unworthy of our calling. Now, let any man reflect what shocking wickedness there must be in grieving the Holy Spirit to such a degree as to compel him to withdraw from us. The same mode of speaking is used by the prophet Isaiah, but in a different sense; for he merely says, that they "vexed his Holy Spirit," (Isa 63:10.) in the same sense in which we are accustomed to speak of vexing the mind of a man. *By whom ye are sealed.* The Spirit of God is the seal, by which we are distinguished from the wicked, and which is impressed on our hearts as a sure evidence of adoption.

Unto the day of redemption, — that is, till God conduct us into the possession of the promised inheritance. That day is usually called *the day of redemption,* because we shall then be at length delivered out of all our afflictions. It is unnecessary to make any observations on this phrase, in addition to what have already been made in expounding Ro 8:23, and 1Co 1:30. In this passage, the word *sealed* may have a different meaning from that which it usually bears, — that God has impressed his Spirit as his mark upon us, that he may recognize as his children those whom he perceives to bear that mark.

31. *Let all bitterness.* He again condemns anger; but, on the present occasion, views in connection with it those offenses by which it is usually accompanied, such as noisy disputes and reproaches. Between *wrath and anger* (Θυμὸν καὶ ὀργὴν) there is little difference, except that the former denotes the power, and the latter the act; but here, the only difference is, that *anger* is a more sudden attack. The correction of all the rest will be greatly aided by the removal of *malice.* By this term he expresses that depravity of mind which is opposed to humanity and justice, and which is usually called *malignity.*

Ephesians 4:32

32. And be ye kind one to another, tender-hearted, forgiving one another, even as God for Christ's sake hath forgiven you.

32. Sitis autem mutuo comes, misericordes, condonantes vobis inter vos, quemadmodum et Deus vobis in Christo condonavit.

32. *And be ye kind one to another.* With *bitterness* he contrasts *kindness,* or gentleness of countenance, language, and manners. And as this virtue will never reign in us, unless attended by *compassion,* (συμπάθεια,) he recommends to us to be *tender-hearted* This will lead us not only to sympathize with the distresses of our brethren, as if they were our own, but to cultivate that true humanity which is affected by everything that happens to them, in the same manner as if we were in their situation. The contrary of this is the cruelty of those iron-hearted, barbarous men, by whom the sufferings of others are beheld without any concern whatever.

Forgiving one another. The Greek word here rendered *forgiving,* (χαριζόμενοι ἑαυτοῖς,) is supposed by to mean beneficence. Erasmus, accordingly, renders it (*largientes*) *bountiful.* Though the word admits of that meaning, yet the context induces me to prefer the other view, that we should be ready to *forgive* It may sometimes happen, that men are *kind* and *tender-hearted,* and yet, when they receive improper treatment, do not so easily forgive injuries. That those whose kindness of heart in other respects disposes them to acts of humanity, may not fail in their duty through the ingratitude of men, he exhorts them to discover a readiness to lay aside resentment. To give his exhortation the greater weight, he holds out the example of

God, who has forgiven to us, through Christ, far more than any mortal man can forgive to his brethren. [152]

Footnotes

138

Τῶς κλήσεως ἧς ἐκλήθητε "Arrian, Epict page 122, 1 3, says, καταισχύνειν τὴν κλῶσιν ἣν κέκληκεν, 'to disgrace the calling with which he has called thee.' He is speaking of a person, who, when summoned to give his testimony, utters what is contrary to that which was demanded or expected from him." — Raphelius.

139

"There are ancient medals now extant, which have the figure of Diana on them, with this inscription, κοινὸν τῶς 'Ασίας, denoting that the cities of Asia were one body or commonwealth. Thus also were all Christians of all nations, Jews and Gentiles, under Christ." — Chandler.

140

For 'the lower parts of the earth,' they may possibly signify no more than the place beneath; as when our Savior said, (Joh 8:23,) 'Ye are from beneath, I am from above; ye are of this world, I am not of this world;' or as God spake by the prophet, 'I will shew wonders in heaven above, and signs in the earth beneath.' Nay, they may well refer to his incarnation, according to that of David, (Ps 139:15,) or to his burial. (Ps 63:9.)" — Pearson.

141

"This was the place of which our Savior spake to his disciples, 'What and if ye shall see the Son of Man ascend up where he was before?' Had he been there before in body, it had been no such wonder that he should have ascended thither again; but that his body should ascend unto that place where the majesty of God was most resplendent; that the flesh of our flesh, and bone of our bone, should be seated far above all angels and archangels, all principalities and powers, even at the right hand of God; this was that which Christ propounded as worthy of their greatest admiration. Whatsoever heaven there is higher than all the rest that are called heavens; whatsoever sanctuary is holier than all which are called holies; whatsoever place is of greatest dignity in all those courts above, into that place did he ascend, where, in the splendor of his Deity, he was before he took upon him our humanity." — Pearson.

142

"The deepest humiliation is followed by the highest exaltation. From the highest heaven, than which nothing can be higher, Christ descended to hell, than which nothing can be lower. And on that account he deserved that he should be again carried up beyond the boundaries of all the heavens, withdrawing from us the presence of his body in such a manner, that from on high he might fill all things with heavenly gifts, and, in a different manner, might now be present with us more effectually than he was present while he dwelt with us on earth." — Erasmus.

143

See Calvin on Corinthians, vol. 1 p. 401.

144

See Calvin on Corinthians, vol. 1 p. 415.

145

“ ’Αληθεύοντες does not seem properly to denote so much ‘speaking the truth,’ as ‘embracing and adhering to it;’ and, to render the Christian perfect, he must add to this regard to truth, love, or universal affection and benevolence. It was a noble saying of Pythagoras, agreeable to this sentiment of our apostle, ‘These are the two loveliest gifts of the gods to men, τό τε ἀληθεύειν καὶ τὸ εὐεργετεῖν, to embrace the truth, and be beneficent.’ AElian. 1. 12, c. 58.)” — Chandler.

146

“ ’Αλγθεύοντες ἐν ἀγάπῃ, means much more than ‘*speaking* the truth in love;’ it signifies thinking, feeling, acting under the influence of ‘the truth, which worketh by love.’” — Brown.

147

“Μαρτύρομαι ἐν κυρίῳ — In this sense μαρτύρομαι is obviously used by Polybius: συνδαραμόντων δὲ τῶν ἐγχωρίων καὶ μαρτυρομένων τοὺς ἄνδρας ἐπανάγειν ἐπὶ τὴν ἀρχήν, when the inhabitants had run together and besought to bring the men to the magistrates. It is more customary to use διαμαρτύρομαι in this sense. Πολλὰ γὰρ τῶν κυβερνητῶν διαμαρτυρομένων μὴ πλεῖν παρὰ τὴν ἔξω πλευρὰν τῶς Σικελίας, because the pilots earnestly implored them not to sail along the opposite coast of Sicily.” — Raphelius.

148

“Il y a bien en l’esprit de l’homme des principes et maximes veritables, qui sont commes estincelles.” “There are, in the mind of man, many true principles and maxims, which resemble sparks.”

149

See Calvin’s Commentary on Corinthians, vol. 2 p. 187.

150

“Stand in awe,” Ps 4:4. (English Version)

151

“According to our view, the verse is a summation of the argument — the climax of appeal. If Christians shall persist in falsehood and deviation from the truth — if they shall indulge in fitful rage, or cherish sullen and malignant dislikes — if they shall be characterized by dishonesty, or insipid and corrupt language, then do they grieve the Holy Spirit of God; for all this perverse insubordination is in utter antagonism to the essence and operations of Him who is the Spirit of truth; and inspires the love of it; who assumed, as a fitting symbol, the form of a dove, and creates meekness and forbearance; and who, as the Spirit of holiness, leads to the appreciation of all that is just in action, noble in sentiment, and healthful and edifying in speech.” — Eadie.

152

See Calvin's Commentary on Philippians, Colossians, etc., page 213.

CHAPTER 5

Ephesians 5:1-2

1. Be ye therefore followers of God, as dear children;

1. Sitis ergo imitatores Dei quemadmodum filii dilecti;

2. And walk in love, as Christ also hath loved us, and hath given himself for us an offering and a sacrifice to God for a sweet smelling savor.

2. Et ambulate in charitate quemadmodum et Christus nos dilexit, ac se ipsum tradidit pro nobis oblationem et hostiam Deo, in odorem bonae fragrantiae.

1. *Be ye therefore followers.* The same principle is followed out and enforced by the consideration that children ought to be like their father. He reminds us that we are the children of God, and that therefore we ought, as far as possible, to resemble Him in acts of kindness. It is impossible not to perceive, that the division of chapters, in the present instance, is particularly unhappy, as it has made a separation between parts of the subject which are very closely related. If, then, we are the children of God, we ought to be *followers of God.* Christ also declares, that, unless we shew kindness to the unworthy, we cannot be the children of our heavenly Father.

"Love your enemies, bless them that curse you, do good to them that hate you, and pray for them who despitefully use you and persecute you; *that ye may be the children of your Father which is in heaven*; for he maketh his sun to rise on the evil and on the good, and sendeth rain on the just and on the unjust." (Matt. 5:44, 45.) [153]

2. *And walk in love as Christ also hath loved us.* Having called on us to imitate God, he now calls on us to imitate Christ, who is our true model. We ought to embrace each other with that love with which Christ has embraced us, for what we perceive in Christ is our true guide.

And gave himself for us. This was a remarkable proof of the highest love. Forgetful, as it were, of himself, Christ spared not his own life, that he might redeem us from death. If we desire to be partakers of this benefit, we must cultivate similar affections toward our neighbors. Not that any of us has reached such high perfection, but all must aim and strive according to the measure of their ability.

An offering and a sacrifice to God of a sweet smelling savor. While this statement leads us to admire the grace of Christ, it bears directly on the present subject. No language, indeed, can fully represent the consequences and efficacy of Christ's death. This is the only price by which we are reconciled to God. The doctrine of faith on this subject holds the highest rank. But the more extraordinary the discoveries which have reached us of the Redeemer's kindness, the more strongly are we bound to his service. Besides, we may infer from Paul's words, that, unless we love one another, none of our duties will be acceptable in the sight of God. If the reconciliation of men, effected by Christ, was *a sacrifice of a sweet smelling savor,* [154] we, too, shall be "unto God a sweet savor," (2Co 2:15,) when this holy perfume is spread over us. To this applies the saying of Christ,

"Leave thy gift before the altar, and go and be reconciled to thy brother." (Mt 5:24.)

Ephesians 5: 3-7

3. But fornication, and all uncleanness, or covetousness, let it not be once named among you, as becometh saints;

3. Scortatio vero et omnis immundities, aut avaritia, ne nominentur quidem inter vos; sicut decet sanctos.

4. Neither filthiness, nor foolish talking, nor jesting, which are not convenient; but rather giving of thanks.

4. Turpitudo, stultiloquium, facetia; quae non conveniunt, sed magis gratia.

5. For this ye know, that no whoremonger, nor unclean person, nor covetous man, who is an idolater, hath any inheritance in the kingdom of Christ and of God.

5. Hoc enim scitis, quod omnis scortator, vel immundus, vel avarus, qui est idololatra, non obtinebit haereditatem in regno Christi et Dei.

6. Let no man deceive you with vain words: for because of these things cometh the wrath of God upon the children of disobedience.

6. Nemo vos decipiat inanibus verbis; nam propter haec venit ira Dei in filios inobedientes (*vel, incredulos.*)

7. Be not ye therefore partakers with them.

7. Ne sitis igitur illorum consortes.

3. *But fornication.* This chapter, and the Col 3, contain many parallel passages, which an intelligent reader will be at no loss to compare without my assistance. Three things are here enumerated, which the apostle desires Christians to hold in such abhorrence, that they shall not even be named, or, in other words, shall be entirely unknown among them. By *uncleanness* he means all base and impure lusts; so that this word differs from *fornication,* only as the whole class differs from a single department. The third is *covetousness,* which is nothing more than an immoderate desire of gain. To this precept he adds the authoritative declaration, that he demands nothing from them but that which *becometh saints,* — manifestly excluding from the number and fellowship of the saints all fornicators, and impure and covetous persons.

4. *Neither filthiness.* To those three — other three are now added. By *filthiness* I understand all that is indecent or inconsistent with the modesty of the godly. By *foolish talking* I understand conversations that are either unprofitably or wickedly foolish; and as it frequently happens that idle talk is concealed under the garb of *jesting* or wit, he expressly mentions pleasantry, — which is so agreeable as to seem worthy of commendation, — and condemns it as a part of *foolish talking* The Greek word εὐτραπελία is often used by heathen writers, in a good sense, for that ready and ingenious pleasantry in which able and intelligent men may properly indulge. But as it is exceedingly difficult to be witty without becoming satirical, and as jesting itself carries in it a portion of conceit not at all in keeping with the character of a godly man, Paul very properly dissuades from this practice. [155] Of all the three offenses now mentioned, Paul declares that they are *not convenient,* or, in other words, that they are inconsistent with Christian duty.

But rather grace. Others render it *giving of thanks;* but I prefer Jerome's interpretation. With the vices which had been formerly mentioned it was proper that Paul should contrast something of a general character, displaying itself in all our communications with each other. If he had said, "While they take pleasure in idle or abusive talk, do you give thanks to God," the exhortation would have been too limited. The Greek word, εὐχαριστία, though it usually signifies *Thanksgiving,* admits of being translated *Grace.* "All our conversations ought to be, in the true sense of the words, sweet and graceful; and this end will be gained if the useful and the agreeable are properly mingled."

5. *For this ye know.* If his readers were at all captivated by the allurements of those vices which have been enumerated, the consequence would be that they would lend a hesitating or careless ear to his admonitions. He determines, therefore, to alarm them by this weighty and dreadful threatening, that such vices shut against us the kingdom of God. By appealing to their own knowledge, he intimates that this was no doubtful matter. Some might think it harsh, or inconsistent with the Divine goodness, that all who have incurred the guilt of fornication or covetousness are excluded from the inheritance of the kingdom of heaven. But the answer is easy. Paul does not say that those who have fallen into those sins, and recovered from them, are not pardoned, but pronounces sentence on the sins themselves. After addressing the Corinthians in the same language, he adds:

"And such were some of you; but ye are washed, but ye are sanctified, but ye are justified, in the name of the Lord Jesus, and by the Spirit of our God."

(1Co 6:11.)

When men have repented, and thus give evidence that they are reconciled to God, they are no longer the same persons that they formerly were. But let all fornicators, or unclean or covetous persons, so long as they continue such, be assured that they have no friendship with God, and are deprived of all hope of salvation. It is called *the kingdom of Christ and of God,* because God hath given it to his Son that we may obtain it through him.

Nor covetous man, who is an idolater. "Covetousness," as he says in another place, "is idolatry," (Col 3:5,) — not the idolatry which is so frequently condemned in Scripture, but one of a different description. All covetous men must deny God, and put wealth in his place; such is their blind greediness of wretched gain. But why does Paul attribute to covetousness alone what belongs equally to other carnal passions? In what respect is covetousness better entitled to this disgraceful name than ambition, or than a vain confidence in ourselves? I answer, that this disease is widely spread, and not a few minds have caught the infection. Nay, it is not reckoned a disease, but receives, on the contrary, very general commendation. This accounts for the harshness of Paul's language, which arose from a desire to tear from our hearts the false view.

6. *Let no man deceive you.* There have always been ungodly dogs, [156] by whom the threatenings of the prophets were made the subject of merriment and ridicule. We find such characters in our own day. In all ages, indeed, Satan raises up sorcerers of this description, who endeavor by unholy scoffs to escape the Divine judgment, and who actually exercise a kind of fascination over consciences not sufficiently established in the fear of God. "This is a trivial fault. Fornication is viewed by God as a light matter. Under the law of grace God is not so cruel. He has not formed us so as to be our own executioners. The frailty of nature excuses us." These and similar expressions are often used by the scoffers. Paul, on the contrary, exclaims that we must guard against that sophistry by which consciences are ensnared to their ruin.

For because of these things cometh the wrath of God. If we consider the present tense to be here used, agreeably to the Hebrew idiom, for the future, these words are a threatening of the last judgment. But I agree with those who take the word *cometh* in an indefinite sense, — *the word of God* usually *cometh,* — as reminding them of the ordinary judgments of God which were executed before their own eyes. And certainly, if we were not blind and slothful, there are sufficiently numerous examples by which God testifies that he is the just avenger of such crimes, — examples of the pouring out of divine indignation, privately against individuals, and publicly against cities, and kings, and nations.

Upon the children of disobedience, — upon *unbelievers* or *rebels.* This expression must not be overlooked. Paul is now addressing believers, and his object is not so much to present alarming views of their own danger, as to rouse them to behold reflected in wicked men, as in mirrors, the dreadful judgments of God. God does not make himself an object of terror to his children, that they may avoid him, but does all that can be done in a fatherly manner, to draw them to himself. They ought to learn this lesson, not to involve themselves in a dangerous fellowship with the ungodly, whose ruin is thus foreseen.

Ephesians 5:8-14

8. For ye were sometimes darkness, but now *are ye* light in the Lord: walk as children of light;

8. Eratis aliquando tenabrae; nunc autem lux in Domino; tanquam filii lucis ambulate;

9. (For the fruit of the Spirit *is* in all goodness, and righteousness, and truth;)

9. (Fructus enim lucis in omni bonitate, et justitia, et veritate:)

10. Proving what is acceptable unto the Lord.

10. Probantes, quid sit acceptum Deo.

11. And have no fellowship with the unfruitful works of darkness, but rather reprove *them*

11. Et ne communicetis operibus infructuosis tenebrarum; quin potius etiam redarguitote.

12. For it is a shame even to speak of those things which are done of them in secret.

12. Quae enim clam fiunt ab illis, turpe est vel dicere.

13. But all things that are reproved are made manifest by the light: for whatsoever doth make manifest is light.

13. Omnia autem, dum coarguuntur, a luce manifestantur; omne enim quod manifestat lux est.

14. Wherefore he saith, Awake thou that sleepest, and arise from the dead, and Christ shall give thee light.

14. Quamobrem dicit: Surge qui dormis, et exsurge ex mortuis; et illucescet tibi Christus.

8. *For ye were once darkness.* The precepts which immediately follow derive greater weight from the motives with which they are mingled. Having spoken of unbelievers, and warned the Ephesians not to become partakers of their crimes and their destruction, he argues still further, that they ought to differ widely from the life and conduct of those men. At the same time, in order to guard them against ingratitude to God, he refreshes their remembrance of their own past life. "You ought," he says, "to be very different persons from what you formerly were; for out of darkness God hath made you light." *Darkness* is the name here given to the whole nature of man before regeneration; for, where the brightness of God does not shine, there is nothing but fearful darkness. *Light,* again, is the name given to those who are *enlightened* by the Spirit of God; for immediately afterwards in the same sense, he calls them *children of light,* and draws the inference, that they ought to walk in light, because by the mercy of God they had been rescued from darkness. Observe here, we are said to be *light in the Lord,* because, while we are out of Christ, all is under the dominion of Satan, whom we know to be the Prince of darkness.

9. *For the fruit of the light.* [157] This parenthesis is introduced, to point out the road in which the *children of light* ought to walk. A complete description is not given, but a few parts of a holy and pious life are introduced by way of example. To give them a general view of duty, their attention is again directed to the will of God. Whoever desires to live in a proper and safe manner, let him resolve to obey God, and to take his will as the rule. To regulate life entirely by his command is, as he says in another Epistle, *a reasonable service,* (Ro 12:1,) or, as another inspired man expresses it, *To obey is better than sacrifice.* (1Sa 15:22.) I wonder how the word Spirit (πνεῦματος) has crept into many Greek manuscripts, as the other reading is more consistent, — *the fruit of the light* Paul's meaning indeed is not affected; for in either case it will be this, that believers must walk in the light, because they are "children of the light." This is done, when they do not live according to their own will, but devote themselves entirely to obedience to God, — when they undertake nothing but by his command. Besides, such obedience is testified by its fruits, such as *goodness, righteousness, and truth.*

11. *And have no fellowship.* As "the children of light" dwell amidst the darkness, or, in other words, in the midst of "a perverse and crooked generation," (De 32:5,) — there is good reason for warning them to keep themselves apart from wicked actions. It is not enough that we do not, of our own accord, undertake anything wicked. We must beware of joining or assisting those who do wrong. In short, we must abstain from giving any consent, or advice, or approbation, or assistance; for in all these ways we *have fellowship.* And lest any one should imagine that he has done his duty, merely by not conniving, he adds, *but rather reprove them.* [158] Such a course is opposed to all dissimulation. Where a manifest offense is committed against God, every man will be eager to vindicate himself from any share in the guilt, but very few will guard against connivance; nearly all will practice some kind of dissimulation. But rather than the truth of God shall not remain unshaken, let a hundred worlds perish.

The word ἐλέγχειν, which is translated *reprove,* answers to the metaphor of darkness; for it literally signifies to drag forth to the light what was formerly unknown. As ungodly men flatter themselves in their vices, (Ps 36:2,) and wish their crimes to be concealed, or to be reckoned virtues, Paul enjoins that they shall be *reproved.* He calls them *unfruitful;* because they not only do no good, but are absolutely hurtful.

12. *Which are done by them in secret.* This shews the advantage of reproving the ungodly. If they do but escape the eyes of men, there is no crime, however shocking to be mentioned, which they will not perpetrate. To use a common proverb, "Night has no shame." What is the reason of this? Sunk in the darkness of ignorance, they neither see their own baseness, nor think that it is seen by God and by angels. But let the torch of God's word be brought forward, and their eyes are opened. Then they begin to blush and be ashamed. By their advices and reproofs the saints enlighten blind unbelievers, and drag forth from their concealment to the light of day those who were sunk in ignorance.

When unbelievers keep the doors of their houses shut, and withdraw from the view of men, *it is a shame even to speak of* the baseness and wickedness with which they rush into all manner of licentiousness. Would they thus lay aside all shame, and give loose reins to their passions, if darkness did not give them courage, — if they did not entertain the hope that what is hidden will pass unpunished? But do you, by reproving them, bring forward the light, that they may be ashamed of their own baseness. Such shame, arising from an acknowledgment of baseness, is the first step to repentance.

"If there come in one that believeth not, or one unlearned, he is convinced of all, he is judged of all; and thus are the secrets of his heart made manifest; and so, falling down on his face, he worships God" (1 Cor. 14:24, 25.)

It may be thought that the word is used here in an unusual acceptation. Erasmus, by substituting another word for *reprove,* has destroyed the whole meaning; for Paul's object is to shew that it will not be without advantage if the works of unbelievers are reproved.

13. *But when all things are reproved.* As the participle, (φανερούμενον,) which is translated, *that which doth make manifest,* is in the middle voice, it admits either of a passive or active signification. It may be either rendered, *that which is made manifest,* or *that which doth make manifest.* If the passive signification, which is followed by the ancient translator, be preferred, the word *light* will denote, as formerly, *that which gives light,* and the meaning will be, that evil works, which had been concealed, will stand out to public view, when they have been *made manifest* by the word of God: If the participle be taken actively, there will still be two ways of expounding it: 1. Whatever manifests is light; 2. That which manifests anything or all things, is light; taking the singular as put for the plural number. There is no difficulty, as Erasmus dreaded, about the article; for the apostles are not in the habit of adhering very strictly to rule about placing every article, and even among elegant writers this mode of using it would be allowable. The context appears to me to shew clearly that this is Paul's meaning. He had exhorted them to reprove the evil works of unbelievers, and thus to drag them out of darkness; and he now adds, that what he enjoins upon them is the proper business of light — *to make manifest* It is Light, he says, which makes all things manifest; and hence it followed that they were unworthy of the name, if they did not bring to light what was involved in darkness.

14. *Wherefore he saith.* Interpreters are at great pains to discover the passage of Scripture which Paul appears to quote, and which is nowhere to be found. I shall state my opinion. He first exhibits Christ as speaking by his ministers; for this is the ordinary message which is every day delivered by preachers of the gospel. What other object do they propose than to raise the dead to life?

"The hour is coming, and now is, when the dead shall hear the voice of the Son of God, and they that hear shall live"

(Joh 5:25.)

Let us now attend to the context. "Unbelievers," Paul had said, "must be reproved, that, being brought forth to the light, they may begin to acknowledge their wickedness." He therefore represents Christ as uttering a voice which is constantly heard in the preaching of the gospel,

Arise, thou that sleepest. The allusion, I have no doubt, is to the prophecies which relate to Christ's kingdom; such as that of Isaiah,

"Arise, shine; for thy light is come, and the glory of Jehovah is risen upon thee" (Isa 60:1.)

Let us therefore endeavor, as far as lies in our power, to rouse the sleeping and dead, that we may bring them to the light of Christ.

And Christ shall give thee light. This does not mean that, when we have risen from death to life, his light begins to shine upon us, as if our performances came before his grace. All that is intended is to show that, when Christ enlightens us, we rise from death to life, — and thus to confirm the former statement, that unbelievers must be recovered from their blindness, in order to be saved. Instead of ἐπιφαύσει, *he shall give light,* some copies read ἐφάψεται, *he shall touch;* but this reading is an evident blunder, and may be dismissed without any argument. [159]

Ephesians 5:15-20

15. See then that ye walk circumspectly, not as fools, but as wise,

15. Videte igitur, quomodo exacte ambuletis; non tanquam insipientes, sed tanquam sapientes:

16. Redeeming the time, because the days are evil.

16. Redimentes tempus, quoniam dies mali sunt.

17. Wherefore be ye not unwise, but understanding what the will of the Lord *is*

17. Quare ne sitis imprudentes, sed intelligentes, quae sit voluntas Domini.

18. And be not drunk with wine, wherein is excess; but be filled with the Spirit;

18. Et ne inebriemini vino, in quo inest lascivia, sed impleamini Spiritu.

19. Speaking to yourselves in psalms, and hymns, and spiritual songs, singing and making melody in your heart to the Lord;

19. Vobis ipsis loquentes psalmis et hymnis, et canticis spiritualibus, canentes et psallentes in corde vestro, Domino;

20. Giving thanks always for all things unto God and the Father in the name of our Lord Jesus Christ.

20. Gratias agentes semper de omnibus, in nomine Domini nostri Iesu Christi, Deo et Patri.

15. *See then.* If believers must not neglect to drive away the darkness of others by their own brightness, how much less ought they to be blind as to their own conduct in life? What darkness shall conceal those on whom Christ, the Sun of righteousness, has arisen? Placed, as it were, in a crowded theater, they ought to live under the eye of God and of angels. Let them stand in awe of these witnesses, though they may be concealed from the view of all mortals. Dismissing the metaphor of darkness and light, he enjoins them to regulate their life *circumspectly as wise men,* [160] who have been educated by the Lord in the school of true wisdom. Our understanding must shew itself by taking God for our guide and instructor, to teach us his own will.

16. *Redeeming the time.* By a consideration of the time he enforces his exhortation. *The days are evil.* Everything around us tends to corrupt and mislead; so that it is difficult for godly persons, who walk among so many thorns, to escape unhurt. Such corruption having infected the age, the devil appears to have obtained tyrannical sway; so that *time* cannot be dedicated to God without being in some way *redeemed.* And what shall be the price of its redemption? To withdraw from the endless variety of allurements which would easily lead us astray; to rid ourselves from the cares and pleasures of the world; and, in a word, to abandon every hinderance. Let us be eager to recover it in every possible way, and let the numerous offenses and arduous toil, which many are in the habit of alleging as an apology for indolence, serve rather to awaken our vigilance.

17. *Wherefore be ye not unwise.* He whose

"delight is in the law of the Lord, and who meditates in it day and night,"

(Ps 1:2,)

will triumph over every obstacle which Satan can oppose to his progress. Whence comes it that some wander, others fall, others strike against a rock, others go away, — but because we allow ourselves to be gradually blinded by Satan, and lose sight of the will of God, which we ought constantly to remember? And observe, that Paul defines *wisdom* to be, *understanding what the will of the Lord is*

"How shall a young man," says David, "direct his way? By attending to thy word, O Lord." (Ps 119:9.)

He speaks of youths, but it is the same wisdom which belongs to old men.

18. *And be not drunk with wine.* When he enjoins them *not to be drunk,* he forbids excessive and immoderate drinking of every description. "Be not intemperate in drinking."

In which [161] *is lasciviousness.* The Greek word ἀσωτία, which is translated "lasciviousness," points out the evils which arise from drunkenness. I understand by it all that is implied in a wanton and dissolute life; for to translate it *luxury,* would quite enfeeble the sense. The meaning therefore is, that drunkards throw off quickly every restraint of modesty or shame; that where wine reigns, profligacy naturally follows; and consequently, that all who have any regard to moderation or decency ought to avoid and abhor drunkenness.

The children of this world are accustomed to indulge in deep drinking as an excitement to mirth. Such carnal excitement is contrasted with that holy joy of which the Spirit of God is the Author, and which produces entirely opposite effects. To what does drunkenness lead? To unbounded licentiousness, — to unbridled, indecent merriment. And to what does spiritual joy lead, when it is most strongly excited? [162]

19. *To psalms, and hymns, and spiritual songs.* These are truly pleasant and delightful fruits. The *Spirit* means "joy in the Holy Ghost," (Ro 14:17;) and the exhortation, *be ye filled,* (ver. 18,) alludes to deep drinking, with which it is indirectly contrasted. *Speaking to themselves,* is *speaking among themselves.* Nor does he enjoin them to sing inwardly or alone; for he immediately adds, *singing in your hearts;* as if he had said, "Let your praises be not merely on the tongue, as hypocrites do, but from the heart." What may be the exact difference between *psalms* and *hymns,* or between *hymns* and *songs,* it is not easy to determine, though a few remarks on this subject shall be offered on a future occasion. [163] The appellation *spiritual,* given to these songs, is strikingly appropriate; for the songs most frequently used are almost always on trifling subjects, and very far from being chaste.

20. *Giving thanks always.* He means that this is a pleasure which ought never to lose its relish; that this is an exercise of which we ought never to weary. Innumerable benefits which we receive from God yield fresh cause of joy and thanksgiving. At the same time, he reminds believers that it will argue ungodly and disgraceful sloth, if they shall not *always* give thanks, — if their whole life shall not be spent in the study and exercise of praising God.

Ephesians 5:21-27

21. Submitting yourselves one to another in the fear of God.

21. Subditi estote invicem in timore Christi (*vel, Dei.*)

22. Wives, submit yourselves unto your own husbands, as unto the Lord.

22. Mulieres suis maritis subditae sint tanquam Domino;

23. For the husband is the head of the wife, even as Christ is the head of the church; and he is the savior of the body.

23. Quoniam vir est caput uxoris, quemadmodum et Christus caput est Ecclesiae, qui idem est servator corporis.

24. Therefore, as the church is subject unto Christ, so *let* the wives *be* to their own husbands in every thing.

24. Caeterum quemadmodum Ecclesia subest Christo, ita et mulieres suis maritis in omnibus.

25. Husbands, love your wives, even as Christ also loved the church, and gave himself for it;

25. Viri, diligite vestras uxores; quemadmodum et Christus dilexit Ecclesiam, et se ipsum tradidit pro ea,

26. That he might sanctify and cleanse it with the washing of water by the word;

26. Ut eam sanctificaret, mundans lavacro aquae in Verbo;

27. That he might present it to himself a glorious church, not having spot, or wrinkle, or any such thing; but that it should be holy, and without blemish.

27. Ut sisteret eam sibi gloriosam Ecclesiam, non habentem maculam, aut rugam, aut quicquam tale; sed ut esset sancta et irreprehensibilis.

21. *Submit yourselves.* God has bound us so strongly to each other, that no man ought to endeavor to avoid subjection; and where love reigns, mutual services will be rendered. I do not except even kings and governors, whose very authority is held for the *service* of the community. It is highly proper that all should be exhorted to be subject to each other in their turn.

But as nothing is more irksome to the mind of man than this mutual subjection, he directs us to *the fear of Christ,* who alone can subdue our fierceness, that we may not refuse the yoke, and can humble our pride, that we may not be ashamed of serving our neighbors. It does not much affect the sense, whether we interpret *the fear of Christ,* passively, thus, — let us submit to our neighbors, because we fear Christ; or actively, — let us submit to them, because the minds of all godly persons ought to be influenced by such fear under the reign of Christ. Some Greek manuscripts read, "the fear *of God.*" The change may have been introduced by some person, who thought that the other phrase, *the fear of Christ,* though by far the most appropriate, sounded a little harsh. [164]

22. *Wives, submit yourselves.* He comes now to the various conditions of life; for, besides the universal bond of subjection, some are more closely bound to each other, according to their respective callings. The community at large is divided, as it were, into so many yokes, out of which arises mutual obligation. There is, first, the yoke of marriage between husband and wife; — secondly, the yoke which binds parents and children; — and, thirdly, the yoke which connects masters and servants. By this arrangement there are six different classes, for each of whom Paul lays down peculiar duties. He begins with wives, whom he enjoins to be subject to their husbands, in the same manner as to Christ, — *as to the Lord.* Not that the authority is equal, but wives cannot obey Christ without yielding obedience to their husbands.

23. *For the husband is the head of the wife.* This is the reason assigned why wives should be obedient. Christ has appointed the same relation to exist between a husband and a wife, as between himself and his church. This comparison ought to produce a stronger impression on their minds, than the mere declaration that such is the appointment of God. Two things are here stated. God has given to the husband authority over the wife; and a resemblance of this authority is found in Christ, who *is the head of the church,* as the husband is of the wife.

And he is the savior of the body. The pronoun HE (αὐτός) is supposed by some to refer to *Christ;* and, by others, to *the husband.* It applies more naturally, in my opinion, to Christ, but still with a view to the present subject. In this point, as well as in others, the resemblance ought to hold. As Christ rules over his church for her salvation, so nothing yields more advantage or comfort to the wife than to be subject to her husband. To refuse that subjection, by means of which they might be saved, is to choose destruction.

24. *But, as the church is subject to Christ.* The particle *but,* may lead some to believe that the words, *he is the savior of the body,* are intended to anticipate an objection. Christ has, no doubt, this peculiar claim, that he is the Savior of the Church: nevertheless, let wives know, that their husbands, though they cannot produce equal claims, have authority over them, after the example of Christ. I prefer the former interpretation; for the argument derived from the word *but,* (ἀλλά,) does not appear to me to have much weight.

25. *Husbands, love your wives.* From husbands, on the other hand, the apostle requires that they cherish toward their wives no ordinary love; for to them, also, he holds out the example of Christ, — *even as Christ also loved the church.* If they are honored to bear his image, and to be, in some measure, his representatives, they ought to resemble him also in the discharge of duty.

And gave himself for it. This is intended to express the strong affection which husbands ought to have for their wives, though he takes occasion, immediately afterwards, to commend the grace of Christ. Let husbands imitate Christ in this respect, that he scrupled not to die for his church. One peculiar consequence, indeed, which resulted from his death, — that by it he redeemed his church, — is altogether beyond the power of men to imitate.

26. *That he might sanctify,* — or, that he might separate it to himself; for such I consider to be the meaning of the word *sanctify* This is accomplished by the forgiveness of sins, and the regeneration of the Spirit.

Washing it with the washing of water. Having mentioned the inward and hidden sanctification, he now adds the outward symbol, by which it is visibly confirmed; as if he had said, that a pledge of that sanctification is held out to us by baptism. Here it is necessary to guard against unsound interpretation, lest the wicked superstition of men, as has frequently happened, change a sacrament into an idol. When Paul says that we are washed by baptism, his meaning is, that God employs it for declaring to us that we are washed, and at the same time performs what it represents. If the truth — or, which is the same thing, the exhibition of the truth — were not connected with baptism, it would be improper to say that baptism is the washing of the soul. At the same time, we must beware of ascribing to the sign, or to the minister, what belongs to God alone. We must not imagine that washing is performed by the minister, or that water cleanses the pollutions of the soul, which nothing but the blood of Christ can accomplish. In short, we must beware of giving any portion of our confidence to the element or to man; for the true and proper use of the sacrament is to lead us directly to Christ, and to place all our dependence upon him.

Others again suppose that too much importance is given to the sign, by saying that baptism is the washing of the soul. Under the influence of this fear, they labor exceedingly to lessen the force of the eulogium which is here pronounced on baptism. But they are manifestly wrong; for, in the first place, the apostle does not say that it is the sign which washes, but declares it to be exclusively the work of God. It is God who washes, and the honor of performing it cannot lawfully be taken from its Author and given to the sign. But there is no absurdity in saying that God employs a sign as the outward means. Not that the power of God is limited by the sign, but this assistance is accommodated to the weakness of our capacity. Some are offended at this view, imagining that it takes from the Holy Spirit a work which is peculiarly his own, and which is everywhere ascribed to him in Scripture. But they are mistaken; for God acts by the sign in such a manner, that its whole efficacy depends upon his Spirit. Nothing more is attributed to the sign than to be an inferior organ, utterly useless in itself, except so far as it derives its power from another source.

Equally groundless is their fear, that by this interpretation the freedom of God will be restrained. The grace of God is not confined to the sign; so that God may not, if he pleases, bestow it without the aid of the sign. Besides, many receive the sign who are not made partakers of grace; for the sign is common to all, to the good and to the bad alike; but the Spirit is bestowed on none but the elect, and the sign, as we have said, has no efficacy without the Spirit. The Greek participle καθαρίσας, is in the past tense, as if he had said, "After having washed." But, as the Latin language has no active participle in the past tense, I chose rather to disregard this, and to translate it (*mundans*) *washing*, instead of (*mundatam*) *having been washed;* which would have kept out of view a matter of far greater importance, namely, that to God alone belongs the work of cleansing.

In the word. [165] This is very far from being a superfluous addition; for, if the *word* is taken away, the whole power of the sacraments is gone. What else are the sacraments but seals of the word? This single consideration will drive away superstition. How comes it that superstitious men are confounded by signs, but because their minds are not directed to the *Word,* which would lead them to God? Certainly, when we look to anything else than to the word, there is nothing sound, nothing pure; but one absurdity springs out of another, till at length the signs, which were appointed by God for the salvation of men, become profane, and degenerate into gross idolatry. The only difference, therefore, between the sacraments of the godly and the contrivances of unbelievers, is found in the Word.

By the *Word* is here meant the promise, which explains the value and use of the signs. Hence it appears, that the Papists do not at all observe the signs in a proper manner. They boast indeed, of having "the Word," but appear to regard it as a sort of enchantment; for they mutter it in an unknown tongue; as if it were addressed to dead matter, and not to men. No explanation of the mystery is made to the people; and in this respect, were there no other, the sacrament begins to be nothing more than the dead element of water. *In the word* is equivalent to "By the word."

27. *That he might present it to himself.* He declares what is the design of baptism and of our being washed. It is, that we may live in a holy and unblamable manner before God. We are washed by Christ, not that we may return to our pollution, but that we may retain through our life the purity which we have once received. This is described in metaphorical language appropriate to his argument.

Not having spot or wrinkle. As the beauty of the wife produces love in the husband, so Christ adorns the Church his bride with holiness as a proof of his regard. This metaphor contains an allusion to marriage; but he afterwards lays aside the figure, and says plainly, that Christ has reconciled the church, *that it might be holy and without blemish.* The true beauty of the church consists in this conjugal chastity, that is, in holiness and purity.

The word *present* (παραστήσ̓Y) implies that the church ought to be holy, not only in the view of men, but in the eyes of the Lord; for Paul says, *that he might present it to himself,* not that he might shew it to others, though the fruits of that hidden purity become afterwards evident in outward works. Pelagians were wont to quote this passage in order to prove the perfection of righteousness in this life, but have been successfully answered by Augustine. Paul does not state what has been done, but for what purpose Christ has cleansed his church. Now, when a thing is said to be done that another may afterwards follow, it is idle to conclude that this latter thing, which ought to follow, has been already done. We do not deny that the holiness of the church is already begun; but, so long as there is daily progress, there cannot be perfection.

Ephesians 5:28-33

28. So ought men to love their wives as their own bodies: he that loveth his wife loveth himself.

28. Ita viri debent diligere suas uxores, tanquam sua corpora. Qui diligit uxorem suam, se ipsum diligit.

29. For no man ever yet hated his own flesh; but nourisheth and cherisheth it, even as the Lord the church:

29. Nemo enim unquam carnem suam odio habuit, sed nutrit et fovet eam; quemadmodum et Christus Ecclesiam.

30. For we are members of his body, of his flesh, and of his bones.

30. Quia membra sumus corporis ejus, ex ejus carne et ex ejus ossibus.

31. For this cause shall a man leave his father and mother, and shall be joined unto his wife, and they two shall be one flesh.

31. Hujus causa relinquet homo patrem et matrem suam, et adhaerebit uxori suae; et erunt duo in carnem unam. (Ge 2:24.)

32. This is a great mystery: but I speak concerning Christ and the church.

32. Arcanum hoc magnum est; ego autem dico in Christo et in Ecclesia.

33. Nevertheless, let every one of you in particular so love his wife even as himself; and the wife *see* that she reverence *her* husband.

33. Caeterum vos quoque singuli, suam quisque uxorem diligat; mulier autem timeat maritum.

28. *He that loveth his wife.* An argument is now drawn from nature itself, to prove that men ought to love their wives. Every man, by his very nature, loves himself. But no man can love himself without loving his wife. Therefore, the man who does not love his wife is a monster. The minor proposition is proved in this manner. Marriage was appointed by God on the condition that the two should be *one flesh;* and that this unity may be the more sacred, he again recommends it to our notice by the consideration of Christ and his church. Such is the amount of his argument, which to a certain extent applies universally to human society. To shew what man owes to man, Isaiah says, "hide not thyself from thine own flesh." (Isa 58:7.) But this refers to our common nature. Between a man and his wife there is a far closer relation; for they not only are united by a resemblance of nature, but by the bond of marriage have become one man. Whoever considers seriously the design of marriage cannot but love his wife.

29. *Even as Christ the church.* He proceeds to enforce the obligations of marriage by representing to us Christ and his Church; for a more powerful example could not have been adduced. The strong affection which a husband ought to cherish towards his wife is exemplified by Christ, and an instance of that unity which belongs to marriage is declared to exist between himself and the Church. This is a remarkable passage on the mysterious intercourse which we have with Christ.

30. *For we are members of his body, of his flesh, and of his bones.* First, this is no exaggeration, but the simple truth. Secondly, he does not simply mean that Christ is a partaker of our nature, but expresses something higher (καὶ ἐμφατικώτερον) *and more emphatic.*

31. *For this cause.* This is an exact quotation from the writings of Moses. (Ge 2:24.) And what does it mean? As Eve was formed out of the substance of her husband, and thus was a part of himself; so, if we are the true members of Christ, we share his substance, and by this intercourse unite into one body. In short, Paul describes our union to Christ, a symbol and pledge of which is given to us in the ordinance of the supper. Those who talk about the torture exercised on this passage to make it refer to the Lord's supper, while no mention is made of the supper, but of marriage, are egregiously mistaken. When they admit that the death of Christ is commemorated in the supper, but not that such intercourse exists as we assert from the words of Christ, we quote this passage against them. Paul says that *we are members of his flesh and of his bones.* Do we wonder then, that in the Lord's supper he holds out his body to be enjoyed by us, and to nourish us unto eternal life? Thus we prove that the only union which we maintain to be represented by the Lord's supper is here declared in its truth and consequences by the apostle.

Two subjects are exhibited together; for the spiritual union between Christ and his church is so treated as to illustrate the common law of marriage, to which the quotation from Moses relates. He immediately adds, that the saying is fulfilled in *Christ and the church.* Every opportunity which presents itself for proclaiming our obligations to Christ is readily embraced, but he adapts his illustration of them to the present subject. It is uncertain whether Moses introduces Adam as using these words, or gives them as an inference drawn by himself from the creation of man. Nor is it of much consequence which of these views be taken; for, in either case, we must hold it to be an announcement of the will of God, enjoining the duties which men owe to their wives.

He shall leave his father and mother. As if he had said, "Let him rather *leave his father and mother* than not cleave to his wife." The marriage bond does not set aside the other duties of mankind, nor are the commandments of God so inconsistent with each other, that a man cannot be a good and faithful husband without ceasing to be a dutiful son. It is altogether a question of degree. Moses draws the comparison, in order to express more strongly the close and sacred union which subsists between husband and wife. A son is bound by an inviolable law of nature to perform his duties towards his father; and when the obligations of a husband towards his wife are declared to be stronger, their force is the better understood. He who resolves to be a good husband will not fail to perform his filial duties, but will regard marriage as more sacred than all other ties.

And they two shall be one flesh. They shall be one man, or, to use a common phrase, they shall constitute one person; which certainly would not hold true with regard to any other kind of relationship. All depends on this, that the wife was formed of the flesh and bones of her husband. Such is the union between us and Christ, who in some sort makes us partakers of his substance. "We are bone of his bone, and flesh of his flesh," (Ge 2:23;) not because, like ourselves, he has a human nature, but because, by the power of his Spirit, he makes us a part of his body, so that from him we derive our life.

32. *This is a great mystery.* He concludes by expressing his astonishment at the spiritual union between Christ and the church. *This is a great mystery;* by which he means, that no language can explain fully what it implies. It is to no purpose that men fret themselves to comprehend, by the judgment of the flesh, the manner and character of this union; for here the infinite power of the Divine Spirit is exerted. Those who refuse to admit anything on this subject beyond what their own capacity can reach, act an exceedingly foolish part. We tell them that the flesh and blood of Christ are exhibited to us in the Lord's supper. "Explain to us the manner," they reply, "or you will not convince us." For my own part, I am overwhelmed by the depth of this mystery, and am not ashamed to join Paul in acknowledging at once my ignorance and my admiration. How much more satisfactory would this be than to follow my carnal judgment, in undervaluing what Paul declares to be a deep mystery! Reason itself teaches how we ought to act in such matters; for whatever is supernatural is clearly beyond our own comprehension. Let us therefore labor more to feel Christ living in us, than to discover the nature of that intercourse.

We cannot avoid admiring the acuteness of the Papists, who conclude from the word *mystery* (μυστήριον) that marriage is one of seven sacraments, as if they had the power of changing water into wine. They enumerate seven sacraments, while Christ has instituted no more than two; and, to prove that matrimony is one of the seven, they produce this passage. On what ground? Because the Vulgate has adopted the word *Sacrament* (*sacramentum*) as a translation of the word *Mystery*, which the apostle uses. As if Sacrament (*sacramentum*) did not frequently, among Latin writers, denote *Mystery*, or as if *Mystery* had not been the word employed by Paul in the same Epistle, when speaking of the calling of the Gentiles. But the present question is, Has marriage been appointed as a sacred symbol of the grace of God, to declare and represent to us something spiritual, such as Baptism or the Lord's Supper? They have no ground for such an assertion, unless it be that they have been deceived by the doubtful signification of a Latin word, or rather by their ignorance of the Greek language. If the simple fact had been observed, that the word used by Paul is *Mystery*, no mistake would ever have occurred.

We see then the hammer and anvil with which they fabricated this sacrament. But they have given another proof of their indolence in not attending to the correction which is immediately added,

But I speak concerning Christ and the church. He intended to give express warning that no man should understand him as speaking of marriage; so that his meaning is more fully expressed than if he had uttered the former sentiment without any exception. The *great mystery* is, that Christ breathes into the church his own life and power. But who would discover here anything like a sacrament? This blunder arose from the grossest ignorance.

33. *Nevertheless, let every one.* Having digressed a little from this subject, though the very digression aided his design, he adopts the method usually followed in short precepts, by giving a brief summary of duties. Husbands are required to love their wives, and wives to *fear* (φοβῶται) their husbands, understanding by *fear* that *reverence* which will lead them to be submissive. Where reverence does not exist, there will be no willing subjection. [166]

Footnotes

153

"To institute an action against one who has injured us is human; not to take revenge on him is the part of a philosopher; but to compensate him with benefits is divine, and makes men of earth followers of the Father who is in heaven." — Clem. Ep., quoted by Eadie.

154

"The offering, in being presented to God, was meant to be, and actually was, a sweet savor to Him. The phrase is based on the peculiar sacrificial idiom of the Old Testament. (Ge 8:21; Lev. 1:9, 13, 17, Lev. 2:9, 12, Lev. 3:5.) It is used typically in 2Co 2:14, and is explained and expanded in Php 4:18 — 'a sacrifice acceptable, well-pleasing to God.' The burning of spices or incense, so fragrant to the Oriental senses, is figuratively applied to God." — Eadie.

155

"He doth not condemn the innocent pleasantries and mirth of a cheerful conversation; but that kind of obscene discourse which we mean by the French expression of *double entendre;* when men, for the sake of merriment and sport, convey lewd sentiments and thoughts to others, under chaste and cleanly expressions. This seems to be the proper meaning of the word εὐτραπελία, *jesting,* in this place. The original sense of it is, 'an artfully turned discourse.' And accordingly it is used either in a good sense, to denote proper wit; or in a bad sense, to signify any kind of lewd and scurrilous discourse, that artfully conveys an ill meaning. And as it is here joined with 'filthiness and foolish talking,' it is plain that the apostle intended by it such ambiguous forms of speech as are intended to raise mirth by dishonest and corrupt meanings." — Chandler.

156

"Mastins." "Mastiffs."

157

The English version reads, *The fruit of the Spirit*; Calvin's, *The fruit of light.* Without attempting, in a brief note, to balance the various readings, it may be proper to mention, that, instead of πνεύματος, (*of the Spirit,*) many Greek manuscripts have θωτὸς, (*of the light,*) and the latter reading has been adopted by Griesbach. — *Ed*

158

"Most expositors supply αὐτοὺς, meaning the doers of the works; and they render ἐλέγχετε, *reprove,* viz., by wholesome correction. This, however, is so harsh, that it is better (with Theodoret, the Pesch. Syr., Wakefield, Schleusner, Photius, and Wahl) to supply αὐτὰ, that is, ἔργα τοῦ σκότους, and to interpret ἐλέγχετε 'bring to the light, and evince their evil nature,' namely, by shewing in contrast the opposite virtues. This sense is required by verse 13, with which the present closely connects; and so ἐλέγχω is used both in the Scriptural and Classical writers." — Bloomfield.

159

"The various spellings of the verb, and the change of φ into ψ, have arisen from inadvertence. This variation is as old as the days of Chrysostom; for he notices it, and decides for the common reading. The verb itself occurs nowhere else in the New Testament, though it is once found in the 'Acts of Thomas,' section 34. That light from Christ flashes upon the awakened and resuscitated; nay, it awakens and resuscitates them. As it streams upon the dead, it startles them into life. It illuminates every topic on which a sinner needs information, with a pure, steady, and mellowed radiance." — Eadie.

160

"In μὴ ὡς ἄσοφοι ἀλλ ' ὡς σοφοὶ we have an antithetical parallelism, (such as is found in the Classical as well as the Scriptural writers,) where, for emphasis' sake, a proposition is expressed both affirmatively and negatively, as in Joh 1:20, ὡμολόγησε καὶ οὐκ ἠρνήσατο, 'he confessed and denied not.' By ἄσοφοι, and σοφοὶ are meant the persons just before denoted by κότος and φῶς, and, a little after, termed ἄφρονες and συνίεντες, by a frequent Hebrew idiom, whereby Wisdom stands for Virtue, and Folly for Vice" — Bloomfield.

161

"The antecedent to ᾧ is not οἶνος, but the entire clause — 'in which vicious inebriety there is profligacy.' The term, if it be derived from α privative and σώζω, is the picture of a sad result. The adjective ἄσωτος is used by the classics to signify one who is, as we say, 'past redemption.' The adverb ἀσώτώς is used of the conduct of the prodigal son in the far country. (Lu 15:13.)" — Eadie.

162

"This is a pleasant kind of drunkenness, which stimulates you, not to wanton dances or foolish songs, by which the Gentiles render homage to their deities, but to psalms, to hymns, to spiritual songs, by which you rejoice, and sing, and offer praise to the Lord, not with indecent roaring, as is the custom of drunk people, but inwardly in your minds and hearts." — Erasmus.

163

See Calvin Commentary on Philippians, Colossians, etc., page217.

164

"Here, indeed, there is great reason to think that Χριστοῦ, (instead of Θεοῦ,) found in very many of the best MSS., ancient Versions, and early Fathers, (and which has been edited by Griesbach, Vater, Tittmann, and Scholz,) is the true reading." — Bloomfield.

165

"Par la parolle." "By the word."

166

"One peculiarity in this injunction has been usually overlooked. What is instructive on either side is not enforced, but what is necessary to direct and hallow such an instinct is inculcated. The woman loves in deep, undying sympathy; but, to teach her how this fondness should know and fill its appropriate sphere, she is commanded to obey and honor. The man, on the other hand, feels that his position is to govern; but, to shew him what should be the essence and means of his government, he is enjoined to love." — Eadie.

CHAPTER 6

Ephesians 6:1-4

1. Children, obey your parents in the Lord: for this is right.
1. Filii, obedite parentibus vestris in Domino; hoc enim est justum.
2. Honor thy father and mother, (which is the first commandment with promise,)
2. Honora patrem tuum et matrem; (quod est mandatum primum cum promissione:)
3. That it may be well with thee, and thou mayest live long on the earth.
3. Ut bene tibi sit, et sis longaevus super terram.
4. And, ye fathers, provoke not your children to wrath; but bring them up in the nurture and admonition of the Lord.
4. Vos etiam, patres, ne ad iram provocetis filios vestros; sed educate eos in disciplina et correptione Domini.

1. *Children, obey.* Why does the apostle use the word *obey* instead of *honor,* 167
which has a greater extent of meaning? It is because *Obedience* is the evidence of that *honor* which children owe to their parents, and is therefore more earnestly enforced. It is likewise more difficult; for the human mind recoils from the idea of subjection, and with difficulty allows itself to be placed under the control of another. Experience shews how rare this virtue is; for do we find one among a thousand that is obedient to his parents? By a figure of speech, a part is here put for the whole, but it is the most important part, and is necessarily accompanied by all the others.

In the Lord. Besides the law of nature, which is acknowledged by all nations, the obedience of children is enforced by the authority of God. Hence it follows, that parents are to be obeyed, so far only as is consistent with piety to God, which comes first in order. If the command of God is the rule by which the submission of children is to be regulated, it would be foolish to suppose that the performance of this duty could lead away from God himself.

For this is right. This is added in order to restrain the fierceness which, we have already said, appears to be natural to almost all men. He proves it to be *right,* because God has commanded it; for we are not at liberty to dispute, or call in question, the appointment of him whose will is the unerring rule of goodness and righteousness. That *honor* should be represented as including *obedience* is not surprising; for mere ceremony is of no value in the sight of God. The precept, *honor thy father and mother,* comprehends all the duties by which the sincere affection and respect of children to their parents can be expressed.

2. *Which is the first commandment with promise.* The promises annexed to the commandments are intended to excite our hopes, and to impart a greater cheerfulness to our obedience; and therefore Paul uses this as a kind of seasoning to render the submission, which he enjoins on children, more pleasant and agreeable. He does not merely say, that God has offered a reward to him who obeys his father and mother, but that such an offer is peculiar to this commandment. If each of the commandments had its own promises, there would have been no ground for the commendation bestowed in the present instance. But this is *the first commandment,* Paul tells us, which God has been pleased, as it were, to seal by a remarkable promise. There is some difficulty here; for the second commandment likewise contains a promise,

"I am the Lord thy God, who shew mercy unto thousands of them that love me, and keep my commandments."

(Exod. 20:5, 6.)

But this is universal, applying indiscriminately to the whole law, and cannot be said to be annexed to that commandment. Paul's assertion still holds true, that no other commandment but that which enjoins the obedience due by children to their parents is distinguished by a promise.

3. *That it may be well with thee.* The promise is — a long life; from which we are led to understand that the present life is not to be overlooked among the gifts of God. On this and other kindred subjects I must refer my reader to the *Institutes of the Christian Religion;* [168] satisfying myself at present with saying, in a few words, that the reward promised to the obedience of children is highly appropriate. Those who shew kindness to their parents from whom they derived life, are assured by God, that in this life it will *be well with them.*

And that thou mayest live long on the earth. Moses expressly mentions the land of Canaan,

"that thy days may be long upon the land which
the Lord thy God giveth thee." (Ex 20:12.)

Beyond this the Jews could not conceive of any life more happy or desirable. But as the same divine blessing is extended to the whole world, Paul has properly left out the mention of a place, the peculiar distinction of which lasted only till the coming of Christ.

4. *And, ye fathers.* Parents, on the other hand, are exhorted not to irritate their children by unreasonable severity. This would excite hatred, and would lead them to throw off the yoke altogether. Accordingly, in writing to the Colossians, he adds, "lest they be discouraged." (Col 3:21.) Kind and liberal treatment has rather a tendency to cherish reverence for their parents, and to increase the cheerfulness and activity of their obedience, while a harsh and unkind manner rouses them to obstinacy, and destroys the natural affections. But Paul goes on to say, "let them be fondly cherished;" for the Greek word, (ἐκτρέφετε,) which is translated *bring up,* unquestionably conveys the idea of gentleness and forbearance. To guard them, however, against the opposite and frequent evil of excessive indulgence, he again draws the rein which he had slackened, and adds, *in the instruction and reproof of the Lord.* It is not the will of God that parents, in the exercise of kindness, shall spare and corrupt their children. Let their conduct towards their children be at once mild and considerate, so as to guide them in the fear of the Lord, and correct them also when they go astray. That age is so apt to become wanton, that it requires frequent admonition and restraint.

Ephesians 6:5-9

5. Servants, be obedient to them that are *your* masters according to the flesh, with fear and trembling, in singleness of your heart, as unto Christ;

5. Servi, obedite dominis secundum carnem, cum timore et tremore in simplicitate cordis vestri, tanquam Christo;

6. Not with eye-service, as men-pleasers; but as the servants of Christ, doing the will of God from the heart;

6. Non quasi ad oculum servientes, tanquam hominibus studentes placere, sed tanquam servi Christi, facientes voluntatem Dei ex animo,

7. With good will doing service, as to the Lord, and not to men:

7. Cum benevolentia, servientes Domino, et non hominibus;

8. Knowing, that whatsoever good thing any man doeth, the same shall he receive of the Lord, whether *he be* bond or free.

8. Scientes quod unusquisque quicquid boni fecerit, recipiet a Domino, sive servus, sive liber.

9. And, ye masters, do the same things unto them, forbearing threatening: knowing that your Master also is in heaven; neither is there respect of persons with him.

9. Et vos, domini, mutuum officium praestate erga illos, remittentes minas; scientes quod illorum et vester Dominus est in coelis; et non est apud eum personarum acceptio.

5. *Servants, be obedient.* His exhortation to servants is so much the more earnest, on account of the hardship and bitterness of their condition, which renders it more difficult to be endured. And he does not speak merely of outward obedience, but says more about *fear* willingly rendered; for it is a very rare occurrence to find one who willingly yields himself to the control of another. The *servants* (δοῦλοι) whom he immediately addresses were not hired servants, like those of the present day, but *slaves,* such as were in ancient times, whose *slavery* was perpetual, unless, through the favor of their masters, they obtained freedom, — whom their masters bought with money, that they might impose upon them the most degrading employments, and might, with the full protection of the law, exercise over them the power of life and death. To such he says, *obey your masters,* lest they should vainly imagine that carnal freedom had been procured for them by the gospel.

But as some of the worst men were compelled by the dread of punishment, he distinguishes between Christian and ungodly servants, by the feelings which they cherished. *With fear and trembling;* that is, with the careful respect which springs from an honest purpose. It can hardly be expected, however, that so much deference will be paid to a mere man, unless a higher authority shall enforce the obligation; and therefore he adds, *as doing the will of God.* (Ver. 6.) Hence it follows, that it is not enough if their obedience satisfy the eyes of men; for God requires truth and sincerity of heart. When they serve their masters faithfully, they obey God. As if he had said, "Do not suppose that by the judgment of men you were thrown into slavery. It is God who has laid upon you this burden, who has placed you in the power of your masters. He who conscientiously endeavors to render what he owes to his master, performs his duty not to man only, but to God."

With good will doing service. (Ver. 7.) This is contrasted with the suppressed indignation which swells the bosom of slaves. Though they dare not openly break out or give signs of obstinacy, their dislike of the authority exercised over them is so strong, that it is with the greatest unwillingness and reluctance that they obey their masters.

Whoever reads the accounts of the dispositions and conduct of slaves, which are scattered through the writings of the ancients, will be at no loss to perceive that the number of injunctions here given does not exceed that of the diseases which prevailed among this class, and which it was of importance to cure. But the same instruction applies to male and female servants of our own times. It is God who appoints and regulates all the arrangements of society. As the condition of servants is much more agreeable than that of slaves in ancient times, they ought to consider themselves far less excusable, if they do not endeavor, in every way, to comply with Paul's injunctions.

Masters according to the flesh. (Ver. 5.) This expression is used to soften the harsh aspect of slavery. He reminds them that their spiritual freedom, which was by far the most desirable, remained untouched.

Eye-service (ὀφθαλμοδουλεία) is mentioned; because almost all servants are addicted to flattery, but, as soon as their master's back is turned, indulge freely in contempt, or perhaps in ridicule. Paul therefore enjoins godly persons to keep at the greatest distance from such deceitful pretences.

8. *Knowing that whatsoever good thing any man doeth.* What a powerful consolation! However unworthy, however ungrateful or cruel, their masters may be, God will accept their services as rendered to himself. When servants take into account the pride and arrogance of their masters, they often become more indolent from the thought that their labor is thrown away. But Paul informs them that their reward is laid up with God for services which appear to be ill bestowed on unfeeling men; and that there is no reason, therefore, why they should be led aside from the path of duty. He adds, *whether bond or free* No distinction is made between a slave and a free man. The world is wont to set little value on the labors of slaves; but God esteems them as highly as the duties of kings. In his estimate, the outward station is thrown aside, and each is judged according to the uprightness of his heart.

9. *And ye masters.* In the treatment of their slaves, the laws granted to masters a vast amount of power. Whatever had thus been sanctioned by the civil code was regarded by many as in itself lawful. To such an extent did their cruelty in some instances proceed, that the Roman emperors were forced to restrain their tyranny. But though no royal edicts had ever been issued for the protection of slaves, God allows to masters no power over them beyond what is consistent with the law of love. When philosophers attempt to give to the principles of equity their full effect in restraining the excess of severity to slaves, they inculcate that masters ought to treat them in the same manner as hired servants. But they never look beyond utility; and, in judging even of that, they inquire only what is advantageous to the head of the family, or conducive to good order. The Apostle proceeds on a very different principle. He lays down what is lawful according to the Divine appointment, and how far they, too, are debtors to their servants.

Do the same things to them. "Perform the duty which on your part you owe to them." What he calls in another Epistle, (τὸ δίκαιον καὶ τὴν ἰσότητα) *that which is just and equal,* [169] is precisely what, in this passage, he calls *the same things,* (τὰ αὐτὰ.) And what is this but the law of analogy? Masters and servants are not indeed on the same level; but there is a mutual law which binds them. By this law, servants are placed under the authority of their masters; and, by the same law, due regard being had to the difference of their station, masters lie under certain obligations to their servants. This analogy is greatly misunderstood; because men do not try it by the law of love, which is the only true standard. Such is the import of Paul's phrase, *the same things;* for we are all ready enough to demand what is due to ourselves; but, when our own duty comes to be performed, every one attempts to plead exemption. It is chiefly, however, among persons of authority and rank that injustice of this sort prevails.

Forbearing threatenings. Every expression of disdain, arising from the pride of masters, is included in the single word, *threatenings.* They are charged not to assume a lordly air or a terrific attitude, as if they were constantly threatening some evil against their servants, when they have occasion to address them. Threatenings, and every kind of barbarity, originate in this, that masters look upon their servants as if they had been born for their sake alone, and treat them as if they were of no more value than cattle. Under this one description, Paul forbids every kind of disdainful and barbarous treatment.

Their Master and yours. A very necessary warning. What is there which we will not dare to attempt against our inferiors, if they have no ability to resist, and no means of obtaining redress, — if no avenger, no protector appears, none who will be moved by compassion to listen to their complaints? It happens here, in short, according to the common proverb, that Impunity is the mother of Licentiousness. But Paul here reminds them, that, while masters possess authority over their servants, they have themselves the same Master in heaven, to whom they must render an account.

And there is no respect of persons with him. A regard to *persons* blinds our eyes, so as to leave no room for law or justice; but Paul affirms that it is of no value in the sight of God. By *person* is meant anything about a man which does not belong to the real question, and which we take into account in forming a judgment. Relationship, beauty, rank, wealth, friendship, and everything of this sort, gain our favor; while the opposite qualities produce contempt and sometimes hatred. As those absurd feelings arising from the sight of a *person* have the greatest possible influence on human judgments, those who are invested with power are apt to flatter themselves, as if God would countenance such corruptions. "Who is he that God should regard him, or defend his interest against mine?" Paul, on the contrary, informs masters that they are mistaken if they suppose that their servants will be of little or no account before God, because they are so before men. "God is no respecter of persons," (Ac 10:34,) and the cause of the meanest man will not be a whit less regarded by him than that of the loftiest monarch.

Ephesians 6:10-13

10. Finally, my brethren, be strong in the Lord, and in the power of his might.

10. Quod superest, fratres mei, sitis fortes in Domino, et in robore potentiae ipsius.

11. Put on the whole armor of God, that ye may be able to stand against the wiles of the devil.

11. Induite totam armaturam Dei, ut possitis stare adversus insidias Diaboli.

12. For we wrestle not against flesh and blood, but against principalities, against powers, against the rulers of the darkness of this world, against spiritual wickedness in high *places*

12. Quia non est nobis lucta adversus carnem et sanguinem, sed adversus principatus, adversus potestates, adversus mundanos principes tenebrarum saeculi hujus, adversus spirituales malitias in coelestibus.

13. Wherefore take unto you the whole armor of God, that ye may be able to withstand in the evil day, and having done all, to stand.

13. Quapropter assumite totam armaturam Dei, ut possitis resistere in die malo, et omnibus peractis stare.

10. *Finally.* Resuming his general exhortations, he again enjoins them to *be strong,* — to summon up courage and vigor; for there is always much to enfeeble us, and we are ill fitted to resist. But when our weakness is considered, an exhortation like this would have no effect, unless *the Lord* were present, and stretched out his hand to render assistance, or rather, unless he supplied us with all the power. Paul therefore adds, *in the Lord.* As if he had said, "'You have no right to reply, that you have not the ability; for all that I require of you is, *be strong in the Lord.*" To explain his meaning more fully, he adds, *in the power of his might,* which tends greatly to increase our confidence, particularly as it shews the remarkable assistance which God usually bestows upon believers. If the Lord aids us by *his mighty power,* we have no reason to shrink from the combat. But it will be asked, What purpose did it serve to enjoin the Ephesians to be strong in the Lord's mighty power, which they could not of themselves accomplish? I answer, there are two clauses here which must be considered. He exhorts them to be courageous, but at the same time reminds them to ask from God a supply of their own deficiencies, and promises that, in answer to their prayers, the power of God will be displayed.

11. *Put on the whole armor.* God has furnished us with various defensive weapons, provided we do not indolently refuse what is offered. But we are almost all chargeable with carelessness and hesitation in using the offered grace; just as if a soldier, about to meet the enemy, should take his helmet, and neglect his shield. To correct this security, or, we should rather say, this indolence, Paul borrows a comparison from the military art, and bids us *put on the whole armor of God.* We ought to be prepared on all sides, so as to want nothing. The Lord offers to us arms for repelling every kind of attack. It remains for us to apply them to use, and not leave them hanging on the wall. To quicken our vigilance, he reminds us that we must not only engage in open warfare, but that we have a crafty and insidious foe to encounter, who frequently lies in ambush; for such is the import of the apostle's phrase, THE WILES [170] (τὰς μεθοδείας) *of the devil*

12. *For we wrestle* [171] *not.* To impress them still more deeply with their danger, he points out the nature of the enemy, which he illustrates by a comparative statement, *Not against flesh and blood.* The meaning is, that our difficulties are far greater than if we had to fight with men. There we resist human strength, sword is opposed to sword, man contends with man, force is met by force, and skill by skill;

but here the case is widely different. All amounts to this, that our enemies are such as no human power can withstand. By *flesh and blood* the apostle denotes men, who are so denominated in order to contrast them with spiritual assailants. This is no bodily struggle.

Let us remember this when the injurious treatment of others provokes us to revenge. Our natural disposition would lead us to direct all our exertions against the men themselves; but this foolish desire will be restrained by the consideration that the men who annoy us are nothing more than darts thrown by the hand of Satan. While we are employed in destroying those darts, we lay ourselves open to be wounded on all sides. To *wrestle with flesh and blood* will not only be useless, but highly pernicious. We must go straight to the enemy, who attacks and wounds us from his concealment, — who slays before he appears.

But to return to Paul. He describes our enemy as formidable, not to overwhelm us with fear, but to quicken our diligence and earnestness; for there is a middle course to be observed. When the enemy is neglected, he does his utmost to oppress us with sloth, and afterwards disarms us by terror; so that, ere the engagement has commenced, we are vanquished. By speaking of the power of the enemy, Paul labors to keep us more on the alert. He had already called him *the devil,* but now employs a variety of epithets, to make the reader understand that this is not an enemy who may be safely despised.

Against principalities, against powers. Still, his object in producing alarm is not to fill us with dismay, but to excite us to caution. He calls them κοσμοκράτορας, that is, *princes of the world;* but he explains himself more fully by adding — *of the darkness of the world.* The devil reigns in the world, because the world is nothing else than darkness. Hence it follows, that the corruption of the world gives way to the kingdom of the devil; for he could not reside in a pure and upright creature of God, but all arises from the sinfulness of men. By *darkness,* it is almost unnecessary to say, are meant unbelief and ignorance of God, with the consequences to which they lead. As the whole world is covered with darkness, the devil is called "the prince of this world." (Joh 14:30.)

By calling it *wickedness,* he denotes the malignity and cruelty of the devil, and, at the same time, reminds us that the utmost caution is necessary to prevent him from gaining an advantage. For the same reason, the epithet *spiritual* is applied; for, when the enemy is invisible, our danger is greater. There is emphasis, too, in the phrase, *in heavenly* places; for the elevated station from which the attack is made gives us greater trouble and difficulty.

An argument drawn from this passage by the *Manicheans,* to support their wild notion of two principles, is easily refuted. They supposed the devil to be (ἀντίθεον) an *antagonist deity,* whom the righteous God would not subdue without great exertion. For Paul does not ascribe to devils a *principality,* which they seize without the consent, and maintain in spite of the opposition, of the Divine Being, — but a *principality* which, as Scripture everywhere asserts, God, in righteous judgment, yields to them over the wicked. The inquiry is, not what power they have in opposition to God, but how far they ought to excite our alarm, and keep us on our guard. Nor is any countenance here given to the belief, that the devil has formed, and keeps for himself, the middle region of the air. Paul does not assign to them a fixed territory, which they can call their own, but merely intimates that they are engaged in hostility, and occupy an elevated station.

13. *Wherefore take unto you.* Though our enemy is so powerful, Paul does not infer that we must throw away our spears, but that we must prepare our minds for the battle. A promise of victory is, indeed, involved in the exhortation, *that ye may be able.* If we only *put on the whole armor of God,* and fight valiantly to the end, we shall certainly *stand.* On any other supposition, we would be discouraged by the number and variety of the contests; and therefore he adds, *in the evil day.* By this expression he rouses them from security, bids them prepare themselves for hard, painful, and dangerous conflicts, and, at the same time, animates them with the hope of victory; for amidst the greatest dangers they will be safe. *And having done all.* They are thus directed to cherish confidence through the whole course of life. There will be no danger which may not be successfully met by the power of God; nor will any who, with this assistance, fight against Satan, fail in the day of battle.

Ephesians 6:14-20

14. Stand therefore, having your loins girt about with truth, and having on the breastplate of righteousness;

14. State igitur succincti lumbos veritate, et induti thoracem justitiae,

15. And your feet shod with the preparation of the gospel of peace;

15. Et calceati pedes praeparatione evangelii pacis;

16. Above all, taking the shield of faith, wherewith ye shall be able to quench all the fiery darts of the wicked.

16. In omnibus assumpto scuto fidei, quo possitis omnia tela maligni ignita exstinguere.

17. And take the helmet of salvation, and the sword of the Spirit, which is the word of God:

17. Et galeam salutaris accipite, et gladium Spiritus, qui est verbum Dei;

18. Praying always with all prayer and supplication in the Spirit, and watching thereunto with all perseverance and supplication for all saints;

18. Per omnem precationem et orationem omni tempore precantes in Spiritu, et in hoc ipsum vigilantes, cum omni assiduitate et deprecatione pro omnibus sanctis;

19. And for me, that utterance may be given unto me, that I may open my mouth boldly, to make known the mystery of the gospel,

19. Et pro me, ut mihi detur sermo in apertione oris mei cum fiducia, ut patefaciam mysterium evangelii;

20. For which I am an ambassador in bonds; that therein I may speak boldly, as I ought to speak.

20. Pro quo legatione fungor in catena; ut confidenter me geram in eo, quemadmodum oportet me loqui.

14. *Stand therefore.* Now follows a description of the arms which they were enjoined to wear. We must not, however, inquire very minutely into the meaning of each word; for an allusion to military customs is all that was intended. Nothing can be more idle than the extraordinary pains which some have taken to discover the reason why *righteousness* is made a *breastplate,* instead of a *girdle.* Paul's design was to touch briefly on the most important points required in a Christian, and to adapt them to the comparison which he had already used.

Truth, which means sincerity of mind, is compared to a *girdle.* Now, a girdle was, in ancient times, one of the most important parts of military armor. Our attention is thus directed to the fountain of sincerity; for the purity of the gospel ought to remove from our minds all guile, and from our hearts all hypocrisy. Secondly, he recommends *righteousness,* and desires that it should be a *breastplate* for protecting the breast. Some imagine that this refers to a freely bestowed righteousness, or the imputation of righteousness, by which pardon of sin is obtained. But such matters ought not, I think, to have been mentioned on the present occasion; for the subject now under discussion is a blameless life. He enjoins us to be adorned, first, with integrity, and next with a devout and holy life.

15. *And your feet shod.* The allusion, if I mistake not, is to the military *greaves;* for they were always reckoned a part of the armor, and were even used for domestic purposes. As soldiers covered their legs and feet to protect them against cold and other injuries, so we must be shod *with the gospel,* if we would pass unhurt through the world. It is *the gospel of peace,* and it is so called, as every reader must perceive, from its effects; for it is the message of our reconciliation to God, and nothing else gives peace to the conscience. But what is the meaning of the word *preparation?* Some explain it as an injunction to be *prepared* for the gospel; but it is the effect of the gospel which I consider to be likewise expressed by this term. We are enjoined to lay aside every hinderance, and to be prepared both for journey and for war. By nature we dislike exertion, and want agility. A rough road and many other obstacles retard our progress, and we are discouraged by the smallest annoyance. On these accounts, Paul holds out the gospel as the fittest means for undertaking and performing the expedition. Erasmus proposes a circumlocution, (*ut sitis parati,*) *that ye may be prepared;* but this does not appear to convey the true meaning.

16. *Taking the shield of faith.* Though *faith* and *the word of God* are one, yet Paul assigns to them two distinct offices. I call them one, because the word is the object of faith, and cannot be applied to our use but by faith; as faith again is nothing, and can do nothing, without the word. But Paul, neglecting so subtle a distinction, allowed himself to expatiate at large on the military armor. In the first Epistle to the Thessalonians he gives both to faith and to love the name of a *breastplate,* — "putting on the breastplate of faith and love," (1Th 5:8.) All that was intended, therefore, was obviously this, — "He who possesses the excellencies of character which are here described is protected on every hand."

And yet it is not without reason that the most necessary instruments of warfare — a sword and a shield — are compared to faith, and to the word of God. In the spiritual combat, these two hold the highest rank. By faith we repel all the attacks of the devil, and by the word of God the enemy himself is slain. If the word of God shall have its efficacy upon us through faith, we shall be more than sufficiently armed both for opposing the enemy and for putting him to flight. And what shall we say of those who take from a Christian people the word of God? Do they not rob them of the necessary armor, and leave them to perish without a struggle? There is no man of any rank who is not bound to be a soldier of Christ. But if we enter the field unarmed, if we want our sword, how shall we sustain that character?

Wherewith ye shall be able to quench all the darts. But *quench* appears not to be the proper word. Why did he not use, instead of it, *ward off* or *shake off*, or some such word? *Quench* is far more expressive; for it is adapted to the epithet applied to *darts* *The darts* of Satan are not only sharp and penetrating, but — what makes them more destructive — they are *fiery* Faith will be found capable, not only of blunting their edge, but of *quenching* their heat.

"This," says John, "is the victory that overcometh the world, even our faith" (1Jo 5:4.)

17. *And take the helmet of salvation.* In a passage already quoted, (1Th 5:8,) "the *hope* of salvation" is said to be a *helmet*, which I consider to be in the same sense as this passage. The head is protected by the best *helmet*, when, elevated by *hope*, we look up towards heaven to that *salvation* which is promised. It is only therefore by becoming the object of *hope* that *salvation* is a *helmet*.

18. *Praying always with all prayer.* Having instructed the Ephesians to put on their armor, he now enjoins them to fight by prayer. This is the true method. To call upon God is the chief exercise of faith and hope; and it is in this way that we obtain from God every blessing. *Prayer* and *supplication* are not greatly different from each other, except that *supplication* is only one branch of *prayer*

With all perseverance. We are exhorted to persevere in prayer. Every tendency to weariness must be counteracted by a cheerful performance of the duty. With unabated ardor we must continue our prayers, though we do not immediately obtain what we desire. If, instead of *with all perseverance*, some would render it, *with all* Earnestness, I would have no objection to the change.

But what is the meaning of *always?* Having already spoken of continued application, does he twice repeat the same thing? I think not. When everything flows on prosperously, — when we are easy and cheerful, we seldom feel any strong excitement to prayer, — or rather, we never flee to God, but when we are driven by some kind of distress. Paul therefore desires us to allow no opportunity to pass, — on no occasion to neglect prayer; so that *praying always* is the same thing with praying both in prosperity and in adversity.

For all saints. There is not a moment of our life at which the duty of prayer may not be urged by our own wants. But unremitting prayer may likewise be enforced by the consideration, that the necessities of our brethren ought to move our sympathy. And when is it that some members of the church are not suffering distress, and needing our assistance? If, at any time, we are colder or more indifferent about prayer than we ought to be, because we do not feel the pressure of immediate necessity, — let us instantly reflect how many of our brethren are worn out by varied and heavy afflictions, — are weighed down by sore perplexity, or are reduced to the lowest distress. If reflections like these do not rouse us from our lethargy, we must have hearts of stone. But are we to pray for believers only? Though the apostle states the claims of the godly, he does not exclude others. And yet in prayer, as in all other kind offices, our first care unquestionably is due to the saints.

19. *And for me.* For himself, in a particular manner, he enjoins the Ephesians to pray. Hence we infer that there is no man so richly endowed with gifts as not to need this kind of assistance from his brethren, so long as he remains in this world. Who will ever be better entitled to plead exemption from this necessity than Paul?

Yet he entreats the prayers of his brethren, and not hypocritically, but from an earnest desire of their aid. And what does he wish that they should ask for him? *That utterance may be given to me.* What then? Was he habitually dumb, or did fear restrain him from making an open profession of the gospel? By no means; but there was reason to fear lest his splendid commencement should not be sustained by his future progress. Besides, his zeal for proclaiming the gospel was so ardent that he was never satisfied with his exertions. And indeed, if we consider the weight and importance of the subject, we shall all acknowledge that we are very far from being able to handle it in a proper manner. Accordingly he adds,

20. *As I ought to speak;* meaning, that to proclaim the truth of the gospel as it ought to be proclaimed, is a high and rare attainment. Every word here deserves to be carefully weighed. Twice he uses the expression *boldly,* — "that I may open my mouth *boldly,*" "that therein I may speak *boldly.*" Fear hinders us from preaching Christ openly and fearlessly, while the absence of all restraint and disguise in confessing Christ is demanded from his ministers. Paul does not ask for himself the powers of an acute debater, or, I should rather say, of a dexterous sophist, that he might shield himself from his enemies by false pretences. It is, *that I may open my mouth,* to make a clear and strong confession; for when the mouth is half shut, the sounds which it utters are doubtful and confused. *To open the mouth,* therefore, is to speak with perfect freedom, without the smallest dread.

But does not Paul discover unbelief, when he entertains doubts as to his own stedfastness, and implores the intercession of others? No. He does not, like unbelievers, seek a remedy which is contrary to the will of God, or inconsistent with his word. The only aids on which he relies are those which he knows to be sanctioned by the Divine promise and approbation. It is the command of God, that believers shall pray for one another. How consoling then must it be to each of them to learn that the care of his salvation is enjoined on all the rest, and to be informed by God himself that the prayers of others on his behalf are not poured out in vain! Would it be lawful to refuse what the Lord himself has offered? Each believer, no doubt, ought to have been satisfied with the Divine assurance, that as often as he prayed he would be heard. But if, in addition to all the other manifestations of his kindness, God were pleased to declare that he will listen to the prayers of others in our behalf, would it be proper that this bounty should be slighted, or rather, ought we not to embrace it with open arms?

Let us therefore remember that Paul, when he resorted to the intercessions of his brethren, was influenced by no distrust or hesitation. His eagerness to obtain them arose from his resolution that no privilege which the Lord had given him should be overlooked. How absurdly then do Papists conclude from Paul's example, that we ought to pray to the dead! Paul was writing to the Ephesians, to whom he had it in his power to communicate his sentintents. But what intercourse have we with the dead? As well might they argue that we ought to invite angels to our feasts and entertainments, because among men friendship is promoted by such kind offices.

Ephesians 6:21-24

21. But that ye also may know my affairs, *and* how I do, Tychicus, a beloved brother and faithful minister in the Lord, shall make known to you all things:

21. Ut autem sciatis vos etiam quae circa me aguntur, quid faciam, omnia vobis patefaciet Tychicus, dilectus frater et fidelis minister in Domino;

22. Whom I have sent unto you for the same purpose, that ye might know our affairs, and *that* he might comfort your hearts.

22. Quem misi ad vos in eum finem, ut statum meum cognosceretis, et consolaretur corda vestra.

23. Peace *be* to the brethren, and love with faith, from God the Father, and the Lord Jesus Christ

23. Pax fratribus, et dilectio cum fide a Deo Patre et Domino Iesu Christo.

24. Grace *be* with all them that love our Lord Jesus Christ in sincerity. Amen.

24. Gratia cum omnibus, qui diligunt Dominum nostrum Iesum Christum in sinceritate. Amen.

21. *But that, ye also may know.* Uncertain or false reports frequently produce uneasiness, chiefly, no doubt, in weak minds, but sometimes also in thoughtful and steady persons. To prevent this danger, Paul sends Tychicus, from whom the Ephesians would receive full information. The holy solicitude which Paul felt about the interests of religion, or, to use his own language, "the care of all the churches," (2Co 11:28,) was thus strikingly evinced. When death stood constantly before his eyes, neither the dread of death, nor anxiety about himself, prevented him from making provision for the most distant churches. Another man would have said, "My own affairs require all the attention I can give. It would be more reasonable that all should run to my assistance, than that they should expect from me the smallest relief." But Paul acts a different part, and sends in every direction to strengthen the churches which he had founded.

Tychicus is commended, that his statements may be more fully believed. *A faithful minister in the Lord.* It is not easy to say, whether this refers to the public ministry of the church, or to the private attentions which Paul had received from Tychicus. This uncertainty arises from these two expressions being connected, *a beloved brother and faithful minister in the Lord.* The former refers to Paul, to whom the second may be supposed also to apply. I am more inclined, however, to understand it as denoting the public ministry; for I do not think it probable that Paul would have sent any man who did not hold such a rank in the church, as would secure the respectful attention of the Ephesians.

23. *Peace be to the brethren.* I consider the word *peace,* as in the salutations of the Epistles, to mean *prosperity.* Yet if the reader shall prefer to view it as signifying *harmony,* because, immediately afterwards, Paul mentions *love,* I do not object to that interpretation, or rather, it agrees better with the context. He wishes the Ephesians to be peaceable and quiet among themselves; and this, he presently adds, may be obtained by brotherly *love* and by agreement in *faith* From this prayer we learn that *faith* and *love,* as well as *peace* itself, are gifts of God bestowed upon us through Christ, — that they come equally *from God the Father and the Lord Jesus Christ.*

24. *Grace be with all.* The meaning is, "May God continue to bestow his favor on all who love Jesus Christ with a pure conscience!" The Greek word, which I follow Erasmus in translating *sincerity,* (ἐν ἀφθαρσίᾳ,) signifies literally *uncorruptedness,* which deserves attention on account of the beauty of the metaphor. Paul intended to state indirectly, that, when the heart of man is free from all hypocrisy, it will be free from all corruption. This prayer conveys to us the instruction, that the only way of enjoying the light of the Divine countenance is to love *sincerely* God's own Son, in whom his love toward us has been declared and confirmed. But let there be no hypocrisy; for most men, while they are not unwilling to make some professions of religion, entertain exceedingly low notions of Christ, and worship him with pretended homage. I wish there were not so many instances in the present day to prove that Paul's admonition, to *love our Lord Jesus Christ in sincerity* is as necessary as ever.

Footnotes

167

"Τιμᾷν properly signifies, 'to perform one's duty to any one;' and here *reverence* must comprehend the cognate offices of affection, care, and support. The same complexity of sense is observable in the classical phrase τιμᾷν τὸν ἰατρόν [to reverence the physician.] — Bloomfield.

168

See volume 1 page 468.

169

See Col 4:1 — *fj.*

170

"Plutarch tells us, (Symp. l. 2., page 638,) that wrestling was the most artful and subtle of all the ancient games, and that the name of it (πάλη) was derived from a word, which signifies to throw a man down by deceit and craft. And it is certain that persons who understand this exercise have many fetches, and turns, and changes of posture, which they make use of to supplant and trip up their adversaries. And it is with great justice, that a state of persecution is compared with it; since many are the arts, arising from the terrors of worldly evil on the one hand, and the natural love which men have to life, liberty, plenty, and the pleasures of life, on the other, that the devil makes use of to circumvent and foil them." — Chandler.

171

"Πάλη is properly a gymnastic term; but the Apostle often unites military with agonistic metaphors; and here the agonistic is not less suitable than the military. So in a similar passage of Max. Tyr. Diss. Version 9, volume 1 page 79, ed. Reisk, we have mention of Socrates wrestling with *Melitus,* with bonds and poison; next, the philosopher Plato wrestling with a tyrant's anger, a rough sea, and the greatest dangers; then, Xenophon struggling with the prejudices of Tissaphernes, the snares of Ariaeus, the treachery of Meno, and royal machinations; and, lastly, Diogenes struggling with adversaries even more formidable, namely, poverty, infamy, hunger, and cold." — Bloomfield.

CALVIN'S VERSION OF THE EPISTLE OF PAUL TO THE GALATIANS.

CHAPTER 1

1 Paul, an apostle, not from men, neither by man, but by Jesus Christ, and God the Father, who raised him from the dead,

2 And all the brethren who are with met to the churches of Galatia;

3 Grace (be) to you, and peace from God the Father, and (from) our Lord Jesus Christ,

4 Who gave himself for our sins, that he might deliver us from the present wicked age, according to the will of God and our Father,

5 To whom (be) glory for ever and ever. Amen.

6 I wonder that ye are so soon removed from Christ who called you in grace, [172] to another gospel;

7 Which is not another thing, than that there are some who trouble you, and wish to subvert the gospel of Christ.

8 But although we, or an angel from heaven preach the gospel to you otherwise than what we have preached to you, let him be accursed.

9 As we said before, now also I say again, if any one shall preach the gospel to you otherwise than what ye have received, let him be accursed.

10 For do I now persuade according to men, or according to God? [173] or do I seek to please men? for if I still pleased men, I should not be a servant of Christ.

11 But I make known to you, brethren, concerning the gospel which was preached by me, that it is not according to man;

12 For I neither received nor learned it from man, but by the revelation of Jesus Christ.

13 For ye have heard of my conversation, which formerly was in Judaism; [174] that, beyond measure, I persecuted the church of God, and wasted it,

14 And profited in Judaism [175] above many my equals [176] in my nation, being exceedingly zealous for the traditions of the fathers. [177]

15 But after that it pleased God, (who had separated me from my mother's womb, and (who) called me by his grace,)

16 To reveal his son to me, that I might preach him among the Gentiles, immediately I conferred not [178] with flesh and blood,

17 Neither did I return to Jerusalem, to those who were apostles before me; but I went away into Arabia, and again returned to Damascus.

18 Next after three years, I returned to Jerusalem, that I might see Peter; and I abode with him fifteen days.

19 But I saw none other of the apostles, except James the Lord's brother.

20 Now the things which I write to you, behold, before God, I do not speak falsely.

21 Afterwards I came into the countries of Syria and Cilicia;

22 And was unknown by face to the churches of Judea, which were in Christ.

23 But there was only this report among them: [179] He who at one time persecuted us, now preacheth the faith which he formerly was destroying,

24 And they glorified God in me.

Footnotes

172

"Par grace, ou, en la grace de Christ." "By grace, or, in the grace of Christ."

173

"Ou, presche-je des hommoes ou de Dieu? ou, humainement, ou, Divinement?" "Or, do I preach from men or from God? or, humanly, or Divinely?"

174

"Quelle a este autrefois ma conversation en la Loi Judaique." "What was formerly my conversation in the Jewish Law."

175

"En la Loy Judaique." "In the Jewish Law."

176

"Plusieurs de mes pareils, ou, de men age." "Many of my equals, or, of my age."

177

"Ou, de mes ancestres." "Or of my ancesters."

178

"Je ne prins point conseil." "I did not take counsel."

179

"Mais ils aveyont seulement ou y dire." "But they had only heard it said."

CHAPTER 2

1 Next, after fourteen years, I went up again to Jerusalem along with Barnabas, having taken Titus also.

2 And I went up according to revelation, [180] and communicated to them the gospel which I preach among the Gentiles; but privately to them who were of reputation, lest by any means I should run, or had run, in vain.

3 But not even Titus, who was with me, being a Greek, was compelled to be circumcised;

4 On account of false brethren, who had secretly entered in order to spy out our liberty, which we have in Christ Jesus, that they might; bring us into bondage;

5 To whom we gave place by subjection, not even for an hour, that the truth of the gospel might remain with you.

6 But of those who appeared to be something, whatsoever they formerly were, it is of no consequence to me; (God accepteth no man's person, De 10:17; 2Ch 19:7; Job 34:19; Wisdom 6:8; Ecclesiasticus 35:16; Ac 10:34; Ro 2:11; Eph 6:9; Col 3:25; 1Pe 1:17;) for they who appeared to be in estimation communicated nothing to me;

7 But, on the contrary, when they saw that the gospel of the uncircumcision was communicated to me, as that of the circumcision (was) to Peter;

8 (For he who was effectual in Peter in order to the apostleship of circumcision, was also effectual in me towards the Gentiles;)

9 And James, and Cephas, and John, (who seethed to be pillars,) having known the grace given to me, gave to me and to Barnabas the right hand of fellowship, that we might discharge the apostleship among the Gentiles, and they among the circumcision.

10 Only that we should be mindful of the poor, which I also was careful to do.

11 And when Peter was come to Antioch, I openly withstood him, because he was worthy of blame.

12 For before that certain persons came from James, he partook of food along with the Gentiles; but when they were come, he withdrew and separated himself from them, dreading those who were of the circumcision.

13 And the other Jews also dissembled along with him, so that Barnabas also was led aside into their dissimulation.

14 But when I saw that they did not walk uprightly, according to the truth of the gospel, I said to Peter before them all 'If thou, being a Jew, livest like Gentiles, and not like Jews, why compellest thou the Gentiles to live like Jews?

15 We, (who are) Jews by nature, and not sinners of the Gentiles,

16 Knowing that man is not justified by works of the law, but through the faith of Jesus Christ, even we have believed in Jesus Christ, that we might be justified by the faith of Christ, and not by the works of the that; for by works of the law no flesh shall be justified.

17 But if, seeking to be justified in Christ, We ourselves also are found sinners, is Christ therefore the minister of sin? By no means.

18 For if I build again those things which I destroyed, I make myself a transgressor.

19 For by the law I am dead to the law. That I might live to God,

20 I am crucified with Christ. [181] Now it is no longer I that live, but Christ liveth in me; and that I now live in the flesh, I live by the faith of the Son of God, who loved me, and gave himself for me.

21 I do not set aside the grace of God; for, if righteousness is by the law, then Christ is dead in vain.

Footnotes

180

"Et y montai par revelation." "And I went up to it by revelation."

181

"Car par la Loy je suis mort a la Loy, et suis crucifie avec Christ, afin que je vive a Dieu." "For by the Law I am dead to the Law, and am crucified with Christ, that I may live to God."

CHAPTER 3

1 O foolish Galatians, who hath enchanted you not to obey the truth, before whose eyes hath been clearly exhibited Jesus, Christ crucified among you?

2 This only I wish to learn from you; Received ye the Spirit by the works of the law, or by the preaching of faith?

3 Are ye so foolish, that, having begun by the Spirit, ye are now completed by the flesh?

4 Have ye suffered so many things in vain? if it be indeed in vain.

5 He therefore that ministereth to you the Spirit, and worketh miracles among you, (doth he it) by the works of the law, or by the preaching of faith?

6 Even as Abraham believed God, and it was imputed to him for righteousness. (Ge 15:6 Ro 4:3 Jas 2:23.)

7 Know ye therefore that they who are of faith are the children of Abraham.

8 And the scripture, because it foresaw [182] that God would justify the Gentiles by faith, formerly preached the gospel to Abraham: In thee shall all nations be blessed.

9 And so they who are of faith are blessed with believing Abraham.

10 For all that are of the works of the law are under a curse; for it is written, (De 22:6,) Cursed is every one that continueth not in all things which are written in the book of the law to do them.

11 Now that by the law no man is instilled before God is evident, for the just by faith shall live. (Hab 2:4; Ro 1:17; Heb 10:38.)

12 And the law is not of faith; but the man who shall do these things shall live in them. (Le 18:5.)

13 Christ hath redeemed us from the curse of the law, having been made a curse for us; (for it is written, (De 21:23,) Cursed is every one that hangeth on a tree;)

14 That the blessing of Abraham may come upon the Gentiles by Christ Jesus; that we may receive the promise of the Spirit by faith.

15 Brethren, (I speak after the manner of men,) though it be but a man's covenant, yet if it be confirmed, no man setteth aside or addeth any thing.

16 Now to Abraham were the promises spoken, and to his seed. He saith not, And to seeds, as of many, but as of one, And to thy seed, which is Christ.

17 And this I say: the covenant (which was) formerly confirmed by God concerning Christ, the law, which began four hundred and thirty years after, doth not annul, so as to abolish the promise.

18 For, if the inheritance (is) by the law, (it is) no longer by promise; but God gave it to Abraham by promise.

19 To what then serveth the law? [183] It was added because of transgressions, till the seed should come, to whom the promise was made; (and it was) ordained by angels in the hand of a mediator.

20 Now the mediator is not of one; but God is one.

21 (Is) the law then against the promises of God? [184] By no means; for, if the law had been given that it might be able to give life, [185] certainly righteousness would have been by the law.

22 But the scripture hath shut up all things under sin, that the promise by faith of Jesus Christ might be given to them that believe.

23 Now before faith came, we were guarded under the law, shut up to the faith which was to be revealed.

24 Wherefore the law was our schoolmaster unto Christ, that we might be justified by faith.

25 But faith being come, [186] we are no longer under a schoolmaster.

26 For ye are all the children of God by faith in Christ Jesus.

27 For as many of you as have been baptized into Christ have put on Christ.

28 There is neither Jew nor Greek, there is neither bond nor free, there is neither male nor female; for ye are all one in Christ Jesus.

29 And if ye are Christ's, then are ye Abraham's seed, and heirs according to the promise.

Footnotes

182
"Prevoyant." "Foreseeing."
183
"A quoy donc sert la Loy?"
184
"Ou, a elle este adjoustee centre les promesses de Dieu?" "Or, was it added against the promises of God?"
185
"Pour pouvoir vivifier." "In order to be able to give life."
186
"La foy estant venue."

CHAPTER 4

1 Now I say: As long as the heir is a child, he differeth nothing from a slave, [187] though he is lord of all;

2 But is under tutors and guardians, till the time appointed by the father.

3 So also we, when we were children, were in bondage under the elements of the world.

4 But when the fullness of the time was come, God sent forth his Son, made of a woman, subjected under the law;

5 That he might redeem those who were under the law, that we might receive adoption. [188]

6 And because ye are sons, God hath sent forth the Spirit of his Son into your hearts, crying, Abba, Father.

7 Wherefore thou art no longer a slave [189] but a son; and if a son, likewise an heir of God by Christ.

8 But at the time when ye knew not God, ye served those who by nature are not gods.

9 But now, after that ye have known God, or rather have been known by God,
why do ye turn again to the weak and beggarly elements, which you again desire to
serve, anew? [190]
10 Ye observe days, and months, and times, and years.
11 I am afraid of you, lest perhaps I have labored among you in vain.
12 Be ye as I; for I also am as you. Brethren, I beseech you; ye have done me no
injury.
13 Now ye knew that, through infirmity of the flesh, I formerly preached the
gospel to you;
14 And the trial of me, which was in my flesh, ye despised not, nor rejected; [191]
but ye received me as an angel of God, as Christ Jesus.
15 Where is then your blessedness? for I bear you witness, that, if it had been
possible, ye would even have plucked out your own eyes, and would have given
them to me.
16 Am I therefore become your enemy by speaking the truth?
17 They are jealous of you, not well; [192] yea, they wish to exclude you, that ye
may be jealous of them.
18 But it is good to be the object of jealousy always in a good thing, and not
only when I am present with you.
19 My little children, for whom I again travail in birth; till Christ be formed in
you,
20 I would wish now to be present with you, and to change my voice; for I am
distressed about you.
21 Tell me, ye who wish to be under the law, do ye not hear the law?
22 For it is written, that Abraham had two sons; one by the bond-maid, the
other by the free-woman.
23 But he who (was) of the bond-maid was born according to the flesh; but he
who, (was) of the free-woman, by promise.
24 Which things are allegorical [193] for there are two covenants; one indeed
from mount Sinai, which gendereth to bondage, that is Agar.
25 For Agar is mount Sinai in Arabia, and, on the other hand, corresponds to
that which is now Jerusalem; for she is in bondage with her children.
26 But Jerusalem, which is above, is free, which is the mother of us all.
27 For it is written: Rejoice, O barren, who bearest not; break forth and cry,
thou that travailest not; for more are the children of the forsaken than of her who
hath a husband. (Isa 54:1.)
28 Now we, brethren, like Isaac, are children of the promise. (Ro 9:7.)
29 But as, at that time, he who was born according to the flesh, persecuted him
who was born according to the Spirit; so also is it now.
30 But what saith the scripture? Cast out the bond-maid, and her son; for the
son of the bond-maid shall not obtain the inheritance with the so, of the free-
woman.
31 Wherefore, brethren, we are not children of the bond-woman, but of the
free.

Footnotes

187

“Il n’est different en rien du serf.” “He is not different in any respect from the slave.”

188

“A celle fin que receussions l’adoption des enfans.” “To this end, that we might receive the adoption of sons.”

189

“Maintenant tu n’es plus serf.”

190

“Ausquels vous voulez derechef servir comme auparavant.” “Which you desire again to serve as formerly.”

191

“Et n’avez point mesprise ne rejette l’espreuve de moy, telle qu’elle estoit en ma chair.” “And ye despised not, nor rejected, the trial of me, such as it was in my flesh.”

192

“Non point pour bien.” “Not for good.”

193

“Lesquelles choses sent dites par allegorie.” “Which things are spoken by allegory.”

CHAPTER 5

1 Stand fast, therefore, in the liberty with which Christ hath made us free; and be not again entangled by the yoke of bondage.

2 Behold, I Paul protest to you, that, if ye be circumcised, Christ will profit you nothing.

3 For I testify again to every man who is circumcised that he is a debtor to do the whole law.

4 Whosoever of you are justified by the law, ye have separated yourselves from Christ; ye are fallen from grace.

5 For we, through the Spirit, by faith, wait for the hope of righteousness.

6 For in Christ Jesus neither circumcision availeth any thing, nor uncircumcision; but faith working by love.

7 Ye were running well. Who hindered you, that ye should not obey the truth?

8 This persuasion is not from him who called you.

9 A little leaven leaveneth the whole lump.

10 I am persuaded concerning you in the Lord, that ye will think nothing else; [194] but he that troubleth you shall bear the condemnation, whoever he be.

11 And I, [195] brethren, if I still preach circumcision, why do I still suffer persecution? The offense of the cross is abolished.

12 Would that they were even cut off who trouble you!

13 For ye, brethren, have been called to liberty; only make not the liberty an occasion to the flesh, [196] but by love serve one another.

14 For the whole law is fulfilled in one word, namely, this: Thou shalt love thy neighbor as thyself.

15 But if ye bite and devour one another, see that ye be not consumed by one another.

16 Now I say: Walk in the Spirit, and ye shall not fulfill the lust of the flesh.

17 For the flesh lusteth against the Spirit; and the Spirit against the flesh; and these are contrary to one another, so that ye cannot do those things which ye would wish.

18 But if ye are led by the Spirit, ye are not under the law.

19 Now the works of the flesh are manifest, which are adultery, fornication, uncleanness, lasciviousness,

20 Idolatry, witchcraft, enmities, strife, emulations, wrath, quarrellings, seditions, heresies,

21 Envyings, murders, drunkenness, revellings, and such like; of which I foretell to you, as I also have foretold, that they who do such things shall not inherit the kingdom of God.

22 But the fruit of the Spirit is love, joy, peace, long-suffering, [197] gentleness, kindness, fidelity,

23 Meekness, temperance; against such there is no law.

24 And they who are Christ's have crucified the flesh with the affections and lusts.

25 If we live by the Spirit, let us also walk by the Spirit.

26 Let us not be desirous of vain-glory, provoking one another, envying one another.

Footnotes

194

"Que vous n'aurez autre sentiment." "That ye will have no other opinion."

195

"Et quant a moy." "And as to myself."

196

"Seulement (gardez) que la liberte ne soit occasion a la chair." "Only beware lest the liberty be an occasion to the flesh."

197

"Patience, ou esprit patient." "Patience, or a patient mind."

CHAPTER 6

1 Brethren, although a man be overtaken in any fault, ye, who are spiritual, restore such a man in the spirit of meekness; considering thyself, lest thou also be tempted.

2 Bear ye one another's burdens, and thus fulfill the law of Christ.

3 For if any one thinketh himself to be something, though he is nothing, he deceiveth himself.

4 But let every one prove his own work; and then shall he have glory in himself alone, and not in another. [198]

5 For every one shall bear his own burden.
6 Let him who is taught in the word communicate to the teacher in all good things.
7 Do not mistake: God is not mocked; for what a man shall have sowed, that will he also reap.
8 For he who soweth to his flesh, shall of the flesh reap corruption; but he who soweth to the Spirit, shall of the Spirit reap everlasting life.
9 And let us not weary in doing good; for if we do not faint, we shall reap in due time. [199]
10 Therefore, while we have opportunity, let us do good to all, but especially to them who are of the household of faith.
11 Ye see what a letter [200] I have written with my own hand.
12 As many as wish to please outwardly in the flesh, [201] they constrain you to be circumcised; only that they may not suffer persecution for the cross of Christ.
13 For neither they who hold by circumcision do themselves keep the law; but they wish you to be circumcised, that they may glory in your flesh.
14 But far be it from me to glory, unless in the cross of our Lord Jesus Christ, by which the world is crucified to me, and I to the world.
15 For in Christ Jesus neither circumcision availeth anything nor uncircumcision; but a new creature.
16 And as many as walk by this rule, peace (be) on them, and mercy, and on the Israel of God.
17 Henceforth let no man give me annoyance; for I bear in my body the marks of the Lord Jesus.
18 The grace of our Lord Jesus Christ (be) with your spirit. Amen.

TO THE GALATIANS IT WAS WRITTEN FROM ROME.

Footnotes

198

"Et alors il aura dequoy se glorifier." "And then will ye have ground of boasting."

199

"Nous moissonnerons en la saison." "We shall reap in the season."

200

"Vous voyez (ou, voyez) quelles grandes lettres." "Ye see, (or, See ye) how long a letter."

201

"Tous ceux qui veuleut selon la face plaire en la chair, ou, Tous ceux qui cherchent belle apparence en la chair." "All those who wish according to the face to please in the flesh, or, All those who seek a fine show in the flesh."

CALVIN'S VERSION OF THE EPISTLE OF PAUL TO THE EPHESIANS.

CHAPTER 1

1 Paul, an apostle of Jesus Christ by the will of God, to all the saints who are at Ephesus, and to the believers in Christ Jesus;

2 Grace (be) to you, and peace, from God our Father, and from the Lord Jesus Christ.

3 Blessed [202] (be) the God and Father of our Lord Jesus Christ, who hath blessed us with every spiritual blessing in heavenly [203] (places) in Christ;

4 As he hath chosen us in him before the creation of the world, that we might be holy and blameless in his sight through love:

5 Who hath predestinated us in adoption in himself through Jesus Christ, according to the good pleasure of his will,

6 To the praise of the glory of his grace, by which he hath made us accepted in the Beloved.

7 In whom we have redemption through his blood, the forgiveness of sins,

8 According to the riches of his grace; in which he hath abounded toward us in all wisdom and prudence;

9 Having made known to us the secret of his will, according to his good pleasure, which he had purposed in himself;

10 In order to the dispensation of the fullness of the times; [204] that he might gather together all things in Christ, both those things which are in heaven, and those things which are on the earth, in him;

11 Through whom also we have obtained an inheritance, being predestinated according to the purpose of him who worketh all things according to the purpose of his will;

12 That we, who first hoped in Christ, might be to the praise of his glory.

13 In whom ye also (trusted,) having heard the word of truth, the gospel of your salvation; in whom also, after having believed, ye were sealed with the Holy Spirit of promise,

14 Who is the earnest of our inheritance, till the redemption of the possession obtained, to the praise of his glory.

15 Wherefore I also, having heard of the faith which ye have in the Lord Jesus, and of the love (which ye have) toward all the saints,

16 Cease not to give thanks for you, making mention of you in my prayers;

17 That the God of our Lord Jesus Christ, the Father of glory, may give to you the spirit of wisdom and revelation, by the knowledge of him, [205]

18 The eyes of your mind enlightened, that ye may know what is the hope of his calling, and what are the riches of the glory of his inheritance in the saints,

19 And what is the surpassing greatness of his power toward us who believe, according to the efficacy of the power of his strength;

20 Which he wrought in Christ, when he raised him from the dead, and caused him to sit at his own right hand in the heavenly (places);

21 Above all principality, and power, and might, and dominion, and every name that is named, not only in this age, but also in (the age) which is to come;
22 And hath put all things under his feet, and hath appointed him head over all things to the church [206]
23 Which is his body, and the fulness of him that filleth all in all.

Footnotes

202
"Benit soit Dieu, ou, Loue soit Dieu." "Blessed be God, or, Praised be God."
203
"Es (choses) celestes, ou, Es lieux celestes." "In heavenly things, or, In heavenly places.""
204
"Afin de le dispenser en la plenitude des temps." "In order to dis-pense it in the fullness of the times."
205
"Pour avoir cognoissance (ou, par la cognoissance) de luy." "*In* order to have knowledge of him, or, By the knowledge of him."
206
"Et l'a constitue sur toutes choses, pour estre chef a l'Eglise."- And hath appointed him over all things, to be head to the Church."

CHAPTER 2

1 And when ye were dead in your trespasses and sins;
2 In which for some time ye walked, according to the course [207] of this world, according to the prince of the power of air, that is, of the spirit that now worketh [208] in the children of disobedience;
3 Among whom we all also, for some time, had our conversation in the lusts of our flesh, executing what was agreeable to the flesh and to the mind; [209] and were by nature children of wrath, even as others.
4 But God, who is rich in mercy, on account of his great love, with which he loved us,
5 Even when we were dead in sins, quickened (us) together with Christ; (by grace ye are saved;)
6 And hath raised us up together, and hath made us sit together in heavenly (places) in Christ Jesus;
7 That he might shew, in the ages to come, the surpassing riches of his grace, in (his) kindness [210] toward us in Christ Jesus.
8 For by grace are ye saved through faith; and that not of yourselves; (it is) the gift of God.
9 Not of works, that no one may boast.
10 For we are his workmanship, having been created in Christ Jesus to good works, which God hath prepared, that we may walk in them.

11 Wherefore remember that you, at one time Gentiles in the flesh, who were called Uncircumcision by that which is called Circumcision, made by the hand in the flesh,

12 At that time were without Christ, having been alienated from the commonwealth of Israel [211] strangers from the tables of promise, [212] not having hope, [213] and without God in the world;

13 But now in Christ Jesus [214] you, who formerly were far off, have been made nigh through the blood of Christ.

14 For he is our peace, who hath made both one, [215] and breaking down the middle wall of partition, the enmities in our flesh;

15 Abolishing in his flesh the law of commandments (which is) contained in ordinances, that he might unite in himself the two into one new man, making peace;

16 That he might reconcile both to God in one body through the cross, slaying [216] the enmities by it;

17 And coming, preached peace to you who were far off, and peace to those who were nigh;

18 For through him we both have access in one Spirit to the Father.

19 Therefore ye are no longer strangers and foreigners, but fellow-citizens of the saints, and of the household of God,

20 Having been built on the foundation of the apostles and prophets, of which Jesus Christ himself is the chief corner-stone;

21 In whom the whole building joined together groweth into a holy temple in the Lord;

22 In whom ye also are built together [217] for a habitation of God in the Spirit.

Footnotes

207

'Secundum saeculum." "Selon le cours."

208

"Qui est l'esprit qui besogne maintenant." "Who is the spirit that now worketh."

209

"Les desirs de la chair et de (nos) pensees." "The desires of the flesh and of (our) thoughts."

210

"*Par* sa benignite." "By his kindness."

211

"N'ayans rien de commun avec la republique d'Israel." "Having nothing in common with the commonwealth of Israel."

212

"Estrangers des tables (ou, alliances) de la promesse." "Strangers to the tables (or covenants) of promise."

213

" N'ayant point d'esperance." "Having no hope."

214
"Par Jesus Christ." "Through Jesus Christ."
215
"Qui de tous les deux a fait un." "Who of both hath made one"
216
"Ayant destruit." "Having destroyed."
217
Or, "In whom also be ye builded together."

CHAPTER 3

1 For this cause I Paul, the prisoner of Jesus Christ, discharge the office of ambassador for you Gentiles;

2 If ye have heard of dispensation of the grace of God, (which was) given me towards you;

3 That through revelation he made known to me the secret, as I wrote a little before;

4 By attending to which ye may understand my knowledge in the mystery of Christ,

5 Which in other ages was not made known to the sons of men, as it hath now been revealed to his holy apostles and prophets through the Spirit,

6 That the Gentiles are fellow-heirs, and of the same body, and partakers of his promise in Christ through the gospel.

7 Of which I was made a minister, according to the gift of the grace of God, which was given to me according to the efficacy of his power.

8 To me, the least of all saints, was this grace given, that I should preach among the Gentiles the unsearchable riches of Christ;

9 And that I should make manifest to all, what is the fellowship of the mystery, which hath been hid from ages in God, who created all things through Jesus Christ;

10 That the manifold wisdom of God might now be manifested to principalities and powers in heavenly places through the church,

11 According to the eternal purpose which he purposed in Christ Jesus our Lord,

12 Through whom we have boldness, and access with confidence, through the faith of him.

13 Wherefore I desire that ye faint not at my afflictions for you, which is your glory.

14 For this cause I bend my knees to the Father of our Lord Jesus Christ,

15 Of whom the whole family in heaven and on earth is named,

16 That he would give to you, according to the riches of his glory, to be strengthened with might through his Spirit in the inner man,

17 That Christ may dwell in your hearts through faith, that ye may be rooted and grounded in love, [218]

18 That ye may be able to comprehend with all saints, what is the breadth, and length, and depth, and height;

19 To know, I say, the love of Christ, which surpasseth knowledge, that ye may be filled with all the fullness of God.

20 Now to him who is able to do abundantly above all that we ask or think, according to the power working in you,

21 Be glory in the church through Jesus Christ, in all ages, for ever and ever. Amen.

Footnotes

218

"Ou, Afin qu'estans enracinez et fondez en charite, vous puissiez comprendre." "Or, That, being rooted and founded in love, ye may be able to comprehend."

CHAPTER 4

1 I therefore, a prisoner in the Lord, beseech you, that ye may walk worthy of the calling to which ye have been called,

2 With all humility and meekness, with patience forbearing one another in love,

3 Endeavoring to keep the unity of the Spirit in the bond of peace.

4 One body and one spirit; [219] as ye have been called in one hope of your calling.

5 One Lord [220] one faith, one baptism.

6 One God and Father of all, who is above all things, and through all things, *(or, above all men and through all men,)* and in you all.

7 But to each of us hath grace been given, according to the measure of the gift of Christ.

8 Wherefore he saith: After having ascended on high, he led captivity captive [221] and gave gifts to men. (Ps 68:18.)

9 Now that (word) he ascended, what is it but that he also descended first into the lower parts of the earth?

10 He who descended is the same also who ascended above all heavens, that he might fill all things. [222]

11 And he gave some apostles, and some prophets, and some evangelists, and others pastors and teachers,

12 For the renewing of the saints, for the work of the ministry, for the edification of the body of Christ;

13 Till we all come into the unity of the faith, and of the knowledge of the Son of God, into a perfect man, into the measure of the age of fulness [223] of Christ;

14 That we may no longer be children, who are tossed and driven about by every wind of doctrine, by the cunning of men, by craftiness for lying in wait to deceive;

15 But, following truth with love, may grow up in all things into him who is the head, that is, Christ;

16 From whom the whole body fitly joined together and compacted by every joint of supply, according to the efficacy in the measure of every part, maketh increase of the body, to the edifying of itself, in love.

17 This I say, therefore, and testify in the Lord, that ye no longer walk, as other Gentiles walk, in the vanity of their mind,

18 Blinded in the understanding, alienated from the life of God on account of the ignorance which is in them, on account of the blindness of their heart;

19 Who, after having ceased to have any feeling, [224] have given themselves up to lasciviousness, to commit all uncleanness with greediness.

20 But ye have not so learned Christ;

21 If indeed ye have heard him, and have been taught in him, as the truth is in Jeεuε;

22 That ye put off, according to the former conversation, the old man, which is corrupted according to the lusts of deceit; [225]

23 And that ye be renewed in the spirit of your mind;

24 And that ye put on the new man, which hath been created according to God, in righteousness and holiness of truth. [226]

25 Wherefore, putting away lying, speak every one the truth with his neighbor;

26 For we are members one of another.

27 Be ye angry, and do not sin. (Ps 4:4.) Let not the sun go down on your wrath; and give not place to the devil.

28 He that stole, let him steal no more; but rather let him labor, by working with his hands what is good, that he may have to give to him that needeth.

29 Let no filthy speech proceed out of your mouth; but if any (speech) is good for the edification of use, that it may impart grace to the hearers.

30 And grieve not the Holy Spirit of God, by whom ye have been sealed to the day of redemption.

31 Let all bitterness, and anger, and wrath, and clamour, and slander, be put away from you with all malice.

32 And be ye kind one to another, merciful, forgiving one another, as God hath forgiven you in Christ.

Footnotes

219

"Soyez un corps et un esprit; ou, Il n'y a qu'un corps et un esprit." "Be ye one body and one spirit; or, There is but one body and one spirit."

220

"Il n'y a qu'un Seigneur." "*There* is but one Lord."

221

"Estant monte en haut, il a mene captive grande multitude de cap-this." "Having ascended on high, he led captive a vast multitude of captives."

222

"Ou, Accomplist, ou, replist le tout, ascavoir, toute l'Eglise de ses dons et graces." "Or, That he might complete, or fill the whole, that is, the whole church, with his gifts and graces."

223

"De l'aage entiere, ou, la parfaicte stature." "*Of* the full age, or, the perfect stature."

224

"Lesquels, sans remors de conscience; ou, Ayans perdu tout sentiment." "Who, without remorse of conscience; or, Having lost all feeling."

225

" Par les concupiscences qui seduisent." "By the lusts which deceive."

226

"Et sainctete de verite, on, vraye sainctete." "And holiness of truth, or, True holiness."

CHAPTER 5

1 Be ye therefore imitators of God, as beloved children;

2 And walk in love, as Christ also hath loved us, and hath given himself for us an offering and sacrifice to God, for a smell of delightful fragrance.

3 But fornication, and all uncleanness, or covetousness, let them not even be named among you, as becometh saints.

4 Or filthiness, foolish talking, jesting; which are not convenient; but rather grace. [227]

5 For this ye know, that no fornicator, or unclean person, or covetous man, who is an idolater, shall obtain inheritance in the kingdom of Christ and of God.

6 Let no man deceive you by vain words; for on account of these things cometh the wrath of God on disobedient *(or, unbelieving)* children, [228]

7 Be not ye therefore their companions.

8 Ye were once darkness; but now ye are light in the Lord; walk as children of light;

9 (For the fruit of the light is in all goodness, and righteousness, and truth;)

10 Proving what is acceptable to God. [229]

11 And have no fellowship with the unfruitful works of darkness; but rather reprove them.

12 For it is a shame even to speak of those things which are done by them in secret.

13 But all things, when they are brought forward, are made manifest by the light; for every thing that maketh manifest is light.

14 Wherefore he saith: Awake, thou that sleepest, and arise from the dead; and Christ shall give thee light.

15 See then how you walk carefully, not as fools, but as wise;

16 Redeeming the time, because the days are evil.

17 Wherefore be ye not imprudent, but understanding what is the will of the Lord.

18 And be not drunk with wine, in which is lasciviousness;

19 But be filled with the Spirit; speaking to yourselves in psalms, and hymns, and spiritual songs, singing and making melody in your heart, to the Lord;

20 Giving thanks always for all things, in the name of our Lord Jesus Christ, to God and the Father.

21 Submit yourselves to one another in the fear of Christ *(or, of God).*

22 Let wives be subject to their own husbands as to the Lord;

23 For the husband is the head of the wife, as Christ also is the savior of the church; and he is the savior of the body.

24 But, as the church is subject to Christ, in like manner (let) wives (be subject) to their own husbands in all things.

25 Husbands, love your wives; as Christ also loved the church, and gave himself for it,

26 That he might sanctify it, cleansing it with the washing of water by the word;

27 That he might present it to himself a glorious church, not having spot, or wrinkle, or any such thing; but that it might be holy and unblamable.

28 So ought husbands to love their wives, as their own bodies. He who loveth his wife loveth himself.

29 For no man ever hated his own flesh, but nourisheth and cherisheth it; as also Christ [230] the church;

30 For we are members of his body, of his flesh, and of his bones.

31 For this reason shall a man leave his father and mother, and shall cleave to his wife; and the two shall be one flesh.

32 This is a great secret; but I speak concerning Christ and the church.

33 Yet let every one of you love his wife; and let the woman reverence her husband.

Footnotes

227

"Grace, on, action de graces." "Grace, or, Thanksgiving.',

228

"Sur les enfans de rebellion, ou, de desobeissance, ou, incredulite." "On the children of rebellion, or of disobedience, or of unbelief."

229

"Au Seigneur." "To the Lord."

230

"Le Seigneur." "The Lord."

CHAPTER 6

1 Children, obey your parents in the Lord; for this is right.

2 Honour thy father and mother; (which is the first commandment with promise;)

3 That it may be well with thee, and that thou mayest be long-lived on the earth.

4 Ye fathers also, provoke not your children to wrath; but bring them up in the instruction and reproof of the Lord.

5 Servants, obey your masters [231] according to the flesh, with fear and trembling, in the simplicity of your hearts, as to Christ;

6 Not with eye-service, as endeavoring to please men, but as the servants of Christ, doing the will of God from the heart: [232]

7 With good-will, serving the Lord, and not men;

8 Knowing that everyone, whether he be bond or free, shall receive from the Lord whatever good he shall have done.

9 And ye, masters, perform your mutual duty toward them, forbearing threatenings; knowing that their Master and yours is in heaven; and there is no respect of persons with him.

10 Finally, my brethren, be strong in the Lord, and in the power of his might.
11 Put on the whole armor of God, that ye may be able to stand against the crafty devices of the devil.
12 For we wrestle not against flesh and blood, but against principalities, against powers, against the princes of the world, of the darkness of this age, against spiritual wickednesses in heavenly places.
13 Wherefore take to you the whole armor of God, that ye may be able to resist in the evil day, and, having accomplished everything: to stand.
14 Stand therefore, having your loins girt with truth, and having put on the breastplate of righteousness,
15 And having your feet shod with the preparation of the gospel of peace;
16 Above all, taking the shield of faith, by which ye may be able to quench all the fiery darts of the wicked one.
17 And take the helmet of salvation, and the sword of the Spirit, which is the word of God;
18 Praying at all times in the Spirit, with all prayer and supplication, and watching for this very purpose, with all perseverance and supplication for all saints;
19 And for me, that speech may be given to me, in the opening of my mouth with boldness, that I may make known the mystery of the gospel; [233]
20 For which I discharge the office of ambassador, in the chain; that I may conduct myself in it courageously, as I ought to speak.
21 But that ye also may know my affairs, what I do, Tychicus, a beloved brother and faithful minister in the Lord, will make known to you all things;
22 Whom I have sent to you for that purpose, that ye might know my affairs, and might comfort your hearts.
23 Peace (be) to the brethren, and love, with faith, from God the Father and the Lord Jesus Christ.
24 Grace (be) with all who love our Lord Jesus Christ in sincerity. Amen.

Footnotes

231
"Obeissez a ceux qui sent (vos) maistres." "Obey those who are your masters."
232
"Faisans de courage la volonte de Christ." "Doing courageously the will of Christ."
233
"Le secret de l'evangile." "The secret of the gospel."

17450818R00140

Printed in Great Britain
by Amazon